T0354300

NEOLIBERALISM ECONOMIC POLICY AND THE
COLLAPSE OF THE PUBLIC SECTOR

How the Jindal Administration
Allowed It to Happen—2008 to 2016

LIONEL D. LYLES, Ph.D.

NEOLIBERALISM ECONOMIC POLICY AND
THE COLLAPSE OF THE PUBLIC SECTOR
HOW THE JINDAL ADMINISTRATION ALLOWED
IT TO HAPPEN—2008 TO 2016

iUniverse books may be ordered through booksellers or by contacting:

iUniverse
1663 Liberty Drive
Bloomington, IN 47403
www.iuniverse.com
1-800-Authors (1-800-288-4677)

ISBN: 978-1-5320-5197-5 (sc)
ISBN: 978-1-5320-5196-8 (e)

Library of Congress Control Number: 2018906836

Print information available on the last page.

iUniverse rev. date: 07/12/2018

DEDICATIONS

This book is dedicated to the hard-working, Louisiana Working Class people, regardless of race, religion, or color, and the American Working Class as a whole, who have struggled to survive the repeated, deep budget cuts the Jindal Administration, and the Louisiana Legislature, have made in various public sector social programs such as higher education and healthcare among others, from 2008 to 2014. Such political action is not unique to Louisiana, but is a common occurrence in every state legislature across America. Nearly every working class man and woman-bottom 80.0 percent- and their children, have suffered a rising tide of poverty, and generalized instability during the Jindal Administration to date, and, too often, good Louisiana people lives have come to a premature end, and far too many others have ended up in a-juvenile or adult-Louisiana Prison serving disproportionately long sentences. Currently, Louisiana incarcerates more of its people per 1,000 population than any other state in the nation, and its incarceration rate is higher than all countries' worldwide!

We also dedicate this work to the thousands of Louisiana people who have a burning question about where our state is headed, and how can we collectively bring it back from the neo-liberalism economic policy collision course it is now on? There are answers to many of the questions some Louisiana people have about how neo-liberalism economic policies have negatively impacted their personal and family lives; many of them are contained in this book. The first step toward changing our social plight is self-education. This re-education process requires *self-reliance and collective, rugged social-determination*, if we will have any hope of ending our belief in scarcity and powerlessness. The outcome of knowledge gained, from a thorough study of the Jindal Administration, will motivate us to reject being *satisfied with nothing,* and, cause us to demand that we, unconditionally, deserve to live our lives in the State of Louisiana, in abundance, with integrity and dignity, free of deception, exclusions, and want.

Lastly, we dedicate this book to Henry, Lionel Lyles II, Harmony, Destini, Zion, Sky, Zoe, and all of the wonderful children in Louisiana, and those who live everywhere on Mother Earth, who deserve a better chance than their parents had.

ACKNOWLEDGEMENT

The vast majority of primary source information contained in this book was taken from The Advocate newspaper online at 2theadvocate.com. This source is based in Baton Rouge, LA, which is the Louisiana Capitol. Every day, since the very first day of the Jindal Administration back on January 1, 2008, the reporters for The Advocate newspaper have consistently written articles related to the Jindal Administration's implementation of neo-liberalism economic policies in Louisiana State Government. We have collected every article of significance written by its reporters, from 2008 to 2014, and they were used to demonstrate exactly how the Jindal Administration carried-out its relentless budget-cutting of social programs in the Louisiana Public Sector in order to provide those taxpayers' dollars to private business to "questionably grow the Louisiana Economy.

In an historical, and systematic fashion, we have included more than 670 footnotes, or references, which, together, shine a very bright light on the massive tax breaks and tax incentives the Jindal Administration gave to private business since 2008 to 2014. Also included are a large number of references related to the privatization of formerly state government operated social programs such as Louisiana Public Hospitals and Prisons. Although we have not met any of The Advocate staff reporters, their reporting on the Jindal Administration's implementation of neo-liberalism economic policies in Louisiana State Government were referenced extensively due to the timeliness and professional quality of their coverage of nearly every action Governor Bobby Jindal initiated against the Louisiana Public Sector.

A thorough examination of this subject could not have been accomplished without the valuable daily reporting of events, by The Advocate staff reporters, as they unfolded during various Louisiana Legislative Sessions, which were directed by Governor Bobby Jindal and other politicians. In addition, we would not be inclusive if we did not also acknowledge the large number of other source materials produced by other authors, organizations, and policy institutes, which were referenced to corroborate the information reported by The Advocate, from 2008 to 2014.

Lastly, neo-liberalism policies and neo-liberalism economic policies are used interchangeably throughout this book, and their meaning outlined on Page 5 is the same.

Although this ideology is primarily associated with Republican politics, it is not exclusively executed by the latter because by June 5, 2018, the John Bel Edwards Administration inherited an enormous budget deficit of over $600 million, and, similar to the Jindal Administration's deep budget cutting of the Louisiana Public Sector, the Edwards Administration is now considering more deep budget cuts in the Louisiana Public Sector, in an attempt to correct the adverse effects of budget cuts and tax breaks left behind by the Jindal Administration.

FOREWORD

Mr. Bobby Jindal, coined an "academic god" by Former Republican Governor Mike Foster, was elected Governor to succeed him with 54% of the vote, and social media reported his election was a *mandate*. During the 2007 Louisiana Governors Race, 1,297,840 Louisiana Registered Voters casted a vote; Mr. Bobby Jindal received 699,275, or 54%. This result is highly misleading, and *Fake News,* given the fact there were 2,884,453 Louisiana Registered Voters in 2007, and if this true denominator was used to calculate the percent of the vote received by Mr. Jindal, he accurately received *only* 24.2 percent of the *eligible vote,* which is 29.8 percent less than he actually received on Election Day. Governor-elect Bobby Jindal spent $13.7 million to get s/elected, making his campaign expenditure the most expensive in Louisiana History! This sum pales in the face of the unheard-of amount of private business tax breaks, rebates, deductions, credits, and exemptions among others that the Jindal Administration was destined to *giveaway* within the first two months of its first term.

When outgoing Governor Kathleen Blanco left office in 2007, she left a $1 billion surplus in the Louisiana Treasury. By the end of the state legislature's second special session, which occurred during the two month old administration of Governor Bobby Jindal, the latter approved a full package of business tax cuts and $1.1 billion in surplus spending (http://blog.nola.comimpact/print.html?entry=/2008/03/jindalbats a thousand at...). This legislative action laid the foundation for the *foreshadowing* of the greatest transfer of Louisiana Taxpayers' Dollars, from the public sector to the private sector, in Louisiana History. In the brief span of two months, the $1.1 billion surplus in the Louisiana Treasury was pillaged.

By the end of the Jindal Administration's first term in 2012, Millhollon informed the Louisiana Public that more than $108 million taxpayer dollars had been diverted from the public sector to the private sector by October 2010 (The Advocate, October 6, 2010, p. 1A.). At the end of 2012, the amount of private business tax breaks *mushroomed* to more than $7 billion! (The Advocate, March 06, 2012, pp. 1 and 2.). The financial trauma, and the social cost to Louisiana Working Class People is incalculable. The financial and social trauma caused by the Jindal Administration continues to have a residual, profound and devastating impact on Louisiana Working Class People today. The information below shows where Louisiana rank nationwide across a number of social indices related to children data included in the **End of Childhood Report, 2018,** which is published by Save The Children.

LA Rank (Avg)	Child Dies	Child is Malnourished	Child Drops Out of HS	Child is Victim of Violence	Child Has A Child
50	47	44	46	47	45

Source: GROWING UP RURAL IN AMERICA: U.S. COMPLEMENT TO THE END OF CHILDHOOD REPORT 2018, Save the Children Publishers, http://www.savethe children.org/us/about-us/resource-library/end-of-childhood, 2018, p. 25.

Without a doubt, there are many right wing apologists who, after reading this information, will hurry to inform you that Louisiana is a bottom performing state *only* because the legislation the Jindal Administration signed into law has not had enough time yet to have their intended impact on the lives of the vast majority of Louisiana Working Class People. Anticipating this tactic, consider the following.

By the end of the Jindal Administration in 2016, marked by the beginning of the John Bel Edwards Administration in December 2016, the massive tax breaks and giveaways to private business resulted in "…one of the largest disparities between [Louisiana's] poorest residents and the richest…: (Elizabeth Crisp, The Advocate, December 15, 2016, p. 1.). Four months later, Elizabeth Crisp reported the John Bel Edwards Administration is currently"...facing a $650 million fiscal cliff..." (Elizabeth Crisp, The Advocate, April 22, 2018, p. 1.). It will take years, decades, even multiple-generations before the affects of the massive budget cuts, in nearly all of the public sector social programs, are no longer a critical danger to the well-being of Louisiana Working People, including children, women, and the elderly.

As evidence of this fact, at the close of the last Louisiana Legislative Session in June 2018, this lawmaking body approved a state budget calling for an end to the state's food stamp program, namely, Supplemental Nutrition Assistance Program commonly referred to as SNAP (Deslatte, Melinda, The Advocate, June 9, 2018, p. 1). Deslatte stated "the Department of Children and Family Services is slated to take a cut of around $34 million in the budget passed by lawmakers in the final minutes of the just-ended special session. The agency says that will force it to shutter the food stamp program in 2019 because it won't be able to pay for administration of the federally funded benefits." If SNAP is done away with as planned, 860,000 Louisiana Working Class Residents, mostly children will be directly impacted. As it is, the $43 million planned budget cut will make it impossible to pay the salaries of 1,000 staff, which will be laid-off, and eight offices will be closed. More illogical is the fact the Department of Children and Family Services will contact the United States Department of Agriculture (USDA), and notify it in September 2018 that SNAP is shutdown, and the $1.4 billion in federal food stamps given to qualified Louisiana Residents will no longer be needed. During the Jindal Administration, the wealthy class received unheard of tax breaks and privatization opportunities, which for the latter, we may refer to the billions of dollars of tax breaks it received as its SNAP (Supreme Non-Competitive Arranged Profit).

Louisiana Children will die(!), and as the data provided earlier shows, Louisiana rank 47th in the nation in the category called "Child Dies." Ironically, many of the same Louisiana Residents, who voted many of the politicians into office, who voted to end SNAP, are the same ones who have rewarded their *love* with the shutdown of SNAP!

In addition to this inhumanity of man against man and woman, the end of SNAP also means "If Louisiana doesn't have a food stamp program, that also means the state can't administer disaster food stamp aid after a hurricane, flood or other calamity." P.2. The 2018 Hurricane Season just begun on June 1, 2018, and many Louisiana Legislators, in spite of the dangers a hurricane posed to Louisiana Residents, felt no love in their hearts for the people, and proceeded to *further collapse the Louisiana Public Sector during the John Bel Edwards Administration, which is using the same budget cutting tactics used by the Jindal Administration, in its attempt to close the $650 million budget deficit left behind by the latter.* Education programs, on all levels, are equally threatened by his runaway train.

For example, the Taylor Opportunity Program, namely TOPS, which provides college scholarships for students, is currently in line to be cut by 20 percent. At least 50,000 students statewide are being heavily impacted. All over Louisiana, in cities, both large and small, social services and infrastructure are crumbling. Roads are in desperate need of repairs, and school districts do not have the funds necessary to build new schools to educate our children. Recently, a tax measure was rejected by the residents of St. Landry Parish, which doomed the children of the same, to continue to attend classes in *antiquated and outdated school facilities.*

Therefore, to help you understand the thought(s) behind this social and economic chaos, this book provides the reader with an in-depth examination of how the Jindal Administration collapsed the Louisiana Public Sector through its implementation of a political ideology called *Neo-Liberalism.* This is a Republican Ideology that aims to shrink government; diminish the public sector via massive budget cuts and tax breaks; and privatize as many social programs formerly operated by state government as possible.

When the American Republic was founded by Thomas Jefferson, George Washington, Alexander Hamilton and others, they used Classical Liberalism to create the *Declaration of Independence, Constitution, and the Bill of Rights aimed at giving the American people a voice in the decision-making process related to how government would operate.* However, by 1980,

Classical Liberalism was rolled-back, and replaced by a Neo-Liberalism Ideology, popularized by the Reagan Administration.

For this ideology to work, the government apparatus must be politically brought under the full control of a class, by using its billions of dollars to elect actors, television celebrities, and athletes among others to public office. This class consists of half of one percent of the Louisiana Population, and own at least 80.0 percent of all wealth. Senator Bernie Sanders highlighted its existence during his 2015 Presidential Campaign. How this Ruling Class used the Jindal Administration to accomplish its economic aim is objectively established.

Marteau, June 2018

PREFACE

Since the 1980s, neo-liberalism philosophy has become a fundamental practice in federal and state government nationwide. By 2014, the Wall Street-induced housing market crash crippled the American Capitalist System, causing the 2008 Depression. Nothing of this magnitude had occurred since the 1929 Depression-85 years ago. The U.S. Congress passed the Dodd-Frank Bill in 2011, which was signed into law by President Barack Obama, and it was aimed at preventing another economic catastrophe. Before 2008, neo-liberalism economic policies replaced the Glass-Steagall Act during the Clinton Administration, which included 85 year old safeguards against the reoccurrence of another economic depression. The 2008 Depression, therefore, has its DNA connected to the end of the Glass-Steagall Act. In October 2014, the Dodd-Frank Bill, which became law after the 2008 Depression, is being, likewise, systematically rolled-back, opening the door for the possibility of another economic depression to occur in the near future. The Associated Press wrote the following:

> "New U.S. rules aimed at getting banks to take on more of the risk when they package and sell mortgage securities are being relaxed with an eye tospurring broader home lending. Federal regulators have dropped a key requirement: a 20 percent down payment from the borrower if a bank didn't hold at least 5 percent of the mortgage securities tied to those loans on its books... The rules, proposed in stricter

form in 2011, were mandated by theoverhaul law enacted
in the wake of the 2008 financial crisis."[1]

Instead of a loud outcry from the Obama Administration about this, there has been no public criticism of this action, and it is representative of how neo-liberalism economic policies influence federal and state government bureaucracy. They leave nothing to chance, which is why the political leadership at the federal and state government levels must be carefully selected and elected, if its economic requirements will be carried-out by them, although such policies impose extreme hardship on the average working class American. The central belief of a selected /elected politician is he or she must first believe, beyond a shadow of personal doubt, that the *only way to grow the American Capitalist Economy is to drastically roll-back government regulations, and, be willing to systematically make deep cuts in public sector expenditures by privatizing public services, and by introducing market incentives in the form of tax breaks, tax incentives, payment of business relocation costs, and the free use of fast track employment training services.* In short, to effectively implement neo-liberalism economic policies, the selected/elected politician must carry-out the following actions:

- Ignore any connections between the past and present history, and effectiveness of a social program, and, without any cause, arbitrarily make deep cuts in its budget.
- Reduce the size of state government by laying-off thousands of working class workers; remove all barriers that inhibit free markets and monopoly development; and, if the government has to enter into the market, the only role it can play is one that enables private businesses in the economic market.
- Redefine the public sector as a service sector, by privatizing existing social programs, and make them operate according to the principles of the market.
- In the event a severe financial crisis is caused by private businesses in the market such as the 2008 Depression, the role of government is to bailout those private businesses that caused the crisis, and,

---

[1] _____ "New rules on banks' risk in mortgage bonds eased," Associated Press, October 21, 2014, p. 1.

then, place the responsibility for repaying the bailout-tax- on the shoulders of the average working class family.

- Oppose any tax increase, and wherever possible, and when the opportunity is created, significantly reduce the income tax rate paid by the one-half of one percent of American families.

- If a market does not exist, the role of government is to create one so private businesses can receive money, via a voucher scheme, for example, from social programs such as the K-12 Public Education Budget, which is protected by constitutional law.

- Discourage ALL criticism related to the impact neo-liberalism policies have on the public sector such as the generalized deterioration of the well-being of citizens in society, and

- In order to insure the smooth functioning of the economic market, use whatever force is necessary, i. e., National Guard, local police, and others, to put down any protest brought against neo-liberalism economic policies by affected working class citizens in society. The Michael Brown Case in Ferguson, MO is a good example, which is representative of how government often responds to the valid desires of working class people.

These are some of the primary requirements a politician must agree to perform if he or she is selected/elected to serve as governor, or President of the United States. Former President Ronald Reagan became the role model for politicians, who aspires to become selected/elected governor or president. By 1987, the year before he left office, former President Ronald Reagan's Fiscal 1988 Budget includes an example of the type of budget cuts he made to public sector social programs, from 1980 to 1987. Table 1.0 below shows how he carried-out the neo-liberalism economic policy agenda at the federal level.

Table 1.0
President Reagan's Fiscal 1988 Budget
Cuts of Selected Public Sector Programs,
January 6, 1987 (in billions of dollars)

SOCIAL PROGRAMS	CURRENT SPENDING	FISCAL 1988 BUDGET CUTS	PERCENT CHANGE
Health	$361.3	-$9.1	-2.5
Education	17.0	-2.3	-13.5
Welfare	9.9	-9.5	-4.0
Housing	14.6	-705.2 million	-4.9
Transportation	26.21	-1.58	-6.0
Agriculture	31.1	-9.83	-31.6
Foreign Aid	14.0	15.2 (no budget cut)	8.5
Defense	282.2	297.6 (no budget cut)	5.5

Source: Wall Street Journal Washington Staff, "What President's Fiscal '88 Budget Does to Programs; Education, Transportation and Housing Face Big Cuts," The Wall Street Journal, January 6, 1987, p. 10.

As we see, former President Ronald Reagan "Raised The Bar," regarding his willingness to apply the neo-liberalism economic policy requirements outlined above. The above data reveals a trend applied by former President Ronald Reagan since he was selected/elected in 1980. That is, to grow the American Economy, he reduced the size of the federal government by making deep cuts in public sector programs. Those taxpayers' dollars classified as budget cuts were given to private industries in the form of tax breaks and incentives. In plain terms, private businesses used the dollars cut out of public sector programs as investments, which minimized the risk and exposure of their own financial investments to changing economic conditions in the market. Simultaneously, former President Ronald Reagan allocated more taxpayers' dollars to defense and foreign aid. Most of the new injections of taxpayers' dollars ended up in the coffers of military industrial contractors. Also, by July 1987, buying guns were more important than the health of the majority of American Working Class people. Michel

McQueen stated "the House Ways and means Committee...voted to cut $8.7 billion from Medicare..."[2]

Following in former President Ronald Reagan's footsteps, the neo-liberalism economic policy lessons learned from the former regarding how to grow the economy, at the expense of the public sector, were applied in Louisiana, beginning in 2008. To replicate the Reagan Neo-liberalism Economic Policy Model in Louisiana, an individual had to be selected/elected to pull it off. Mr. Bobby Jindal was groomed for the job when he was appointed to serve as head of the Louisiana State Colleges and Universities System at a very young age. Then Louisiana Governor, Mike Forster, once said Mr. Bobby Jindal was the smartest man he had ever known. In addition, Mr. Bobby Jindal left this position, and was appointed to another high level federal government position in the Bush Administration. With his meteoric rise in political stature secured, his qualifications to be governor quickly became a non-issue, and, as a result of his "political grooming," he easily won the 2007 Louisiana Gubernatorial Election as planned by his neo-liberalism benefactors. The Louisiana Public Sector was seldom mentioned during Mr. Bobby Jindal's Gubernatorial Campaign; however, the Reagan Neo-Liberalism Economic Policy Model was prepared before the governor's race for implementation, similar to the way a Jumbo 777 Jetliner waits its turn for takeoff on the tarmac with its engines and flight plan ready to go. By 2008, the Reagan Neo-Liberalism Economic Policy Model achieved wheels up with the selection/election of Mr. Bobby Jindal as Louisiana governor.

In Chapter I, some insight about what was already in the pipeline was expressed in Governor Bobby Jindal's 2007 Louisiana Gubernatorial Victory Speech. Several of the neo-liberalism economic policy cornerstones mentioned above were identified in this speech, and in his 2012 Election Victory Speech. Both contain a clear message of Governor Bobby Jindal's intent to use neo-liberalism economic policies to grow the Louisiana Economy at the expense of its public sector. In order to make sure we include as much information as possible about the origin of neo-liberalism

---

[2] McQueen, Michel, "House Panel Votes To Trim Medicare By $8.7 Billion," The Wall Street Journal, July 31, 1987, Section 2, p. 34.

ideology, regarding where it came from, we trace its beginning back to 16th Century Europe, and England in particular. It is revealed that neo-liberalism evolved directly out of Classical Liberalism Philosophy, which was initially used by the Founding Fathers to set up the first American Government. Ironically, since 1776 to today, there has been a continuous, conservative political chorus calling for less government. Chapter II establishes a link between neo-liberalism economic policies and criminal aggression. The motor that drives this ideology is consecutive, deep budget cuts in public sector social programs. Thus, when a deep cut-back is made in a social program's budget during time period (X), the devastating impact it has on human life, or social well-being-takes its greatest toll five years later, by (Y) time period. This theory is called the Distributed Lag Relationship. During Governor Bobby Jindal's first term in office, a discussion is provided that reveals there was a sustained 1.5 percent unemployment rate, for five years during this time; and, by his fifth year in the Governor's Office, there was an increase in crime and health problems among others. Moreover, the Distributed Lag Relationship was developed by Dr. Harvey Brenner as part of a study commissioned by the Joint Economic Committee, 94th Congress, 2nd Session, Congress of the United States. An expanded discussion of the Distributed Lag Relationship is included in Chapter VIII.

Meanwhile, underlying the sustained unemployment rate during the Jindal Administration's first term in office, and throughout the first two years of his second one, is its privatization and subsidization neo-liberalism policies, which are address at length in Chapter III. Some attention is given to the neo-liberalism policies passed into law by the Louisiana Legislature, which provided the Jindal Administration with a legal cover-up and foundation upon which it could provide massive tax breaks and incentives to private business. Those private businesses, and the amount of the tax breaks they received, are also discussed. Since investment capital is required for a private business to engage in production of a commodity or service and so forth, and since we already know neo-liberalism policies rely on government to give taxpayers' dollars to private business to produce for the market, the only place for government to turn to get the taxpayers' dollars required for them to engage in production, is the public sector. Given the massive social program budget cuts, from 2008 to 2014, The Advocate Staff quoted Governor Bobby Jindal saying, "Today, Louisiana is the epicenter of an industrial renaissance surpassing anything we've witnessed since perhaps the industrial revolution in 19th-century America..."[3] However, on the other hand, in the midst of Governor Bobby Jindal's Industrial Renaissance, is a growing trail of worsening unemployment. For example, The Advocate Staff recently reported "Houston-based Hercules Offshore says it will lay off 324 offshore Gulf of Mexico workers, about 15 percent of its workforce, because of a decline in business... The layoffs involve employees who work out of Port Fourchon, Grand Isle, Berwick, Cameron, Abbeville, Lafitte, Larose and Venice."[4] These layoffs are not unique, but they are the latest in a continuing and escalating trend during the Jindal Administration. According to the Associated Press, "the state labor department says first-time claims for unemployment insurance in Louisiana for the week ending Nov. 1 increased to 2,178 from the previous week's total of 2,171... Continued unemployment claims for the week ending Nov. 1 increased to 19,190 compared to 19,123 the previous week."[5]

Moreover, The Council of Economic Advisers and the Department of Labor stated "the Emergency Unemployment Compensation (EUC) program authorized by Congress in 2008 has provided crucial support to the economy and to millions of Americans who lost jobs through no fault of their own."[6] In its referenced report, and in column one, the "Number of People Who Received EUC Benefits from January 2008 through September 2013 [, for the State of Louisiana, was] 174,083."[7] Does this idleness of Louisiana Working Class people have any influence

---

[3] The Advocate Staff, "Sasol gives final approval to $8.1 billion Louisiana Project," The Advocate, October 28, 2014, p.1.

[4] _____ "Hercules Offshore to lay off 324 workers," The Advocate, November 5, 2014, p.1.

[5] _____ "Initial unemployment claims rise in Louisiana," The Advocate, November 8, 2014, p. 1.

[6] _____ The Council of Economic Advisers and the Department of Labor, Executive Office Of The President Of The United States, THE ECONOMIC BENEFITS OF EXTENDING UNEMPLOYMENT INSURANCE, http://www.whitehouse.gov/sites/default/files/docs/uireport-2013-12-4.pdf, December 2013, p. 1.

[7] Ibid., p. 11.

on the Industrial Renaissance that Governor Bobby Jindal says is going-on in Louisiana today? It should not be overlooked that this large number of Louisiana Residents, who received EUC/EB Benefits, increased during Governor Bobby Jindal's First Term in office, and continued rising at the beginning of his Second Term as governor.

To prime his budget cutting pump during this time, Chapter IV reveals the first thing the Jindal Administration did was place a message in the social media about Louisiana State Government not having enough money to operate its public sector. This message was cloaked in the language of a shortfall illusion. Before the latter was sent out into cyberspace, massive tax breaks and incentives were already given away to private businesses. Therefore, since the average Louisiana Working Class Resident is clueless about the workings of neo-liberalism policies, and when Governor Bobby Jindal gave the signal to his administration to drop the budget ax on social programs in the public sector, the average Louisiana Resident had no leg to stand on to protest the budget cuts that were made against their working class interest. Rather, a vast majority of the people remained silent, and they suffered more hardships; and many, many innocent people ended up committing violent crimes, and engaging in many antisocial behaviors, ranging from drug abuse to suicide among others.

Once the tax breaks and incentives were given away to private business, we also discuss in Chapter IV the heavy toll budget cuts had on the Louisiana Higher Education Budget, from 2008 to 2014. Although the Louisiana K-12 Budget is protected from budget cuts by constitutional law, the Jindal Administration created a new market for private business by instituting a Report Card Scheme that allegedly evaluates the academic health of a public school. It is discussed in detail how the Jindal Administration used a "voucher scheme" to steer around the constitutional law that protects the K-12 Budget, similar to the way a Category 5 Hurricane steers itself around a high pressure system. By allowing Minimum Foundation Program Funds to follow public school children from so-called "D and F" failing ones, our analysis of the "voucher scheme" continues with a discussion of how it allows millions of taxpayers' dollars to flow into Charter Schools, which have sprung up over much of the Louisiana Public School Landscape.

At the end of Chapter IV, we included a detailed discussion related to Superintendent John White and his Executive Staff. This discussion focuses on the minimal educational backgrounds of his Executive Staff, and some attention is given to Superintendent John White's rise out of the Teach for America Program to become Superintendent of the Louisiana Department of Education. Also addressed is the usually high salaries paid to Mr. John White and his Executive Staff.

After this discussion, Chapter V deals with the privatization of the vast majority of Louisiana Public Hospitals. The names of each privatized public hospital are identified as well as the business the Jindal Administration allowed to take it over. A detailed analysis of the Cooperative Endeavor Agreement is also explained in detail. In addition, information related to healthcare budget cuts is also considered. The Affordable Care Act (ACA), commonly known as Obamacare, is discussed, which reveals that President Obama did not play a role in drafting it, although most Americans inaccurately believe that the ACA is a federal government program that removed healthcare out of the market. The information provided indicates there has not been any significant change in the way healthcare is consumed in the market after the ACA became a law. In addition, some attention is given to a discussion of the Jindal Administration's refusal to expand Medicaid in Louisiana, and what this decision means regarding the number of Louisiana Working Class Residents who, as a result of the non-expansion of Medicaid, will not have access to any affordable healthcare. Chapter V also includes a consideration of the budget cuts made in the Department of Environmental Quality's (DEQ) Operating Budget, from 2008 to 2014. Similar to the massive budget cuts made in the social programs in the public sector, the Louisiana Environment is at risk of further deterioration due to cutbacks in the DEQ's operating budget.

By the time Governor Bobby Jindal's first term in office came to an end, and given his use of the Reagan Neo-Liberalism Economic Policy Model to grow the Louisiana Economy, ironically, there was a simultaneous increase in poverty in Louisiana. All boats did not rise with the rising economic tide Governor Bobby Jindal earlier called an industrial renaissance; more sank than rose. Chapter VI includes a discussion of the extent to which poverty increased in Louisiana, from 2008 to 2013. Neo-liberalism Economic Policies have created an income gap in Louisiana that widened significantly between the "haves" and the "have nots" during the Jindal Administration's first term. Chapter VII provides information that shows the Louisiana Ruling Class, or the top one-half of one percent of its families, earned more money during this time than the vast majority of the Louisiana Working Class Population, and the former paid significantly less of its income in taxes than the latter. Is this neo-liberalism economic policy trend unique to Louisiana, or does its roots extend from the federal government to our state, similar to the way spokes in a bicycle wheel radiate out from its axle to the other forty-nine?

An answer to this question is established in Chapter VIII, in which available information shows there has been a systematic dismantling, or rollback, of the New Deal Era federal government regulations that were put in place to prevent another catastrophic financial crisis after the 1929 Depression. During the discussion, the information reveals former President Bill Clinton was selected/elected to politically oversee Congress' vote to throw the Glass-Steagall Act in the dust bin of American History. With its end, the door was opened through which the Reagan Neo-Liberalism Economic Policy Model took a giant step at the federal government level. The consequences were dramatic, and it is revealed that the conditions that gave birth to the 2008 Depression flourished after the Glass-Steagall Act was dismantled. Afterwards, the Dodd-Frank Bill was enacted by Congress, and before the ink dried, many of the government regulations put in place to prevent another 2008 Depression were thrown-out by the Obama Administration. Although Governor Bobby Jindal has consistency criticized President Barack Obama, both selected/elected politicians have systematically implemented the Reagan Neo-Liberalism Economic Model at the federal and state government level.

Chapter IX provides a detailed discussion of how Governor Bobby Jindal put neo-liberalism economic policy into practice in Louisiana. One result of his massive social program budget cuts was a sustained level of unemployment. The Distributed Lag Relationship provides a way to explain the pathological impact neo-liberalism policies continue to have on the health of the vast majority of Louisiana Working Class people, beginning in 2008. A detailed discussion of antisocial behaviors, which paralleled the implementation of neo-liberalism policies, include, but not limited to, suicide, state prison admissions, incarceration rate, prison privatization boom and the overrepresentation of Afro-Americans in the Louisiana Criminal Justice Plantation System, Afro-American Profiling, murder of women in Louisiana, and declining health of a majority of Louisiana Residents. Regarding the social index during the Jindal Administration, Louisiana ranked at or near the bottom of every social index.

More interestingly, and as we already know, neo-liberalism economic policies call for the non-interference of government in the day-to-day functioning of the market. In Chapter X, information is provided that indicates Governor Bobby Jindal was a "Road Scholar" during a majority of his first and second terms in office. Louisiana State Government was left rudderless. While the budget ax fell on many Louisiana Public Sector Programs, Governor Bobby Jindal was away from the state campaigning for a possible 2016 run for the President of the United States. Marsha Ballard stated "Jindal also told a news conference that he was not interested in any other future office but president of the United States."[8] This is a paradox inasmuch as the social and economic condition of the vast majority of the Louisiana People is shown to be at an all-time historic low. And worse, his out-of-state travel was paid for by the vast majority of Louisiana Working Class residents, whose social needs have been grossly disrespected and, at best, neglected. In Chapter XI, a number of conclusions are presented, including a review of the Louisiana State Budget for 2014. The prospects for the Louisiana environment are addressed with emphasis on what we call the coming drowning of New Orleans, LA and the Louisiana Coast.

After six years of the Jindal Administration, and by October 2014, Elizabeth Crisp reported a majority of Louisiana Residents feel the state's neo-liberalism economic policies have it moving in the "wrong direction." She stated "a majority of Louisiana voters say the state is heading in the "wrong direction." The state's biggest problems are education and unemployment, they told researchers from the University of New Orleans

---

[8] Ballard, Marsha, "Bobby Jindal: Only office I'd seek is presidency," The Advocate, October 22, 2014, p. 1.

in a recent survey. Both Republican Gov. Bobby Jindal and Democratic President Barack Obama are not well liked — earning 40 percent and 38 percent job approval ratings, respectively."[9] If the neo-liberalism economic policies applied in Louisiana, which are given primary attention throughout this book, were making a positive difference in the lives of the vast majority of Louisiana Working Class people, it follows Governor Bobby Jindal's approval rating by the masses would be much, much higher than 40.0 percent. On the other hand, if the UNO Poll would conduct another approval rating survey, and include only responses from Louisiana Residents who make up the top one-half of one percent of household income, Governor Bobby Jindal's approval rating would be more than 90.0 percent. Information discussed later will prove this fact beyond any doubt.

In the Epilogue, a discussion is included to demonstrate how neo-liberalism economic policies have politically, and unfortunately, captured state and federal government nationwide. The discussion shows there is an increasing income gap in Louisiana and nationwide. The income gap is not limited to the United States, but it is international in scope. Thus, as the income gap continues to widen, this is evidence of the growing use of neo-liberalism economic policies to grow the Louisiana Economy at the state and federal government level. As we shall see shortly, what growth the Louisiana Economy has enjoyed during the Jindal Administration thus far, has come with a high price tag, namely, consecutive, deep, year-to-year cuts in the social programs in the Louisiana Public Sector.

Lastly, an Afterword is provided that highlights The Advocate newspaper's eight part series related to its detailed presentation of the various tax giveaway incentives, by the Jindal Administration, in such areas as industrial, enterprise zone, inventory, hydraulic fracking, and the film industry among several others. The eight part article series represents some of the best information published to date, regarding the total amounts of the Louisiana Taxpayers' Dollars, which fall in the general category called *Giving Away Louisiana*. The eight part article series was published in late November and early December 2014.

---

[9] Crisp, Elizabeth, "UNO Poll: Louisiana headed in 'wrong direction,'" The Advocate, October 30, 2014, p. 1.

CONTENTS

I.   Neo-Liberalism Ideology Unmasked..1
     Introduction 1
     Classical Liberalism by 1650...4
     West European Migration to America......................................5
     Classical Liberalism in America..8
     Ownership of African Slaves by Selected Founding Fathers and
     Presidents by 1869 18
          Thomas Jefferson 18
          George Washington 19
          Presidents who Owned African Slaves, From George
          Washington To The Civil War 21
     Neo-Liberalism: Attack on Public Sector Human Rights Made Public. 24
          Neo-Liberalism Rise In America During The Reagan
          administration, 1980 to 1988 24
          Neo-Liberalism And The Role Of The State....................28
          Transformation Of The Public Sector Into A Privatized
          And Commodified Market...31
          Absence Of Criticism Of Neo-Liberalism Policies.........40
          Embedded Neo-Liberalism Policies in Mr. Bobby Jindal's
          Selected 2007, 2012 Election Victory Speeches And in his
          2013 Speech To The Republican National Committee,
          Charlotte, NC..45
          Dividends And Liabilities Of Neo-liberalism Policies
          During The Jindal Administration, 2008 to 2014 61

II. Neo-Liberalism and Human Aggression 64
     Forest Fire Metaphor 67
     Joint Economic Committee 94th Congress, 2nd Session
     Congress of the United States...68

Distributed Lag Relationship...71
Violence and Criminal Aggression Framework........................73

III.   Privatization and Subsidization Policies of the Jindal
    Administration 76
    Wolf and Sheep 78
    Neo-Liberalism Economic Policy: Industrial Tax Breaks and
    Incentives, 2008 to 2014 82
        Louisiana Legislature And Neo-liberalism Economic
        Policies Passed Into Law...83
        Business Tax Breaks By The End Of The Jindal
        Administration's First Term, 2012.....................................86

IV.   Social Program Cuts: Actions Taken by the Jindal
    Administration to Balance the Louisiana State Budget, 2008-
    2014 100
    Cause of Higher Education Budget Cuts, 2008 to 2014......................100
    Higher Education Budget Cuts, 2008 to 2010 104
        Higher Education Budget Cuts by 2013.......................................105
        Summary of Impact on the Higher Education Budgets,
        2008 to 2013...114
    Public Education Budget: K-12 119
        Charter School And Its Underlying Financial Goal 121
        Classification Of Louisiana Public Schools: "D" or "F"? 123
        Clearing The Way For Charter School Development:
        BESE, Jindal Administration, And The Louisiana Legislature 127
        Charter School Depletion Of The Minimum Foundation
        Fund Program 131
        Charter Schools And Federal Desegregation Orders Disregarded 133
        Charter Schools And Budget Shortfall Consequences At
        The Local School Districts Level 141
        More Failing Public Schools Means Increased Number Of
        Charter Schools...145
        Louisiana Legislature, Charter Schools, Public School
        Failures, And Teacher Retirement 149
    John White, Superintendent of Education and his Executive Staff.......158
        John White, Superintendent Of Education's Executive Staff........160
        Executive Staff Organizational Chart And Position Title.............167

V.   Healthcare Program Privatization and Staff Layoffs 173

Healthcare Budget Cuts, 2008 to 2013 173

    Louisiana Public Hospitals And Health Related Programs............174

    Impact of Neo-Liberal Economic Policy On The Louisiana

    Healthcare Budget, Fiscal Year 2013 175

    Bruce Greenstein: Privatization Architect Of The Louisiana

    Public Hospitals, 2008 to 2013 199

    Impact Of Privatization Of Louisiana Public Hospitals On

    Hospital Employees And Patients, 2013 205

Obamacare: Its Authors, Who Benefits And What Is Insured?............217

Jindal Administration And Medicaid: No Expansion Of

Coverage, 2013... 227

Louisiana Mental Health Program, 2013 244

Inefficiencies Of Neo-Liberal Economic Policy, And Its Inability

to Provide Practical Solutions to Social Problems 248

Department of Environmental Quality (DEQ) Budget, 2008 to 2014 252

VI.   Poverty Among the Louisiana Citizenry During the Jindal

Administration, 2008 to 2013 261

Poverty In The United States, 2011 261

Poverty In Louisiana During The Jindal Administration's First

And Second Terms In Office, 2008 to 2013 262

    Jindal Administration's Explanation For Rising Poverty In

    Louisiana, 2008 to 2013... 265

    Economic Impact Of The Federal Government's Oil-

    Drilling Moratorium On The Louisiana Economy, 2008 to 2013 268

VII.   Louisiana Ruling Class and Taxes Paid During the Jindal

Administration 271

Louisiana Ruling Class Definition 271

Taxes Paid by the Louisiana Ruling Class, January 2013 272

Taxes Paid By The Louisiana Ruling Class, 2013 273

Taxes Paid by the Louisiana Working Class, 2013............................... 274

VIII.   Dismantling of the New Deal Regulations, and Paving the Road

for the 2008 Depression.. 277

End Of New Deal Regulations Insuring Another 1929 Great

Depression 277

Post-Glass-Steagall Act Repeal And Rise Of Neo-Liberal

Privatization Economic Policy... 279

Post 2008 Depression And The Wall Street Compromise Of The
Dodd-Frank Bill's Investment Bank Regulations 286

IX.   Louisiana Unemployment During the Jindal Administration,
        2008 to 2013 295
        Neo-Liberal Privatization Economic Policy And Rising
        Unemployment 295
        Rising Tide Of Louisiana Unemployment 296
        Cumulative Impact Of The Sustained 1.8 Percent Rise In
        Unemployment During The Jindal Administration's First Five
        Years In Office, 2008 To 2013 299
            Brief Review Of The Distributed Lag Relationship Theory 299
            Distributed Lag Relationship And Neo-Liberal
            Privatization Economic Policy 301
        Pathological Impact Of Neo-Liberal Privatization Economic
        Policy On The Health Of The Louisiana Working Class, 2008
        to 2012 302
            Suicide In Louisiana During The Jindal Administration 302
            State Prison Admissions During The Jindal Administration 304
            Louisiana Residents Incarcerated Since The Jindal
            Administration Took Office, 2008 to 2013 305
            Origin Of The Louisiana State Prison Population And The
            Part Played By Neo-Liberal Privatization Economic Policy
            In The Modern Era 308
            Prison Privatization Boom: A Perfect Marriage Between
            The Availability Of Incarcerated Labor Power Of African-
            Americans And Private Business Interests 313
            Racist Laws And The Criminal Justice System Plantation 314
            Doing Time In Louisiana During The Jindal Administration 319
            Louisiana Criminal Justice System Plantation And The
            Prison Industrial Complex (PIC) 321
            Homicides Reported In Louisiana During The Jindal
            Administration, 2008 to 2013 337
            Murder of Women In Louisiana And Sexual Assault
            During The Jindal Administration, 2008 to 2013 341
            Sexual Assault Against Women In The American Military,
            2008 to 2013 346
            Cardiovascular Deaths In Louisiana During The Jindal
            Administration, 2008 to 2013 352

X.   Governor Bobby Jindal: A Louisiana Road Scholar...............359
        TURTLE ON A POLE.. 361
        Road Scholar, 2008 to 2014 364
            Governor Bobby Jindal: A Frequent Flyer 366
            Road Scholar Travel Expenses Paid For By The Louisiana
            Taxpayers 369

XI.   Conclusion 372
        Louisiana State Budget, 2014 373
        Environmental Deprivation, 2014 380
        The Coming Drowning Of New Orleans, LA And The
        Louisiana Gulf Coast 392

Epilogue.. 405
        Income Inequality Worldwide, 2014 421
        Income Inequality In The United States, 2014 422

Afterword.. 437
        Film Industry Tax Incentives By December 2014.............. 439
        Hydraulic Fracking Tax Incentives By December 2014 440
        Enterprise Zone Tax Incentives By 2014............................ 442
        Industrial Tax Incentives by 2014..................................... 446
        Inventory Tax Refund By 2014.. 447
        Solar Energy Tax Credit By 2014 449

LIST OF TABLES

Preface

Table 1.0   President Reagan's Fiscal 1988 Budget Cuts of
             Selected Public Sector Programs, January 6, 1987
             (in billions of dollars)... xviii

Chapter I

Table 1.1   Signers Of The Declaration Of Independence By State.... 9
Table 1.2   Signers Of The U. S. Constitution by State................... 10
Table 1.3   Selected "Founding Fathers," Their Birthplace,
             And Class: Delegates To The Constitutional
             Convention... 13

Chapter II

Table 1.4   Cumulative Impact of the 1.4 Percent Rise in
             Unemployment During 1970..................................... 72

Chapter III

Table 1.5   Louisiana Legislature Laws Authorizing Business
             Tax Breaks During the First Term of the Jindal
             Administration 92
Table 1.6   Implementation of Laws Authorizing Business Tax
             Breaks by the Louisiana Economic Development
             Agency, Office of the Governor, Jindal
             Administration, 2008 to Present............................... 93

Chapter IV

Table 1.7 Louisiana State Budget Deficits, 2009 to 2013 102
Table 1.8 Six Figure Salaries of Superintendent of Education
           John White's Executive Staff, Including his Own,
           October 2012 161
Table 1.9 Superintendent of Education John White's
           Executive Staff 167

Chapter V

Table 1.10 Total Annual Amount of Louisiana Taxpayer
            Dollars Given to Private Business as a result of the
            Privatization of All Louisiana Public Hospitals,
            Fiscal Years 2013 and 2014 196
Table 1.11 Number of Uninsured Louisiana Residents
            Denied Health Insurance Due to the Jindal
            Administration's Non-Expansion of the New
            Obamacare Medicaid Program in Louisiana, By
            Mental Health Conditions, February 26, 2014 232
Table 1.12 Louisiana National Ranking Regarding Selected
            Diseases, 2013 249
Table 1.13 Louisiana National Ranking Regarding Seniors
            Health Condition, 2013 250

Chapter VI

Table 1.14 Employment Changes from April 2010 to July
            2010 for Five oil Industry Intensive Parishes in
            Louisiana 269

Chapter VIII

Table 1.15 Income Inequality in American Class Society For
            Selected Corporations, 2014 285

Chapter IX

Table 1.16 Violent Crimes and Murders/Homicides In
            Louisiana During the Jindal Administration, 2008
            to 2012 339

Table 1.17   Percutaneous Coronary Intervention Rate Per
1,000 Louisiana Residents For Selected Cities, 2013.....357

Table 1.18   Cumulative Impact Of The Sustained 1.8 Percent
Rise in Unemployment During The Jindal
Administration: 2008 to 2013 358

Chapter X

Table 1.19   Governor Bobby Jindal's Out-Of –State Travels
On Non-Louisiana State Government Business
During His First And Second Terms In Office 368

Chapter XI

Table 1.20   Gulf of Mexico And Louisiana Wildlife Affected
by the BP Deepwater Horizon Oil Spill Disaster
Four Years Later-April 2014 382

Epilogue

Table 1.21   Louisiana Unemployment and Obesity Rates, by
the Third Year of the Second Term of the Jindal
Adminstration, by Selected Parishes, June 26, 2014 408

CHAPTER I

Neo-Liberalism Ideology Unmasked

A. Introduction

During the Middle Ages, from around 1300 to 1500, or the "Dark Ages," human rights were non-existent, and human beings were viewed as "subjects," who were subordinated to the singular dictatorship of a monarchy form of rule. Throughout this period, "...hereditary privilege, state religion, absolute monarchy, and the Divine Right of Kings..."[10] were common practices throughout societies in Western and Eastern Europe. Unable to continue living under these oppressive conditions, absolute monarchy, and many of its mentioned customs, gave way to a new political form called Classical Liberalism. The latter took root at the beginning of the "Age of Enlightenment," from 1650 to 1800. "Enlightenment thinkers in Britain, in France and throughout Europe questioned traditional authority and embraced the notion that humanity could be improved through rational change...The American and French Revolutions were directly inspired by Enlightenment ideals..."[11] It was during this period that Classical Liberalism gained a foothold in Western Europe, and later in America.

As it was, tradition and absolute government was on the way out, and

---

[10] _____ Boundless Political Science, http://www.boundless.com/politicalscience/textbooks/boundless-political-science-textbooks/American-politics-1/

[11] _____Enlightenment, www.history.com/topics/enlightenment

1

liberal "talk" about the value of human rights was finding its way into law. For example,

> "Liberalism first became a powerful force during the Enlightenment, when it became popular among philosophers and economists in the Western world. Liberalism rejected the notions, common at the time, of hereditary privilege, state religion, absolute monarchy, and the Divine Right of Kings. The early liberal thinker John Locke, who is often credited with the creation of liberalism as a distinct philosophical tradition, employed the concept of natural rights and the social contract to argue that the rule of law should replace both tradition and absolutism in government; that rulers were subject to the consent of the governed; and that private individuals had a fundamental right to life, liberty, and property."[12]

Just before the Age of Enlightenment started in 1650, England engaged in The Thirty Years War, from 1618 to 1648. Peter H. Wilson stated "The Thirty Years War (1618-48) was the most destructive conflict in Europe before the twentieth-century world wars."[13] This war not only resulted in massive loss of lives; it brought extreme poverty and suffering to the British Working Class. For the typical British Working Class individual, life in England was horrible. Andrea Stewart's book titled *Sugar In The Blood*, 2012 offers a graphic portrayal of the socio-economic and political hardship the vast majority of British Working Class people endured by the end of The Thirty Years War, which coincided with the onset of the Age of Enlightenment. She wrote the following:

> "The wider political situation also contributed to the depressed mood of the country and the general suffering during this period. The Thirty Years War (1618 -1648), which had seen warring Protest ant and Catholic forces

---

[12] _____Boundless Political Science, Op. Cit.
[13] Wilson, Peter H., "The Causes of The Thirty Years War, 1618 -1648," <u>English Historical Review</u>, CXXIII (502): pp. 554-586. (Abstract)

reduce much of Europe to a corpse-strewn battleground, further depleted the nation and contributed to profound collective dissatisfaction with the status quo. The decades from the 1630s through to the end of the 1650s were, according to the historian Peter Bowden, "probably amongst the most terrible years through which the country had ever passed."[14]

Moreover, besides the three decades war, there were many other mounting socio-economic problems facing the vast majority of British Working Class people at this time. Stuart further explained the depressed plight of the British Working Class population as such:

> "In the late sixteenth and early seventeenth centuries, rapid population growth and periodic agricultural depression, culminating in a series of terrible famines, caused genuine hardship. In the countryside large numbers of people had been deprived of their ancient rural security. The lack of land to cultivate frustrated many, while unemployment threatened agricultural laborers as well as village artisans. The rise of the cost of living and the simultaneous fall in the value of wages meant that many people were surviving on the very margins of existence. Housing was inadequate at best; in cold weather fuel was scarce and expensive. Health scares were frequent, with regular outbreaks of tuberculosis and plague. Effective medical treatment was almost non-existent and so the mortality rate-already high-rose even higher. Resentment against these conditions focused and crystallize on a lavish, self-indulgent monarch…from 1629, the people had been governed by arbitrary monarchial rule."[15]

The vast majority of the British Working Class did not own any property

---

[14] Stuart, Andrea, *Sugar In The Blood: A Family's Story Of Slavery And Empire,* Vintage Books, New York, 2012, p. 13.

[15] Ibid., p. 12.

by 1629, a time when the British Monarchy owned nearly every useful asset in the country. Stuart stated "only one in seven English heads of households owned freehold land and almost all of them owed at least token payments to a manorial lord..."[16] To say the least, everyday life in England was, generally speaking, depressing. England, at the time, was the wealthiest nation on Earth; yet, the British Working Class, whose labor power made this great wealth possible, hardly had clothes to wear; food to eat; and shelter from the cold weather.

B. Classical Liberalism by 1650

Alongside the rising poverty of the British Working Class, there was a simultaneous upsurge in the latter's desire for a better life, characterized by the inalienable human rights of "being free" to satisfy their basic needs such as freedom of speech, right to work, freedom of religion, freedom of assembly and more without any absolute, monarchial government dictating their individual lives. The right to self-determination was gaining more strength as daily social and economic life continued to rapidly deteriorate for the vast majority of British Working Class people.

As the Age of Enlightenment gained momentum, and more discussion spread through West European Societies, including England and France, but not limited to them, a surge of interest, in the working class people, swept through these nations regarding the possibility of realizing their human rights. John Locke, Western Philosophers, "...credited with the creation of liberalism, argued that the rule of law should replace both tradition and absolutism in government; that rulers were subject to the consent of the governed; and that individuals had a fundamental right to life, liberty, and property."[17] With these thoughts being burned into their imagination, tens of thousands of poor, uneducated, property less, working class people, from England, and other West European Nations, *having nothing to lose and everything to gain, that is, their freedom in particular, found a way to make the long voyage across the Atlantic Ocean to America, in search of freedoms they were historically denied in their*

---

[16] Ibid., p. 26.

[17] Boundless Political Science, Op. Cit.

own homeland. What drove millions from their European homeland was a belief in liberty. According to the National Center For Public Analysis, John C. Goodman stated "...classical liberalism is the belief in liberty."[18] Having lived without liberty for so many centuries that by the time the Age of Enlightenment came into existence, thousands of West Europeans were ready to uproot from their homelands and make the journey to America.

C. West European Migration to America

If the Native American Indians had refused West Europeans, from England and other West European nations, entry into America, their native homeland, beginning in 1607, thousands of them would have perished in the sea and back in Western Europe. The descendants of many of the first migration of West Europeans to America have forgotten the *compassion extended to them, given the upsurge in their energy to block Latin American Working Class people from entering America today.*

Regarding the West European Working Class people's search for freedom, which they could not find in their own homelands, Andrea Stuart wrote the following:

> "the migration had begun as a trickle in 1607 with the settling of Jamestown, the first permanent colony in what is now the United States. It had increased to a recognizable stream by 1629 and became a veritable flood in the 1640s, when over 100,000 people left a country with a population of just under five million. (Between1600 and 1700 over 700,000 people emigrated from England, about17 percent of the English population in 1600)...one ship depart[ed] from England every day..."[19]

As the socio-economic conditions in England, and other Western

---

[18] Goodman, John C., "What Is Classical Liberalism?," www.ncpa.org, Washington, D. C., 2010, p.1.
[19] Stuart, Andrea, Op. Cit., p. 10.

European Countries continued to worsen, the flood of emigrants became a tidal wave. The Lancashire Cotton Famine, was triggered by the outbreak of the Civil War in the United States. Former imports of baled cotton, from America, came to halt. Thus, between 1861 and 1865, the shortage of baled cotton shutdown the textile industry located in North West England. Textile workers, among many others, were laid-off, and joined the ranks of the most impoverished people in England. The Cotton Famine, war, and a monarchy government created a general socio-economic climate, characterized by poverty and hopelessness. A vast majority of British Working Class people did not have any human rights at the time, although many were waking up to the fact they did not have any freedom. With no hope of producing a better life for themselves, millions of working class people departed England and other Western European Countries between 1600 and 1920. Ayers, Schulzinger, et. al, stated "between 1840 and 1920, the country experienced its largest period of immigration, an influx of 37 million people...Because of the potato famine and European upheavals [mentioned earlier], Irish and German arrivals dominated..."[20]

> Who were these immigrants, and how did most of them obtain their passage to America, if, at the time of their departure from England, they lived in poverty?

From the outset of the great immigration to America, most of the emigrants obtained their passage as indentured servants. Andrea Stuart stated "the indentured system was first trialed in 1620, by a Virginia planter who began purchasing labor of servants for a specified period in return for paying their passage to the colony. The system had spread rapidly across the Americas, only dying out when these same colonies embraced African slavery."[21] Most of the European Emigrants pre-paid their passage to America with a lien on their labor power. Stuart added "the Irish were particularly plentiful because of frequent food shortages, high

---

[20] Ayers, Edward L., Schulzinger, Robert D., et. al., *American Anthem: Modern American History*, Holt, Rinehart and Winston, 2007, p. 767.
[21] Stuart, Andrea, Op. Cit., p. 43.

unemployment and English military disruptions in their homeland."[22] The British Working Class Emigrants were producers with a diverse mixture of skills. Andrea Stuart provided the following information about the skills of the European emigrants:

> "These emigrants were unrepresentative of the population of their various homelands in that they were overwhelmingly young, male and unmarried. While history has highlighted the stories of ambitious adventurers and privileged second and third sons who made their reputations in the New World, the vast majority were, in fact, ordinary people. As the passenger manifests of the day attest, it is men of modest means who were listed page after page: rope-makers and butchers, masons and farmers. Their numbers swelled by the streams of involuntary migrants who went to the Americas in chains: indentured servants who were tricked aboard ship by "spirits" (agents paid by the settlement companies to recruit laborers by any means necessary); political prisoners who were exiled as punishment; vagrants and or phans and criminals who had been deposited there like so much rubbish."[23]

Female emigrants were rounded up wherever they could be found and sent to America. Stuart wrote the following about the social and economic condition of most women who made the voyage to America and the so-called New World:

> "These were throwaway women with rough lives. Some were prostitutes, some were criminals, some were mentally ill, some were victimized or unlucky-but mad or bad, virtuous or fallen, once these girls arrived in the New World they were in demand. Despite their colorful reputation, the real defining characteristics

[22] Ibid., p. 43.
[23] Ibid., p. 16.

of these women's lives was not their immorality but
their powerlessness. Many were desperate-discarded by
family, abandoned by husbands, broken by poverty and
abuse."[24]

As we see, the plight of the West European Immigrants does not
coincide with the romantic version so often written into the American
History book by historians and many other scientists. They were slaves
without chains-nearly penniless. Indentured servants were enslaved for
years once they arrived in the American Colonies. Before a majority of
the British Working Class people left England for America, only 1 of
7 owned any land; when they arrived in America, the Native American
Indians gave them land free of charge. Almost overnight many of the
West European Immigrants became landowners; and many others
assumed this status after they served their indentured servant terms.
In their new American homeland, the former British Immigrants, in
due time, were now free to put their Classical Liberalism Philosophy
into practice.

D. Classical Liberalism in America

The vast majority of European Immigrants, who came to America,
were primarily poor, illiterate, and property less. Yet, they left England,
and other West European Countries, in waves. We should remember
that most of the European Immigrants came to America in search
of human rights and freedom, but, most were uneducated. Who,
then, were the European Immigrants, among them, who put Classical
Liberalism Philosophy into a written form so the vast majority of
uneducated European Immigrants would feel America could become
a better place than the economically depressed British Society they
recently fled? A careful examination of the backgrounds of the so-
called "Founding Fathers" reveal the individuals who brought Classical
Liberalism to America were still significantly influenced by Monarchy
Government Principles and Royal Etiquettes, which their parents were
conditioned by during their lifetimes before they left England. The

---

[24] Ibid., p. 52.

parents of the "Founding Fathers" taught their children what they learned about Monarchy Government, while living in England, during their childhoods in America. Table 1.1 below shows the names of the "Founding Fathers," who signed the Declaration of Independence.

Table 1.1
Signers Of The Declaration Of Independence By State

Massachusetts	Connecticut	Pennsylvania	Maryland	North Carolina
John Hancock	Roger Sherman	Robert Morris	Samuel Chase	William Hooper
Samuel Adams	Samuel	Benjamin Rush	William Paca	Joseph Hewes
John Adams	Huntington	Benjamin	Thomas Stone	John Penn
Robert Treat	William Williams	Franklin	Charles Carrol	
Paine	Oliver Wolcott	John Morton		**South Carolina**
Elbridge Gerry		George Clymer	**Virginia**	Edward Rutledge
	New York	James Smith	George Wythe	Thomas Heyward
New Hampshire	William Floyd	George Taylor	Richard	Thomas Lynch
Josiah Bartlett	Philip Livingston	James Wilson	Henry Lee	Arthur Middleton
William Whipple	Francis Lewis	George Ross	Thomas Jefferson	
Matthew	Lewis Morris		Benjamin	**Georgia**
Thornton		**Delaware**	Harrison	Button Gwinnett
	New Jersey	Caesar Rodney	Thomas	Lyman Hall
Rhode Island	Richard Stockton	George Read	Nelson, Jr.	George Walton
Stephen Hopkins	John	Thomas M' Kean	Francis	
William Ellery	Witherspoon		Lightfoot Lee	
	Francis		Carter Braxton	
	Hopkinson			
	John Hart			
	Abraham Clark			

Source: Colonialhall.com/biography.php

In addition, Table 1.2 shows the names of the "Founding Fathers" by state, who signed the U.S. Constitution.

Table 1.2
Signers Of The U. S. Constitution by State

New Hampshire	Pennsylvania	Virginia
John Langdon	Benjamin Franklin	John Blair
Nicholas Gilman	Thomas Mifflin	James Madison, Jr.
	Robert Morris	George Washington
Massachusetts	George Clymer	
Rufus King	Thomas FitzSimons	**North Carolina**
Nathaniel Gorham	Jared Ingersoll	William Blount
	Gouverneur Morris	Richard Dobbs Spaight
Connecticut	James Wilson	Hugh Williamson
Roger Sherman		
William Samuel Johnson	**Delaware**	**South Carolina**
	George Read	John Rutledge
New York	Gunning Bedford, Jr.	Charles Cotesworth
Alexander Hamilton	John Dickinson	Pinckney
	Richard Bassett	Charles Pinckney
New Jersey	Jacob Broom	Pierce Butler
William Livingston		
David Brearley	**Maryland**	**Georgia**
William Paterson	James McHenry	William Few
Jonathan Dayton	Daniel Carroll	Abraham Baldwin
	Dan of St. Thomas Jenifer	

Source: Colonialhall.com/biography.php

These men created the Declaration of Independence and the U.S. Constitution, and given this fact-ALL-carried within them a strong sympathy for British Monarchy Government when these two documents were created. Their philosophy was Classical Liberalism, which basically mean a belief in liberty for all human beings, although British Monarchy Government Principles were subtly incorporated into these two documents. Frank Prochaska, Yale University Professor, wrote the following:

> "In September 1761, the colonial Englishman Benjamin Franklin, on tour in the Low Countries, eagerly anticipated a return to his home in London to attend the coronation of George III... Franklin's admiration for his monarch had few limits. After a dinner at Versailles hosted by Louis XV in 1767, he reported that 'no Frenchman shall go beyond

me in thinking my own king and queen the very best in
the World and most amiable'…As Franklin's devotion to
royalty illustrates, it was no easy matter to break with so
universal a system of government as monarchy, especially
for colonial subjects who thought of themselves as patriotic
Englishmen and their King as a guardian of the Protestant
faith and the 'father of his people'…Royal authority was
slow to weaken in a land of English-speaking emigrants
on the fringes of the known world, whose leaders looked
to the King for political legitimacy. As the colonists
believed the monarchy to be the guarantor of their rights,
even the disaffected were hesitant to blame the King for
their discontents…The colonial tradition of looking to the
Crown for redress was powerful… Dismissing the monarch
was more difficult given the deep roots of royalism in the
colonies… Americans, as Franklin's grandson Benjamin
Franklin Bache put it in 1797, created a constitution
before they 'had sufficiently *un-monarchized* their ideas
and habits' (his italics)… hereditary monarchy was the
principal constitutional model on which Americans
had to draw before the French Revolution. The forms
of government on offer to the Founding Fathers were
essentially variations of monarchy, 'the rule of one'…
Though few Americans said it openly after 1776, many
of them believed that limited hereditary monarchy was a
practical system of government."[25]

What has emerged thus far is a majority of the signers of the Declaration
of Independence and the U. S. Constitution were heavily influenced by the
British Monarchy Government inasmuch as it was the political model most
familiar to them, and the American Colonists in general. Prochaska stated
"not all the Founding Fathers were averse to kingship… Various American

[25] Prochaska, Frank, "The American Monarchy," History*Today*, http://www.
historytody.com/frank-prochaska/american-monarchy, Published in History Today
(/taxonomy/term/43)Volume:57Issue:8 (/taxonomy/term/108),2007 (/taxonomy/
term/14781), pp. 1, 2, and 3.

thinkers, most notably John Adams (d. 1826) and Alexander Hamilton (d.1804), leaned towards incorporating monarchical elements in the American constitution..."[26] There was a deep-rooted belief in the British Monarchy form of government by a majority of Alexander Hamilton's contemporaries. As it was, Prochaska added Alexander Hamilton's mind "... had been shaped by the British constitution, which he believed, like many of his contemporaries, to be the finest in the world."[27] Before and during the writing of the mentioned documents, Prochaska noted "in looking for a viable constitutional model, the Founding Fathers turned naturally to British precedent...they strained to reconcile egalitarianism with mixed government, their colonial experience eased the translation of King, Lords and Commons into President, Senate and the House of Representatives."[28] By changing the names with some timely substitutes such as King with President, and so forth, the Founding Fathers were able to remain true to the British Monarchy Model of Government while on the surface, an appearance was given that they had forged a new U. S. Constitution, overwhelmingly distinct from British Monarchy Rule. Prochaska added "every parent believes in the hereditary principle. The want of a hereditary monarchy, what Bagehot called 'a family on the throne', has only propelled the emergence of political dynasties in the United States, from the Adamses to the Bushes."[29] We should not lose sight of the fact that the vast majority of European Immigrants fled Europe, hoping that Classical Liberalism would bring liberty into their then hopeless, pessimistic, unhappy, and impoverished lives.

Thus, the dilemma faced by the "Founding fathers," at the time of the development of the Declaration of independence and the U.S. Constitution, was on one hand, write Classical Liberalism ideas into these documents to the satisfy the vast majority of the American Colonists and a vast majority of Americans throughout the coming generations, and on the other, incorporate underneath the *flowery language of optimism, freedom,*

---

[26] Ibid., p. 3.

[27] Ibid., p. 4.

[28] Ibid., p. 4.

[29] Ibid., p. 5.

happiness, and the "American Dream" hidden principles of British Monarchy Government.

As we have already seen, the "Founding Fathers" were not the everyday, average European Immigrant, who found his or her way to America as a poor, impoverished indentured servant, or someone who paid his or her way to America with the few possessions they had, leaving them *penniless upon arrival.* To the contrary, in Table 1.3, a vast majority of the "Founding Fathers," were the children of very wealthy families, regardless if they were born in Europe or America.

Table 1.3
Selected "Founding Fathers," Their Birthplace, And Class: Delegates To The Constitutional Convention

NAME	BIRTHPLACE	YEAR	CLASS
James Madison	Port Conway, Virginia	1751	Planter Aristocracy
George Washington	Wakefield Plantation, Virginia	1732	Landed Gentry
Thomas Mifflin	Philadelphia, PA	1744	Rich Merchant
Gouverneur Morris	Westchester County, NY	1752	Wealthy Family
James Wilson	St. Andrews, Scotland	1741	Wealthy family
Alexander Hamilton	Nevis, British West Indies	1757	Merchant and Planter Aristocracy
Thomas Jefferson	Charlottesville, Virginia	1743	Elite Planter Aristocracy*
John Adams	Braintree, Massachusetts	1735	Planter Aristocracy
John Marshall	Germantown, Virginia	1755	Wealthy Family
Patrick Henry	Hanover, Virginia	1736	Planter Aristocracy

Source: www.archives.gov/exhibits/charters/constitution_founding_fathers.html and www.biography.com

> *"…third U. S. president…born into one of the most prominent families of Virginia's planter elite."

From the above information, it is easily understood that the majority of the so-called "Founding Fathers" were born into wealthy families, whose parents were descendents of the British upper-class. As such, the vast majority of the Founding Fathers had more in common with the British Monarchy than the ordinary British Working Class Immigrant at the time the Declaration of Independence and the U. S. Constitution were written and approved. The challenge for the so-called Founding Fathers was to write language into these documents that would make the vast majority of European Immigrants, who migrated to America, feel *optimistic about their future, while, underlying their colorful language about freedom, life, and happiness, they incorporated in them a self-serving, elective monarchy government*. Most European Immigrants could not understand the hidden details beneath the language because, as we already know, a vast majority of them were illiterate, or having had only minimal schooling. Prochaska wrote the following

> "America's adaptation of 'elective monarchy' and the borrowing of British ceremonial suggests just how deeply indebted the new nation was to its colonial past. In Britain, as Bagehot and a host of constitutional writers agreed, a republic had 'insinuated itself beneath the folds of a Monarchy'. In America, a monarchy had insinuated itself beneath the folds of a republic. The phrase 'Monarcho-Republicanism' was sometimes used to describe the British Crown in the nineteenth century. It had a variant in the US presidency, which many a participant in the Revolution recognized. Even Jefferson...felt that the spirit, if not the letter of monarchy, had persisted. He feared an eventual tyranny of executive power in Washington, which he believed to be a feature of Federalist politics. As he wrote to James Madison in 1789: 'We were educated in royalism; no wonder, if some of us retain that idolatry still'...a penchant for 'the rule of one' had a recurring echo in the republic, which the constitution did little to silence. Throughout American history references to the President as a king have been a feature of the nation's conversation about its political leadership. Such references have increased of late, as a glance at many a newspaper will attest. Stephen Graubard's recent survey of presidents from Theodore Roosevelt to George W. Bush sees them as a breed of would be monarchs surrounded by courtiers, with vastly

expanded executive authority and 'unmistakable signs of having assumed the trappings traditionally bestowed on European heads of state'. Brought up on trappings of royalty many Americans continue to succumb to the idolatry and charm of kingship."[30]

Well, royalty and British Monarchy remained alive in the Declaration of Independence and the U.S. Constitution as one of its primary writers, Thomas Jefferson voiced in a letter to James Madison in 1789. Who better to know what is written into these documents than the writer of them himself? Of course Classical Liberalism took front and center stage for working class people to consume for generations to come. John C. Goodman, President of the national Center for Policy Analysis, wrote the following in his article titled "What Is Classical Liberalism?"

"Prior to the 20th century, classical liberalism was the dominant political Philosophy in the United States. It was the political philosophy of Thomas Jefferson and the signers of the Declaration of Independence and it permeates the Declaration of Independence, the Constitution, the Federalist Papers and many other documents produced by the people who created the American system of government. Basically, classical liberalism is the belief in liberty."[31]

As we shall see shortly, the Declaration of Independence is filled with words that talk about liberty, and that people have human rights that cannot be given to them by government. For example, in the American History textbook titled *American Anthem: Modern American History*, 2007, Edward L. Ayers, Jesus F. de la Teja, Deborah Gray White, Robert Schulzinger, and Sam Weinburg published the Declaration of Independence in their book in which the following was written by Thomas Jefferson:

---

[30] Ibid., p. 7.
[31] Goodman, John C., "What Is Classical Liberalism?," www.ncpa.org, national Center for Policy Analysis, Washington, DC, 2010, p. 1.

> "When in the course of human events, it becomes
> necessary for one People to dissolve the political bands
> which have connected them with another, and to assume
> the Powers of the earth, the separate and equal station
> to which the Laws of Nature and of nature's God entitle
> them, a decent respect to the opinion of mankind requires
> that they should declare the causes which impel them to
> the separation."[32]

This is Classical Liberalism at its best inasmuch as Thomas Jefferson made a call beyond the British Monarchy to the human heart, and, rather than the former issuing human rights to man and woman, he accurately noted that such human rights are granted independent of monarchy government, and-instead-by the "Laws of Nature." Thomas Jefferson explained what he meant by human rights being decreed by the Laws of nature only in the second paragraph of the Declaration of Independence. There, he wrote the following:

> "We hold these truths to be self-evident, that all men are
> created equal, that they are **endowed** by their Creator
> with certain unalienable Rights, that among these are
> Life, Liberty, and the pursuit of happiness."[33]

Remember, in England during the reign of King George III, women, and people of color in the known world at the time, did not have any human rights, and, as we have previously mentioned, Thomas Jefferson, and the other Founding Fathers, followed the line of Absolute Monarchy by omitting women and people of color because, like King George III, they-too-believed that women and people of color were not "endowed by their Creator with certain unalienable Rights. This can be easily verified by the fact that Thomas Jefferson went to great lengths in the Declaration of Independence, for the purpose of outlining "the history of the present

---

[32] Ayers, Edward L. Schulzinger, Robert D., Teja, Jesus F. de la, White Gray, Deborah, and Sam Wineburg, <u>American Anthem: Modern American History</u>, Holt, Rinehart And Winston, New York, 2007, p. 38.
[33] Ibid., p. 38.

King of Great Britain is a history of repeated injuries and usurpations, all having in direct object the establishment of an absolute **Tyranny** over these States. To prove this, let Facts be submitted to a **candid** world."[34] Thomas Jefferson outlined 18 specific injuries against the American Colonies caused by King George III.[35] Actually, Thomas Jefferson included 19 specific injuries in the draft of the Declaration of Independence he submitted to the U. S. Congress. What happened to the mysterious **19th Injury**? Before we answer this question, let us state what the **19th Injury is**:

> "He has waged cruel war against human nature itself, violating its most sacred rights of life and liberty in the persons of a distant people whomever offended him, captivating and carrying them into slavery in another hemisphere, or to incur miserable death in their transportation thither."[36]

When the Founding Fathers read this injury, among the others, caused by King George III, England was heavily engaged in the International Slave Trade. However, it would be very simplistic to conclude the above was written into the Declaration of Independence as a means of getting King George III to end England's involvement in the International Slave Trade. The Founding Fathers removed the **19th Injury, from the Declaration of Independence,** because a large number of them, as we have already seen, were members of the American Planter Aristocracy, which also depended on slave labor. "In 1776, Jefferson's strong attack on the slave trade in the draft of the Declaration of Independence was deleted by the Continental Congress."[37] Who would replace the indentured servants if the **19th Injury remained in this document?** Thus, to charge King George III with destroying the lives of human beings "who never offended", and who lived in distant lands, would close the door to slavery in America also.

---

[34] Ibid., p. 38.

[35] Ibid., pp. 38, 39, and 40.

[36] Ibid., p. 41.

[37] _____ "Jefferson and Slavery," The Monticello Classroom, http://classroom. monticello.org/kids/resources/profile/263/Middle/Jefferson-and-Slavery/, 2007 Thomas Jefferson Foundation.

This is why the Founding Fathers took out the 19th Injury so the practice of slavery could expand beyond the American Colonies during the 17th and 18th Centuries.

E. Ownership of African Slaves by Selected Founding Fathers and Presidents by 1869

a. Thomas Jefferson

At the time Thomas Jefferson wrote the Declaration of Independence, he owned more than 500 African Slaves. According to available information, his ownership of African Slaves is documented as follows:

> "Thomas Jefferson spent his entire life in the company of African-American slaves. Jupiter, born in 1743 (the same year Jefferson was born) was his childhood companion. He later became Jefferson's personal servant, traveling with his master all over Virginia. Slaves accompanied Jefferson to Philadelphia, where he wrote the Declaration of Independence...Over his lifetime, Thomas Jefferson owned over six hundred slaves. When Jefferson was twenty-one, he inherited about thirty slaves from his father. Later, he inherited 135 more from John Wayles, his wife's father. By 1796, Jefferson owned about 170 slaves. At Monticello, Jefferson and his family we surrounded by African Americans. They were necessary for running the 5,000-acre plantation, which consisted of four separate farms. En-slaved workers plowed the fields, planted the wheat, drove the wagons, cared for the livestock and constructed the buildings. In the house they stoked the fires, prepared the food, washed the clothes and cared for the children... by law, Jefferson's slaves were his property. And he treated them as property. When circumstances required it, he bought and sold them, gave them as wedding gifts, and hired or leased them out. Slaves who refused to obey were punished and some were sold "South." By the time he was

twenty-one, slaves had been in the colonies for about145 years. Jefferson owned slaves throughout his lifetime." [38]

This information leaves no doubt that when Thomas Jefferson wrote the Declaration of Independence, he owned a large number of African Slaves. His words "We hold these truths to be self-evident that all men are created equal…" did not apply to Africans enslaved by him. Yet, as a proponent of Classical Liberalism, Thomas Jefferson's writings tell us he believed in *liberty for all men and women.* Absolute Monarchy practiced in England, and in other European countries up to the time of the Age of Enlightenment, did not believe human beings-working people-had any human rights. Thomas Jefferson, if he felt otherwise, would not have been able to write the Declaration of Independence because some human beings would be excluded.

b. George Washington

Like Thomas Jefferson, George Washington was a slave owner. Available information states "at the time of George Washington's death, the Mount Vernon estate's enslaved population consisted of 318 people. Washington himself had been a slave owner for fifty-six years, beginning at eleven years of age when he inherited ten slaves from his deceased father."[39] Dr. Henry Louis Gates, Jr. added "of our first five presidents, four owned slaves… Washington and his wife Martha together owned about 200 slaves at the beginning of the Revolution, but at the end of his life the couple owned 317 slaves together."[40] Dorothy Twohig stated George Washington's "… slave inventories indicate the number of slaves employed at Mount Vernon at various times: in 1759 he owned 24 slaves under the age of sixteen; in 1786 he owned slightly over 100 slaves on his own, with 113 dower

---

[38] Ibid.

[39] _____ "Slavery," George Washington's Mount Vernon, file:///G:/Founding%20 Fathers-George%20Washington%20Slave%20Ownership.htm

[40] Gates, Henry Louis, Jr, George Washington's Runaway Slave, Harry, The Root, http://www.theroot.com/articles/history/2012/12/ george_washington_slave_owner_and_the_people_he_owned.html

slaves; in 1799 there were 164 Washington slaves and 153 dower slaves."[41] George Washington's ownership of African Slaves is further proof that the Declaration of Independence, including all of its Classical Liberalism statements about freedom, did not apply to Africans brought to America and turned into slaves. Moreover, it did not apply to White Women either. It would take another 140 years or more before White Women were allowed to vote in America.

White Women would be counted for representation and taxation purposes, and only three-fifths of the African Slave population would be counted for the same. Neither, of course, could vote or participate in the new American Government. Edward L. Ayers et. al. stated "in the Three-Fifths Compromise, delegates agreed that all whites plus three-fifths of the slave population (referred to as "all other persons") would be counted for both representation and taxation. Native Americans would not be counted."[42] Interestingly, the Founding Fathers established the same political restrictions against human rights in America, which caused a vast majority of European Immigrants to flee Europe, and England in particular, in hopes of beginning a new life. Native Americans, who were already free when the European Immigrants arrived, were strangely perceived by the Founding Fathers as not being free.

Worse, when the Founding Fathers, including George Washington, wrote the U.S. Constitution, nothing was written into it related to the safeguard and preservation of the human rights of working people, freedom of the African Slaves, and recognition of the Native American people as just owners of everything the European Immigrants found in America when they arrived. The Bill of Rights, written by George Mason of Virginia, was amended to the U.S. Constitution in order to get it ratified. Edward L. Ayers, et. al. wrote the following:

> "Before agreeing to ratify the Constitution, most Antifederalists first wanted a **Bill of Rights.** They wanted

---

[41] Twohig, Dorothy, "That Species of Property": Washington's Role in the Controversy Over Slavery," http://gwpapers.virginia.edu/history/articles/species/#2
[42] Ayers, Edward L., et. al., Op. Cit., p. 46.

to see basic rights added to the document to be sure that individual liberties would be protected. Adding a Bill of Rights to the Constitution became the main focus of the struggle over ratification...By the end of 1791, 10 amendments were approved. These first 10 amendments to the Constitution became the Bill of Rights."[43]

After 1776, it took 15 years, or a generation, to get the Bill of Rights added to the U. S. Constitution. This shows just how opposed the Founding Fathers were against applying Classical Liberalism principles of freedom and justice to the lives of the vast majority of White working class people, enslaved Africans, and Native American people. Even though the Bill of Rights were added to the U.S. Constitution, this did not prevent, or inhibit future presidents of the United States from owning slaves, including the Planter Aristocracy located in the North and South.

c. Presidents who Owned African Slaves, From George Washington To The Civil War

The first eighteen presidents of the United States owned African Slaves, or someone in their immediate family did. It is worthwhile repeating here that although Classical Liberalism was the driver behind the Development of the Declaration of Independence and the U.S. Constitution, it follows, based on African Slave ownership by the Founding Fathers, that the spirit of these documents were not meant to include the former, White women, and Native American Indians. According to Rob Lopresti, American Presidents owned African Slaves, from George Washington to Ulysses S. Grant. He wrote,

> "Of the first five presidents, **four** owned slaves. All **four** of these owned slaves while they were president. Of the next five presidents (#6-10), **four** owned slaves. Only **two** of them owned slaves while they were president. Of the next five presidents(#11-15), **two** owned slaves. Both of these **two** owned slaves

---

[43] Ibid., p. 49.

while they were president. Of the next three presidents (#16-18) **two** owned slaves. **neither** of them owned slaves while serving as president. The last president to own slaves while in office was the twelfth president, **Zachary Taylor** (1849-1850).The last president to own slaves at all was the eighteenth president, **Ulysses S. Grant** (1869-1877). So **twelve** of our presidents owned slaves and **eight** of them owned slaves while serving as president."[44]

Nothing changed related to Thomas Jefferson's claim in the Declaration of Independence that "We hold these truths to be self-evident that all men are created equal." From 1776 to 1877, a period spanning 101 years-a century-the Founding Fathers, and their descendants, or selected representatives, continued to practice the British Monarchy Doctrine of Governance despite their claims, during this time, that all men are created equal, and that they should share equally in the bounty and abundance of life, liberty, optimism, and happiness in the New World. Shortly after 1877, and by 1896, the United States Supreme Court ruled the following in the Plessey vs. Ferguson Case:

> "The statute of Louisiana, acts of 1890, c. 111, requiring railway companies carrying passengers in their coaches in that State, to provide equal, but separate, accommodations for the white and colored races, by providing two or more passenger coaches for each passenger train, or by dividing the passenger coaches by a partition so as to secure separate accommodations; and providing that no person shall be permitted to occupy seats in coaches other than the ones assigned to them, on account Page 163 U. S. 538 of the race they belong to; and requiring the officer of the passenger train to assign each passenger to the coach or compartment assigned for the race to which he or she belong; and imposing fines or imprisonment upon passengers insisting on going into a coach or compartment other than the one set aide for the race to which he or

---

[44] Lopresti, Rob, which U.S. Presidents Owned Slaves?," file:///E:/ FoundingFathers%20U.S.%20Presidents%20Owned%20Slaves-George%20 Washington%20to%20Ulysses%20GrantCivil%20War.htm, p. 1.

she belongs; and conferring upon officers of the train power to refuse to carry on the train passengers refusing to occupy the coach or compartment assigned to them, and exempting the railway company from liability for such refusal, are not in conflict with the provisions either of the Thirteenth Amendment or of the Fourteenth Amendment to the Constitution of the United States."[45]

This U.S. Supreme Court Decision was not surprising, given a number of facts we have already discussed. For example, Thomas Jefferson, primary author of t he Declaration of Independence, owned the largest number of African Slaves; some of his slaves accompanied him to Philadelphia, PA where he wrote the document. During the century following the beginning of the American Republic in 1776 to 1877, every American president, or someone in his extended family, owned African Slaves. Thus, the doctrines that originated out of Classical Liberalism, namely, the Declaration of Independence and the U.S. Constitution, did not have any affect on discouraging the limitation of liberty of freed African Slaves, Native American Indians, and White women descendants of European Immigrants. In addition, the Plessey vs. Fergusson U.S. Supreme Court decision played a part in sustaining the terror that a majority of freed African Slaves experienced after the Civil War. White men could vote but White women could not, and, the freedom of both were sharply curtailed by their transformation into factory wage workers, which was hardly much different than the plight of the African Slaves before the Civil war, and as freed Africans after it.

Soon after the Plessey vs. Ferguson U.S. Supreme Court Decision, Jim Crow was born, and from the end of the Civil War to the Civil Rights Movement during the 1960s, the human rights of American Working Class people, regardless of race, were continuously abused by the descendants of the elite class of Founding Fathers, who, similar to their British Ancestors, carried the torch of human rights abuse forward throughout every generation

[45] _____ Justia U.S. Supreme Court, Plessey vs. Ferguson, 163 U.S. 537 (1896), U.S. Supreme Court Case, Plessey vs. Ferguson, No. 210, Argued April 18, 1896, May 18, 1896, https://supreme.justia.com/cases/federal/us/163/537/case.html

after 1776. This was the norm, although every American Public and Private School developed a history curriculum in which the Declaration of Independence and the U.S. Constitution were given repeated accolades being two of the greatest documents ever written. Theoretically, this is true. However, isn't a truly great document, which professes liberty for all, is one that *actually delivers that freedom-to all-through the various judicial, political, educational, and economic institutions set up to safeguard the human rights of the vast majority of American Working Class people?* Otherwise, as American History has proven so far, there is a disconnect between Classical Liberalism and the human rights of the vast majority of American people.

Since the 1929 Great Depression, many New Deal Laws, or government regulations, such as the Glass-Steagall Act, which we will discuss later in this book, have been undermined, weakened, or outright repealed. Presently, we intend to show that Classical Liberalism has undergone a metamorphosis, namely, it has been intentionally changed to a new form known as Neo-Liberalism, which originated during the Reagan Administration in1980. As we shall see, Neo-Liberalism is a more aggressive attack on the social programs that are aimed at meeting the basic needs of the vast majority of American people, namely the *Public Sector.*

F. Neo-Liberalism: Attack on Public Sector Human Rights Made Public

a. Neo-Liberalism Rise In America During The Reagan administration, 1980 to 1988

In the beginning of the American Government Experiment, Classical Liberalism was used by the wealthy Class of "Founding Fathers" to form a new society independent of the old, oppressive ones in Europe that the vast majority of European Immigrants fled before 1776. The two documents that were *suppose to guarantee human rights for all of those thousands of original European Immigrants, and for generations of their unborn descendants to come,* were the Declaration of Independence and the U.S. Constitution. We discovered, however, that the Founding Fathers, who wrote these documents, and signed off on them, remained quietly, privately, and supportive of the British Monarchy Principles of government that their own parents, and their ancestors, supported for many generations before migrating to America. Their allegiance to a monarchy form of government could not be overtly made known to the vast majority of other European Immigrants, who fled Europe, and in many cases, they did so with just the clothes on their backs. They were landless and homeless. Thus, Classical Liberalism provided hope and optimism for the weary and the oppressed masses of European Immigrants. Yet, the liberty and freedom promised would come at an astronomical human costs through the years to come.

Neo-Liberalism Policies were "...developed in the US in the 1980s."[46] After 1980, the façade of Classical Liberalism was taken down, and an all out attack on the Public Sector, which consists of the descendants of the original European Immigrants today, including other peoples of color, began. To confuse us about this attack, the social media, during this time, has presented, for our unwitting consumption, a steady diet of *wars, and rumors of war-related terrorism, and mounting fears, that is used as a diversionary tactic, and acting as anesthetizing drugs, this causes us to not feel the pain of the internal attacks on the Public Sector, and as planned, in our numbed state of awareness, we have, therefore, unwittingly confused the source of our real pain with the wars in Iraq and Afghanistan, when, upon closer inspection, its real source is the fiscal crises here at home, in America, that we have continuously suffered through, since 1980 to date.* Many American Working Class people have not left the hometown where they grew up; yet, large numbers live with the fear that ISIS, Al queda, or some other dragons, are constantly plotting to do them harm daily. Herein lay the truth when the anesthetizing drugs are counter-posed with the truth.

Former President Ronald Reagan was the face of Neo-Liberalism Policies during his two administrations. Lorenz wrote the following:

---

[46] Lorenz, Charles, "If You're So Smart, Why Are You under Surveillance? Universities, neoliberalism, and New Public Management," <u>Critical Inquiry</u>, Volume 38, The University of Chicago, Spring 2012, p. 603.

"Since the 1980s...an entirely different wind has been blowing...The fiscal crisis of the welfare states and the neoliberal course of the Reagan and Thatcher governments made the battle against budget deficits and against government spending into a political priority...As the eighties went on, the neoliberal agenda became more radical—smaller state and bigger market—attacking the public sector itself through efforts to systematically reduce public expenditure by privatizing public services and introducing market incentives."[47]

Two things need to be understood before we move forward. First, Classical Liberalism, as used by Thomas Jefferson and the other Founding Fathers before 1776, was focused on forming a government. Since 1980, Neo-Liberalism is being used to shrink that government through a drastic reduction in regulations, and, at the same time, greatly expanding existing markets. When Former President Ronald Reagan was elected in 1981, his first act as president was to reduce government by attacking the Public Sector, and expand markets by sharply reducing the amount of taxes paid by the top one-half of one percent of Americans. The information below verifies the "coming out of the closet of Neo-Liberalism:"

"In 1981, newly elected President Reagan abandoned long-fashionable Keynesian economic policies--the interventionist, big-government, "stimulus" approach... Instead, he explicitly campaigned on, and then implemented, four specific economic policy components that became known as Reaganomics: [1]Tax cuts to restore incentives for economic growth. The topincome tax rate of 70 percent was cut leaving just two rates--28 percent and 15 percent. [2] Spending reductions, including a $31 billion cut in 1981. This was close to 5 percent of the federal budget then, or the equivalent of about $180 billion of spending cuts in year nowadays. [3] Deregulation, cutting

---

[47] Ibid., p. 599.

red tape, and reducing bureaucracy saved consumers an
estimated $100 billion per year in lower prices."[48]

As we see, from the starting gate, Former President Ronald Reagan cut
$31 billion out of the Public Sector Budget in 1981. And, he expanded
markets by cutting the top income tax rate, from 70 percent to 28 and
15 percent respectively. In addition, Former President Ronald Reagan
drastically eliminated government regulations, shifting more than $100
billion to the private sector.

Thus, Former President Ronald Reagan became the "Founding Father"
of modern day Neo-Liberalism. The Reagan Administration, in its zeal
to eliminate government regulations, opened the floodgate for the 2008
Depression. The following information is informative:

> "The new era of deregulation resulted in a boom time for
> the rich getting richer. Reagan opened wide the door for
> companies to gamble with taxpayers' money. In 1999,
> the Glass-Steagall Act was repealed, and a real free-for-all
> began. It was passed in 1993 to keep separate the low-
> risk commercial banks where we put our deposits, and
> the brokerage banks that engage in high-risk speculative
> investments. This worked just fine for more than 50
> years. During the Reagan years, the lobbyists for the
> finance, insurance, and real estate outfits started pushing
> to dump the law; then the rules of the game changed
> totally. Mergers and commercial/investment partnerships
> skyrocketed. Now banks could start taking multiple home
> mortgage loans and turning them into securities to trade
> on Wall Street. They could all gamble like crazy, and with
> very little regulation. How insane was it to destroy one of
> the main protection devices created out of the pain of the
> Great Depression."[49]

---

[48] _____ "Ronald Reagan on Budget & Economy," On The Issues, http://
www.ontheissues.org/Celeb/Ronald_Reagan_Budget_+_Economy.htm
[49] Ibid.

Later, we will mention a few more drastic cuts in government programs during the Reagan Administration. Presently, we will further unravel the meaning of Neo-Liberalism, which will make an understanding of its implementation in Louisiana, by the Jindal Administration, much easier to comprehend.

b. Neo-Liberalism And The Role Of The State

For the capitalists, Neo-Liberalism Policies is a dream come true. Reduce government regulations, and increased market expansion via privatization of the Public Sector, according to Lorenz, "...is the neoliberal dream of the free market economy and *homo economicus*, and it shows no necessary connection with the economic reality of today or of the past. This is tellingly illustrated by the present crisis in private financial markets in the US and Europe, which only keep on functioning through continual massive injections of public funds (in other words, taxpayers' money) by the state..."[50] Neo-Liberalism does not have a connection with reality. Arbitrary actions in the marketplace are taken without reference to any historical precedent. When a financial crisis occurs, as they inevitably must, taxpayers dollars are injected into the economy such as the massive $850 billion bailout of Wall Street in 2008 by the Obama Administration. This was nothing short of a tax increase on the American Working Class, and on its unborn children. One of the primary functions of state government, including federal and local governments, is to set up the conditions for the privatization of various social programs in the Public Sector such as education, health, military, and crime, among others. The aim is twofold: (1) To expand private business control of the marketplace and (2) To reduce government size and interference in the marketplace, regarding the removal of regulations, or the prevention of any new ones from being set up to safeguard the human rights of American Working Class people.

As such, Thorsen and Lie stated economic liberalism, or neo-liberalism, is a political ideology that believes states "...ought to abstain from intervening in the economy, and instead leave as much as possible up to individuals

---

[50] Lorenz, Op. Cit., p. 601.

participating in free and self-regulating markets."[51] Lorenz wrote the following regarding the role of the state in today's American Economy driven by Neo-Liberal Policies:

> "It is the task of the state therefore to remove all obstacles in the way of free markets, like preventing the rise of monopolies... The legitimacy of the state in neoliberalism is not given but is dependent on its enabling functions for the economic market. The state and the citizen are thus primarily conceived in economic rather than legal terms; the state emerges primarily as a shareholders' state and not as a state under the rule of law *(Rechtstaat)*. The individual is basically represented as an entrepreneur... Neo-liberalism simultaneously shifts its focus from rights to risks; it represents "risk society," job insecurity...Neo-liberalism thus silently uncouples the globalized individual from fundamental rights formerly connected to national citizenship, like the right to schooling and welfare. It trades all these civil rights for one new right: the right to buy services on the privatized service market."[52]

Dr. David Harvey defined the role of the state in his book titled *A Brief History Of Neo-liberalism,*2005 as follows:

> "Neo-liberalism is in the first instance a theory of political economic practices t hat proposes that human well-being can best be advanced by liberating individual entrepreneurial freedoms and skills within an institutional framework characterized by strong private property rights, free markets, and free trade. The role of thestate is to create and preserve an institutional framework appropriate to such practices. The state has to guarantee, for example, the quality and integrity of money. It must also set up

---

[51] Thorsen, Dag Einar and Lie, Amund, What is Neoliberalism?, Department of Political Science, University of Oslo, http://folk.uio.no/daget/neoliberalism.pdf, p. 2.
[52] Lorenz, Op. Cit., p. 602.

those military, defense, police, and legal structures and functions required to secure private property rights and to guarantee, by force if need be, the proper functioning of markets. Furthermore, if markets do not exist (in areas such as land, water, education, healthcare, social security, or environmental pollution) then they must be created, by state action if necessary. But beyond these tasks the state should not venture. State intervention In markets (once created) must be kept to a bare minimum because, according to the theory, the state cannot possibly possess enough information to second-guess market signals (prices) and because powerful interest groups will inevitably distort and bias state interventions (particularly in democracies) for their own benefit."[53]

The state, as we shall see later in the Louisiana case, is, in the first instance, mainly an enabler and promoter of the smooth functioning and expansion of the marketplace. It only takes *an authoritative, leadership role in cases where law enforcement is needed to beat back the human rights desires of working class people (The demonstrations in Ferguson, MO associated with the brutal, cold-blooded murder of Michael Brown is a recent example of state intervention to save the market from so-called "looting," etc.).* At the federal level in 2008, the Obama Administration stepped in decisively to temporarily save the American Marketplace with an $850 billion tax increase Bailout. Also, the Obama Administration again acted to attempt to protect the international marketplace when it ordered air-strikes against ISIS in Syria and Iraq. Besides this role, government is barred from performing any other function, especially when it comes to strongly advocating resources and programs that serve the basic needs of working class people, regardless of level of government. In fact, Lorenz mentioned above that working class people are disconnected from their "fundamental civil and human rights." Human rights, in the Neo-Liberalism environment, are traded for a so-called new right to purchase goods and services, from the mall and online. Lorenz does not stop here with the overthrow of our human rights for an

---

[53] Harvey, David, *A Brief History Of NEOLIBERALISM*, Oxford university Press, New York, 2005, p. 2.

object; he accurately points-out the state's role is remove all barriers from the smooth functioning of the marketplace inclusive of doing away with as much government as possible.

Moreover, Dr. David Harvey's research clearly pointed-out the role of the state, and as we shall see clearly later, the Jindal Administration, since 2008, has maintained the integrity of money markets; it has created a market in the Louisiana Educational System with the use of vouchers; it has privatized Louisiana's Public Hospitals; and most importantly, the Jindal Administration has not ventured to establish any significant social programs for the Louisiana Working Class people. To the contrary, we systematically show the Louisiana State Government made very deep cuts in the budgets geared toward serving the social needs of the vast majority of its working class people. We shall also see later that the capitalists donated $13 million to Mr. Bobby Jindal's Gubernatorial Campaign by 2007. Furthermore. Lorenz added "all former state activities in the domains of education, social security, and healthcare can be privatized and commodified so that they can be made efficient and profitable. In neo-liberalism collective goods don't exist, in contrast with classical liberalism."[54] We have already shown that even during the historical era leading up to July 4, 1776, White Women were excluded from the collective good as well as Africans transported to America, and turned into slaves. Native Americans were not even counted when various states applied for statehood in which large numbers of Native Americans lived on their own homeland.

c. Transformation Of The Public Sector Into A Privatized And Commodified Market

Under the influence of neo-liberalism policies, the Public Sector is transformed into a *service sector*. Lorenz stated "the public sector is redefined by…[neo-liberalism] as a service sector that functions best when it operates in accordance with the principles of the free market."[55] It should be pointed-out here that "free market" refers to limited, or no

---

[54] Lorenz, Op. Cit., p. 602.
[55] Ibid., p. 603.

state government intervention in it save insuring its smooth operation. The most insidious action taken by state governments, which are under the influence of neo-liberalism policies, is the promotion and allowance of deep budget cuts in the former Public Sector, which is transformed into a service sector by state governments, for the purpose of channeling money out of social programs to cover the so-called budget shortfalls left behind as a result of tax breaks and incentives given to private business. The Louisiana Experience during the Jindal Administration's first and second term is addressed at length in this book. Meantime, Lorenz provides an excellent, detailed insight into what actually takes place in the Public Sector, when neo-liberalism transforms it into a service sector. Lorenz wrote the following:

> "...it is not surprising that the introduction of ...[neo-liberalism] into the former public sector has manifested itself in the guise of permanent reductions in costs, that is, permanent spending cuts. This trend is evident in the typical combination of (1) a constant decrease in the level of service; (2) a constant decrease in the level and quality of employment in the former public sector, which comes down to a steady process of deprofessionalization and a reduction in the number and quality of jobs; (3) constantly rising prices for the consumers of services such as education, healthcare, and social security..."[56]

Taking a brief look at Louisiana housing, which was part of the former Public Sector, and the influence of neo-liberalism policies on it, Timothy Boone wrote the following about rising rent prices:

> "The part of Louisiana where residents are feeling the most "rent stress" from rising rates for housing isn't in New Orleans or Baton Rouge — it's in rural East Carroll Parish in the northeast corner of the state. That's what LSU professors Jim Richardson and Roy Heidelberg told the Louisiana Housing Corp. Wednesday when they went

---

[56] Ibid., p. 605.

before the LHC board to discuss their ongoing assessment of the state's housing market. Households are considered "rent stressed" if they are spending 35 percent or more of their monthly income on rent. Almost 80 percent of the households in East Carroll with annual incomes of between $10,000 to $20,000 are rent stressed. In contrast, 39 percent of the households in Louisiana with incomes between $10,000 and $20,000 are rent stressed."[57]

This is neo-liberalism policies at work. Nearly 80 percent of the households in east Carroll Parish, which earn an income between $10,000 and $20,000, currently spend 35.0 percent of their household income on rent. As we see, the household income in East Carroll Parish is among the lowest in Louisiana and the nation. In short, there is no market, according to neo-liberalism "thinking (?)," that suggest, from a dollar perspective, more affordable housing need to be constructed in East Carroll Parish to reduce the rising rent stress among most of its residents. There is no market demand for housing, and Louisiana State Government, as we have already seen, must not venture into the housing market in East Carroll Parish in an effort to subsidize the development of affordable housing for the Louisiana Working Class people who reside there. Instead, rather than providing housing to meet the basic needs of the rent stressed residents of East Carroll Parish, neo-liberalism policies are directed toward constructing housing for Louisiana residents in cities where there is a strong demand, thus, generating profits for private business.

The Louisiana Housing Commission, a government agency, is the driver of where the housing market will be developed based on *money and not human rights*. Boone shows just how neo-liberalism policies always favors money over the satisfaction of the basic human rights needs of the Louisiana Working Class people. He wrote

"the discussion highlighted a philosophical split within the LHC: Should the organization focus on building

---

[57] Boone, Timothy, "Rent stress felt most in rural areas of Louisiana," The Advocate, October 9, 2014, p. 1.

affordable housing in areas that are growing rapidly like New Orleans, Baton Rouge or Lake Charles, where there are needs to develop places for support workers to live? Or should it address poor areas of the state where the populations are shrinking?"[58]

It is the role of Louisiana Government to develop an equitable strategy to reduce the rent stress in the most impoverished region(s) of Louisiana. However, since we now know that the role of government is to allow the market to act freely, one can safely conclude that housing will be developed where the maximum amount of profit will be realized on a minimum investment. Another example of how neo-liberalism is undermining the Public Sector, is education (We will address the massive budget cuts made in the Louisiana Education Budget later; we will also reveal most of the Louisiana State Department of Education's top management, during the Jindal Administration, have a *corporate background, and many do not have a formal professional doctoral degree in education, which was earned from an accredited four year university with an accredited graduate school).*

From 2008 to 2014, many of Louisiana's colleges and universities experienced deep cuts in their operational budgets. The Southern University System stands out because, as of October 2014, it is faced with a $7million deficit in its operational budget due to neo-liberalism policies implemented by the Jindal Administration. Elizabeth Crisp stated

> "after years of state budget cuts, Southern University is facing significant financial struggles... The university is bracing for an estimated $7 million shortfall during the fiscal year that began July 1 and already has been dipping into reserves to prop up its budget in recent years. Southern University's Baton Rouge campus and two others recently failed to meet the benchmarks outlined in the state's 2010

---

[58] Ibid., p. 1.

GRAD Act, so it's barred from increasing tuition to bring in more money."[59]

Moreover, the so-called GRAD Act is a tool used by the Jindal Administration to tighten its stranglehold on the Southern University System. The underlying aim is set very high academic standards that are impossible for it to achieve, then allocate state taxpayers' dollars based on how successful the GRAD Act was implemented during a given time period. The financial situation of the Southern University System is so bad as evidenced by the fact none of its three campuses-New Orleans, LA, Shreveport, LA, and Baton Rouge, LA-passed the GRAD Act Standards set by the neo-liberalism policies of the Jindal Administration. Crisp wrote the following:

> "Three of the Southern University System's campuses were the only ones in the state that didn't meet the measures outlined in the GRAD Act, which incentivise performance by giving schools the authority to raise tuition and granting other autonomies... The efforts, outlined in a recent report to the state Board of Regents, are a direct response to the university's failure to meet the state's GRAD Act measures, which are meant to improve student outcomes... colleges that fail to meet the GRAD Act benchmarks have an opportunity to gradually earn back some of their funding if they enter into a contract with the board and build a remedy-action plan."[60]

The only other point that need to be made here is, we wonder if the existing Southern University Board of Supervisors, including the University's Academic Community and Alumni, are aware now that the institution has entered into a contract with the Louisiana Board of Regents, all of its power has been transferred to it, and on any given day, the Southern

[59] Crisp, Elizabeth, "Southern board member calls for Mason's resignation," The Advocate, August 22, 2014, p.2.
[60] Crisp, Elizabeth, "Southern submits improvement plan," The Advocate, October 28, 2014, p. 1.

University System can be transformed into a community college, some other arrangement, or closed down completely? This is how neo-liberalism policies keep draining taxpayers' dollars out of the public sector into private business to, in the words of Governor Bobby Jindal, grow the Louisiana Economy. Grambling State University, the other Historically Black College and university, is also being slammed by the Jindal Administration's Neo-liberalism Policy Hammer.

Recently, due to the cumulative impact of the Governor Bobby Jindal-led drain of vital taxpayers' dollars out of the public sector higher education budget, which was motivated by his attempt to offset the massive tax breaks given to private business to grow the Louisiana Economy for a few, the Interim President of Grambling State University announced some internal deficit measures that will further undermine the academic integrity of the quality of higher education training Afro-Americans, in particular, will receive. Crisp wrote the following:

> "Facing a more than $3 million deficit, Grambling University plans to increase faculty teaching loads while requiring furloughs, provide incentives for 15 faculty members to retire, and possibly even shutter the Grambling Laboratory Schools. Interim President Cynthia Warrick announced the drastic measures to help cash-strapped Grambling regain sound financial footing during a meeting with faculty and staff on campus Thursday... But she also laid blame with the Louisiana Legislature and Gov. Bobby Jindal's administration. "State budgets have been cut -- all these Republican governors have decided they can balance their budgets on higher education," she said. State funding for higher education has been drastically reduced in Louisiana through repeated cuts in recent years. According to the national Center on Budget and Policy Priorities, Louisiana's per student higher ed funding fell more than any other state's between fiscal 2008 and 2014 -- plunging 43 percent. Warrick said she's hopeful the state will step in and provide $762,000 for

Grambling's lab schools to stay open past May 2015. "It will be up to the Legislature and the governor and the Louisiana Board of Education," Warrick said. "[61]

Later in this book, we will demonstrate the extent to which Governor Bobby Jindal ordered outrageously deep cuts in the Louisiana Higher Education Budget during his first term in office. Crisp noted "Louisiana's per student higher ed funding fell more than any other state's between fiscal 2008 and 2014-plunging 43 percent." To try to stay afloat, Grambling State University's Interim President Cynthia Warrick has ordered an increase in faculty teaching loads, and she has offered 15 faculty members incentives to retire. More than likely, these faculty members are full-time, tenured, full professors, and they are the experienced ones who Grambling State University's students need to teach them. Interim President Warrick says Grambling State University's enrollment has fallen; yet, we wonder what she thinks is going to happen to the school's enrollment when the tenured full professors are gone? Sadly, the money needed to pay their salaries was given away to private businesses in the form of tax breaks and other incentives. The public sector suffers, and the working class parents' children surely will receive an inferior education. Worse, Grambling State University has its "hat in its hand," and its fate is dependent on the Louisiana Legislature, Governor Bobby Jindal, and the Louisiana Board of Education; these are the same people who choreographed the neo-liberalism policies that put Grambling State University, Southern University System, and all of Louisiana Higher Education in the shape they're in today.

In addition, the management and financial situation at Southern University has become so dysfunctional that its Board of Supervisors voted, first, to not extend Chancellor James Lloren's contract, who, at the time, was the Chancellor of the Baton Rouge Campus, beyond July 1, 2014, and second, it subsequently voted to not extend President Ron Mason's contract beyond July 1, 2015. Neo-liberalism policies, no doubt, have a taken their toll on the Southern University System. As reported by Elizabeth Crisp, "on Saturday, the Southern Board of Supervisors voted overwhelmingly

---

[61] Crisp, Elizabeth, "Grambling leader outlines plan to address deficit," The Advocate, October 31, 2014, p. 1.

against a proposed one-year contract extension for embattled system President Ronald Mason. Mason's contract expires June 30, 2015."[62] So, as it currently is, President Ron Mason is lame duck, and the lack of leadership of the Southern University System, is just one example of how the Jindal Administration's neo-liberalism policies have devastated the higher education component of the Louisiana Public Sector. Much more will be said about this later on.

Presently, if you are wondering what this devastation at Southern University looks like, and at other institutions of higher education in Louisiana, Lorenz accurately provides a roadmap. He summed up the devastation as follows:

> "...(1) a continuous worsening of the faculty/student ratio, which manifests itself in among other things ever increasing teaching loads for faculty and continuing enlargements of scale in education...Online instruction is therefore increasingly replacing face-to-face education (2) Faculty are decomposing into a shrinking core of tenured faculty and a growing periphery of part-time, temporary faculty hired for one year, one semester, or one course. This boils down to structural substitution of inflexible and expensive faulty-especially tenured, full-time professors-by flexible and cheap staff-especially untenured, part-time adjuncts, teaching assistants, and symbolic professors...In the risky neoliberal world, jobs and social security for faculty are definitely passe. In the US almost two thirds of teaching is now done by untenured faculty under increasingly worsening conditions, creating a class of "scholar gypsies... (3) Teaching and research are continuously dissociated; the proportion and quantity of teaching is increasing. More and more faculty are hired only to teach temporarily. Simultaneously academic research is being outsourced and commodified. (4) Tuition fees are increasing...Increasing

---

[62] Crisp, Elizabeth, "Southern system president's term to end in 2015," The Advocate, August 24, 2014, p. 1.

student debt and decreasing faculty income therefore are
direct consequences of …[neo-liberalism] policies."[63]

As horrible and terroristic as this is, Lorenz says there is not any rationale
behind the budget cuts in higher education, and in other areas of the
Louisiana Public Sector, including those of other states nationwide. The
budget cuts are not aimed at improving higher education and so forth; *they
are expressly made to shift financial resources to private businesses in the form of
huge tax breaks and tax incentives.* Therefore, the $7 million budget deficit
that the Southern University System currently face, is not representative
of any improvements in the overall operation of the university. To the
contrary, the mentioned budget deficit has only made the operation of
the university worse, and turned it, as we pointed-out above, into a place
in which it is nearly impossible to engage in the art of higher, critical
thinking at the undergraduate and graduate levels of study. Lorenz added
"because there are no substantial aims at all behind…[neo-liberalism]
policy, each cut in spending is simply a springboard to the next…"[64]
Neo-liberalism policy has no purpose but to rob financial resources from
the Public Sector, and this being the case, it is economic anarchy. Lorenz
supports this viewpoint given he termed neo-liberalism policies "…as the
McDonaldization of society."[65] He also noted that the university has been
turned "…into a fast-food outlet that sells only those ideas its managers
believe will sell, that treats its employees as if they were too devious and
stupid to be trusted…"[66]

One other defining feature must be mentioned about neo-liberalism policies
before we move ahead, namely, there is a holy grail against taxation! No
matter how bad is the devastation to the Public Sector, never can state
government mention this: To repair the social services such as education,
taxes must be raised. To raise taxes would defeat neo-liberalism policies
because the aim is just to accumulate capital indefinitely, and in ever
increasing amounts. Throughout the Jindal Administration, not once has

---

[63] Lorenz, Op. Cit., pp. 605 and 606.
[64] Ibid., p. 606.
[65] Ibid., p. 606.
[66] Ibid., p. 608.

Governor Bobby Jindal proposed any tax increases; however, on numerous occasions, he has repeatedly said he will not call for a tax increase. Later, we will show just how much money the Louisiana Ruling Class-upper one-half of one percent of the population-has accumulated since it selected/elected Mr. Bobby Jindal, governor of Louisiana in 2007. Meantime, one of the prerequisites for ne-liberalism to work is there must be a complete absence of criticism of it by individuals-both in-and-out of state government.

d. Absence Of Criticism Of Neo-Liberalism Policies

Although the neo-liberalism policies of the Jindal Administration have wreaked havoc on the the social programs of the Public Sector, which are designed to care for the basic needs of the Louisiana Working Class people, and on a daily basis, hardly any information is discussed publicly related to what impact this or that decision will have on the well-being of the lives of millions of Louisiana Working Class people. There has not been one public town hall meeting to discuss whether privatizing Louisiana's Public Hospitals will improve their access to needed healthcare. There has not been any public discussion focused on how the enormous tax breaks and tax incentives *given to private business will be paid for.* In short, only those state government employees and business executives have knowledge about these, and other adverse impacts neo-liberalism policies are having on Louisiana Working Class people. As it is, all decisions are made behind closed doors in the Louisiana Governors Mansion, the Louisiana Legislature, and the corporate boardrooms of the various private businesses that are currently benefiting financially from the Jindal Administration's implementation of their neo-liberalism policies. A detailed listing of the beneficiaries of neo-liberalism policies during the Jindal Administration is provided later.

Lorenz included this information eclipse in his research. He stated neo-liberalism policies are "...totalitarian because it leaves no institutionalized room for criticism, which it always sees as subversion..."[67] At the same time neo-liberalism policies took root, as a political ideology to siphon money out of the Public Sector like a parasite sucks blood out of its host, in the

---

[67] Ibid., p. 608.

early 1980s, or at the beginning of the Reagan Administration, social media was monopolized by fifty giant corporations. Ben H. Bagdikian, University of California, Berkeley Professor, wrote the following in his book titled *The Media Monopoly*, 1983:

> "Modern technology and American economics have quietly created a new kind of authority over information-the national and multinational corporation. By the 1980s, the majority of all major American media-newspapers, magazines, radio, television, books, and movies were controlled by fifty giant corporations. These corporations were interlocked in common financial interest with other massive industries and with a few dominant international banks...fifty men and women, chiefs of their corporations, control more than half the information and ideas that reach 220 million Americans..."[68]

In view of this monopoly, and social media's increased concentration since the 1980s to date, it is easy to understand, given the interlocking directorates of the Fortune 500 Corporations today, the neo-liberalism policies information eclipse. As it is, everyday in Louisiana during the 5PM and 6PM News Hour, *the only information that is consistently broadcasted pertains to crime, namely, who committed a violent crime, ranging from murder, rape, burglary, and traffic accidents.* In addition, the Louisiana residents, who tune into the television during these times, are also given a good dose of information related to terrorism threats as far away as Afghanistan, Iraq, Israel, Syria, and more; yet, it is neo-liberalism policies that cause a daily deterioration in the mental and physical well-being of the majority of Louisiana Working Class people. There is a complete absence of any criticism of neo-liberalism policies, regardless of the areas of the Public Sector that they eat away at like an uncontrollable cancer. Even on the Louisiana Public Broadcasting Channels, usually when an issue is superficially addressed, and if there are two or more people being interviewed, both present the same side of it. It is rare to see and

---

[68] Bagdikian, Ben H., *The Media Monopoly*, Beacon Press, Boston, 1983, pp. xv and xix.

hear a dissenting voice about any issue. In short, the mind of a majority of Louisiana Residents, and those of every state, is shaped by filtered information, which is generally void of any critical thinking. Ben H. Bagdikian stated "each citizen's fate is shaped by powerful forces in distant places. The individual now depends on great machines of information and imagery that inform and instruct. The modern systems of news, information, and popular culture are not marginal artifacts of technology. They shape the consensus of society."[69] Thus, no information is shared publicly related to neo-liberalism policies, while the minds of Louisiana Residents are filled with meaningless information about crime, conspicuous consumption, and war.

Bagdikian informed us that "...the individual now depends on great machines of information and imagery that inform and instruct." Today, this great machine is the I-phone, or Smartphone. Well before its invention and common use by 2014, the average Louisiana Resident, and Americans as a whole, according to David Shenk "in 1971 the average American was targeted by at least 560 daily advertising messages. Twenty years later, that number had risen sixfold, to 3,000 messages per day."[70] The number of messages skyrocketed by 2012. The Science Daily summed up the high consumption of information as follows:

> "U.S. media consumption totaled 3.5 zettabytes, an average of 33 giga bytes per consumer per day (One byte is one character of text. A giga-byte is 109 bytes. A zettabyte is 1021 bytes.). By 2012, total U.S. consumption had increased to 6.9 zettabytes, an average of 63 gigabytes per person per day. Put another way, researcher Short said, if we printed 6.9 zettabytes of text in books, and stacked those books as tightly as possible across the United States, including Alaska and Hawaii, the pile would be almost 14 feet high.• In 2008, Americans talked, viewed and listened to media for 1.3 trillion hours, an average of 11

---

[69] Ibid., p. xvi.
[70] Shenk, David, *DATA SMOG: Surviving the information glut*, HarperEdge, San Francisco, 1997, p. 30.

hours per person per day. By 2012, total consumption had increased to 1.46 trillion hours, an average of 13.6 hours per person per day, representing a year over year growth rate of 5%. **2015: What's Ahead** • By 2015, the data indicate that Americans will consume media for more than 1.7 trillion hours, an average of approximately 15.5 hours per person per day. The amount of media delivered will exceed 8.75 zettabytes annually, or 74 gigabytes -- 9 DVDs worth -- of data sent to the average consumer on an average day."[71]

This is both the tip of the iceberg and the other part of it beneath the surface of the water. Shenk stated "as the amount of information and competing claims stretches toward infinity, the concern is that we may be on the verge of a whole new wave of indecisiveness; paralysis by analysis. (In this way, technology brings with it yet another internal contradiction: As it speeds up our world in the name of efficiency and productivity, it also constricts rational thinking."[72] Overwhelmed by information is an understatement; Louisiana Residents, and Americans in general, are inundated and submerged beneath an ever expanding tower of information eclipse. Neo-liberalism policies are similar to a needle in a haystack; it is intentionally thrown in it and hidden from public debate in our American Democracy. Oddly and strangely, the more sophisticated the great Smartphones become, and the more information its consumers can access 24/7, the less aware they become of self and other people in their immediate households, community, and the world. Shenk stated "...our information mania has sparked a behavioral *devolution.*"[73] In short, we lose more of our capacity to think critically every time we turn on our cherished, great machine-smartphone. Shenked accurately explains what is subtly happening to our humanism as follows:

---

[71] _____ "Media Consumption to Average 15.5 hours a day by 2015," Science daily, University of California, Marshall School of Business, http://www.sciencedaily.com/releases/2013/10/131030111316.htm, October 30, 2013.
[72] Shenk, Op. Cit., p. 94.
[73] Ibid., p. 159.

> "As our information supply increases, our common discourse and shared understanding decrease. Technically, we posses an unprecedented amount of information; however, what is commonly known has dwindled to a smaller and smaller percentage every year...we face a paradox of abundance-induced amnesia. The more information we come upon, the more we narrow our focus. The more we know, the less we know...This severely limits much of what it means to be human..."[74]

The data overload, or data pollution in our individual and collective minds, causes us to lose our ability to distinguish between reality and non-reality, between "lies and fantasies" and "truth." Shenk confirmed this fact when he wrote "...the danger is that in our increasing distraction and speediness, the lies...move so much faster than the truth, they will too often become the truth."[75] Later, we shall see how the Jindal Administration orchestrated, with the help of the Louisiana Legislature and the Board of Elementary and Secondary Education (BESE), a framework for classifying Louisiana Public Schools as "D" and "F" schools. Behind all of the data pollution and rhetoric is a hidden fact that *in order to rob the Louisiana K-12 Budget, which is protected from budget cuts by the Louisiana Constitution, a clever scheme, or lies, was created, packaged, and sold to weary working class parents, whose children are performing two to three or more grade levels behind where they should be.* The scheme is a voucher lie that profess to be able to take African-American children in particular, and with a voucher, allow them to enroll at a Charter School, and somehow, and way, these children, and others, will *miraculously catch up to their appropriate grade level, and then perform academically and socially as well as any child who is on the honor roll in any public or private school in Anywhere, Louisiana.* During the Jindal Administration's first term in particular, there were railcar loads of information written and spoken about the right of Louisiana Working Class Parents to exercise their right to determine where they desire to enroll their children. By attaching their academic failure to a building with bricks and mortar, and simultaneously downplaying the history of

---

[74] Ibid., pp. 124, 125, and 126.

[75] Ibid., p. 162.

poverty among Louisiana Working Class people, then, the data pollution overrode the fact children fail academically because their parents, due to generational poverty, did not have the available resources to parents their children, and it is the *purpose of state government to provide financial resources, and opportunities, for parents, and prospective ones, to develop emotionally and academically so this energy could be transferred to their children and so forth.* As we have already seen, state government, which has been captured by neo-liberalism policies as Louisiana's has been, is prevented from the development of any social and economic programs that will promote individual and collective social development among people. How the Jindal Administration advanced neo-liberalism policies will be addressed in detail later in this book.

Meantime, we shall, for added emphasis, briefly examine some of Mr. Bobby Jindal Campaign Speeches, which he made in 2007, to determine if he ever explained to the vast majority of Louisiana Working Class people that his plan, if elected governor of Louisiana, is to collapse the Public Sector, thereby bringing about mounting social and economic hardship for the majority of Louisiana Residents.

e. Embedded Neo-Liberalism Policies in Mr. Bobby Jindal's Selected 2007, 2012 Election Victory Speeches And in his 2013 Speech To The Republican National Committee, Charlotte, NC

"Hidden in plain sight" best explains how Governor Bobby Jindal conveyed, in the above speeches, his intentions to implement neo-liberalism policies in Louisiana, beginning with his election/selection as governor in 2007. The average Louisiana Resident would not be able to discern the approaching deep budget cuts, government workers layoffs, tax breaks and incentives giveaways to private businesses, privatization of social services, including public hospitals, and the general cut-back in Public Sector services, if one did have a clear understanding of neo-liberalism policies before the 2007 Louisiana Gubernatorial Governors Election/Selection. Without some working knowledge, and awareness of what neo-liberalism policies are, Governor Bobby Jindal told us in his speeches that the budget ax will be taken to the Public Sector, leaving a trail of poverty and social destruction of a quality not seen in Louisiana since the days of the American Slavery Institution. We know this may be hard to believe, but when some of Governor Bobby Jindal's speeches are examined, his neo-liberal policy intentions are clear to see.

Let us begin sifting out Governor Bobby Jindal's neo-liberalism policy intentions embedded in his Louisiana Gubernatorial Election Victory Speech delivered on October 20, 2007.

To drain the Louisiana Public Sector Program Budgets of Louisiana Taxpayers Dollars, a smokescreen was used to divert our attention away from the Jindal Administration's continuation of the massive government corruption that has become as commonly accepted as boudin and cracklins in everyday Louisiana Life. In short, Governor Bobby Jindal had to create a fantasy impression that the "corrupt and greedy," regardless of whether they are politicians, business CEOs, or others, would be identified, fingerprinted, and put out of the business of corruption. In his own words, Governor Bobby Jindal stated the following:

> "I don't want to mislead anyone -- this ain't going to be easy... I suspect that some of those who oppose making big changes in Louisiana government will try to mount a counter-offensive. And some who've been feeding at the trough may not go quietly, but that is up to them. They can either go quietly or they can go loudly, but either way they will go."[76]

"Feeding at the Trough" is as common as apple pie in Louisiana, and no amount of reform is going to change that fact. In fact, the point is to increase this corruption. To hide this coming avalanche of corruption, Governor Bobby Jindal called a special session of the Louisiana Legislature to pass an ethic reforms law. He expressed his smokescreen as follows:

------

[76] Jindal Bobby, Louisiana Gubernatorial Election Victory Speech, http://www.americanrhetoric.com/speeches/bobbyjindallouisianagovvictory.htm. October 20, 2007, p. 2.

"As I promised in the campaign, right after I'm sworn in, I'm going to notify the legislature that I'll be calling them in for a special session to pass real ethics reform with real teeth…Ethics reform is the first step in winning the public trust. It is the first step to unlocking our future. It is the first step to growing our economy and bringing great jobs to Louisiana. Before we can create real economic growth, we must show the voters and the entire country that we are serious about changing our reputation."[77]

Behind the smokescreen of ethics reform, Governor Bobby Jindal set the table, which he referred it to the key to unlock "our" future[78]. This was the first step to allowing people to continue to "feed at the trough" at the expense of the demolition of the Louisiana Public Sector, including education, healthcare and so forth. Those who are "feeding at the trough" are the one's who Governor Bobby Jindal has unlocked the future for. We shall give a detailed account of this situation later in this book. At the moment, there is more information in Governor Bobby Jindal's 2007 Speech that shows how he intends to use neo-liberalism policies to unlock the future for those who are feeding at the trough of state government at the expense of the vast majority of Louisiana Working Class people.

With the first step completed, namely Ethics Reform, which dressed up the corrupt in saints clothing, Governor Bobby Jindal ended his 2007 Election/Selection Victory Speech with an invitation to private business that the Louisiana Public Sector Budgets are open for business, effective his

[77] Ibid., p. 3.

[78] Our Future: This is a phrase, similar to the often used one-American People-that, on an emotional level, would suggest that the opportunities and money to be derived, as a result of the implementation of neo-liberalism policies, will be shared equally by all Louisiana Residents, regardless of class, race, educational background, political affiliation, and religion among others not mentioned. The phrase our future is used to get the majority of Louisiana Working Class people, in a moment of emotional excitement, to believe that they will be included in the abundance, when in reality, the latter's taxpayer dollars will be used to pay for the Tax breaks and tax incentives and so on that were given to private businesses during the Jindal Administration's first term in office, from 2008 to 2012.

first day in office in 2008. Governor Bobby Jindal stated in closing "this state -- This state wants change, and I've got one more message tonight: If you're a business looking at expansion, and especially if you're a young person trying to decide where you will make your home, change is not just on the way: Change begins tonight!"[79] As we shall see later, millions of dollars of tax breaks and tax incentives giveaways, including privatization of government run social programs, were "given" to business looking for expansion. We shall see later, the Jindal Administration, in order to lure businesses looking for expansion, went so far as to pay for the relocation cost of a number of them during its first term. Paying for their relocation cost was on top of millions of dollars in various tax breaks and incentives already provided, depending on the business.

In sum, Governor Bobby Jindal's words in his 2007 Gubernatorial Election/Selection Speech foreshadowed the ushering in of *the greatest Louisiana taxpayer dollars giveaways in Louisiana History during his first term.* After Governor Bobby Jindal was selected/elected to a second term as governor in 2012, in his inaugural speech, he placed everyone on notice that his neo-liberalism policy mission was not over yet.

As we have already seen, one of the cornerstones of neo-liberalism policies is the drastic reduction in the size of state government. In his 2012 Inaugural Speech, Governor Bobby Jindal stated "As long as there is waste and inefficiency in government service -- our mission is not accomplished."[80] Government services are wrongly compared to the operation of a private business, and if something is not functioning properly at a given moment, then government is judged to be inefficient. Lorenz stated "the dogma of the free market can best be expressed by a formula: free market=competition=best value for the money=optimum efficiency for... owners of private property..."[81] Therefore, every Louisiana Public Sector

---

[79] Ibid., p. 4.
[80] Text of Gov. Bobby Jindal's inaugural speech, Associated Press, file:///G:/JINDALADMINText%20of%20Gov.%20Bobby%20Jindal's%20inaugural%20speech%20%20%20NOLA.com%20January%209%202012.htm, January 9, 2012, p. 3.
[81] Lorenz, OP. Cit., p. 601.

Program, from education to healthcare, was judged by Governor Bobby Jindal as being run inefficiently. Efficiency means profits in the language of the neo-liberalism policy world. Social services provided by government to Louisiana Residents is always considered an inefficient endeavor.

Thus, to correct Louisiana government inefficiency, Governor Bobby Jindal oversaw the layoffs of thousands of government workers. Marsha Shuler reported the impact neo-liberalism policies had on state government workers, from 2008, when Governor Bobby Jindal took office, to October 2014, as follows:

> "As Bobby Jindal prepared for his 2008 inauguration as governor, state government workers numbered about 93,500. Today, that work-force hovers at 62,000 employees — fewer than it's been in more than two decades. Spending on payroll has decreased by about $1 billion annually. At the Louisiana State Employees Retirement System, retirees now exceed the number of active employee members — another consequence of the downsizing... The shrinking of the state government workforce by one-third stems largely from Jindal's privatization of many government functions and facilities, most notably in the health care arena. The biggest hit to state employment ranks — about 7,000 jobs — came as LSU turned over the management of nine of its 10 charity hospitals to private managers, a process that wrapped up during the last budget year. The privatization push — part of Jindal's political agenda — started early on, and the pace picked up in his second term in office. Reorganization of department operations has eliminated many jobs during the Jindal years, as did consolidation of agency procurement and information technology operations within the governor's management arm, the Division of Administration. Legislative Auditor Daryl Purpera said it would be "a massive, massive project" to undertake a full-blown review of Jindal's privatization in itiatives and government downsizing..."Are the same

services being delivered?" he asked. "Is there a savings, or did we just redirect into professional services costs? You would have to analyze."[82]

As we see, Governor Bobby Jindal talked about ethics reform in his 2007 Louisiana Gubernatorial Election Victory Speech; yet, underneath the rhetorical talk, the neo-liberalism policy plan of those wealthy Louisiana Business people, who elected him, called for a drastic reduction in state government workers in the Public Sector in the form of layoffs. From 2008 to October 2014, 31,500 state government workers were laid-off-a decrease of -33.7 percent. State government payroll spending simultaneously decreased by $1billion annually. In short, one-third of state government workers were eliminated, and the big, big question is: Where has the $1billion annual savings in Louisiana State Government Payroll Expenditures gone? From 2008 to 2014, this means $6 billion was saved. Where did it go? It was used by Governor Bobby Jindal to pay for tax breaks and tax incentives. We are certain it was not used to assist Louisiana Working Class people with acquiring their basic needs. We shall see later this was definitely not the case. We will also observe that most of the state government worker layoffs can be attributed to the Jindal Administration's privatization of Louisiana Public Hospitals. Moreover, there are more retired state government workers today than there are active state government workers. And, we also know that ethics reform had no influence inasmuch as Louisiana Legislative Auditor Daryl Pupera said it is not clear whether any improvements have been made in state government operations because no analysis, from a cost effective perspective, has been done to make a determination. From an efficiency-free market-profit perspective, every neo-liberalism policy-backer of Governor Bobby Jindal claim the layoff of thousands of government workers in the Public Sector, was a great success.

A tsunami is a massive ocean wave that is nearly benign while it is far out in the ocean away from the shoreline. However, as the tsunami moves closer to the shoreline, it suddenly rises from the ocean, and crashes onshore in a

---

[82] Shuler, Marsha, Government workers down 30K over 6 years," The Advocate, October 13, 2014, pp. 1and 2.

series of successive waves. Similar to the Jindal Administration, the wave of its implementation of neo-liberalism policies dealt with a sharp cutback in state government workers; the second wave was its massive giveaway of tax breaks and incentives to private businesses, including the privatization of vital social services in the Louisiana Public Sector; the third wave was its use of a voucher scheme designed to funnel millions of dollars out of the Louisiana K-12 Budget. Governor Bobby Jindal alerted us about his voucher scheme in his 2012 Inaugural Speech. This voucher scheme was glossed over by Governor Bobby Jindal's Ethics Reform Act, which attempted to give Louisiana Residents a fantasy feeling that corruption in Louisiana State Government had been cleaned-up.

At the heart of Governor Bobby Jindal's 2012 Inaugural Speech is a long narrative of primarily one sentence paragraphs, which most Louisiana Public High School Teachers would probably place a failing mark on their students' essays, if turned in written this way. The Associated Press reported the following:

> "And as long as there are children who are not receiving a quality education here in Louisiana -- our mission is not accomplished. And let me stop on that point and say this: In America, we believe that every child deserves an equal opportunity to a quality education. Regardless of income or status, male or female, black or white, ALL are precious in His sight...Allow me to be blunt here for a moment on the subject of equal opportunity in education. For most, if not all, of the families represented here today, our kids will be fine. We will make sure that we either live in an area with good public schools, or we will send our kids to highly functioning nonpublic schools that better meet their needs. We will make sure our kids get a good education. But the simple truth is there are many children -- very many -- who do not have the same opportunity. They may live in an area with public schools that are failing, and they cannot afford to move to an area with better public schools and they cannot afford private school...America

promises equal opportunity to have success, but America does not promise equal success. That part is up to you, the student, the worker, the individual…"[83]

The above is a description of the "haves," who have access to the best opportunities and schools, and the "have nots," who do not have access to the same educational opportunities as the "haves," whom Governor Bobby Jindal represents. Inside of this idea, the neo-liberalism backers of Governor Bobby Jindal hatched a voucher scheme that, on an emotional level, is suppose to correct this class problem, which has a history that dates back to the American Slavery Institution. It is very simplistic for anyone to think, let alone believe, that a voucher is all that is required to *even the playing field so heavily tilted in favor of the "haves."* At least, we must give Governor Bobby Jindal credit for recognizing that the playing field is highly distorted in favor of wealthy Louisiana residents. He wrote "… America does not promise equal success." To fix the distortion, Governor Bobby Jindal outlined his neo-liberalism voucher-CHOICE- scheme, which is cloaked in Ethics Reform. Consider the following:

> "In some places the traditional public schools are functioning well. But in others, the traditional public schools are failing our kids….Real reform lies in providing more choices and more opportunities for parents, for families and for children.Kids only grow up once. Waiting for the system to reform itself is not an option; it is time to act. I'm confident that when we reform our education system, Louisiana will become an even better place to start or move a business and our economic outlook will improve even more."[84]

The most striking thing here is Governor Bobby Jindal said more choices made available to parents of Louisiana Working Class Public School Children would level the opportunity playing field currently enjoyed by his neo-liberalism backers' children. By us believing what Governor

---

[83] Text of Governor Bobby Jindal Inaugural Speech 2012, Op. Cit., pp. 2 and 3.
[84] Ibid., p. 4.

Bobby Jindal said in his 2012 Inaugural Speech, and acting from a totally emotional position, which was void of any concrete data, we jumped on his educational voucher reform, choice bandwagon, and, many of us, pulled our working class children out of their so-called failing public schools and enrolled them in Charter Schools. The latter was expressly designed to funnel Minimum Foundation Program funds out of the Louisiana Constitutionally protected K-12 Budget, which consists of $5 to 8 billion. We will discuss, in detail, how the Jindal Administration orchestrated its predatory plunder of this budget. Similar to higher education, hundreds of Louisiana Tenured Public School Teachers were forced to take an early retirement, and other hundreds of younger-age public school teachers were placed in a nearly impossible position of earning tenure due to the draconian evaluation process they are being forced to comply with as part of the Jindal Administration's Compass Program. In either case, the fraud is clear: By chasing seasoned veteran public schoolteachers out of the classroom statewide, and by making it very difficult for young teachers to earn their deserved tenure, this would on one hand, insure that more public schools would be judged "D and F" failing public schools, and on the other, more public school children, who are enrolled in them, would continue to fail academically, causing their working class parents to accept Governor Bobby Jindal's Voucher Scheme Plan, which is nothing more than a pipeline for Minimum Foundation Programs Funds to flow into Charter Schools like crude oil that flows through pipelines to the refinery. If there is another purpose of this Voucher Scheme, we would like to know what it is, given the vast majority of children who have enrolled in Charter Schools are African-Americans, who live in poor, poverty-stricken households. Governor Bobby Jindal even acknowledged Louisiana Working Class people's children do not have the same opportunity as the wealthy, elite class. And, what is worse, he also knew when he made this statement that it was not real, and yet, he made it to make poor families feel they have a choice to improve the educational opportunity for their children. This is what we see on the surface, but beneath it, many African-American children continue to fail in Charter Schools while millions of dollars of Minimum Foundation Program Funds flow into the "bottom lines of the private businesses that own them.

Before we proceed, it is necessary to point-out here that the Louisiana Supreme Court upheld Governor Bobby Jindal's neo-liberalism policy aimed at making it nearly impossible for new Louisiana Public Schoolteachers to obtain tenure, and, its ruling will also insure that the exodus of veteran tenured public schoolteachers will continue to leave their chosen teaching profession. Will Sentell wrote

> "In a victory for Gov. Bobby Jindal, the Louisiana Supreme Court on Wednesday upheld a hotly debated state law that makes it harder for public school teachers to earn and retain a form of job protection called tenure. The ruling, for the second time, reversed a decision by state District Judge Michael Caldwell, of the 19th Judicial District Court in Baton Rouge. Caldwell concluded that the overhaul was illegally approved by the Louisiana Legislature because it jammed too many subjects into a single bill. The court disagreed, and handed the governor a big legal win on one of the most contentious issues of his 2012 public schools overhaul. "This is good news," Jindal said in a prepared statement. "Act 1 was created to help ensure we have a great teacher in every classroom, and we're pleased that it will continue improving Louisiana's schools for children and families across our state."... State Superintendent of Education John White, who was a key ally of Jindal when the tenure law won approval, praised Wednesday's ruling by the Louisiana Supreme Court... Aside from being harder to earn tenure, teachers who already have the job protection can lose it and even be fired if they are repeatedly rated as ineffective in the classroom."[85]

This is neo-liberalism policies working at its best. The Louisiana Supreme Court ruled against Louisiana Public Schoolteachers in favor of Charter schools and money. Superintendent of Education, John White has not earned a doctoral degree in education from any four year accredited academic

---

[85] Sentell, Will, "Louisiana Supreme Court upholds state's teacher tenure law," The Advocate, October 16, 2014, pp. 1 and 2.

institution in America, yet he is the Superintendent. His executive staff will be examined in detail later in this book, and similar to Mr. John White, none of them have a doctoral degree in education, although Superintendent John White, and his Executive Staff, oversees the implementation of the Jindal Administration's Act 1, which is designed intentionally to harass tenured and non-tenured Louisiana Public Schoolteachers, ultimately, causing them to become disillusioned and leave the teaching profession altogether. This action takes the hinges off of the door, allowing a flood of poor Louisiana Working Class people's children to enroll in Charter Schools so millions of dollars of Minimum Foundation Program Funds can be siphoned out of the Louisiana K-12 Budget.

Interestingly, while the collapse of the Louisiana Public Sector was in full swing, Governor Bobby Jindal, holding true to state government having almost no role in day-to-day decision-making on such issues as education budget cuts, public schoolteacher tenure, privatization of public hospitals, and massive tax breaks and incentives, he, as we shall see later, spent a significant amount of his time away from Louisiana campaigning to make a possible run for president of the United States in 2016. No, you are not dreaming this; it is true, and we analyze in detail Governor Bobby Jindal's premature campaign for president, which contrary to popular belief, many Louisiana Residents erroneously believe he has championed a strong government role in Louisiana Affairs. Governor Bobby Jindal is a Road Scholar, and the last speech we will spend a moment analyzing, is the one he gave at the Republican National Convention in Charlotte, NC on Friday, January 25, 2013.

On Friday, January 25, 2013, Governor Bobby Jindal addressed the Republican National Convention (RNC) in Charlotte, NC, and what is interesting about the speech he delivered, is what he proposed to the RNC are the exact same neo-liberalism policies that he oversaw the implementation of in Louisiana, from 2008 to January 25, 2013. His speech to the RNC also gave its members an opportunity to study Governor Bobby Jindal to determine if he would be someone they could rely on to continue the advancement of the neo-liberalism policies the Reagan Administration used to severely attach the Federal Government's

Public Sector, if he is chosen as the Republican Presidential Candidate in the 2016 national election. In view of what was at stake, Governor Bobby Jindal did not miss the opportunity to tell the RNC that the federal government's role in America must be drastically limited. From the outset of his speech, Governor Bobby Jindal spoke the following words about the federal government:

1. Federal Government

> "The first concept I want to talk about is simply this – America is not the federal government.Take a minute to let that thought sink in. America is not the federal government. In fact, America is not much about government at all. In America, government is one of those things you have to have, but you sure don't want too much of it…kind of like your in-laws."[86]

As we have already seen, limited, or no government, is one of the most prized cornerstones of neo-liberalism policy. Nothing can happen, regarding the robbery of the Public Sector, until the one-half of one percent of the American Population is absolutely certain that the *door to the vault of the federal and state public sectors are held opened by the government's governor or president, who, before their selection and election, must already be in complete accord with a limited government role in the day-to-day affairs of governance, especially when the American Working Class masses are concerned.* Their hopes, optimism, aspirations, goals and so forth must always remain a dream, and the federal government must take no action to bring any of them into reality in the form of social programs that spend money on meeting the basic needs of the masses. When former President John Kennedy tried to do something for the downtrodden negroes, and other American Working Class people of all colors, he was assassinated; and Dr. Martin Luther King, Malcolm X, and too many others to name here,

---

[86] Jindal, Bobby Governor, FULL TEXT: BOBBY JINDAL'S SPEECH TO THE RNC IN CHARLOTTE, http://illinoisreview.typepad.com/illinoisreview/2013/01/full-text-bobby-jindals-speech-to-the-rnc-in-charlotte.html, FRIDAY, JANUARY 25, 2013, P. 1.

tried to do something concrete for the masses, they-too-met the same fate. Governor Bobby Jindal understands this lesson well, which is why he said in plain words that the federal government is like our "in-laws." Moreover, he told the RNC that the "...challenge...[is to not let] government...[grow] ever larger..."[87] As Governor Bobby Jindal proceeded with his speech to the RNC, he leaked-out some more information about how to grow America.

He stated "...we as conservatives must dedicate our energies and our efforts to growing America, to growing the American economy...That path does not lie in government...The health of America is not about government at all...Our objective is to grow the private sector."[88] Before there was anything called an America, the vast majority of Europeans lived in countries, from England to Russia, which did not have any government. Most were administered by hereditary monarchies. An excellent example of why the neo-liberalism backers of Governor Bobby Jindal do not want a state, or federal government, interference in the market, can be understood by considering the federal government's recent audit of the privatization of Louisiana Public Hospitals, which he oversaw and approved.

First, the reason Louisiana Public Hospitals were privatized in the first place was to increase the profit of the private hospitals that took them over, and healthcare services they provide to Louisiana Residents remains a secondary concern. Recall, Governor Bobby Jindal's first order of business in 2008 was he called the Louisiana Legislature into Special Session to pass an Ethics Reform Law. However, behind closed doors, Marsha Shuler unraveled the on-going fraud promoted by the Jindal Administration as follows:

> "The federal government has postponed Medicaid payments to 57 Texas hospitals over questions about a financial scheme similar to one Louisiana adopted... The arrangements are worth billions of dollars in Texas and hundreds of millions in Louisiana. Other states use a different method... Under the federal microscope is an

---

[87] Ibid., p. 2.
[88] Ibid., p. 3.

arrangement Texas uses, which is similar to Louisiana's
$400 million...Low Income and Needy Care Collaboration
Agreements program has been used to get extra funding
to public LSU hospitals, which now have contracted with
private operators... Under the deals, a private company
agrees to provide the health care services that had been
provided by a public entity. The arrangement frees the
government dollars that had been spent by the public
entity. The public funds are directed to Medicaid coffers
to increase the state's match, which in turn brings
more federal funds. The private company then receives
supplemental payments from Medicaid."[89]

This fraud, or financial scheme as Marsha Shuler calls it, has only one goal,
and that is, to funnel higher profits into the bank accounts of the private
hospitals that Governor Bobby Jindal allowed to take them over. A detailed
discussion is included in later part of this book. Without any federal
government intervention into the market, which is what neo-liberalism
policy demands, and Governor Bobby Jindal is a practitioner *par excellence*,
the $400 million or more will flow unnoticed into the coffers of the private
businesses that now operate the former Louisiana Public Hospitals. It
should be more clear now why Governor Bobby Jindal spent so much of
the Louisiana Taxpayers money to call a special session of the Louisiana
Legislature! It's the old schoolyard game of "throw a stone and hide your
hand" behind the Ethics reform Law. It remains to see whether the Barack
Obama Administration will stop this racing fraud train in Louisiana, or
allow it to proceed unstopped, given its past experience of buckling under
to neo-liberalism policy during the 2008 Depression, which resulted in an
$850 billion bailout of Wall Street investment bankers.

2. Growing The Private Sector

Neo-Liberalism policies work best where government is non-existent, and
if it does exist, it must play a passive role in the market, allowing the

[89] Shuler, Marsha, "Federal questions on Medicaid funding worry Louisiana hospitals," The Advocate, October 19, 2014, pp. 1 and 2.

private sector to pillage the public sector, which serves the basic needs of the American masses, whether at the federal, state, or local level. To grow the private sector, Governor Bobby Jindal told the RNC what action is needed to do so at the federal level:

> "This means re-thinking nearly every social program in Washington. Very few of them work in my view, and frankly, the one-size fits all crowd has had its chance. If any rational human being were to create our government anew, today, from a blank piece of paper – we would have about one fourth of the buildings we have in Washington and about half of the government workers. We would replace most of its bureaucracy with a handful of good websites."[90]

Every social program's budget would be cut to the bone similar to what Governor Bobby Jindal, and the Louisiana Legislature have done since 2008. This is what neo-liberalism policies demands. Compassion for working class people is trodden under the foot of profit, which his realized via social program budget cuts. The reader will see firsthand how the Jindal Administration allowed this to happen later on. Another major cornerstone of neo-liberalism policies is no tax increase.

3. No Tax Increases

Since Governor Bobby Jindal has been in office, there has not been one tax increase that he has ask the Louisiana Legislature to pass to bring revenue to take care of the needs of the people of the state of Louisiana. The infrastructure in Louisiana is collapsing, and its roadways of representative of the generalized degeneration going-on. Will Sentell reported the Louisiana infrastructure deterioration as follows:

> "Movassaghi said the state needs $2.7 billion just to tackle it structurally deficient bridges, ranks 44th in its rate of highway fatalities and features the highest

---

[90] Ibid., p. 5.

annual auto insurance rates in the nation at $1,277. "Louisiana's highway network is in a deplorable state," he told the committee... House Transportation Committee Chairwoman Karen St. Germain, D-Pierre Part, said... the state...[has a] $12 billion backlog of transportation projects.... Gov. Bobby Jindal opposes any tax hikes, the Jindal administration dismissed Movassaghi's overhaul proposals..."[91]

Louisiana Residents continue to die in larger numbers on Louisiana roadways that are in drastic need of repairs, Yet, Governor Bobby Jindal, remaining true to neo-liberalism policies, inasmuch as he is against any tax increases, and, without any basis to make an informed decision, he dismissed Movassaghi's proposal to overhaul Louisiana Highways. While speaking to the RNC, Governor Bobby Jindal stated "higher taxes still do not create prosperity for all."[92] This is the root cause of the widening income gap America, and of its ever increasing budget deficit. We have included data in this book that verifies the poor pay more taxes than Louisiana Residents who earn more than $100,000 annually. On this point, Governor Bobby Jindal is right; Louisiana Working Class people pay much higher taxes than millionaires who live in the state. This is the underlying reason Governor Bobby Jindal is opposed to any new tax increases.

Back in Louisiana, Governor Bobby Jindal, and the Louisiana Legislature, passed laws allowing for working class parents to take their children out of so-called failing schools, and enroll them in Charter Schools using a voucher scheme. In his speech to the RNC in Charlotte, NC, Governor Bobby Jindal gave the real reason for it when he stated "let us feature the success of child-centered education solutions that meet the needs of the digital age, education where the dollars follow the child."[93] In short, the education of the child is not important; neo-liberalism policies are the

[91] Sentell, Will, "Officials: roads in 'deplorable state,' The Advocate, October 5, 2014, p. 1.
[92] Full Text of Governor Bobby Jindal Speech to the RNC, Op. Cit., p. 6.
[93] Ibid., p. 6.

disguised burglars, who steal Minimum Foundation Program Funds from the Louisiana K-12 Budget every time a voucher is used to enroll a former public school student in a Charter School. The last topic we will address is called dividends and liabilities of neo-liberalism policies. A larger, and more in depth examination of the Jindal Administration's use of neo-liberalism policies to shrink state government and collapse the Public Sector is forthcoming.

f. Dividends And Liabilities Of Neo-liberalism Policies During The Jindal Administration, 2008 to 2014

Earlier, Governor Bobby Jindal was quoted saying "our objective is to grow the private sector." In a capitalist economy, this means invest a minimum of one's own money and, in return, receive a maximum profit. Private business would leave Louisiana en masse if it was the other way around: Maximum investment for a minimum profit. This is where neo-liberalism policies enter the play. Governor Bobby Jindal has given several billion dollars in tax breaks to private businesses since 2008 to 2014. Rather than use their own money to relocate to Louisiana for example, the Jindal Administration, as we shall see later, paid the relocation cost for a private business to set up its operation in the state. Moreover, most, if not all of them, were also exempted from paying any taxes for several years. These neo-liberalism policies have created an industrial boom for private business. Their dividends are great. Richard Thompson stated "Louisiana is enjoying its biggest industrial boom since the oil bust in the 1980s, and much of the action — tens of billions of dollars of investment — is happening along the 70-mile corridor between New Orleans and Baton Rouge... State economic officials estimate about $75 billion will be spent on industrial projects in Louisiana during that span in what they say is the biggest such expansion in the state's history."[94] A very large portion of the state remains impoverished despite this tax break stimulated economic development. How were the massive tax breaks paid for by the Jindal

---

[94] Thompson, Richard, "River corridor between N.O., BR is home for much of state's industrial boom," The Advocate, November 17, 2013, p. 1.

Administration? The short answer is deep budget cuts were made in Public Sector social programs such as healthcare and education.

Together, the deep budget cuts, when added up, have left a giant so-called shortfall in revenue to pay for social services for the Louisiana Working Class people. Elizabeth Crisp wrote "Next year's state spending plan could be off by as much as $1.2 billion, but the projected shortfall was only briefly discussed during a meeting at the State Capitol on Thursday."[95] Even though this is a great liability, no one involved expressed any criticism. In fact, Crisp stated "...the message from Jindal's top budget advisers on Thursday was, again, not to worry about next year's budget..."[96] The coolness in which the news of this massive budget deficit was received by Barry Dusse, Director of the governor's Office of Planning and Budget[97] is reflective of another one of the cornerstones of neo-liberal policy, namely, criticism is equal to subversion. No one raises any concerns because it is a known fact that, beginning July 1, 2015, if more deep cuts must be made in the Louisiana Public Sector, they will be made to balance the state budget, regardless of the added hardship this action will continue to have on the Louisiana Working Class people. To buy some more time, or pushing the inevitable budget deficit train wreck a little further into the future, Marsha Shuler stated "the Legislature's top money committee punted Friday on Jindal administration reports of a $178.5 million surplus at the June 30 end of last fiscal year."[98] This let us know just how terrible the budget deficit situation is when Governor Bobby Jindal claimed the state has a $178.5 million surplus, yet it cannot be verified, and no one in or out of state government, who knows anything about the "magical surplus," is speaking out about the camouflage.

In all, we have seen the transformation of Classical Liberalism into Neo-Liberalism. The latter is a political ideology that comes very close to the

---

[95] Crisp, Elizabeth, "State face $1.2 billion budget shortfall," The Advocate, August 15, 2014, p. 1.

[96] Ibid., p. 1.

[97] Ibid., p. 1.

[98] Shuler, Marsha, "Budget panel defers action on surplus," The Advocate, October 17, 2014, p.1.

old hereditary monarchy form of rule, where human rights did not matter, nor did they have any value to the monarchs except people lives could be wasted during war and in the factory. Every word written forward will demonstrate how the Jindal Administration used neo-liberalism ideology-policies-to shrink state government, give tax breaks, and others to the wealthy, and pillage Public Sector social programs to pay for them. This action insures that Louisiana will continue to be buried at or near the bottom of every social index, and human rights, similar to 16th Century Europe, are rapidly being replaced by conspicuous consumption in the market.

CHAPTER II

Neo-Liberalism and Human Aggression

Regarding nearly every social index that point to the well-being of people, such as education, health, employment, environmental quality, family, and crime, including incarceration among many others, Louisiana *ranks at, or near the bottom of every index.* The prevailing perception of many Louisiana Residents, ranging from state government officials, judicial representatives, public schoolteachers, and university professors to sanitation workers, is our state is in the shape it is in now because Louisiana is an economically poor state. On the surface, this is a fashionable, sexy explanation for the generalized deterioration of the social fabric of life in Louisiana today. However, if we go beyond the surface, commonly known to many as "getting out of the box," illusions, fantasies, and myths will progressively disappear, and reality, or what is actually underlying and promoting the social deterioration of the Louisiana social fabric can be seen more clearly without emotion and unsubstantiated opinions.

Given the anger that is fueling a wave of violence across America, variously acted out as shopping mall shootings, shootings inside of churches, shootings on college campuses, movie theater shootings, public school shootings-Sandy Hook Elementary School-, Boston Marathon Bombing, Navy Yard Massacre, University of California, Santa Barbara Massacre, Chicago Murder Epidemic, Zimmerman-Travon Martin Murder, Darren Wilson-Michael Brown Murder, Eric Garner strangulation in New York, Sean Bell in Oakland, CA, 12 year old Tamir Rice, and the hundreds of other homicides that routinely take place everyday among many other violent crimes, one simple question demands an answer: Are Louisiana Residents being placed at risk of becoming a direct or indirect victim of this type of violence too? Something serious is taking place "outside of the box," and yet, our best and brightest minds seem preoccupied with trivial matters, which have questionable significance, such as stock market gains and losses, super bowls, ice water challenge, who won the latest mega-lottery, cell phone mania in all its forms, or with the generalized corruption of politicians and others. It reminds us of the Dark Ages, or when an Apollo Spacecraft travels around the backside of the moon, when all communication with Earth is lost. In his book titled *Democracy At Work: A Cure For Capitalism*, 2012, Richard Wolff stated the following about the absence of any criticism of capitalism in the American Democracy:

> "...our economic system-capitalism-has been almost entirely exempted from critical discussion, as if some taboo precludes criticism. Business and political leaders, the mainstream mass media, and the bulk of the academic community have substituted celebration and cheerleading for serious criticism and debate of capitalism. This was their response to the Cold War-and even more an intrinsic part of the conservative resurgence after the Great Depression, the New Deal, and the United States' wartime alliance with the Soviet Union frightened and galvanized such forces into reaction. They insistently treated capitalism as beyond criticism, debate, or basic change-and demanded no less of others."[99]

For example, in the aftermath of the Sandy Hook Shootings of innocent, vulnerable, and defenseless elementary school age children, which is one of the worst, violent actions imaginable, this slaying of defenseless children rapidly, almost overnight, faded into the distance, and the *cause underlying this American made tragedy* has been all but drowned-out by an orgy of meaningless debates centered around gun control. Even the murder of 20 Sandy Hook Elementary School children could not wake us up out of

---

[99] Wolff, Richard, *Democracy At Work: A Cure For Capitalism*, Haymarket Books Chicago, Illinois, 2012, p. 24.

our Rip Van Winkle type sleep. Alan Fram stated "a bipartisan effort to expand background checks faced almost certain defeat Wednesday as the Senate approached a long-awaited vote on the linchpin of the drive to curb gun violence… Rejection of the provision would mark a jarring setback for gun control advocates, who had hoped Decembers slayings of 20 children and six aides at a Newtown, Conn., elementary school propelled firearms violence into a national issue."[100] As Fram predicted, the U. S. Congress voted against tougher gun laws, and the American public went about its daily "survival routine" as usual. Jordan Blum wrote, "the congressional effort to expand criminal background checks — the only form of gun control that was still on life support…was… soundly defeated Wednesday-[April 17, 2013]-on the Senate floor."[101] At best, the latter is merely an effect, or immoral cover-up, of a deeper cause few, if any, Americans are aware of, and if any are aware of the real, underlying root cause of violence, the mass media has successfully sequestered their voices, which, on one hand, bars the truth on the other side of the door, and, on the other, hold open another door for more tragic shootings to occur again and again.

When a tragedy such as the one that recently occurred in January 2013 in Newtown, Connecticut takes place, the first card that is played is the *emotional card*. The perpetrator of the violent action is called "mentally disturbed," and the act of violence itself is called "senseless." This has worked so far to soothe our pain generated by the increasing lost of human life; for the past two decades, the "stop the violence" slogan has become very tattered, faded, and torn around the edges because it has been used so many times with little or no results. This slogan is used by those who subscribe to "inside the box thinking." In short, violence cannot be stopped; it must be ended, and to do so, like a toothache, it cannot be stopped; an action must be taken to uproot it, and put a permanent end to the capitalist system in which it, and all other antisocial behaviors spring. Reform is nothing but wishful "inside the box" thinking. American History is a witness to this fact.

---

[100] Fram, Alan, "Background check bill faces likely Senate defeat," <u>The Advocate</u>, April 17, 2013, p. 1.
[101] Blum, Jordan, "Landrieu votes "yes" but gun control fails in U.S. Senate," <u>The Advocate</u>, April 18, 2013, p. 1.

A. Forest Fire Metaphor

Earlier we made note that *anger* is currently fueling the wave of violence spreading across America like a wild fire being fueled by trees that died five years ago. The trees that died during Year 1 serve as dry kindling, which also serves as current day fuel, allowing millions of acres of green, youthful forest to burn. Without a significant amount of available kindling accumulated over five years or more, enough fuel would not be available to sustain a forest fire for weeks at a time, or longer.

This simple Forest Fire Metaphor contains within itself the missing link that can help us gain a deeper understanding of the cause of violence in our society today. In reflection, inside of the Forest Fire metaphor, three factors are essential, and at work: (1) time (2) delayed time, and (3) dead, dried tree kindling. Those trees that died during the 2000 to 2005 time period for example, embodies a period in which a delay occurred; the delay allowed dead trees to dry, or cure into a mass of *potential* kindling. Thus, by 2005, those trees that died in 2000 are prime, potential kindling that can fuel a forest fire when ignited by an outside source such lightning, improper management of a campfire, or a lone cigarette thrown out of a car window.

Mr. Bobby Jindal was elected governor of Louisiana in 2008; to date, he has completed his first four year term, and he was re-s/elected to his second four year term, in 2012. Governor Bobby Jindal is in his fifth year in office, and this is enough of a time delay to examine the impact his economic policies are having on the Louisiana Citizenry. Moreover, it should be pointed-out here that Governor Bobby Jindal-himself- is not the focus of this research. For example, we are dealing with a political time continuum that goes back to 2000 when Governor Mike Foster was elected governor of Louisiana. Former Governor Mike Foster selected Mr. Bobby Jindal to serve in his cabinet. Therefore, from 2000 through 2013, this time period is available for us to examine, although our immediate focus will be on the neo-liberal economic policies of the Jindal Administration, which are a continuation of the same economic policies of the Foster Administration, dating back to 2000.

Having knowledge of the three essential factors that exists within the mentioned Forest Fire Metaphor, it is easy to take the next step toward acquiring a deeper understanding of the *underlying cause* of the violence that is sweeping across America like a forest fire today. In short, at the root of the violence is not *a so-called excessive use of force by law enforcement police officers; rather, it is inseparably linked to the existing economic system, which allows neo-liberal economic policies to predominate.* More violence will occur as this type of economic policy inject increasing hardship in the lives of American Working Class people, regardless of race. Moreover, what most observers know is another major forest will inevitably occur, and, similarly, for those of us who are thinking "outside of the box," we equally know another violent crime will inevitably occur. Therefore, of all the crime research conducted over the past 50 years, there is one study commissioned by the 94th Congress, 2nd Session that provides a definitive answer to what is the kindling, or fuel, underlying the spread of violent crime in our society.

B. Joint Economic Committee 94th Congress, 2nd Session Congress of the United States

The above Congressional Committee of the Congress of the United States commissioned Dr. M. Harvey Brenner, associate professor, John Hopkins University, to conduct a comprehensive study on the following topic: Achieving The Goals of The Employment Act of 1946-Thirtieth Anniversary Review. On October 26, 1976, Senator Hubert H. Humphrey, dem, Minnesota, stated the following in his Letter of Transmittal:

> "To the Members of the Joint Economic Committee...
> Transmitted herewith for the use of the Members of
> the Joint Economic Committee and other Members of
> Congress is the study entitled, "Estimating the Social

Costs of National Economic Policy: Implications for
Mental and Physical Health, and Criminal Aggression."[102]

The above study has been in existence for 37 years. Given its landmark
feature that link economic policies, particularly employment with stress
caused by unemployment, inflation, and per capita income with their social
costs, government planners and others, if they had implemented the above
study in their planning processes routinely, at the national, state, and local
level, they would have taken an opportunity years earlier to save thousands
of American lives during this time, including Michael Brown, Travon
Martin, Eric Garner, and many others. Senator Hubert H. Humphrey
stated what policy planners knew as early as 1976:

> "Policy planners know...that contradictory economic
> policies generate unemployment. In turn, this
> unemployment will reduce incomes and output and enlarge
> Federal budget deficits as tax receipts fall and outlays rise
> for jobless benefits. They also know that unemployment
> creates stressful situations for laid-off workers and their
> families as well. And stress has long been recognized as
> a major contributor to a variety of physical and mental
> illnesses. Yet, no systematic evaluation of this straight
> forward relationship—the link between job loss and stress
> related illness—has occurred covering a long period of
> time...Similarly, no evaluation has been made of the
> long-term links between unemployment; income of price
> changes, and the social indices of criminal aggression such
> as homicides and imprisonment."[103]

In his landmark study, Dr. Brenner worked out the straight forward link
between economic policy (" Per capita income, rate of unemployment,

---

[102] Joint Economic Committee Congress Of The United States, 94th Congress,
2nd Session, A Study: Estimating The social Costs Of National Economic Policy:
Implications For Mental And Physical Health, And Criminal Aggression, October
26, 1976, Prepared For The Use Of The Joint Economic Committee Congress Of
The United States, U.S. Government Printing Office, Washington: 1976.
[103] Ibid., p. III.

and rate of inflation) and a series of *pathological indices*, namely, age and sex-specific mortality rates, cardiovascular-renal disease mortality rates, suicides mortality rates, homicide mortality rates, mental hospital admissions rates, and imprisonment rates."[104] Before we demonstrate how to substitute the three essential factors at work inside the Forest Fire Metaphor presented earlier, which are also at work in our *Violence and Criminal Aggression Framework* (VACA), it is necessary to point out here that the latter affect all races in a similar fashion. Accordingly, Dr. M. Harvey Brenner stated the following:

> "The most consistent pattern of relationship between national [state and local] economic changes and each of the measures of social cost was demonstrated with the unemployment rate. Unemployment plays a statistically significant role in relation to social trauma for each of the indices of social cost and for virtually all ages, both sexes, and for whites and non-whites in the United States..."[105]

This fact does away with any subjective thinking such as maybe unemployment has varying pathological effects on different ethnic groups? As Dr. Brenner pointed-out in his study, the pattern is consistent across all racial groups. Moreover, the Brenner Study further stated the following:

> "...actions which influence national [state and local] economic activity especially the unemployment rate-have a substantial bearing on physical health, mental health, and criminal aggression...To the extent, therefore, that economic policy has acted to influence economic activity, it has always been related to the nation's [,or state's] social health. It would appear that on a day-to-day basis, nearly all political and deliberate economic decisions which affect the national, regional, and local economic

---

[104] Ibid., p. 2.
[105] Ibid., p. 4.

situations also are associated with many aspects of the nation's well-being."[106]

In effect, the pathological indices used by Dr. M. Harvey Brenner, in his groundbreaking study conducted for the Joint Economic Committee of the 94th Congress 2d Session, concluded that "…pathological reactions will follow increased unemployment, increased inflation, and decreased per capita income."[107] Dr. Brenner reached this conclusion based on his discovery of what he called a "Distributed Lag Relationship" that exists between the former economic policy indicators and the pathological indices identified earlier, i. e., mortality rates (age, sex, and race specific), suicide rate, homicide rate, rate of first admissions to mental hospitals, and rate of imprisonment, among others.

C. Distributed Lag Relationship

Using the mentioned economic stress indicators already identified, Dr. Brenner defined his Distributed Lag Relationship as follows:

> "In the cases of each of these three economic sources of distress, we expect what is referred to as a "distributed lag" relationship. This means that the relationships to economic stress are dispersed over time so that during each of several years, a certain proportion of the economic stress initiated during the first year takes its toll…increases in the unemployment rate, regardless of the causal basis, will be followed by increases in the various pathology indices estimated in this report."[108]

What follows are some of the dramatic findings Dr. Brenner discovered. Table 1.4 below shows the pathological effects of a 1.4 percent rise in unemployment during 1970. Dr. Brenner added "in 1970, unemployment

---

[106] Ibid., p. 7.
[107] Ibid., p. 22. The three sources of economic distress and stress are as follows: (1) Increased unemployment
[108] Ibid., p. 23.

rose 1.4 percent to 4.9 percent. This 1.4 percent increase has been sustained since that time…through 1975."[109]

Table 1.4
Cumulative Impact of the 1.4 Percent Rise
in Unemployment During 1970

Social Stress Indicator	Stress Incidence 1975	Chg in Stress Indicator for a 1.4 Percent Rise in Unemployment	Increase in Stress Incidence Due to the Rise in Unemployment
Suicide:	29,960	5.7%	1,540
State Mental Hospital Admission:	117,480	4.7	5,520
Homicide:	21,730	8.0	1,740
Cirrhosis of the Liver Mortality:	32,080	2.7	870
State Prison Admission:	136,875	5.6	7,660
Cardiovascular-Renal Disease Mortality:	979,180	2.7	51,570
Total Mortality:	1,910,000	2.7	51,570

Source: Brenner, M. Harvey, Estimating The Social Cost of National Economic Policy: Implications For Mental And Physical Health, And Criminal Aggression, Washington, D. C., 1976, p. vii.

The above data clearly indicates how the Distributed Lag Relationship, or link between economic policy-unemployment in particular-result in an increased pathological affect on the American people. Guessing, speculations, apologies, assumptions, and opinions are rendered useless in face of the above data showing, for example, that between 1970 and 1975, the 1.4 percent sustained rise in unemployment resulted in an 8.0 percent change in the stress indicator for homicides, which, during the mentioned period, resulted in 1,740 new homicides. Stated another way, Americans took the lives of 1,740 of their fellow Americans due to the rise in stress caused by the 1.4 percent sustained increase in unemployment.

---

[109] Ibid., p. vi.

Dr. Brenner adds a valued explanation of exactly what effect sustained unemployment has on an affected individual. He wrote

> "In all of the sources of aggression thus far identified and scientifically supported, the connection with economic distress can be seen. Put directly, the fear, or actuality, of loss of income or employment is a profound source of frustration and a potential source of major loss. Moreover, it is not difficult to imagine that the unexpected mental trauma due to losses of income, employment or social position would be regarded as an unjust attack by the society upon many of the individual's subject to it."[110]

Herein lies the three factors that were already pointed-out in our Forest Fire Metaphor, which we will consider next in our Violence and Criminal Aggression Framework (VACA).

D. Violence and Criminal Aggression Framework

In the Forest Fire Metaphor, the three essential factors are time, delayed time, and dried wood kindling. Embedded within the Violence And Criminal Aggression Framework (VACA) are time, delayed time, and profound individual frustration and stress. Profound means characterized by extreme intensity of feeling and unexpected mental trauma. Our VACA Framework neatly overlays the Forest Fire Metaphor. Of course, the one main difference is the latter deals with trees in a forest, and individuals are the centerpiece of the VACA Framework. As we have already seen, Dr. M. Harvey Brenner's landmark 1976 Study focused mostly on the affects economic policies had on Americans at the national level; we will, to the contrary, use Dr. Brenner's Distributed Lag Relationship (DLR), and apply it to Louisiana during the 2000 to 2013 time period, emphasizing the 2008 to 2013 time period, which corresponds to the first and second term of the Jindal Administration. In the VACA Framework, the 2008 to 2013 years represent time; analysis of the *privatization and subsidization*

---

[110] Ibid., p. 13.

economic policies at the state level during the identified time period, refers to delayed time. And, the DLR, which reflects what affects the privatization and subsidization economic policies of the Jindal Administration has had on sustaining unemployment, will demonstrate that a proportion of the *profound frustration and economic distress caused by unemployment in 2008, or the first year of the Jindal Administration, will take its toll on the Louisiana Citizenry by the fifth year-2012.* Thus, the result of the Distributed Lag Relationship (DLR), as we have already seen from Dr. Brenner's Study, and the economic distress caused by sustained unemployment inevitably results in the cause of violence and criminal aggression in Louisiana, and in our society as a whole. We already mentioned earlier that Senator Hubert H. Humphrey stated "policy planners know…that contradictory economic policies generate unemployment."[111]

Policy planners, and most all public policy officials, have known this fact for years. Over the past 37 years, since Dr. M. Harvey Brenner first submitted his completed report to the 94th Congress, numerous graduate schools have sprung up in Louisiana, and nationwide, that grant doctoral degrees in public policy, or the study of the affect economic policy has on people. Policy planners know that such contradictory economic policy, such as privatization and subsidization inevitably generate economic distress and profound frustration. They also know that the latter, over time, result in the creation of violence and criminal aggression, and other antisocial diseases in our state and the nation. Interestingly, Nobel Prize Awards are consistently given out annually to researchers who discover new technologies that have implications for creating products that can be sold on the *market for a profit.* How many social scientists, regardless of their field of study, have received this award for coming up with a way to *end violence and aggression,* as Dr. M. Harvey Brenner did in 1976?

Had quality attention been devoted to social research that could end violence and aggression, those young, elementary school age children, who were gunned down in cold blood at Sandy Hook Elementary School, would be alive today. Of course, many apologists, from all walks of American life, will rush to say otherwise, but this fact has not changed, namely, policy

---

[111] Ibid., p. iii.

planners know contradictory, privatization and subsidization economic policies generates violence and aggression.

Rather than speculate one way or the other, we intend to demonstrate that many of the Findings in Dr. M. Harvey Brenner's 1976 Study, are still relevant in Louisiana 37 years after the latter was submitted to the 94th Congress of the United States of America.

CHAPTER III

Privatization and Subsidization Policies of the Jindal Administration

The best way to enter this discussion is for us to get a consensus understanding of what is meant by privatization. The root word inside of privatization is privatize. And, what does it mean? According to the *Webster's Ninth New Collegiate Dictionary*, 1984, privatize refers "to make private...to change (as a business or industry) from public to private control or ownership." [112] Privatization is simply an on-going intent to change what is in the public domain to the private. The next logical question we need to answer is as follows: Why is privatization useful? As an economic policy, it is a useful tool for extremely, wealthy individuals because, as a ruling class, they collectively act by donating large sums of money to selected politicians, who agree, beforehand, to carry-out the systematic *privatization of public resources at either the national, state, or local levels of government.* It should be clearly understood by every wage-worker that he or she is not ever suppose to understand the privatization of resources, that is, their transfer from the public domain to the private, are not designed to support their individual and collective well-being directly. Wage-workers only find out about privatization after they go to the voting polls and elect a governor or president, who, in turn, immediately set the wheels of privatization to turning once the elected politician is safely in office. Meantime, during the political campaign, a lot of name-calling and crude exchanges are volleyed, like a tennis ball, for the purpose of attacking one or the other politician's

---

[112] Page 936.

character and values. Mr. Donald Trump, presidential candidate, is an excellent example of someone who uses this tactic. This is purposefully done to wear down the concentration of the wage-worker, or Louisiana voters. At some point, the latter drops-out of the political campaign, feeling like it is futile and a waste of time to continuously listen to the mudsling going-on between this or that politician. But wait. By no slight of imagination is this an accident. The main goal of the ruling class we mentioned earlier is to get its politician, and in Louisiana's Case Mr. Bobby Jindal, elected as governor so he can safely crank-up the privatization engine, changing public, social programs to private control. Great secrecy is required to get this done because enormously, huge amounts of taxpayer dollars are at stake. By privatizing, or eliminating a social or educational program, simply means this is taxpayer dollars that formerly served the needs of Louisiana Residents, which, once privatized, those same taxpayer dollars now end up as profit for the individuals of the wealthy, Louisiana Ruling Class, which elected Mr. Bobby Jindal to carry forward its privatization economic policy in the first place. Similar to privatization, subsidization economic policy works the same way. Subsidization refers to the promotion of private business with public money. Privatization is the right hand, and subsidization is the left hand of the Louisiana Ruling Class' neo-liberal economic policies. We cannot stress the fact enough that after Mr. Bobby Jindal was elected governor, *it then became vastly more effortless for him to arbitrarily slash one social program after the next in order for the wealthy, Louisiana Ruling Class to gain control over our taxpayer dollars budgeted for social programs, which, after his election, have fallen steadily in the hands of his benefactors via their privatization and subsidization economic policies.* Because all of this privatization and subsidization economic policies are held in utmost secrecy during the political campaign seasons, even the Louisiana mass media, academia, public education officials, and everyday Louisiana Citizenry-All-believe that their *hard earned tax dollars, which are taken out of our paychecks, somehow have mysteriously vanished into thin air. Many echo the habitual practice that the privatized and subsidized tax dollars are what is called a shortfall.*

With this better understanding of privatization, we shall now examine the economic policies of the Jindal Administration in order to systematically demonstrate that, since Governor Bobby Jindal took office, every political move he has made has been the driver behind a wave of privatization that began during his first term in office, beginning in 2008, and continues to dominate his policy agenda during his second term in office.

To effectively demonstrate that the Jindal Administration's economic agenda is dominated by privatization and tax breaks, we will use a series published articles by The Advocate newspaper since 2008.

A. Wolf and Sheep

In order for privatization to work, namely yield unheard of profits through the movement of as many economic resources, including those with profit-generating potential, from the public to the private domain, first merchants and later capitalists needed to devise a trusted, fail-safe way to enter into the nation, or state government treasury; rob it via privatization, without anyone-taxpayers- being robbed able to discern, on any conscious level, what is taking place right before their own eyes. Thus, the Jindal Administration, regarding the Louisiana Case, is the most recent installment of a *political protector that allows the modern day capitalist ruling class to carry-out its economic policy of privatization and tax breaks.* How this is achieved goes all the way back to the Roman Empire days and before. Richard Hoskins documents the coming into being, or merger of the capitalist ruling class with the state as follows:

> "Rome was no longer a nation of honest independent farmers. It was a feudal Empire. The international merchant had arrived, paid the Roman priests to bless them and allow them to trade, and paid a king to protect them. The king was now an emperor, but he was still on the payroll of the international Trade Cartel."[113]

From the Roman Empire era to the Jindal Administration, the Capitalists, or ruling class, still need a protector to gain direct access to the treasury

---

[113] Hoskins, Richard Kelley, *In The Beginning…:The story of the International Trade Cartel*, Virginia Publishing Company, 1995, p. 98.

at all levels of government. Hoskins defined the Wolf and The Sheep (The Wolf is the capitalists, or ruling class, and The Sheep is the everyday working class man and woman) this way:

> "Political rulers protect the merchant and his wares. Students do well to remember: "In order for a wolf to eat sheep he must first enter the sheepfold. Unless properly introduced by the watchman, the rams will surround a wolf and kill him. First, the wolf must bribe the watchman, who then proclaims that the wolf has been magically transformed into a sheep. As a sheep he is entitled to enter into the sheepfold. Once in the sheepfold he hires rams to protect him while he kills an eats sheep…It makes no difference to the wolf how many strive to obtain the lucrative position of protector. The wolf can work with one contender [Democrat or Republican] as easily as the next. The successful protector is given a generous share of the prey."[114]

Without a protector, the wolf would be destroyed. But his or her protector-politician-constantly glorifies the wolf until the people-sheep-come to believe that the wolf is a sheep. The Roman Empire perfected The Wolf and Sheep relationship. Providing further evidence of this fact, Hoskins wrote

> "The Roman emperors were like schoolboys playing "king of the mountain." Whoever struggled to the top was acceptable to the trade-priests, became their "protector," and received an allowance that came from the empire's trade-profits. In time the emperor was replaced by a contender-and a victor in turn was put on the payroll. Emperors came and went-but the church held the title, kept the records, collected the rents, was of God, and continued on without end."[115]

---

[114] Ibid., p. 99.
[115] Ibid., p. 104.

Nothing has changed from the Roman Empire Period. Protector politicians, some call themselves Democrats, and others call themselves Republicans, engage in the "king of the mountain" ritual in the name of democracy. To the capitalists, or ruling class, it matters not if the protector is one or the other (This distinction only matters to the sheep, wage-worker, taxpayer, etc. for democracy promotion purposes.); what matters to this class is there is a politicians who will willingly introduce the former into state government treasury, and in the process, reveal the tax records, titles and deeds, and bank account sums. Mr. Bobby Jiindal was groomed for the protector role that he is currently carrying-out during his second term in office. In *The Creature from Jekyll Island*, 2010, G. Edward Griffin wrote the following:

> "Secrecy…is essential for the success of a cabal. And the Rothchilds perfected the art. By remaining behind the scenes, they were able to avoid the brunt of public anger which was directed, instead, at the political figures which they largely controlled. This is a technique which has been practiced by financial manipulators ever since, and it is fully utilized by those who operate the Federal Reserve System today…Clandestiny was and remained a feature of Rothchild political activity. Seldom were they to be seen engaging in open public debate on important issues. Never did they seek government office…Yet all the while they were helping to shape the major events of the day: by withholding funds; by providing statesmen with an official diplomatic service; by influencing appointments to high office; and by an almost daily intercourse with the great decision makers…Rothchilds often financed both sides in a conflict…placing money on both sides of the conflict were exactly the kinds of maneuvers for which the Rothchilds had become famous throughout Europe and were now practicing in America."[116]

---

[116] Griffin, G. Edward, *THE CREATURE FROM JEKYLL ISLAND: A Second Look at the Federal Reserve*, American Media, Fifth edition, 2010, pp. 219, 220, and 383.

In either case, and regardless of the politician or issue, whichever one made it to the top of the mountain did not matter to the American Ruling Class at the national, state, or local level of government. What mattered to its financially wealthy members is protection from the sheep, or people, while they siphoned off taxpayer dollars from the treasury. For their stated goal to be realized, ambitious men were carefully selected who could not distinguish between the trappings of power (i.e., Office, titles, clothing, jewelry, bank accounts, parties, vacation trips, etc.) and authentic, personal power, namely, providing for the real welfare of the people through practical deeds such as housing all of the people, providing medicine for all of the people, and, equally important, providing full employment for all of the people.

Peter Schweizer, in his book titled *Throw Them All Out*, demonstrates that the Top of the Mountain Game created as early as the Roman Empire Era by its Ruling Class, is still going strong today at all levels of government in the United States. Schweizer wrote the following:

> "Honest graft is so insidious because it piggybacks on legitimate service, and cloaks both in the name of public good... Give someone the chance to feel that they are serving the public and getting rich at the same time and you have created nightmare. Always a practical observer of human nature, Benjamin Franklin in 1787 expressed" There are two passions which have powerful influence in the affairs of men. These are *ambition* and *avarice;* the love of power and the love of money. Separately, each of these has great force in prompting men to action; but when united in view of the same object, they have in many minds the most violent effects. Place before the eyes of such men a post of *honor* that shall at the same time be a place of *profit*, and they will move heaven and earth to obtain it."[117]

---

[117] Schweizer, Peter, *THROW THEM ALL OUT*, Houghton Mifflin Harcourt, New York, 2011, pp. xxiii and xxiv.

In our Louisiana Case, Mr. Bobby Jindal fits this description perfectly. As you may recall, we stated earlier that he was appointed by former Governor Mike Foster to his cabinet as Secretary of Health. Is there a better way to serve the Louisiana people? and earn a six figure salary? Benjamin Franklin's warning came true in Louisiana in 2008 when Mr. Bobby Jindal was elected governor. Since this time, if you ask the average Louisiana Citizen, or working class man or woman do you feel your life has improved?, you will likely learn they have been living the nightmare that Benjamin Franklin expressed to the Constitutional Convention in 1787.

Therefore, the protector of the Louisiana Ruling Class since 2008, and during his second term, is Governor Bobby Jindal. Using data related to the Jindal Administration's Privatization Economic Policy taken directly from The Advocate, a Baton Rouge, LA newspaper, we will document how the latter has convinced a many Louisiana Citizens that the Jindal Administration's Privatization Economic Policy serves their best interest when, in reality, it only has created a nightmare for the majority of Louisiana Citizens. Before we proceed with this important task, recall that the aim of this study is to show that the Jindal Administration's Privatization Economic Policy, within the context of Dr. M. Harvey Brenner's Distributed Lag Relationship, results in the creation of what we mentioned earlier, and that is namely, a Violent and Criminal Aggression Framework.

B. Neo-Liberalism Economic Policy: Industrial Tax Breaks and Incentives, 2008 to 2014

On his own merit, free of any support from the Louisiana Ruling class, it is highly unlikely that Mr. Bobby Jindal would ever be elected governor of Louisiana. He was selected to open the Louisiana Budget to his benefactors, and provide them with legal protection in order to implement their neo-liberalism economic policies. This is how it was done during the Caesar's Rule in Rome, and nothing has changed to this day.

The first essential requirement necessary to implement neo-liberalism economic policies is to have a governor in place who truly believes that the way to serve the public good is to move as many financial resources from the public sector to the private. In short, a floodgate of public taxpayer dollars must be open; and kept open; to allow the maximum amount of public funds in the Louisiana State Budget to flow smoothly, and legally, into the private, corporate domain. As taxpayer dollars are steadily drained out of the public domain in the Louisiana State Budget, a decrease in public sector funds becomes a major problem. This occurrence is commonly referred to by the social media as a *shortfall*. As we move ahead with our study, it will be seen that the term shortfall is a misrepresentation of the fact; there is neither a shortfall or a deficit in the budget. To the contrary, there is a deliberate drain of taxpayer dollars out of the Louisiana State Budget as a result of the hidden agenda of the Louisiana Ruling Class' neo-liberalism economic policies. In an attempt to cover up the effects of this neo-liberalism ideology, *the Jindal Administration has carried-out a slash and burn budget reduction campaign aimed directly against the social programs that serve the critical needs of the majority of the Louisiana citizens.* The situation is simple: The more public funds are privatized, the more budget cuts are arbitrarily and capriciously enacted. Before we document the massive privatization of social program funds and tax breaks since the Jindal administration took office in 2008, it is interesting to note here a significant contradiction. That is, The Jindal Administration has mentioned, on many occasions, that the purpose of his neo-liberalism economic policies is *the creation of jobs.* The contradiction here is why is it necessary to eliminate social programs and existing jobs to create jobs?

a. Louisiana Legislature And Neo-liberalism Economic Policies Passed Into Law

The protector Jindal Administration also includes the Louisiana Legislature. If the former proposed a neo-liberalism economic policy, and the latter opposed it, and voted it down fifty percent of the time, then this is what we call precarious protection, a kind that is not consistently dependable. For neo-liberalism economic policies to yield the maximum profit for the Louisiana Ruling Class every time, the Jindal Administration must have them approved by the Louisiana Legislature every time. And, to keep up the illusion of democracy, the Louisiana Legislature must periodically convene to debate *so-called house and Senate Bills*, and after all is said and done, Privatization Economic Policies must be consistently approved by the Louisiana Legislature, and signed into law by Governor Bobby Jindal, a modern day Protector.

Within the first three months of the Jindal Administration, which took office in 2008, 100 percent of its proposed neo-liberalism economic policies were approved by the Louisiana Legislature. In his article titled "Jindal 'bats a thousand' at session, Ed Anderson quoted Governor Bobby Jindal saying, "this group should be proud of batting a thousand," Jindal said."[118] The group newly elected Governor Bobby Jindal referred to is the Louisiana Legislature. Ed Anderson also stated the following in his article:

> "The state Legislature on Friday wrapped up its second special session during the 2-month-old administration of Gov. Bobby Jindal by completing a full sweep of the governor's proposed package of business tax cuts and 1.1 billion in surplus spending…"[119]

There was never a doubt in the mind of the Louisiana Ruling Class that every proposed bill by the Jindal Administration would not pass easily. This is how the Protector-Wolf and Sheep game-operates. Nothing is left to chance because too much money is at stake. Moreover, Ed Anderson offers an idea of just how much money began to move out of the public sector into the private. He wrote the following:

> "Jindal and his legislative allies won all the initiatives they set out to accomplish during the six-day session, including a controversial bill to grant a partial tax deduction for private school tuition…Lawmakers passed bills to eliminate a 1 percent sales tax that businesses pay on utilities, an estimated annual savings to Louisiana

---

[118] Anderson, Ed, "Jindal 'bats a thousand' at session," The Times-Picayune, http://blog. nola.com/news_impact/print.html?entry=/2008/03/jindal_bats_a_thousand_at_…, Published Friday, March 14, 2008, 10/22/2010, p. 1 of 3.
[119] Ibid., p. 1.

companies—as well as loss of state revenue—of $69
million. They also passed an expedited phase out of taxes
on manufacturing machinery and equipment...Hose
and Senate members struck a historic compromise Friday
[March 14, 2008] on a bill to create a state income tax
deduction for 50 percent of the tuition paid for private
school education, up to $5,000 per student."[120]

In addition, "the Legislature acceded to the wishes of Jindal by breaking the
state spending cap by $1 billion...increasing the spending limit from $11
billion to $12 billion."[121] Although the new $ 1 billion was mostly approved
for infrastructure improvements, by the time this money was allocated in
the form of contracts and others, the vast majority ended up in the pockets
of the same businesses that received the large tax breaks mentioned earlier.
Of everything mentioned so far about the Louisiana Legislative Special
Six-Day Opening Session in 2008, the one tax deduction measure that
demonstrates the "greed mentality" at work since was the $5,000 tax
deduction for private school tuition. Ask yourself, why would anyone
who makes $1 million per year, or $200,000 per year, need a $5,000 tax
deduction on his or her private school tuition bill? The only real explanation
is greed, and as we go forward, we shall consistently be amazed at how the
Jindal Administration's implementation of the Louisiana Ruling Class'
Privatization Economic Policies *one-sidedly benefited the Louisiana wealthy
Ruling Class to the stark disadvantage of the so-called poor working class.* In
addition, the Protector Jindal Administration, and its Legislative Allies, are
not unfamiliar with *false generosity.* That is to say, while claiming to want
to improve public education in Louisiana by "giving" working class parents
a choice-voucher- of where they send their children to public school, Will
Sentell stated "the measure, House Bill 976, will allow low-and middle-
income students attending "C," "D" and "F" public schools to switch to
private and parochial schools, and use state dollars traditionally reserved for
public schools to help pay for tuition."[122] One of the key disguises of House

[120] Ibid., p. 1.
[121] Ibid., p. 2.
[122] Sentell, Will, "Schools chief to set rules for subsidies, " The Advocate, April 4,
2012, p. 1A.

Bill 976 is the *private and parochial schools* referred to in House Bill 976 are, to the contrary, charter schools. And, the majority of students who have left so-called "D" and "F" public schools are African-Americans. The other key disguise is charter schools are privately owned and operated, and when a student elects to attend a charter school, the Minimum Foundation Funds follow the enrolled student to the charter school, and it, not surprisingly, ends up in the hands of their business owners. This is a clever way the Louisiana Ruling Class has been allowed, by the Jindal Administration and its allies, to divert taxpayers dollars from the state budget's social program line items into private ownership.

The Six-Day Special Session in 2008 set the foundation for an avalanche of neo-liberalism economic activity. Having secured the force of law behind it, millions of taxpayer dollars have been diverted, by the Jindal Administration, from health and education programs, and from other much needed infrastructure improvements such as simple highway pavements statewide.

b. Business Tax Breaks By The End Of The Jindal Administration's First Term, 2012

More than $108 million taxpayer dollars had been diverted from the public sector to the private sector by October 2010. According to Millhollon,

> "State government ended last fiscal year more than $100 million in the red. Commissioner of Administration Paul Rainwater said Tuesday that he is working on a plan for dealing with the $108 million shortfall from the $29 billion budget for the fiscal year that ended June 30 [2010]. That plan-likely to involve cuts in spending for state services... "Its going to be a tough year for Louisiana government and for our citizens," state Sen. Lydia Jackson predicted."[123]

---

[123] Millhollon, Michelle, " State budget $100 million in red in last fiscal year," The Advocate, October 6, 2010, p. 1A.

What drove the budget shortfall? Did the $108 million miraculously disappear from the Louisiana State Budget? If someone robbed the Department of Treasury and arrested, he or she would be put on trial and sent to Angola State Prison for 40 years or more. No. The $108 million was allowed to be taken out of the state budget by the Protectors of the Louisiana Ruling Class, namely the Jindal Administration and the Louisiana Legislature. To makeup for the Privatized $108 million, Millhollon mentioned the money would likely involve cuts to social services. More about the drain of taxpayers dollars from the Louisiana State Budget is provided later. Currently, we will continue to follow the money trail carved by the neo-liberalism economic policies of the Jindal Administration and its allies in the Louisiana Legislature.

Earlier, Millhollon reported Commissioner of Administration, Paul Rainwater, "...is working on a plan for dealing with the $108 million shortfall"[124] on October 6, 2010. Two weeks later, pieces of it began to surface in the media. Millhollon captured the neo-liberalism economic policies at work, where on one hand, taxpayers dollars were diverted from the Louisiana State Budget, and on the other, those same dollars were then re-directed to a business in the form of a "sweetheart" tax break. Accordingly, Millhollon reported the following:

> "the Jindal Administration wants to chop state construction dollars [Taxpayers Dollars] for LSU, a north Baton Rouge YMCA and other Projects to generate $30 million for a St. James Parish Iron Facility. Legislators knew some projects would have to go on the chopping block to make room for spending on the Nucor Corp. plant in the state construction budget...A number of area projects lost funding in the state construction budget to carve out $30 million for Nucor. The projects-and the amount they lost-include: Louisiana Animal Disease Diagnostic Laboratory, receiving $3.3 million instead of $6 million; Homeland Security and Environmental Technical Center, $825,000; Louisiana State Police and

---

[124] Ibid., p. 1A.

Wildlife and Fisheries Enforcement Training Academy, $600,000; LSU Fire and Emergency Training Institute, new dormitory, $600,000; Renovation of old engineering Shops for the LSU Art Department, $1.1 million; La 1/ Interstate 10 connector, La 415 Bridge at Intercoastal Canal, $2 million; [and] North Baton Rouge YMCA, $400,000."[125]

Behind these numbers, as we shall see later, there are real Louisiana Working Class people, who have been forced to take drastic pay cuts, or suffer the ultimate injustice-unemployment. Neo-liberalism economic policies do not cut one way; some people in the Jindal Administration were adversely affected by the Millhollon "Chopping Block." For example, Millhollon reported by February 2012, the top administrator in the Jindal Administration, Commissioner Paul Rainwater, was arrested in December 2011 for Driving While under the Influence of Alcohol-DWI. She stated the following, which demonstrates the affect cutting the Louisiana State Budget, which makes taxpayers dollar giveaways available to businesses to the detriment of Louisiana families, had a significant psychological impact on Commissioner Paul Rainwater:

"Police arrested Rainwater in December on one count each of first-offense DWI, reckless operation of a vehicle and failure to obey a stop sign or yield sign. According to the affidavit of probable cause, a Baton Rouge police officer saw Rainwater run a stop sign and drive on the wrong side of the road on Christian Street. The affidavit said Rainwater performed "very poor" on a field sobriety test and registered a 0.170 blood-alcohol level, or more than twice the legal limit of 0.08 percent to operate a motor vehicle in Louisiana."[126]

---

[125] Ibid., p. 1A.
[126] Millhollon, Michelle, "Jindal aide to do DWI program," The Advocate, February 8, 2012, p. 1B.

As part of Commissioner Paul Rainwater's pre-trial diversion program, Millhollon also stated "Baton Rouge City Court Prosecutor Lisa Freeman said Rainwater will have to breathe into an interlock device to start his car, pick up litter and undergo alcohol screenings as part of the program."[127] Imagine the impact neo-liberalism economic policies have had, and continue to have, on the Louisiana Citizenry?

By the end of the Protector Jindal Administration first term, the neo-liberalism economic policies of the Louisiana Ruling Class had resulted, in just four short years, in a multiple billion dollar diversion of taxpayer dollars from the Louisiana State Budget. According to Millhollon, the amount was more than $7 billion. Specifically, she reported the following

> "A report released Monday by the Legislative Auditor's Office shows corporations and individuals cut their tax liabilities in Louisiana by nearly $5 billion through tax credits and other exemptions over a six-year period. Corporations reduced $5.4 billion in tax liabilities by $3 billion over six years. Individuals reduced $16.5 billion in tax liabilities by $1.8 billion over the same time period. As of February 2011, Louisiana allowed 464 tax credits and other exemptions. One such tax break is a state income tax deduction 50 percent of private-school tuition up to $5,000 per child... During debate on the state Senate floor last year, then-state Sen. Rob Marionneaux, D-Grosse Tete, stood on a ladder and allowed a stack of the state's more than $7 billion in tax breaks, credits, exemptions and rebates to spill from his hand to the floor."[128]

Moreover, the LFT Connection Newsletter, which is published by

---

[127] Millhollon, Michelle, The Advocate, "Rainwater to do community service on DWI arrest," The Advocate, February 08, 2012.
[128] Millhollon, Michelle, "Report: Tax breaks benefits unclear," The Advocate, March 06, 2012, pp. 1 and 2.

the Louisiana Federation of Teachers, the latter includes the following information: "The state's general fund comes largely from individual and business taxes. But over the years, our elected leaders[-Protectors-] have routinely passed hundreds of statutory tax expenditures-*tax credits, exemptions, and deductions*-which amount to more than $7 billion... If the state were to collect all the taxes that are on the books, general fund revenues would be closer to $15 billion."[129] Thus, what is the point of speaking about a so-called shortfall, when more than 400 statutory tax credits, exemptions, and deductions are written in plain sight in the Louisiana State Budget. And yet, the Louisiana Citizenry is scared nearly to death by talk we hear over-and –over in the social media claiming the Louisiana Economy is about to go over a *mysterious fiscal cliff.* Unbelievable does not even come close to the emotional panic that the average Louisiana Citizen has experienced since the Protector Jindal Administration was selected/elected to office in 2008.

Millhollon added "the report said determining what the state received between 2005 and 2010 is difficult...Tax breaks reduce the amount of revenue that finance state services."[130] So far, the Jindal Administration, and its Legislative Allies, have constantly talked about a state budget shortfall. Well, now it is clear that shortfall is a word used to cover up the harmful affects of the neo-liberalism economic policies of the Louisiana Ruling Class. By March 6, 2012, the last year of the first term of the Jindal Administration, Millhollon reported "the state is facing a nearly $900 million shortfall in the budget year that starts July 1 [2012]. The shortfall is based on the gap in revenue needed to fund state services at their current levels."[131] As we have already seen, the "shortfall" came to $108 million by 2010, or the end of the Jindal Administration's first term. This sum increased 733 percent over the $108 million shortfall by the last year of the first term of the Jindal Administration. The opposite of short is long; and, this means the Louisiana Ruling Class received long billions of dollars of taxpayers money from the state budget clandestinely, or in the disguise that Louisiana is truly benefiting from giving its citizens tax dollars away

---

[129] Monaghan, Steve, Your LFT Connection, September 2010.
[130] Ibid., p. 2.
[131] Ibid., p. 2.

to promote neo-liberalism economic growth in the state. There is nothing farther from the truth according to Michelle Millhollon's investigation of the matter. She wrote the following

> "The Louisiana Budget Project is part of the Center on Budget Policy Priorities network in Washington, D. C...The director of the Louisiana Budget Project, Jan Moller, said in a statement that...The report confirms that Louisiana's tax code is riddled with costly loopholes benefitting a few, big profitable corporations at the expense of job-creating investments in education, transportation, public safety and other building blocks of a strong economy."[132]

During the 2009 tax year, which corresponds with the second year of the Jindal Administration, Millhollon stated "five entities claimed 78 percent of the motion picture investor tax credits. Five entities claimed 94 percent of the research and development tax credits. [And] five entities claimed 68 percent of the enterprise zone-jobs tax credits."[133] This unheard-of outflow of taxpayers dollars that subsidize private businesses, will, no doubt, increase more than the accumulated 733 percent total by the end of the Protector Jindal Administration first term. Before we show some of the businesses that received enormous tax incentives, credits, etc., Table 1.5 shows the major Tax Breaks Laws approved for business by the Protector Jindal Administration during the last months of its first term. These are guaranteed to add larger outflows of taxpayer dollars to the bank accounts of business, and, the money that ends up in them was, and will continue, to be taken directly from the public sector line items in the State budget, which are specifically aimed at taking care of the basic needs of the majority of Louisiana Working Class people.

---

[132] Ibid., p. 1.
[133] Ibid., p. 2. More detailed, and up-to-date information related to the Jindal Administration's massive tax break "giveaways" to private business is located in the Epilogue and Afterword Sections at the end of this book.

Table 1.5
Louisiana Legislature Laws Authorizing Business Tax Breaks During the First Term of the Jindal Administration

NAME	PURPOSE	DECISION	REVENUE LOSS
House Bill 729	Allow business to lower corporate income and franchise taxes.	Louisiana House voted 100-0 for it.	Reduce state revenue by $5 million in fiscal year 2016-2017.
House Bill 937	25% rebate over five years for businesses that move corporate headquarters to Louisiana.	Louisiana House voted 81-13 for it.	Reduce state revenue by $5 million in fiscal year 2017-2018.
House Bill 937	Offer 10-year property tax exemption to targeted sectors such as corporate headquarters, data centers, digital media, and software developers.	Louisiana House voted 81-13 for it.	Reduce state revenues ranging from $2.5 million to $25 million for parishes in 2016 -2017.
House Bill 958	Give a payroll subsidy of up to 15 percent for next generation automotive companies.	Louisiana House voted 87-8 for it.	Reduce state revenue by $6 million in fiscal year 2016-2017.

Source: Millhollon, Michelle, " House Oks business tax incentives, The Advocate, April 14, 2012, p. 6A, and Millhollon, Michelle, "Jindal's target is good jobs," The Advocate, February 03, 2012, pp. 1 and 2.

The above legislation can be further understood by using a simple "door and lock" analogy. The above legislation is the key that was designed to unlock the Louisiana State Budget so the existing taxpayers dollars allocated to social programs and services could be siphoned off by the Protector Jindal Administration, and, then, given to businesses in the form of massive tax breaks. Thus, once the billions of dollars of tax breaks and incentives were given away to subsidize the operations of businesses, the state budget is famously said to have shortfalls, and the solution to resolve it, is to cutback on every social program possible, from education, health, environment, infrastructure, and more. We will take a close look at how the Louisiana Ruling Class' neo-liberalism economic policies have ravaged the Louisiana Public Sector since the Jindal Administration took office in 2008.

Meantime, we will identify the businesses and the tax breaks given to each of them by the Jindal Administration. While enormously, large sums of taxpayers' dollars flow quietly into the bank accounts of businesses like the *unseen,* fast moving waters, which flow rapidly at the bottom of the Mississippi River to the Gulf of Mexico without ever being seen, or detected, the average tax paying Louisiana Citizens does not see the steady outflow of their tax payers' dollars flowing quietly into the coffers of private businesses. This information is included in Table 1.6 below.

Table 1.6
Implementation of Laws Authorizing Business Tax Breaks by the Louisiana Economic Development Agency, Office of the Governor, Jindal Administration, 2008 to Present

NAME	YEAR	CITY	TAX BREAKS	AMOUNTS
Aeroframe Services	2008	Lake Charles	Install New tail Dock; 5 to 6 Percent Cash Rebate of Annual Gross Payroll Up To 10 Years.	$375,000
Albermarle	2008	Baton Rouge	Headquarters Relocation Expenses	$4.2 Million
Baton Rouge Coca-Cola Bottling Company	2007-2008	Baton Rouge	Support a Water Line Extension And Upgraded Water Main Pressure Stability. Received Industrial Tax Exemption on Buildings, Machinery and Equipment; Rebates on Income and Sale Taxes; Rebates on Local Sales Taxes Through the Enterprise Zone Program.	$1.4 million
Bercen Inc.	2008	Denham Springs	Offered Infrastructure and Headquarters Relocation Expenses.	$450,000

CenturyLink	2009	Monroe	Support Headquarters Personnel Relocation; Support Offset of Transportation Costs. Support Created a new Clarke M. Williams Memorial Endowed Professorship. 150, 000 sq. Ft. Discounted Lease Space.	$5 Million $600,000 $900,000 $14.9 million $3.3 million $1.2 Million
LambWeston	2009	Delhi	Support for Plant Processing Equipment and Site Infrastructure.	$34.7 million
Dr. Reddy's Laboratories	2011	Shreveport	Upgrade facility Packaging Equipment.	$2.1 million
Dynamic Fuels	2008	Geismar	Support Fuel Production Plant.	$100 million Gulf Opportunity Bonds and 100 Percent Property Tax Abatement for up to 10 years.
Gardener Denver Inc.	2009	Monroe	Received a Grant for Relocation Expenses	$8.7 million
Globalstar	2008-2009	Covington	Relocate its Headquarters to Louisiana.	$4.4 million
Nucor	2010	St. James Parish	Support Building a Five Phase Steel Plant.	$160 million
Schumacher Group	2011	Lafayette	Support Headquarters Expansion.	$9 million
Zagis USA	2008	Lacassine	Support Building two Cotton Spinning Mills.	$2.4 million
		TOTAL		**$1,244,625,000**

Source: Office of the Governor, Louisiana Economic Development Department, http://www.opportunitylouisiana.com/index/key-industries and http://www.opportunitylouisiana.com/.

Business giveaways, another name for tax breaks and incentives, have been completed at the local government level as well during the Jindal Administration's first term in office. Brett H. McCormick stated in an article "Donaldsonville plant gets $2.1 billion expansion," the following:

"CF Industries Inc. Will expand the nation's largest nitrogen plant, investing $2.1 billion into its Ascension Parish complex...Local officials, too, were pleased with CF Industries investment decision...Teri Casso, an Ascension Parish councilwoman, called the announcement a "tremendous expansion," while Mike Eades, president of the Ascension Economic Development Corp., labeled the project "substantial"...The parish offered CF Industries a rebate of 0.45 percent on its sales and use tax for construction material and initial equipping of the plant, Eades said, while Ascension Parish Sheriff Jeff Wiley said the Sheriff's Office will rebate 0.25 percent. Together, that will save more than $6 million...The state, meanwhile, offered an incentive package consisting of a $3 million tax credit, a $2 million loan that is forgivable if the company meets payroll targets...Gov. Bobby Jindal said."[134]

In another tax break giveaway, Timothy Boone, Advocate business writer, wrote "a Florida company announced plans to build five plants in Pointe Coupee Parish that will convert agricultural waste into fertilizer. BioNitrogen Corp., of Doral, Fla., said it has been granted preliminary approval by the Louisiana Community Development Authority to issue up to $1.25 billion in tax-exempt bonds to acquire land for the plant and build and develop the facilities."[135] The East Baton Rouge Metro Council through its hat into the tax break/incentives-subsidization ring, as recently as May 8, 2013, when it *gave Costco Wholesale a $7million incentive deal.* Rebekah Allen stated the details as follows:

"Costco Wholesale is moving to Baton Rouge, thanks to a $7 million incentive deal that city-parish officials said was essential to lure the superstore to the city... The $7 million deal will pay for $5.5 million in road improvements, to

---

[134] McCormick, Brett H., "Donaldsonville plant gets $2.1 billion expansion, " <u>The Advocate</u>, November 02, 2012, pp. 1 and 2.
[135] Boone, Timothy, "5 fertilizer plants planned in Pointe Coupee, <u>The Advocate</u>, February 28, 2013, p. 1.

alleviate traffic back ups in the area, and $1.5 million
toward the $4.5 million cost of tearing down the old
Coca-Cola bottling facility…The city-parish will also pay
Costco a 4.5 percent interest rate over an estimated four
years, which will bump the city-parish's total allocation
to about $7.8 million."[136]

The North Baton Rouge Community, which has been affected by the awful smells of sewage, and other airborne pollution for decades, tried desperately to get the City of Baton Rouge to lead an effort to get a business-buyout of their homes so they could move to another more healthy environment. Nothing came of this effort except talk and more talk, and eventual defeat and disillusionment. Yet, in one stroke of a pen, the EBR Metro Council approved a $7.8 million tax incentive package to lure Costco Wholesale to relocate in the city. But, nothing at all was done to help North Baton Rouge Residents relocate to another part of the city to escape the life-threatening air pollution. No economic incentives were provided.

Moreover, the pace of the Jindal Administration's extension of tax breaks, privatization, and subsidization monetary packages to business has not slowed down one bit as Governor Bobby Jindal enters the first year of his second term in office. In his article "IBM selects BR," Timothy Boone wrote the following:

"Today's announcement is a game changer that will have
a generational impact on Baton Rouge and our state,"
Gov. Bobby Jindal said. IBM announced Wednesday
it will establish a first-of-its-kind software development
center at the former site of The Advocate… LED offered
IBM a performance-based incentive package that includes
grants totaling $29.5 million over 12 years, including
a $1.5 million contribution from the city-parish to
reimburse costs related to recruiting personnel, relocation
and other workforce-related costs; internal training; and

---

[136] Allen, Rebekah, "EBR Metro Council approves incentives deal," The Advocate, May 08, 2013, pp. 1 and 2.

facility operating expenses.... The office building will be
funded by $14.8 million from the state of Louisiana, $3
million from the city-parish and $12.7 million in federal
Community Development Block Grant money.[137]

LED offered IBM this money to come to Baton Rouge, LA. The Louisiana
Economic Development Department is the same one that offered the
previously mentioned businesses more than $1 billion in tax breaks
and incentives, creating a so-called $1 billion plus hole in the FY 2013
Louisiana State Budget.

The generalized pattern of Jindal Administration tax breaks did not
end by the end of the former's first term in 2012; to the contrary, the
mentioned pattern of tax breaks, and the budget shortfalls they created,
carried right over into Governor Bobby Jindal's second term in office.
According to David Mitchell, "Jindal said...that the Department of
Economic Development offered BASF a discretionary incentive of a $1.2
million modernization tax credit over five years if BASF meets payroll
and investment targets. He added the company is expected to use the
state's Quality Jobs and industrial tax exemption programs and potentially
the Fast Start workforce training program."[138] How many working class
people do you know are offered a discretionary salary, meaning they can
raise their own salary anytime that they choose to? Contrary to what
Governor Bobby Jindal is telling the Louisiana Citizenry that all of these
identified tax breaks result in increased employment, the fact is, in just a
short period of time, many businesses provided a tax break actually end up
laying off a significant portion of their work force. An excellent example
of this situation is Entergy's recent layoff of hundreds of working people.
Thompson and Ballard stated the following:

"Entergy Corp. said Tuesday it will lay off 800 people
— 240 or nearly one-third of them-in Louisiana — in
an effort to improve the company's performance. The

[137] Boone, Timothy, "IBM selects BR," The Advocate, March 27, 2013, pp. 1,2 and 3.
[138] Mitchell, David J., "BASF announces $42.6 million project, 22 jobs," The
Advocate, September 12, 2013, p. 2.

job cuts, about 5 percent of the New Orleans-based power provider's workforce of nearly 15,000 employees companywide, were part of its second-quarter earnings report. Entergy's second-quarter earnings plunged to $163.7 million, or 92 cents per share, compared with $365.0 million, or $2.06 per share, a year earlier. Entergy's earnings fell short of Wall Street analysts' expectations. Analysts surveyed by Thomson Reuters had forecast Entergy's earnings at $1.16 per share... Eliminating the jobs will save Entergy $200 million to $250 million by 2016, the company said. Chanel Lagarde, an Entergy spokesman, said about 160 jobs are being cut in the New Orleans area, 25 in Baton Rouge and another 55 around the state. The layoffs have begun and should be completed by the end of the year [2013], he said."[139]

In addition to these layoffs, by September 2013, Entergy raised the electric bills of many of the same workers it laid-off back in July 2013. Ballard stated "about 700,000 Entergy customers from the New Orleans suburbs to the Arkansas line already are paying to repair the Waterford 3 nuclear plant that has only 11 years left on its license. Since January, Entergy Louisiana's typical residential customers — who buy about 1,400 kilowatt hours of electricity monthly — have been paying $5.81 more each month for the nuclear plant repairs, according to the company's calculations."[140] Entergy stockholders do not create any value; yet, the working class people who do create all value with their labor power, are laid-off and charged more for electricity. How will a laid-off worker provide lighting in his or her home for their children to do their homework for school the next day? What is more hypocritical is the tax break policy of the Jindal Administration is, on paper at least, suppose to create jobs for Louisiana Citizens; however, in the Entergy Case, and many others, layoffs are commonplace.

---

[139] Thompson, Richard and Ballard, Mark, "Entergy to layoff 240 in La.," The Advocate, July 30, 2013, p. 1.

[140] Ballard, Mark, "Entergy seeks bill increase to pay for nuclear plant repairs," The Advocate, September 7, 2013, p. 1.

As we see, the budget deficit, shortfall, or whatever you choose to call it, is growing larger, and, as we have already pointed-out, Louisiana is mandated by law to have a balanced budget annually. This brings us to the next main question which we will address next, and that is, How will the Jindal Administration balance the FY 2013 Louisiana State Budget? How? Rather than speculate, to follow is an answer to this question taken directly from the Jindal Administration's implementation of the Louisiana Ruling Class' neo-liberalism economic policies.

CHAPTER IV

Social Program Cuts: Actions Taken by the Jindal Administration to Balance the Louisiana State Budget, 2008-2014

A good place to begin is with K-12 education and higher education. Our focus is on the devastating cuts to Louisiana Higher Education since Governor Bobby Jindal was s/elected to office.

A. Cause of Higher Education Budget Cuts, 2008 to 2014

These represent a few examples of the tax breaks trend that has radiated out from its source in the Jindal Administration, which, in a matter of two to three years, has taken root in a majority of the largest Louisiana cities, including some rural parishes. In sum, the tax breaks and incentives shown in Table 1.6 above have one very interesting quality, namely, the $1.244,625,000 *aggregate tax breaks and incentives equal to the exact amount of missing tax revenues in the 2013 Louisiana State Budget proposed by Gov. Bobby Jindal.* This $1.2 billion is called a shortfall by the mass media. The upcoming Regular Session of the Louisiana Legislature is going to spend most, if not all, of its time trying to figure out just what can be done to compensate for the FY 13 Budget Shortfall? Later, we will provide information that demonstrates just how the mounting Louisiana State Budget Shortfalls have been addressed during the Jindal Administration.

Table 1.6 has, using the reported Louisiana Economic Development Tax Breaks Case Studies Data, proves, beyond a shadow of a doubt, that a proportional relationship exists between the Louisiana Economic Development's approval of business tax breaks and incentives and the existence of a recognized, reported revenue shortfall in the Louisiana State Budget. As we have already seen, for Fiscal Year 2013, the shortfall in the Louisiana State Budget is $1,244,625,000 (This is the amount that has accumulated since Gov. Bobby Jindal was s/elected to office in 2008). As noted previously, the shortfall was $108 million in 2010; it grew to $900 million in 2012; and at the start of Gov. Bobby Jindal's first year of his second term in office, the total leaped to $1,244,625,000. Since 2010, the shortfall in the Louisiana State Budget increased a whopping1,052 percent!! While the latter is turned into a mystery by the Louisiana Social Media, other agencies outside of Louisiana know about the $1.2 billion FY 2013 Louisiana State Budget Shortfall.

According to The Bob Williams Report, a weekly update on state budgets, "**LOUISIANA:** State has $1.2 billion budget shortfall. WBRZ.com. January 18, 2013."[141] This state budget update was reported on January 23, 2013. After viewing the tax breaks and incentives data in Table 1.6, the mystery and illusion of a so-called shortfall has been exposed because we now know where the $1.2 billion originated, and what it was used for. Had the $1.2 billion remained in the Louisiana State Budget, there would not be any discussion about a shortfall. However, to the contrary, the Center on Budget and Policy Priorities reported that for Fiscal Year 2013, Louisiana has a total shortfall of $1.2 billion, which is 14.3%[142] of the Louisiana State Budget. Table 1.7 shows the history of Louisiana State Budget deficits caused by tax breaks and incentives since Governor Bobby Jindal was s/elected to office in 2008.

---

[141] Williams, Bob, The Bob Williams Report, State Budget Update January 23, 2013, http://www.statebudgetsolutions.org/The_williams_report, 2013, p. 1.

[142] Oliff, Phil, Mai, Chris, and Palacios, Vincent, "States Continue to Feel Recession's Impact," Center on Budget and Policy Priorities, http://www.cbpp/cms/index=view&id=711, June 27, 2012, p. 5.

Table 1.7
Louisiana State Budget Deficits, 2009 to 2013

YEAR	FY DEFICIT	% OF FY REVENUES
2013	$1.2 billion	14.3
2012	2.1 billion	25.1
2011	1.1 billion	14.3
2010	2.5 billion	27.8
2009	341 million	3.7
TOTAL	**$7.24 billion**	

Source: Center on Budget and Policy Priorities, center@cbpp.org, June 27, 2012, pp. 5, 8, 9, 10, and 11.

As we see, when the Jindal Administration assumed office in 2008, the Louisiana State Budget was manageable, given the fact that when Former Gov. Kathleen Blanco left office in 2007, Louisiana had a roughly $1billion surplus. However, as the Jindal Administration, under the leadership of Gov. Bobby Jindal, implemented the Louisiana Ruling Class' neo-liberalism economic policies beginning in 2008, the Fiscal Year budget deficits-shortfalls-have steadily risen with no slowing down in the foreseeable future. As a matter of fact, between 2009 and 2013, the Louisiana State Budget Deficit increased 265.0 percent! The all call for more social program budget cuts has already been sounded statewide. The reason is simple. Louisiana, like 49 other states, is required by its constitution to have a balanced budget. "The National Conference of State Legislatures (NCSL) has traditionally reported that 49 states must balance their budgets, with Vermont being the exception...State balanced budget requirements can be categorized as consisting of one of more of the following: The governor's proposed budget must be balanced; The enacted budget must be balanced; [And,] no deficit can be carried forward from one fiscal period to the next."[143] That being so, the Jindal Administration, having no other alternatives to balance the Louisiana State Budget short of revoking its neo-liberalism economic policies, which is totally off of

---

[143] _____NCSL FISCAL BRIEF: STATE BALANCED BUDGET PROVISIONS, National Conference of State Legislatures, http://ncsl.org/documents/fiscal/statebalancedbudget, October 2010, p. 2.

the table for consideration, the former embarked on a course of *enacting a continuous series of social program cuts, affecting adversely the vast majority of Louisiana Citizenry, ranging from the unborn to the elderly.* Do not overlook the fact that the billions of dollars awarded for tax breaks and incentives are not revenue placed in the Louisiana State Budget by an alien angel, but, in fact, the vast majority of it is was derived from taxes paid by the majority of the Louisiana Citizenry against whom steady and yearly budget cuts have been directed. As you have traveled back and forth in your own communities statewide, you have seen the housing for sale signs in the yards of residents; you have seen the for sale by owner signs; you have seen cars, boats, motorcycles, and many others listed as for sale; you have driven on interstate highways in Louisiana, and all of a sudden, you hit a pothole, and your vehicle makes a loud sound while you are driving 75 plus miles per hour; you have driven on secondary highways in your own communities where the streets are becoming so riddled with asphalt patches that it feels like you are driving constantly on back roads in some Third World undeveloped countries. When it rains, water ponds in the potholes, and you are at risk of hydroplaning off of the street into a nearby ditch. We can go on longer with this trend because it stretches statewide. Instead, we will transition to the next phase of this study in which we will demonstrate what impact the Jindal Administration's budget cuts have had on the social programs that are designed to serve the basic needs of the Louisiana Citizenry, regardless of race, color, religion, and so forth. This is not about race or color; however, the longstanding illusion that it is is designed to call up racism and racist outbursts by one race of people against another, who, unknowingly, are not the cause of each others' problem, but enacted budget cuts aimed at trying to balanced a growing deficit in the Louisiana State Budget is the cause of all of our problems, regardless of race, color, religion, and so forth.

One of the actions taken by Governor Bobby Jindal to balance the Louisiana State Budget, thus far, has been making consecutive fiscal year-deep-cuts in the higher education budget line item. Why has the higher education budget been a prime target of the Jindal Administration's budget cuts? Because the higher education budget is not protected by the Louisiana Constitution when it comes to which ones cannot be cut to achieve a balanced budget, which is required by law. As a result, the axe has fallen heavily on higher education. Wouldn't it make good use of time for all of the presidents of higher education institutions in Louisiana to "lobby" to have higher education protected from *any budget cuts?* Since 2008, the Protector Jindal Administration has held the door open for the criminal-like plunder of the Louisiana Higher Budget. Shortfalls is the prop the Jindal Administration continues to use to convince the Louisiana Citizenry that the budget cuts to higher education are necessary and unavoidable. Let the Jindal Administration record speak for itself.

B. Higher Education Budget Cuts, 2008 to 2010

According to Tom Hall, Governor Bobby Jindal placed higher education in his budget cutting cross hairs early in his first term in office. He stated the following:

> "Louisiana Republican Governor Bobby Jindal has proposed deep budget cuts to education and health care for the poor…While pledging not to increase taxes on business, the governor is targeting higher education and health care-two areas of state funding that are relied upon by the working class and poor but neither of which are constitutionally mandated…$350 million[have] already [been] slashed from the higher budget over the last two years…forcing workers and students to shoulder the burden of the state's $1.6 billion deficit."[144]

Given what we now know about the so-called shortfall/deficits and so forth, Tom Hall recognized that the "burden" is no mystery but what we have already seen, namely the unheard-of tax breaks and incentives given to business by Governor Jindal via his Louisiana Economic Development Department in the Governors Office. Victoria Shirley added "the shortfall is forcing law makers to cut $270 million dollars. With the constitution

---

[144] Hall, Tom, "Louisiana governor plans cuts t oeducation, health care," http:// wsws.org/en/articles/ 2011/03, March 3, 2011, p. 1.

and federal mandates protecting 70% of the operating budget, lawmakers have little choice about where the axe will fall...Cuts like these aren't a new thing, since 2008, $585 million dollars have been cut from the state's higher education fund."[145] Alyson Gaharan stated "since 2008, Gov. Bobby Jindal and the Louisiana Legislature have cut more than $425 million from the higher education budget, according to The Advocate."[146] Consecutive deep cuts were made in the Louisiana Higher Education Budget between 2008 and 2010. By the end of the Jindal Administration's first term in office, an unimaginable amount of taxpayer's dollars were subtly, very quietly so, shifted from the higher education budget in an attempt to patch up the giant hole in the state budget created by Governor Bobby Jindal's giveaways of tax breaks and incentives to business.

a. Higher Education Budget Cuts by 2013

Overall, by the end of the Jindal Administration's first term in office, irreparable damage had been done to higher education in Louisiana. For a state that is ranked at, or near the bottom nationally, in nearly all indices of social well-being, for many, in and outside of Louisiana, it is difficult to imagine why the one area-education-that can help alleviate many of our state woes, is the self-same area that has been the victim of astronomical budget cuts? We have already answered this heart-wrenching question earlier. Koran Addo stated just how serious the budget cutting in higher education had become by January 12, 2013. She stated "Louisiana's colleges and universities have lost more than $625 million to state budget cuts in the past four years, according to an accounting that Purcell[,State commissioner of Education,] presented to the Louisiana Board of Regents."[147] Moreover, Addo mentioned what impact this budget slashing is having on the Louisiana Citizenry. She wrote State Commissioner of Education, Jim Purcell, "...added that continued budget cuts are

---

[145] Shirley, Victoria, "Louisiana budget cuts: higher education on chopping block," http://www.knoe.com/story18441433/louisiana-budget, May 16, 2012, p.1.

[146] Gaharan, Alyson, "Midyear cuts were more modest than anticipated," The Daily Reveille, January 13, 2013, p. 1.

[147] Addo, Koran, "Board urged to stop education budget slashing," The Advocate, January 12, 2013, p. 1.

hampering school's ability to train students who can meet workforce demands."[148] Addo reported the following:

> "LSU's Baton Rouge campus has lost $102 million, or 44 percent of its budget. Southern University's Baton Rouge campus lost $25 million, or 47 percent of its budget. The University of New Orleans lost $34 million in state funding, or 48 percent of its budget...'BRCC is in the fastest-growing city in the state, and they've gone from $20 million to $9 million. That's more than a 50 percent cut,'Purcell said."[149]

The situation is worse in March 2013 than it was when Governor Bobby Jindal began his higher education budget cutting frenzy back in 2008. In early April 2013, the Louisiana Legislature will convene its regular session, and its top priority is to plug the $1.2 billion so-called shortfall in the 2013 Fiscal Year state budget. More higher education budget cuts will be made. Edie Talley stated "Another $209 million dollars – that's the amount Governor Jindal is proposing to cut from Louisiana's higher education 2013-2014 budget... If it passes in its current form, Louisiana's public colleges and universities will have had their funding cut by 84.5 percent, $1.24 billion, since 2008.[150] Addo added"This year's proposed $209 million budget cut would make six straight years that the governor and legislators have taken an ax to college and university state revenues. The governor's $24.7 billion overall, comprehensive budget proposal reduces higher education funding 21 percent to $774 million, down from $983 million in the current year."[151] According to The Times-Picayune, the budget ax will once again be used by Governor Bobby Jindal and the Louisiana Legislature to slash and chop the higher education budget. The following information was reported on March 21, 2013:

---

[148] Ibid., p. 1.

[149] Ibid., p. 1.

[150] Talley, Edie, "Jindal's latest higher ed proposal: More cuts, shaky money, higher tuition, Driftwood, http://driftwood.uno.edu/jindal's-lates-higher-ed-prop, March 17, 2013, p. 1.

[151] Addo, Koran, "College funding in question," The Advocate, March 18, 2013, p.1.

"For the sixth year in a row, Louisiana's public colleges and universities are girding for a state budget that once again takes an ax to their funding. Regents say they must brace for $209 million in cuts that are included in Gov. Bobby Jindal's budget proposal for the coming year... According to Jindal's $24.7 billion budget proposal, the state outlay for higher education in the fiscal year starting July 1 would draw $284.5 million from the state's general fund, plus $489 million from sources that will be available only once, or expected collections that may not be as much as predicted... "All units (of higher education) will be at risk for reduction should any of these funds not materialize," according to a report from the state Board of Regents, which coordinates all public higher education in Louisiana... Since 2008, Louisiana has cut state funding for higher education by almost $650 million..."[152]

During the Fall 2011, the Jindal Administration's consecutive fiscal year slashing of the higher education budget had gathered enough devastating momentum to cause the Southern University Board of Supervisors, for the Baton Rouge Campus, to *declare financial exigency, or bankruptcy.* Jordan Blum, journalist for The Advocate, reported the following obituary:

"The Southern University Board of Supervisors declared a financial emergency on the main campus [in October 2011]... The decision gives university administrators more leeway to furlough and lay off faculty as well as terminate academic programs. Southern Chancellor James Llorens and Southern University System President Ronald Mason Jr. made the exigency request again. They argued that staff layoffs did not save as much money as expected and that a voluntary faculty furlough plan ended up a mess. Mason said exigency is needed to address recurring money

---

[152] Pope, John and Adelson, Jeff, " Regents claim Jindal proposing more cuts to higher education next year; greater reliance on one-time revenues, tuition," Times-Picayune: Greater New Orleans, March 21, 2013, pp. 1 and 2.

> problems… Llorens said exigency is a "dramatic" step.
> Llorens initially had said at least 90 percent of the faculty
> needed to voluntarily accept the furloughs in order to
> balance the university budget without exigency."[153]

Similar to cattle being herded out to pasture led by the one with a bell around its neck, President Ronald Mason and Chancellor Jim Llorens bought into the Jindal Administration's otherworldly reasoning that by declaring financial exigency, Southern University would really be an improved academic institution. Earlier, we quoted Jim Purcell, State Commissioner of Education, saying massive budget cuts to higher education is "…hampering school's ability to train students who can meet workforce demands." How can any higher education institution of any worth prepare students to meet workforce demands after declaring financial exigency? Mr. Purcell is correct on this point; and yet, he praised Drs. Mason and Llorens for declaring financial exigency on the Baton Rouge Campus. Mr. Purcell stated "today's vote indicates the board's willingness to support proactive realignment of the institution to best meet its new priorities and goals and that's an excellent indicator of their commitment to the university's success, Purcell said in a prepared statement." [154]What a contradiction!!On one hand, we have thus far seen the massive higher education budget cutting that continues through March 2013, and on the other, Mr. Purcell said the Southern University Board of Supervisor's declaration of financial exigency will not "hamper the university's ability to train students who can meet workforce demands." Had Grambling State University still been an independent, stand alone academic institution with its own Board of Supervisors, it-too-probably would have declared financial exigency also, and Mr. Purcell would likely have praised that action as well. Regardless, the damage is done.

On Saturday, June 15, 2013, the premiere national organization of university professors concluded in its recent report that the Southern University Baton Rouge Campus, under the leadership of Drs. Ron Mason and

---

[153] Blum, Jordan, "SU Board OKs exigency," <u>The Advocate</u>, October 29, 2011, pp. 1and 2.
[154] Ibid., p. 3.

James Llorens, did not need to declare financial exigency in October 2011, which, as we have already seen, led to the wrongful layoffs of numerous tenured professors and administrative staff. According to Jordan Blum, "the top national organization of university professors...voted to place Southern University on academic censure for its handling of a declared financial emergency and the resulting faculty layoffs during the past two years."[155] During September 2012, a team of AAUP representatives visited the Southern University Baton Rouge Campus, during which time, they interviewed a number of laid-off professors and administrative staff. Based on the AAUP's assessment of the data they collected, the identified campus was placed on academic censure. The latter finding by the AAUP supports our research, given the fact we already know that there was *never a budget shortfall because millions of dollars were removed intentionally, from the Louisiana State higher Education Budget to cover more than a billion dollars worth of tax breaks and incentives given carte blanche to private business.* Because both Drs. Ron Mason and James Llorens were purposely kept unaware of this fact. Dr. Llorens, as late as June 15, 2013, the day the AAUP's report was released, still believes, however erroneously, that it was the right thing to do to request a declaration of financial exigency on the Southern University Baton Rouge Campus. To contribute money to Governor Bobby Jindal's Tax Break Machine, Jordan Blum added the following:

> "By laying off 19 senior professors on short notice, while simultaneously deducting 10 percent from the salaries of all faculty members through mandatory furloughs, the (Southern) administration managed to combine the worst of two worlds," AAUP Associate General Secretary Jordan Kurlans said about the determinations. Southern ultimately eliminated roughly 70 faculty positions and several dozen non-faculty positions through layoffs... during the eight-month exigency period."[156]

In face of what we now know about the tax break plundering of the

---

[155] Blum, Jordan, "AAUP censures Southern," <u>The Advocate</u>, June 15, 2013, p. 1.
[156] Ibid., pp. 1 and 2.

Louisiana State Higher Education Budget, and the fact the above layoffs were part of Governor Bobby Jindal's Plundering Plan, Chancellor James Llorens thinks the declaration of financial exigency on the Southern University Baton Rouge Campus was required to make the latter a better academic institution, when, to the contrary, it was necessary because the Louisiana Taxpayers' Dollars previously paid to the more than 70 laid-off employees before financial exigency, was redirected into the tax break money given to private business. Yet, Blum stated "Llorens said he stands by the decisions made and the university's policies. "We're just confident the exigency was much needed to get out of a very serious financial situation," Llorens said."[157]

We do not disagree with Chancellor James Llorens that the Southern University System, and its Baton Rouge Campus, faced a "very serious financial situation" by October 2011, nearly three years after Governor Bobby Jindal took office in 2008. What Dr. Llorens failed to understand is he directly participated in a robbery while not having a clue that the serious financial situation he referred to was caused by a massive pattern of tax breaks given to private business, as we have already seen, beginning in earnest by 2008. For their participation, silence, and indifference in this tragedy-comedy, the Jindal Administration pays Drs. Mason and Llorens very well; together, their salaries alone exceed more than a half million dollars annually. This is small change relative to the enormous sums of operating funds, which were taken out of the Southern University Baton Rouge Campus' Budget, which were converted into tax breaks for private business.

By now, a few Louisiana Residents may have caught on to just what is the real reason Southern University Baton Rouge Campus was forced into declaring financial exigency, or bankruptcy, as previously mentioned in October 2011. Since Dr. Felton Clark, former President of Southern University, left office in 1969, the latter evolved a culture of corruption at the highest administrative levels of the university. Friends of friends became president without appropriate qualifications, and nepotism among many others, has gone on unabated. The most recent revelation of this

---

[157] Ibid., p. 2.

historical pattern of corruption is the case of former president of the Southern University System, Dr. Ralph Slaughter. Joe Gyan Jr. stated the following:

> "the foundation — the university's private fundraising arm — sued Slaughter in late 2009, claiming he received $400,000 in salary supplements without foundation board approval, although the Southern Board of Supervisors authorized the payments as the result of a 2007 settlement of a Slaughter lawsuit against Southern. The foundation's board of directors never approved the salary supplement payments, foundation attorneys argue, and the foundation was not a party to Slaughter's employment contract... Slaughter is appealing the rulings Kelley made last summer. The judge ordered him to repay the foundation $400,000 in combined salary supplements for the years 2007, 2008 and 2009, plus $75,000 in foundation money that Slaughter used to pay a lawyer after he sued Southern over his dismissal."[158]

As we see, if the $400, 000 in Southern University foundation funds were not fraudulently taken out of it, including the $75,000 used by Dr. Ralph Slaughter for attorney fees, this money could have *significantly helped the university to avoid having to declare financial exigency.* Moreover, the Board of Supervisors for the Southern University System, its supreme decision-making body, authorized Dr. Ralph Slaughter to remove the $475,000 out of the Southern University Foundation in 2007, four years before Chancellor James Llorens encouraged the same Board of Supervisors to approve a declaration of financial exigency in 2011.

Moreover, on June 27, 2013, the chickens came home to roost. Jow Gyan reported a state district judge rules that former President of the southern University System, Dr. Ralph Slaughter, willfully intended to defraud the

---

[158] Gyan, Joe, Jr. "Lawyers face off over Slaughter asset transfer," The Advocate, June 13, 2013, pp. 1 and 2.

Southern University Foundation while serving as president. He stated the
matter this way:

> "System Foundation by transferring much of his estate
> to his wife last year while the private Former Southern
> University System President Ralph Slaughter intended
> to defraud the SU group was seeking to recover nearly
> half a million dollars from him, a judge ruled Thursday.
> State District Judge Tim Kelley's ruling allows the
> foundation to attempt to seize the Slaughters' Moss Side
> Lane home, automobiles and other property in order to
> collect $475,000 — plus running legal interest — that
> the judge ordered Slaughter to pay the foundation last
> summer... At the foundation's urging, Kelley revoked
> Slaughter's July 12, 2012, donation of his interest in the
> couple's $1.3 million home to his wife, Shalonda Denise
> Slaughter. The judge also revoked Slaughter's transfer of
> property — including a 2007 Mercedes-Benz, a 2009
> GMC Yukon, jewelry and a share of his retirement income
> from the Louisiana State Employees Retirement System
> — to his wife that same day... His monthly retirement
> income is $14,000."[159]

Amazing but believable, given the culture of fraud that continues to run
rampant within the Southern University System. We wonder if Chancellor
James Llorens realize that part of the reason a declaration of financial
exigency was necessary was due to the rampant fraud flowing through the
veins of the Southern University System. If the average Southern University
professor, or staff employee, retires with a monthly retirement income of
$3,000, this sum would be considered a good one after 30 years or more of
service. However, Former President, Dr. Ralph Slaughter, by the end of his
short tenure as president-less than five years-retired with a monthly income
of $14,000. Many Louisiana residents work hard all of their lives and retire
with a monthly retirement income far, far less than $14,000. The only way

---

[159] Gyan, Joe, "Judge: Assets transfer done to defraud SU Foundation," The Advocate,
June 27, 2013, pp. 1 and 2.

anyone can retire with a monthly income of $14,000 or more is some form, or multiple forms, of exploitation is directly involved. Gyan added "[State District Judge] Kelley, in rulings last summer on July 31 and Aug. 13, ordered Slaughter to repay a combined $475,000 to the foundation. That money included $400,000 in combined salary supplements for the years 2007, 2008 and 2009, plus $75,000 in foundation money that Slaughter used to pay a lawyer after he sued Southern over his dismissal."[160] In addition, given Dr. Ralph Slaughter's $14,000 monthly retirement income, it is interesting to point-out here that his monthly retirement income in two months amounts to $28,000, which is more income than a majority of Louisiana Working Class people earn in one year!! Regarding Louisiana per capita income, 2011, "the ACS survey shows **the median per capita income for Louisiana was $22,882 in 2011.**"[161] Moreover, since 2005 to 2011, Louisiana per capita income never exceeded $25,000 annually,[162] yet, every two months, Dr. Ralph Slaughter's monthly retirement income amounts to $28,000. Dr. Ralph Slaughter's case is merely symbolic of the political and economic corruption played out within the Southern University System, which is a part of the larger culture of corruption we have systematically documented-thus far- that has engulfed all levels of Louisiana State government. One of the biggest impacts of the culture of corruption on Southern University Baton Rouge Campus is its steadily declining student enrollment.

As a consequence of the culture of corruption mentioned earlier, Koran Addo stated the Southern University Baton Rouge Campus "...student population has dipped from about 9,500 students in 2004 to about 6,600 students currently [May 2013]."[163] Since the parents of many Louisiana Citizens, who have college age children, know about the on-going culture of corruption, a significant number do not send their children elsewhere. Ina desperate attempt to increase its student enrollment, Chancellor James

---

[160] Ibid., p. 1.
[161] _____ Louisiana Household Income, Department of Numbers, http://deptofnumbers.com/income/louisiana/, 2011, p. 1.
[162] Ibid., p. 1.
[163] Addo, Koran, "Southern to welcome Brazilian students," The Advocate, July 03, 2013, p. 1.

Llorens has plans to bring in students from Brazil. Addo added "recruiting international students has been one of the main strategies Southern has undertaken in recent years to boost enrollment... On Tuesday [July 2, 2013], Llorens said he believes the initial 36 students coming this fall could balloon to 500 students in a matter of years."[164]

In the end, thousands of college students have been impacted; many academic programs have been done away with; and numerous full professors have been laid-off because of this *gross and irresponsible decision-making.* It is worth noting here that Dr. Ralph Slaughter recently transferred all of his property assets into his wife's name to avoid having to repay any of the illegally received money given to him, by the Southern University Foundation, and approved by the Southern University Board of Supervisors, while he served as president of the Southern University System.

Consequently, take a look at the following fiscal climate that Southern University, including all of the other higher education institutions is operating in, and you decide whether this or that one can flourish and grow academically?

b. Summary of Impact on the Higher Education Budgets, 2008 to 2013

Beginning with state expenditures for students enrolled in higher education, Louisiana ranks fourth in the nation, regarding percentage change in outlays-money-provided to support Louisiana children who chose to pursue a higher education degree between FY08 and FY13, a period that coincides perfectly with Governor Bobby Jindal's first and second terms in office. According to the Center on Budget and Policy Priorities, and according to Phil Oliff, Vincent Palacios, et.al., Louisiana cut higher education spending by 42.0 percent.[165] We wonder how the Southern University Baton Rouge Campus, for example, is ever going

---

[164] Ibid., p. 1.

[165] Oliff, Phil, Palacios, Vincent, Johnson, Ingrid, and Michael Leachman, "Recent Deep State Higher education Cuts May Harm Students and the Economy for years to Come," Center on Budget and Policy Priorities, March 19, 2013, P. 4.

to realize Dr. Ron Mason's vision of a "new Southern?" Maybe he has a private benefactor who is going to shower millions of dollars on Southern University, making the Jindal Administration's higher education budget cutting policy mute? The other thing that is worrisome about the Southern University Baton Rouge Campus' declaration of financial exigency is Drs. Mason and Llorens truly believe their action was motivated by their desire to improve the academic climate of the university; however, as we have pointed-out in detail thus far, the *declaration of financial exigency was triggered as a direct reaction to Governor Bobby Jindal's plunder of the higher education budget between 2008 and 2012.* We remind Drs. Mason and Llorens that reducing academic and administrative program offerings, terminating professor contracts, laying off staff, and failing to reverse the recent enrollment downturn among others, and, taken together, do not move the university toward any "New Vision," but, to the contrary, financial exigency is speeding up the inevitable collapse of the Southern University System. Can the university operate from one year to the next with less operating state funds for the current fiscal year than the amount allocated for the previous one? Once Drs. Mason and Llorens declared financial exigency on the Southern University Baton Rouge Campus, they, along with their Board of Supervisors, thought that the budget problem at Southern University was now solved. This, of course, was far from the truth because Jordan Blum quoted Dr. Mason five months after declaring financial exigency saying the following:

> "Southern University System President Ronald Mason Jr. said the struggling main campus in Baton Rouge is forced to take yet another heavy financial hit after declaring a financial emergency, called exigency, last year[October 2011]."If you're already in a state of emergency, then how do you get out of that emergency with what you're facing down the road?" Mason said. "Give the campus that's in distress a little breathing room with a year to dig itself out," Mason pleaded. "If the flagship goes, so goes the (Southern) system."[166]

---

[166] Blum, Jordan, "Higher ed leaders see funding method flaws," The Advocate, March 21, 2012, p. 1.

Dr. Mason's statement did not take into consideration two things: One, the Jindal Administration "gives" tax breaks to business only, and two, the so-called flagship-LSU-is not going anywhere; the Southern University System will disappear before LSU goes out of existence. How can Southern University dig itself out of a financial hole when the hole the latter is in is being dug by the Jindal Administration? As we have already seen, Southern University, and all other Louisiana universities, is facing a deeper hole in its operating budget because Governor Bobby Jindal has already "given" business $1.2 billion in tax breaks; he must cut the state higher education budget in order to balance the Louisiana State Budget, which is required by the constitution. Excluding LSU, the hole, for most other Louisiana Colleges and Universities, is growing deeper similar to the Texas Brine Sinkhole in Assumption Parish. Koran Addo stated the following:

> "From buildings filled with mold to faulty water and sewer systems that back up into classrooms, higher education leaders across Louisiana are growing increasingly concerned with the state's backlog in repairing and renovating campus facilities. The state Board of Regents estimates that colleges and universities are looking at a $1.7 billion price tag to address maintenance that's been put off year after year for lack of state funds."[167]

Southern University Baton Rouge Campus is suffering the affects of Governor Bobby Jindal's tax breaks and subsidies given to private business since he has been in office. If Chancellor Jim Llorens is aware of this fact, he has not publicly voiced it. The fact, however, is the Southern University Campus' physical plant is rapidly undergoing increased decay. According to Addo, Chancellor Jim Llorens can only watch Southern University Baton Rouge Campus' infrastructure decay because there is no money available to repair the mounting problems. She added

> "Across town, at Southern University, Chancellor James Llorens said his school doesn't have the donor base that other schools have to pay for new buildings and major

---

[167] Addo, Koran, "BACKLOG," The Advocate, May 19, 2013, p. 1.

renovations as campus buildings fall into disrepair. This past academic year, Southern had to do patchwork fixes when water lines backed up into T.H. Harris Hall and when leakage from heavy rains forced the university to close the School of Nursing's classroom auditorium, Llorens said. Officials estimate that just getting Southern's water and sewer infrastructure up to date will cost the university $10 million."We've just not been able to address our needs for many, many years," Llorens said. "We have older labs in need of complete replacement. We have issues with roofs and leaking windows. It really affects our students' ability to go into their classrooms and have an adequate learning environment."[168]

Maybe Chancellor Llorens might decide, in another moment of desperation, to recommend the Southern University Board of Supervisors declare financial exigency again. By doing so, more professors would be laid-off, and the dollar savings could be used to patch up the deepening sinkhole on the Southern University Baton Rouge Campus. All of the ingredients for the closure of Southern University are now in place; the overall situation will continue to deteriorate to a point that Drs. Mason and Llorens will come out publicly and ask the Jindal Administration, or the next one, to shut down the institution because it will not be able to operate any longer because of a lack of sufficient state budget funds. It may already be too late to salvage the ailing institution.

The information that follows shows that tuition is now being relied on to operate most public four-year colleges.

Not only did the Jindal Administration reduce state higher education spending per student by 42.0 percent between FY08 and FY13, Louisiana, according to Oliff, Palacious, et. al., noted that this 42.0 percent reduction in state spending per higher education student was equivalent to a -$4,715[169], ranking Louisiana second in the nation behind only New Mexico with

---

[168] Ibid., p.2.
[169] Ibid., p. 5.

a -$4,775 reduction. How can a "New Vision" for the Southern university System, or any university, take root in a fiscal climate like the one the Jindal Administration has created? Moreover, those Louisiana students, who pursued a higher education degree between FY08 and FY13, were forced to shoulder a significant portion of the burden, or cost, of the so-called state higher education budget cuts, in the form of sharply rising tuition. During this time, Louisiana's tuition cost rose 38.0 percent, ranking the state tenth in the nation in the "percent change in average tuition at public, four-year colleges..."[170] The 38.0 percent increase in tuition amounted to an average of $1,599[171] that each Louisiana higher education students were forced to pay to enroll in a four-year public college in Louisiana. The irony of this tax is, as we have already seen, the money to support higher education was in the Louisiana State Budget (There was no such thing as a so-called shortfall.); it was removed to support tax breaks and incentives for business; and, as a result, the typical higher education student's parents, who already paid their taxes to support Louisiana Higher Education during FY08 to FY13, found themselves, once again, being forced to pay a second tax in the form of higher tuition costs. Many Louisiana Higher Education Graduates are shackled with enormous debt by the time they graduate; and, unfortunately, it takes them years to pay back their student loans. Oliff, Palacious, et. al., added the following regarding the debt Louisiana Higher Education Students had to pay during the Jindal Administration's first term:

> "...rising tuition burdens students with mounting levels off debt. Indeed, student debt levels have swelled...Between the 2007-08 and the 2010-11 school years, the amount of debt incurred by the average bachelor's degree recipient at a public four-year institution grew from $11,800 to $13,600 (in 2011dollars), an inflation adjusted increase of $1,800, or15 percent. The average level of debt incurred had grown from $11,100 to $11,800, an increase of$700, or about 6 percent, over the previous eight years.[172]

---

[170] Ibid., p. 9.

[171] Ibid., p. 10.

[172] Ibid., p. 15.

The "New Vision" most higher education students would like to see become a reality is one where they do not have to pay huge amounts of money back to the government because there was, little or no, money available in the Louisiana State Budget to support their pursuit of an education. Worse, in the Southern University System's Case, whose Mission, since its inception, is to take students from low socioeconomic status backgrounds, and train them to become skilled professionals in a chosen profession. Because of rising tuition costs, tax breaks and incentives, and subsidization of business, many Louisiana children's parents cannot afford to send them to college. Oliff, Palacious, et. al., stated "students from low income families are far less likely to attend college."[173] Moreover, by 2008, only 44.0 percent of the children, from the lowest socioeconomic backgrounds, could afford to attend a 4-year public college.[174]

All-in-all, the prospect for new higher education funding, during the Jindal Administration's second term, is very remote, or non-existent. If the Louisiana Higher Education Budget has been plundered by the Jindal Administration, what has happened to the K-12 public education budget, which is commonly called Minimum Foundation.

C. Public Education Budget: K-12

The K-12 Budget, or Minimum Foundation, which provides operating funds for the 64 Parish School districts throughout the state, is protected, from budget cuts, by the Louisiana Constitution. That is, this budget cannot be cut like the unprotected higher education budget, but it can be manipulated. Privatization is the pipeline through which taxpayer dollars flows to business in the form of tax breaks and vouchers. On the other hand, a different pipeline is used, which is equally effective, to legally drain taxpayer dollars from the protected K-12 Minimum Foundation (MFP) Budget. According to Tulane University's Cowen Institute, the Louisiana's MFP is regulated by the state constitution as follows:

---

[173] Ibid., p. 15.
[174] Ibid., p. 15.

"The primary source of state and local funding for schools in Louisiana is the Minimum Foundation Program (MFP). The Louisiana Constitution requires the State Board of Elementary and Secondary Education (BESE) to annually develop and adopt a formula which determines the cost of a minimum foundation program of education in all public elementary and secondary schools as well as to equitably allocate the funds to parish and city school systems. Once BESE adopts the formula, the Legislature passes it by Concurrent Resolution without making changes to the formula."[175]

The Amount of money in the Louisiana Budget for K-12 public school use was more than $8 billion in Fiscal Year 2012. That year, the Louisiana Department of Education website reported the following:

"In Fiscal Year 2012, Louisiana's education budget for kindergarten through high school is $8.7 billion, including $8 billion for local school districts and a half billion for the Recovery School District. More than 99% of the funding goes directly to school districts. The budget for the Louisiana Department of Education is less than one percent of the state's Education budget... State tax dollars fund approximately 38% of the total education budget. For Fiscal Year 2012-2013, Louisiana provided an estimated $3.4 billion for the Minimum Foundation Program."[176]

---

[175]   Public School Funding in Louisiana, Minimum Foundation Program (MFP), Cowen institute For Public Education Initiatives, Tulane University, March 2010, p. 5.

[176]   Department of EDUCATION, http://wwww.louisianabelieves. com/funding/revenue.

a. Charter School And Its Underlying Financial Goal

With $8.7 billion protected by the Louisiana Constitution, the Louisiana Ruling Class, and through a timely use of its Jindal Administration and Legislative allies, cobbled together a Privatization Economic Policy, which has allowed a significant amount of MFP revenue to flow out of the K-12 Budget into organizations that have an educational shell, and on the other hand, the latter serves as a conduit, or pipeline, for significant amounts of protected taxpayer dollars to flow *quasi-legally* into the hands of private business. The quasi-legal organization devised to plunder the Louisiana K-12 Budget is the *Charter School*. During the Jindal Administration's first term, a significant number of them began to operate. The Louisiana Department of Education website reported the following:

> "In Louisiana, 104 charter schools are educating nearly 58,000 students. An additional 11 charter schools will open in the 2012-2013 school year...Charter schools are publicly-funded schools that are run independently of the school district. Charter schools are run by... business leaders in the community. Charter schools can be converted from existing schools or be start-up schools established by businesses... Charter schools are authorized by a local school district or the Board of Elementary and Secondary Education for five years. Charter schools enter a contract with the authorizing body and must meet the terms of the contract... to continue to operate."[177]

By now, is the picture becoming more clear? A business, or group of businesses, set up a Charter School; the Board of Elementary and Secondary Education enter into a contract with the Charter School; and, yes, protected K-12 public education dollars follow every public education student who enrolls in a Charter School. As we have seen, more than 100 Charter Schools have started operation since Governor Bobby Jindal's first term began in 2008, and more of them are expected to open during

---

[177] Ibid.

the 2012-2013 school year. This is all quasi-legal, and a sly, lizard-like way of going around the Louisiana Constitution to vet the Louisiana K-12 Public Education Budget. Setting up the quasi-legal Charter School is the first big step; the second is to formalize a document that has exchange value, which can be transacted as money between a former public school student and the business owner of a Charter School. *Webster's Ninth New Collegiate Dictionary* defined voucher as "a documentary record of a business transaction...a form or check indicating a credit against future purchases or expenditures."[178] As such, by 2012, the Education Reporter published the following voucher information under the following heading: "Louisiana Voucher Program Privatizes Education:

> "Louisiana's voucher program is now the most comprehensive in the country, thanks to a new law that will allow more low and middle-income students in substandard public schools to use public funds to attend private schools. Beginning this fall, students whose parents make less than $60,000, and who attend a public school where at least 25% of students test below grade level, will be eligible to take up to $8,800 annually to the charter school of their choice. Louisiana currently has 120 of these schools, and that number is expected to rise as demand for vouchers increases. At least 6,000 students have already applied for the 5,000 available spots. 380,000 students are eligible for vouchers — more than half the state's total student population... The voucher program will expand further next year, when students of all income levels will be able to use mini-vouchers worth up to $1,300 per student per class to pay private-sector vendors for classes not offered in the public schools. This voucher money, which is subtracted from public school funding, can be

---

[178] _____ *Webster's Ninth New Collegiate Dictionary*, A Merriam-Webster Inc., Publishers, Springfield, Mass., 1984, p. 1323.

used to pay... online schools, businesses [and] industry trade groups"[179]

b. Classification Of Louisiana Public Schools: "D" or "F"?

The Louisiana Legislature passed HB 976 in April 2012, bringing together the Charter School and voucher as the primary apparatus currently being used to go around the Louisiana Constitution to openly rob the Louisiana K-12 Budget in broad daylight. While this is the unspoken goal of public education reform, namely, to steal money from the latter, Governor Bobby Jindal, in typical hypocritical fashion, or in genuine public gesture, stated "we have a moral imperative to improve the education system for our children, our state, and our country, and these new laws will be a game changer for Louisiana,"[180] The "game changer" Governor Bobby Jindal referred to is through the use of the Charter School and the voucher, the Louisiana K-12 Budget can be pillaged, plundered, and outright robbed. If a man or woman goes into a bank and robs it of $200, and, if he or she is caught, no doubt, he will spend at least 40 years in prison. Yet, the Education Reporter stated "its estimated that the newly expanded voucher program may remove as much as $3.3 billion annually from public schools..."[181] and nobody is going to be held accountable! The vast majority of MFP revenue is being siphoned into the private sector in the Orleans Parish School District. In fact, the Tulane University Cowen Institute stated "...Orleans Parish has the highest rate of charter attendance of any district in the nation at 71%."[182]

Moreover, we can see how the charter school-voucher robbery of the Louisiana State K-12 Education Budget works by observing the fact that once a public school is classified as being a "D" or "F" school, the Louisiana

---

[179]   Education Reporter, http://www.eagleforum.org/publications / educate/july1, July 12, 2012.

[180] Ibid.

[181] Ibid.

[182]   K-12 Public Education in Louisiana: 2011 Regular Session of the Louisiana Legislature, Cowen Institute Report, Tulane University, April 2011, p. 3.

State Department of Education rushes in, takes over the affected school, then farm it out to a private business to operate as a newly formed charter school. Keep in mind the fact that every public education student[183], who formerly attended the taken-over so-called failing public school, is given a choice to attend a charter school. If an affected student chooses to attend a charter school, the Minimum Foundation Funds follow that student to the charter school, bringing the voucher-robbery scheme full circle. Consider a recent case involving the East Baton Rouge School District. Charles Lussier reported the following:

> "The state on Thursday shot down an East Baton Rouge Parish school system proposal to reconfigure two low-performing schools, a move aimed at averting a state takeover... State Superintendent John White laid out his reasons for rejecting the Delmont and Mayfair requests in a letter Thursday to Taylor. "The schools have both earned academically unacceptable status and 'F' letter grades for the past three years," White wrote... The seven schools RSD runs in Baton Rouge have all struggled since their takeover, undergoing many leadership and personnel changes. The state is seeking charter schools to operate them as early as fall 2014."[184]

Even though Superintendent Bernard Taylor-East Baton Rouge Parish School District-presented a thoroughly written plan to rework Delmont Elementary and Mayfair Middle School into schools that can work themselves back to high levels of academic performance without Louisiana

---

[183] A public education student, who attends a so-called failing public school, usually has a low academic achievement history. The charter school is presented to him or her as a magical wand that can reverse his academic underachievement, and, in just a very short period, bring the affected students academic performance up to grade level and above. This sounds good to the affected students since their academic performance is at its lowest level, and any option that claims it can work an academic miracle is grabbed for like a drowning man reaching for a rope as his last and only hope before drowning.

[184] Lussier, Charles, "State denies plan for two EBR schools to avoid takeover," The Advocate, July 12, 2013, pp. 1 and 2.

Department of Education takeovers, State Superintendent John White denied Superintendent Bernard Taylor's action plan for the mentioned schools. The reason for the denial is found in the last line of Charles Lussier's above quote. That is, Superintendent John White, carrying-out his orders, has two more fish on his charter school line, and no matter how much Superintendent Bernard Taylor wiggles or resist, those schools will be given to a private run charter school to operate, including the MFP funds, which will follow every student who elects to attend this or that charter school. Lussier also pointed-out that the seven schools, which are part of the East Baton Parish Recovery School District, are also struggling academically, and if their records are analyzed, they may need to be classified as failing by Superintendent John White also. However, since charter schools are operated by private business, student academic records are the private property of the former who run them.

Similar to the tax break trend we spoke about earlier, there has been no let up in the pace of the Board of Elementary and Secondary Education-BESE-authorization of new charter schools during Governor Bobby Jindal second term in office. In fact, Will Sentell stated the following:

> "A committee of Louisiana's top school board Tuesday authorized up to 10 new charter schools for East Baton Rouge Parish during the next two years amid continuing debate about their value... officials said, Tuesday's action could pave the way for up to four more charter schools in East Baton Rouge Parish for the 2014-15 school year and five or six more the following year depending on building availability and other issues...That would roughly double the current tally of parish charter schools. Louisiana has about 120 charter schools in the current school year. About 58,000 students were enrolled in 2012-13. The charter plans were approved by BESE's School Innovation and Turnaround Committee... The committee approved seven charter management firms that were recruited by New Schools for Baton Rouge, which was formed in 2012 as part of a bid to upgrade struggling public schools in

north Baton Rouge. That list includes Celerity Educational Group, which is based in Los Angeles; Democracy Prep Public Schools, based in New York City and Family Urban Schools of Excellence, which is based in Hartford, Conn… Charter schools are public schools run by non-governmental boards."[185]

Furthrmore, Lussier further exposed the charter school privatization voucher scheme. He stated "Charter Schools USA operated 48 charter schools in five states last year. It has plans to run five elementary schools in the Baton Rouge metro area by 2015."[186] In addition, in mid-October 2013, the Louisiana Board of Elementary and Secondary Education (BESE), approved the spread of charter schools in the Lafayette Parish School District. Specifically, Marsha Sills reported the following development:

"The Louisiana Board of Elementary and Secondary Education approved the applications from Lafayette Charter Foundation to open two K-8 schools by August and a high school by 2017, and an application from Louisiana Achievement Charter Academies to open one K-8 school by August and another K-8 school in 2015. Lafayette Charter Foundation's schools will be managed by Charter Schools USA, which signed letters of intent to purchase property for its one of its K-8 schools in the northern part of the parish in the new neighborhood development of Couret Farms. and for its other K-8 school in the existing neighborhood development of Sugar Mill Pond. Both schools are on target for an August [2014] opening, said Mary Louella Cook, president of the Lafayette Charter Foundation. Louisiana Achievement Charter Academies is a statewide network of schools that will be operated by National Heritage Academies, said Jay

---

[185] Sentell, Will, "EBR charter schools win approval," The Advocate, August 14, 2013, pp. 1and 2.
[186] Lussier, Charles, "EBR School board to take up strategic plan, charter school request," The Advocate, August 15, 2013, P. 2.

Miller, one of two Lafayette Parish residents who serves on the LACA board... "The two areas we're looking at now on the north side are extremely close to the at-risk children we're hoping to reach and the families that we're trying to provide for," Miller said."[187]

Once the door is swung open to charter school development in the Lafayette Parish School District, we can be reasonably certain that more such schools will follow. Sills noted the new charter schools will be developed on the Northside of Lafayette, LA, which is where the vast majority of low income African-American households currently reside. The charter school acts like a straw in a soda cup; when the consumer sucks on it, liquid flows into his or mouth. The charter school is a straw in the Minimum Foundation Fund Program, which will siphon out of it approximately $9,000 per African-American public education student who elects to enroll in one of the approved charter schools. All of the usual rhetoric is the same: "hoping to reach African-American public education students," "hoping to reach their families," and "trying to provide for them and their children." These platitudes are just that. Platitudes. Most of the people who will serve as administrators of the two new charter schools do not even live in a neighborhood located on the Northside of Lafayette, LA. They can be thought of as modern day Carpetbaggers.

c. Clearing The Way For Charter School Development: BESE, Jindal Administration, And The Louisiana Legislature

Sentell's article exposes the whole charter school scheme. Before we identify the steps in the process of the charter school scheme, Kevin Zeese and Margaret Flowers defined a scam as follows: "A scam is a fraudulent operation designed to make money. A scam unfolds over time with a team of swindlers seeking to rob the victim without the victim ever knowing they have been

---

[187] Sills, Marsha, "BESE approves charter schools in Lafayette," The Advocate, October 17, 2013, p. 1.

scammed."[188] First, in order for the charter school fraud to move forward, BESE had to legally authorize them. Second, BESE had to evaluate each public school as being either "A thru F," regarding academic performance. Third, BESE had to approve the charter school applications submitted to it by non-governmental boards, or private business. Fourth, once private businesses from as far away as Los Angeles, CA, Hartford, Conn. and so forth were approved to operate a charter school in Louisiana by BESE, significant amounts of the $8 billion of constitutionally protected Minimum Foundation Program funds could then be funneled to private business by the latter's encouragement of public school students to leave the so-called "F" rated public schools, or failing public schools, and enroll in charter schools.

Moreover, the Louisiana BESE Board has the whole charter school scheme standing on its head. When it is turned back upright on its feet, the true situation causing some of the Louisiana Public Schools to be classified "F," or failing schools, becomes clear. Specifically, no public school can be classified as a "F" school; public schools are what they are: Classrooms made out of steel, bricks, wood, glass, and electrical wires among other inanimate materials. What is conveniently omitted from the BESE, Governor Bobby Jindal, and Superintendent John White's "F" school discussion is the *socioeconomic condition of the households in which Louisiana Residents live in in the respective communities where the so-called "F" schools exists.* By 2012, the last year of the first term of Governor Bobby Jindal, Louisiana was ranked among the poorest states in America. Sauter, Alexander, and Frohlich, defined the economic health of Louisiana households as follows by 2012, the end of Governor Bobby Jindal's first term in office:

> "almost 20% of Louisiana residents lived below the poverty line in 2012, better only than Mississippi and New Mexico. Last year, nearly 18% of households in the state received food stamps...Income inequality in the state has become worse in the past decade. As measured by the Gini Index, Louisiana is among the five states with the highest income inequality. It also had the fourth-highest

---

[188] Zeese, Kevin and Flowers, Margaret, "Obamacare: The Biggest Insurance Scam in History," Truthout, http://www.truth-out.org/opinion/item/19692-obamacare-

percentage of households earning less than $10,000 in 2012."[189]

Given Governor Bobby Jindal is the current governor of one of the poorest states[190] in America, the children growing up in the majority of economically depressed households usually attend public schools classified by BESE as "F" schools, or Failing academically. To stand the charter school scheme upright, it is right to mention here that the American Capitalist System in operation in Louisiana need to receive an "F" failing economic system classification because it has *Failed many Louisiana working class households, in which a majority of public school students live, many of whom are leaving their so-called "F" failing public school to attend various charter schoosl.* In sum, Louisiana capitalism is failing a growing number of Louisiana Working Class households, and not the public school BESE want us to believe is, which the latter has classified as Failing. Nevertheless, BESE classified public schools as Failing, hiding capitalism's hand, so private businesses could come into Louisiana, and legally rob the constitutionally protected K-12 Louisiana Budget via a voucher scheme. The charter school scheme is now seen in its naked exploitation of the Louisiana Citizens, and their public school age children.

To avoid any legal challenges to this money laundering scheme, or robbery of the Louisiana K-12 State Budget, Governor Bobby Jindal, and his Ruling Class Republican backers, figured-out a way, by having the money placed first in the General fund Line Item of the Louisiana State Budget. This is the scheme that is at work well into the first year of the second term

---

[189] Sauter, Michael B., Alexander, E. M., and Frohlich, Thomas c., "America's Richest (and Poorest) States," 24/7 Wall St., September 19, 2012.

[190] The term "poorest" must be placed in the proper context. Regarding the aggregate value of oil and natural gas for example, each year the oil and gas industry produce as much as $10 billion worth of oil revenues and an equal amount or more of natural gas annually via its onshore and offshore oil and natural gas drilling wells. The vast majority of this revenue does not go toward social program development for the Louisiana people. When other Louisiana industries are considered, the pattern continues to hold true. Thus, it is this reason that Louisiana is erroneously called a poor state by historians, sociologists, businesspeople, and politicians among many others in the social media.

of Governor Bobby Jindal. To follow is information that demonstrates why the latter took this action to insure that millions of dollars could flow to private business, without disruption, after the Louisiana Supreme Court ruled, in a 6-1 decision, that the paying of vouchers from the Minimum Foundation Program is unconstitutional.

When Governor Bobby Jindal, and the Louisiana Legislature, approved the voucher-robbery charter school scam, he, and everyone else inside his inner political circle, knew the mentioned scam was illegal, but they went ahead with its approval anyway. Arrogance, and thinking they are above the law everyone else is demanded to follow, clearly shows their "So What" attitude and disrespect for the legal system. However, after the Louisiana Supreme Court overturned the voucher-robbery scam by a vote of 6-1, the latter sent a shockwave through Governor Bobby Jindal's inner political circle. According to Will Sentell, "the court ruled 6-1 Tuesday that paying for vouchers out of the state's public school financing program — called the Minimum Foundation Program — is unconstitutional."[191] Rather than end the voucher-robbery scam immediately, and publicly admit to their wrongdoings, so the children all over Louisiana, who look up to them as role models, could witness Governor Bobby Jindal taking responsibility for his illegal actions, his appointed State Superintendent of Education, John White, recently said he is "…trying to decide how to make the school year's final $6 million payment for vouchers after the state Supreme Court scuttled the way the aid is allocated."[192] There is no remorse observed in John White's statement even though the highest Louisiana Court ruled the voucher program is unconstitutional. Why? Because private business want their voucher money, regardless if it is acquired illegally. Long before the Louisiana Supreme Court declared the voucher program unconstitutional, State Superintendent John White has allowed another 8,000 public school students to enroll in charter schools for the 2013-14 school year. Sentell stated "nearly 5,000 students at 118 schools get the aid now, and around 8,000 students are set to do so for the 2013-14 school year."[193]

---

[191] Sentell, Will, "Voucher payments under review," The Advocate, May 9, 2013, p. 1.
[192] Ibid., p. 1.
[193] Ibid., p. 1.

d. Charter School Depletion Of The Minimum Foundation Fund Program

Worse, a significant amount of the Minimum Foundation Program Budget has already been funneled into the bank accounts of private business. Sentell wrote the following:

> "Gov. Bobby Jindal faces budget and political hurdles in his bid to continue funding for vouchers after the Louisiana Supreme Court ruled that the current spending method is unconstitutional... At the top of Jindal's to-do list is finding the money to continue the aid. State Superintendent of Education John White said Thursday the state is spending $24 million in the current school year to underwrite vouchers for nearly 5,000 students... That means the tab for the 2013-14 school year — nearly 8,000 are signed up for vouchers — could be about $41 million."[194]

Thus, we see $24 million have already been illegally drained from the Minimum Foundation Program as a result of Governor Bobby Jindal's voucher robbery scam. And, in typical arrogant and disrespect for the Louisiana Supreme Court, Governor Bobby Jindal, and his accomplices in his inner political circle, are moving ahead to find other ways to get more funds out of the Minimum Foundation Program to give to private business. At the conclusion of the recent Legislative Session, which ended on June 6, 2013, legislators approved a $25.4 billion budget for FY 2013-2014. What is interesting is this budget includes a skillful way around the recent Louisiana Supreme Court Ruling that says using any MFP Funds to operate private run charter schools, or other private, parochial schools, is unconstitutional.

To get around this court ruling, the Louisiana Legislature shifted MFP Funds from the K-12 Public Education Budget, and placed it in the General Fund Line Item in the approved FY 2013-2014 budget. How much money was taken out of the MFP Budget? Will Sentell stated "The budget...

---

[194] Sentell, Will, "State's school voucher funding questioned," The Advocate, May 12, 2013, pp. 1 and 2.

includes about $45 million for roughly 8,000 students to attend private and parochial schools using vouchers, which are state aid for students who previously attended public schools rated C, D or F by the state... Under the bill approved on Thursday [June 6. 2013], vouchers would be paid for from the state's general revenue fund."[195] The other component of this smoke and mirror deal involved *buying out Louisiana Public School Teachers, who, for the most part, have expressed greater displeasure for Governor Bobby Jindal's so-called overhaul of public education, making it vastly more difficult for tenured teachers to hold on to their tenure status, and harder for new, first year teachers to acquire tenure.* To smooth out this aggravation, and more importantly, divert public school teacher unions, and teachers, from understanding that the MFP Fund is still being plundered by the Louisiana Legislature's placement of the MFP Funds in the General Fund, the latter also included a pay raise in the FY 2013-2014 Louisiana State Budget for public school teachers. Sentell added "Public school teachers will see pay raises of about $500 under a budget compromise that won final approval less than an hour before adjournment Thursday... Under the plan, half of the money would be used for certificated personnel — teachers and others..."[196] For all intent and purpose, this $500 pay raise is nothing more than *hush money.* When the math is done by an 8th grade public school student, by dividing the $500 over the 12 month school year, each certificated public school teacher will receive only $41.70 per month extra. And, when Uncle Sam takes his income tax bite out of that total, the affected public school teachers will receive even less money monthly. Thus, in the end, who will truly benefit from the approved $25.4 billion FY 2013-2014 state budget is private business owners of charter schools and other private parochial schools. While the latter will take in a cumulative $45 million, each public school teacher will receive $41.70 before taxes are taken out. Politically, this smoke and mirror game worked because Joyce Haynes, president of the Louisiana Association of Educators, was quoted saying "I believe that teachers and the public school employees have done a yeoman's job on talking and speaking and lobbying with legislators..."[197]

---

[195] Sentell, Will, "Budget deal includes teacher pay raise, " The Advocate, June 06, 2013, p. 2.

[196] Ibid., p. 1.

[197] Ibid., p. 2.

e. Charter Schools And Federal Desegregation Orders Disregarded

Since Governor Bobby Jindal first term in office began in 2008, the charter school-voucher scheme took front and center stage among an array of budget-cutting actions carried-out that resulted in deep cuts in the Louisiana Higher Education Budget. While all of this robbing of the Louisiana Treasury was taking place with the blessings of the BESE Board and the Board of Regents, the former, and John White's Louisiana Department of Education, allowed the charter school money laundering to go on, although as many as 34 school districts throughout Louisiana are still operating under federal desegregation orders dating back to the pre-Civil Rights Era of the 1950s.. The reason Governor Bobby Jindal's charter school-voucher scheme has run head-on into resistance from the U.S. Department of Justice, is the *majority of students, who have left the public school system, are African-Americans.* According to Andrew Vanacore, "about 90 percent of the state's 8,000 voucher students are black. Only low-income families from C, D or F rated schools can qualify for the program."[198] Millhollon added "the Jindal administration said nearly 90 percent of students in the voucher program are minorities."[199]

The head-on collision is, once again, between segregation and racial integration. We will use Andrew Vanacore research to sum up this contradiction shortly. First, however, it is worth remembering that the entire Civil Rights Movement, led by Dr. Martin Luther King, Fannie Lou Hamer, Malcolm X, Sam Cooke, Medgar Evers, and many others, was about integration of public schools, and not segregating them. By allowing African-American public school students to move out of the 34 Louisiana School Districts that are still under federal desegregation orders, by using the charter school-voucher scheme rhetoric that charter schools will magically bring their academic performance up to grade level and above, many of the school districts that are still under federal desegregation

---

[198] Vanacore, Andrew, "Legal challenge from Obama contends Louisiana vouchers collide with integration efforts, " The Advocate, August 28, 2013, p. 2.

[199] Millhollon, Michelle, "Jindal rebukes federal challenge of school voucher," The Advocate, August 25, 2013, p. 2.

orders are becoming more segregated than they were more than 50 years ago. We have included a lengthy quote from Vanacore's research, which supports this fact:

> "for decades, education activists have argued that giving families a choice about where they send their children to school will improve public education for minority and low-income students. Now that idea is colliding with an even older strategy for improving education among the historically underserved: racial integration... The Justice Department cites two cases in particular, one in which a number of black students used vouchers to leave a majority white school, and another in which a group of white students used vouchers to leave a majority black school. Each of those schools already had a racial balance that was out of whack with the rest of their district. For instance, Independence Elementary School in Tangipahoa Parish was already 61.5 percent black in a district that is only 47.5 percent black; losing five white students to the voucher program, the federal government argues, reinforced "the racial identity of the school as a black school.".... Nelson Taylor, an attorney for the plaintiffs in an on-going desegregation case against the Tangipahoa Parish School Board — one of 34 parishes in the state under an active desegregation order — argues that Louisiana's voucher program is another attempt to interfere with federal attempts to bring about integration."[200]

Even though it is obvious to a blind person that improving the academic plight of African-American public school students, who enroll in charter schools, is "smoke and mirrors," and privatization of K-12 public schools is the priority, Governor Bobby Jindal has made "smoke and mirror" public statements that the former is true, and the charter school profit motive machine has nothing to do with the situation. For example, Millhollon stated the following:

---

[200] Vanacore, Op. Cit., pp. 1 and 3.

"This is shameful. President (Barack) Obama and Attorney General (Eric) Holder are trying to keep kids trapped in failing public schools against the wishes of their parents," Jindal said in a prepared statement released Saturday…"Giving every single child — no matter their race or their income — the opportunity to get a great education is a moral imperative. We will not sit by while folks in Washington, D.C., try to tell Louisiana parents that they are not able to attend the school of their choice," the governor said."[201]

Since the U. S. Justice Department raised severe concern about charter school vouchers turning the hands of the clock back to pre-1950 segregation for a growing number of Louisiana Public Schools, it is not surprising that Governor Bobby Jindal has publicly attacked the former's effort to insure that Louisiana Public Schools do not return to the days of segregation. Blum stated "the U.S. District Court in New Orleans ordered Louisiana to undertake an analysis of the voucher program and provide it to the federal government by Nov. 7[,2013].[202] Blum added "Jindal called the Justice Department's claims a disingenuous stunt. "While attempting to rebrand its legal challenge as merely an attempt to seek information about implementation of the scholarship program, the administration's real motive still stands — forcing parents to go to federal court to seek approval for where they want to send their children to school," Jindal said in a prepared statement."[203] The only reason Governor Bobby Jindal issued his prepared statement is he is afraid of the possibility there will be a cut-off of Minimum Foundation Funds going to charter schools via the voucher scheme we are now familiar with. If Governor Bobby Jindal was truly, and genuinely concerned about the U.S., Justice Department disrupting the education of African-American children, who are largely enrolled in charter schools, wouldn't it make good sense for him to speak directly to the affected African-American parents' of those children publicly, rather than send

---

[201] Millhollon, Michelle, "Jindal rebukes federal challenge of school vouchers," The Advocate, August 25, 2013, pp. 1 and 2.

[202] Blum, Jordan, "Jindal criticizes Justice Department letter on voucher lawsuits," The Advocate, September 26, 2013, p. 1.

[203] Ibid., pp. 1 and 2.

a prepared statement to the news media? His failure to do so demonstrates his own prejudice toward allowing Minimum Foundation Program Funds to be shifted to charter schools under the pretense that affected African-American public education students can receive a better education from a charter school, although many come from households submerged in poverty. To further confused the charter school voucher scheme as a direct cause of re-institutionalizing racial segregation in Louisiana Public School Districts, the Jindal Administration, and its ruling class backers, quickly had a hastily done research study done to counter the U.S. Department of Justice claim that such schools, in fact, are not causing racial segregation.

In an attempt to sway Louisiana Public Opinion in particular, Will Sentell reported the following:

> "Disputing the U. S. Department of Justice, a report issued Thursday says Louisiana's voucher program aids public school desegregation."The evidence suggests that use of private school vouchers by low-income students actually has positive effects on racial integration," according to a study released by the academic quarterly journal Education Next, which is produced by Harvard and Stanford universities... The Education Next study says its review shows voucher tranfers "overwhelmingly improve integration in the public schools that students leave, bringing the racial composition of the schools closer to that of the broader communities in which they are located."[204]

Harvard and Stanford Universities are two of the educational arms of the American Ruling Class. It is no surprise that their study found to the contrary, charter school vouchers improve racial integration at the public schools where African-Americans have left to enroll in a charter school. Whoever conducted this study for Harvard and Stanford should have, before coming to the mentioned conclusion, researched the civil rights movement because they would have discovered that the aim to remove racial segregation from Louisiana Public Schools, or any similarly

---

[204] Sentell, Will, "Vouchers aid desegregation," <u>The Advocate</u>, October 3, 2013, p. 1.

affected states' public schools, had *absolutely nothing to do with insuring that the racial balance in a Louisiana public school was based on the racial composition of the local community in which an affected public school exists.* The main goal, during the civil rights movement then, as it is now, was to balance the racial composition within the public school itself. It is useful here to point-out to our Harvard and Stanford colleagues that *the whole justification for busing public school students from one local community to another 10 miles or more across town, for example, was to insure that the racial composition in two spatially separated public schools would have a correct racial balance, and not the local community itself.* Moreover, white flight, from one local community to another, is driven mainly by the desire to establish a new community that is racially segregated. Under pressure from the millionaires and billionaires that elected President Barak Obama in 2008, the latter called off the U.S. Justice Department's aim to put a stop to the charter school scheme going-on in Louisiana today-December 2013.

Will Sentell stated quoted Governor Bobby Jindal saying,

> "we are pleased that the Obama Administration has given up its attempt to end the Louisiana Scholarship program with this absurd lawsuit... Jindal said in a prepared statement that U.S. District Judge Ivan Lemelle, who is presiding over the case in New Orleans, said Justice Department officials had essentially abandoned their bid to stop the aid, which the governor called a victory."[205]

Where are the Louisiana masses suppose to turn to for help now, given the fact their U.S. Department of Justice has caved in to the charter school robbery scheme? The K-12 Minimum Foundation Program Fund's door is swung wide open, and the dollars are walking out of the Louisiana Public Schools every time an African-American Public School Student signs up to attend a charter school, and every time any public school student, regardless of race, walks out and enroll in a charter school. If the so-called terrorists had come up with this charter school robbery scheme, it would

---

[205] Sentell, Will, "Jindal criticizes fed's new school voucher review plan," The Advocate, November 20, 2013, p. 1.

be, in the minds of many Louisiana Residents, a justification for war. Charles Lussier provides information that shows just how widespread the charter school robbery scheme had become, by the end of the first year of Governor Bobby Jindal's Second Term in office. He wrote the following:

> "As it enters its second year, student participation in Louisiana's embattled experiment with private school vouchers has grown by 37 percent, a fast pace but slower than state leaders estimated before an adverse court Supreme Court ruling in May. The number of participating schools increased — 120 to 127 — as did the number of participating students — 4,994 to 6,775, according to totals released by the Louisiana Department of Education... New Orleans, where vouchers began as a pilot program in 2008, continues to outpace the rest of the state. Almost 2,800 students at 28 schools in that city receive vouchers, nearly half of all students in the program, and 500 more student than participated last year. That's also more than double the participation level of runner-up East Baton Rouge Parish where about 1,300 students are taking public money to attend private school, up from about 700 last year... The vouchers allow children attending Louisiana public schools with academic grades of C, D or F to transfer to approved private schools."[206]

How much of the Minimum Foundation Program Fund has been stolen as a result of this increase in charter school enrollment? Lussier added "this year the Louisiana Scholarship Program is estimated to cost taxpayers about $36 million, or an average of about $5,300 per child. Originally, the state estimated this year's cost at $41 million."[207] Give us the $41 million, and the first thing we would do is work with the households-parents-in which so many African-Americans children now live in poverty. We would change the households from "F" households to "A" households,

---

[206] Lussier, Charles, "Voucher participation on increase, but at a slower rate than expected," The Advocate, October 22, 2013, pp. 1 and 2.
[207] Ibid., p. 1.

and, in the process, there would be a remarkable change in the academic achievement of the African-American children, who would now live in an "A" household. In short, there would be no need for a charter school, or band aid. As it stands today, the $41 million will flow into the hands of private business owners of charter schools, and this means there will be a net outflow of Minimum Foundation Program Funds, from the communities where the so-called "F" failing public schools are located. The vast majority of the MFP Program Funds will become privatized, and there will be no lasting impact on the local community because many of the African-Americans currently enrolled in charter schools will inevitably end up in jail or prison. If you do not believe what we are saying, just turn on your TV to the local News channel 24/7, and you will see the human carnage reported daily as news.

Although $41 million is the amount of the charter school drain on the K-12 Budget during the 2013-2014 Academic School Year, the overall academic performance of Louisiana Public Schools remains very poor. On November 7, 2013, Will Sentell reported the depressing news as follows:

> "Public school students in Louisiana again Thursday finished near the bottom nationally in reading and math in the latest update of the nation's report card. The exam is called the National Assessment of Educational Progress... The exam is considered one of the most reliable indicators of student achievement and state-to-state comparisons. The latest results for fourth- and eighth-graders show that Louisiana students were:
>
> -- Tied for 50th in fourth-grade math.
>
> -- 48th in fourth-grade reading.
>
> -- Tied for 48th in eighth-grade math.
>
> -- Tied for 48th in eighth-grade reading.

The state failed to show statistically significant gains or losses in any of the four sections."[208]

As we already have seen earlier, Louisiana's experience with charter schools took root with the beginning of the Jindal Administration. We also have seen Governor Bobby Jindal sending out prepared statements telling the Louisiana Public that charter schools are really making a significant difference in the lives of African-Americans who enroll in them, and, therefore, the academic achievement among K-12 students is greatly improved. Not so fast. After four years or more, Louisiana, based on the above data, is still bogged-down at the bottom of public education achievement nationally. Yet, $41 million have been drained-out of the K-12 Budget in one year, and there has been no academic improvement, given the fact Louisiana still ranks between 48th and 50th nationally in fourth and eighth-grade reading and math. The charter school scheme/scam, as defined earlier, is working perfectly.

Knowing the fraudulent water flowing under the bridge, Governor Bobby Jindal attempted to put a band-aid on the hemorrhaging of the constitutionally protected K-12 Budget, by surrounding the Louisiana Ruling Class Charter School Voucher Scheme in a glowing, moral light. His statement even comes of like one made by someone who truly has the best interest of the Louisiana people at heart. The frightening thing about the governor's statement is he actually believes the illusion he is a part of carrying-out. This is merely "shop talk;" and, a written statement some aide put in front of him to read. Millhollon put a big hole in Governor Bobby Jindal's charter school educational fantasy with the following:

> "Jindal led the charge to expand a New Orleans program
> that allowed public school children to use taxpayer dollars
> to pay for attending private schools. Hundreds of children
> statewide currently participate in the voucher program...
> The Jindal administration forcefully pushed through
> voucher laws with an "ideological ... privatized, choice

[208] Sentell, Will, "Louisiana ranks low on nation's math, reading report card," The Advocate, November 7, 2013, pp. 1 and 2.

agenda" without paying attention to actual sound policy or desegregation laws, Monaghan said[Steve Monaghan is the President of the Louisiana Federation of Teachers]."[209]

As we see, Governor Bobby Jindal is waste deep in the charter school voucher scheme. He led the charge to get the Louisiana Legislature to legalize it. Yet, he makes public statements about how good charter schools are, and talks about the scheme as the modern day savior for African-Americans, many of whom are in high school but who cannot write a clear paragraph about anything relevant to them, their culture, the nation, or the world. Moreover, charter schools are segregated! Yet, Governor Bobby Jindal denies charter school vouchers do not return public schools to pre-1950 segregation. Everything civil rights workers died for are undermined and destroyed by the charter school voucher scheme. Don't hang up because there is much more going on we need to talk about.

f. Charter Schools And Budget Shortfall Consequences At The Local School Districts Level

Who can stop them now(?) but the Louisiana Citizenry. In addition, the $24 million already taken out of the K-12 Budget during FY 2012-2013 is having a drastic impact on school districts statewide. In short, the $24 million is a so-called shortfall, and because superintendents of school districts statewide are unaware of how Governor Bobby Jindal's voucher-robbery scam works, most, if not all, believe there is a *mysterious shortfall and, in order to address it, actions are taken that create D and F labeled public schools*. Marsha Sills wrote the following action is being taken by the Lafayette Parish School District to address the so-called shortfall.

> "Rather than take $6.7 million from its rainy day fund to balance next school year's $258 million budget, the Lafayette Parish School Board decided Tuesday to allow district staff more time to devise a list of cuts to offset the shortfall... In lieu of using the rainy day money, staff

---

[209] Ibid., pp. 1 and 2.

proposed other options, such as the elimination of teaming instructional models in middle schools (nearly $1.3 million) and annual pay raises ($2.3 million)... School Board members debated funding for 37 instructional strategist positions previously paid for with federal Title I money. The district receives about $9 million in Title I funding, designed to help high-poverty schools, but expects a 10 percent reduction in that funding next school year.[210]

In a recent e-mail Dr. Pat Cooper sent to every teacher employed by the Lafayette Parish School District, including Board members, the same old budget cutting theme dominated its primary content. Dr. Pat Cooper stated the information below in his internal communication:

"The alternative is to make what I deem to be drastic cuts that will harm the students and teachers academically, exacerbate discipline problems, and make it even harder to retain teachers. These cuts could include eliminating elementary physical education programs causing teachers to lose much of their planning time, removing teaming as a middle school tool making it impossible for the teachers to have their grade level planning time, placing more students in teachers' classrooms creating even more difficulty for teachers to teach and children to learn, removing Assistant Principals and Deans of Students thereby making the discipline problems even more difficult to prevent and to deal with quickly, and implementing a one mile walk zone as is allowed by the State, making transportation of students less convenient for the parents."[211]

Therefore, while private business quietly received the $24 million funneled

---

[210] Sills, Marsha, "Lafayette schools budget talks to continue," The Advocate, May 15, 2013, p. 1.

[211] Dr. Pat Cooper's E-Mail to the Lafayette Parish School District Board Members and employed Lafayette Parish Schoolteachers, May 13, 2013.

to Louisiana Charter Schools during the 2012-2013 Academic School Year, the huge hole left in the Lafayette Parish School District's Operating Budget is the latest *imaginary shortfall that creates D and F public schools.* Charter Schools are a front, or voucher-robbery pass-through. How can a Charter School, having hardly no proven history, educate Louisiana children better than public schools, which have more than a century of experience? The Lafayette Parish School District so-called shortfall problem is Louisiana Ruling Class made, for the purpose of taking Minimum Foundation Program Funds that are designed to prevent public schools from becoming D and F school. Without proper state funding, any public school will become a D or F school eventually. Next door to the Lafayette Parish School District is the St. Martin Parish School District, which, similar to Dr. Pat Cooper, Dr. Lottie Beebe, Superintendent of the latter, bought into the budget shortfall fantasy. Henri C. Bienvenu wrote about the impact Governor Bobby Jindal's tax breaks to private business is having on the St. Martin Parish School District. Specifically, Bienvenu stated

> "facing a...$2.5 million budget deficit for the fiscal year[2013-1014], the St. Martin School Board's finance committee...endorsed a proposal to trim almost $1 million in expenses by eliminating 15 teachers across the parish... In addition, mileage reimbursements for employee travel would be reduced from 44[cents] to 30[cents] per mile. **The total estimated savings would amount to an estimated $1,065,255...**The cuts at Stephensville will save almost $250,000 while the elimination of approximately 12 teacher positions through the change in student/ teacher ratios across the parish will trim an estimated $793,490. The reduction in mileage reimbursements will save...$20,000."[212]

Several things make this St. Martin Parish School System Budget vetting most interesting, but not unique. First, with the elimination of 15 teacher positions, the pupil/teacher ratio will increase from 21/1 to 22/1 in grades

---

[212] Bienvenu, Henri C., "Teacher positions at risk: school system facing $2.5 M budget shortfall," Breaux Bridge Banner, Vol. 27, No. 17, June 5, 2013, p. 1.

K-5; it will rise from 22/1 to 23/1 in grades 6-8. Second, for high school, the pupil/teacher ratio will rise from 22/1 to 23/1. Third, with many of St. Martin Parish School District's Public Schools already classified by the Louisiana Department of Education with an overall evaluation grade of C or below, the increase in pupil/teacher ratio will definitely aggravate an already serious academic achievement problem across the school district.[213] And lastly, Dr. Lottie Beebe, Superintendent of the St. Martin Parish School District, is, as of June 23, 2013, a member of the Board of Elementary and Secondary Education, the governing body that make all decisions related to K-12 education in Louisiana. This means Dr. Lottie Beebe, knowingly or unknowingly, participated in the approval of millions of public education taxpayer dollars for charter schools; yet, in her own St. Martin Parish School District, she approved the above budget cuts to address the so-called *budget shortfall*. Since this is not rocket science, one would think Dr. Lottie Beebe would be able to see the contradictory character of her decision-making. Given the nature of the long standing academic problems within the public schools in St. Martin Parish, the latter actually need the $1.1 million that was cut out of the St. Martin Parish School District's Budget, and several million more, to begin to

---

[213] In December 2010, the Board of Elementary and Secondary Education (BESE) set standards for schools to earn letter grades. BESE established its own Student Performance Scores (SPS). The new system's SPS Benchmarks are as follows: (1) Top-performing school must earn a 120 or above to receive a letter grade "A;" any school with a SPS of 65 or below will receive a letter grade "F." Based on this new BESE System, St. Martin Parish School District earned a District Performance Score (DPS) of 87.3 in 2010. Based on the BESE SPS System, St. Martin Parish School District's 87.3 DPS fell within the range 65.0-89.9, which means the latter's public schools across the school district cumulatively received a letter grade "D," or failing. In short, Dr. Lottie Beebe helped develop the BESE SPS System; the St. Martin Parish School District earned a "D" letter grade in 2010; and by June 2013, Dr. Beebe approved a budget reduction of $1.1 million to address a so-called budget shortfall caused by huge tax breaks given to private business by Governor Bobby Jindal. The game is on one hand, use the BESE SPS System to set up the Louisiana School Districts for failure, and on the other, politically get BESE to take MFP funds and place it in the General Fund line item in the Louisiana State Budget so it can be given to private business; the latter has set up numerous charter schools to receive MFP Funds that follow "academically –failing" children from "academically-failing" public schools to "flow-through" charter schools.

effectively address the learning problems of the children of the parents who reside in St. Martin Parish.

g. More Failing Public Schools Means Increased Number Of Charter Schools

Moreover, although the Louisiana Supreme Court ruled it is illegal and unconstitutional to take funds out of the Minimum Foundation Program to financially support private-owned and operated charter schools, and even when the Louisiana Legislature sent the proposed K-12 Budget back to the Board of Elementary and Secondary Education (BESE) and ask the latter to remove MFP Funds from charter schools to comply with the Louisiana Supreme Court Ruling, Governor Bobby Jindal and Superintendent John White disregarded the high court ruling and found a way around it. Will Sentell reported the information below:

"A state Senate panel Wednesday rejected a $3.5 billion funding request for public schools, further muddling an already confused picture on how classrooms will be funded. The Senate Education Committee approved a resolution, without objection, that asks the state Board of Elementary and Secondary Education to submit a new request in light of last week's ruling by the state Supreme Court. The court's 6-1 decision held that the state cannot use the Minimum Foundation Program — the key source of state aid for public schools — to also finance vouchers for some students to attend private and parochial schools. Gov. Bobby Jindal has said state aid for vouchers will continue... In a related development, state Superintendent of Education John White said the state faces an unexpected $30 million expense this year because of last week's ruling. About $12 million of the charge stems from dollars owed by the state to local school districts as part of the costs for vouchers, which are being used by nearly 5,000 students in the current school year."[214]

As the old saying goes, "Governor Bobby Jindal, and his Louisiana Legislative inner political circle, was caught red handed." Public School Districts all across Louisiana are suffering because they do not have enough MFP Funds to give teachers a raise, or make critically needed improvements in their curriculum offerings, and to various school facilities desperately in need of repairs for years. Thirty million dollars is no small change; yet, it has been siphoned off to private business under the disguise that charter schools will give already failing public school students, who are for the most part, African-American, and, who mostly live in poverty, a better education and future. Just when we thought some of the Jindal Administration's, and the Department of Education's arrogance, would likely decrease as a result of the Louisiana Supreme Court's recent ruling that use of MFP Funds to financially support charter schools is unconstitutional, Charles Lussier's article paints an entirely opposite picture; their arrogance and disregard for the mentioned Louisiana Supreme Court Ruling has, in fact, increased. Lussier added

> "Thirty-five organizations submitted applications to start about 100 new charter schools in 19 parishes in Louisiana, the state Department of Education reported Thursday. The organizations turned their applications in by the May 1 deadline and are seeking to open their new schools in 2014, 2015 or 2016. Twenty-two of the applicants want to start schools in East Baton Rouge Parish — the most applications to open charter schools in Baton Rouge since the mid-'90s, when the state first authorized the creation of the charter schools. Orleans and Jefferson parishes tied for second place with eight organizations applying in each of the parishes. New Orleans has the highest percentage of children in charter schools in the U.S. Baker and Caddo Parish were next with four applicants each... Of the 35

---

[214] Sentell, Will, "Panel sends public school funding bill back to BESE," The Advocate, May 16, 2013, pp. 1 and 2.

applicants, 19 are based in Louisiana and 16 are from out-of-state... Those organizations are: Celerity Educational Group, based in Los Angeles; Collegiate Academies, based in New Orleans; Democracy Prep Public Schools, based in New York City; Family Urban Schools of Excellence or FUSE, based in Hartford, Conn; Green Dot Public Charter Schools, based in Los Angeles; Knowledge is Power Program or KIPP, based in San Francisco; and YES Prep Public Schools, based in Houston."[215]

Private businesses as far away as Los Angeles, CA, San Francisco, CA, and New York City have applied to open up a charter school in Louisiana in order to cash in on some of the easiest money to be made anywhere in America in today's lingering 2008 Depression. New York City business people are supposed to know how to educate children down here in the Deep South. Really? Who is going to pay for the potentially new charter school openings, now that MFP Funds cannot be used to do so any longer? Your guess is right...While we are all watching Lebron James, and the Miami Heat NBA Basketball Team battle the San Antonio Spurs for the 2013 NBA Championship on National and worldwide TV, in the shadows, more MFP Funds have been diverted to a private owned charter school located in Arkansas. Anything will be done to get money similar to a vampire, which will do anything to acquire its victim's blood. Will Sentell reported the following.

"the state Board of Elementary and Secondary Education has approved plans for up to 100 students in northwest Louisiana to attend school in Arkansas with the state aid routed through a charter school in northeast Louisiana... Aid for the students could total up to $700,000."[216]

The academic interests of the 100 students are secondary; getting the

[215] Lussier, Charles, "DOE: 35 groups apply for charter schools, " <u>The Advocate</u>, May 17,2013, pp. 1 and 2.
[216] Sentell, Will, "La. students get aid to attend Arkansas schools," <u>The Advocate</u>, June 22, 2013, pp. 1 and 2.

$700,000 is primary importance. After 500 years of American slavery, a vast majority of the students caught up in the charter school movement are African-Americans. Huge sums of money are still being generated off-of the illiteracy of the descendents of their enslaved ancestors, who actually lived, worked for nothing, and died during the American Slavery experience. In addition to the charter school privatization frenzy, the Louisiana Board of Elementary and Secondary Education-BESE-recently approved a sizable sum of money to support a nationwide educational operation called Teach for America. A brief of consideration of the latter shows the contradictions and illogical decision-making going-on with the approval of Governor Bobby Jindal. Later, we will provide information that proves, any of the individuals, including Superintendent of Education John White, were trained by the Teach for America (TFA) organization. Meantime, Will Sentell stated the following:

> "...Louisiana's top school board has approved $1.2 million in aid for Teach for America... TFA recruits top college students, puts them through five weeks of training and... later and sends them to some of the nation's most troubled public schools for at least two years... The $1.2 million contract approved for TFA will allow them to recruit 25 first-year teachers and retain 23 others..."[217]

Interestingly, the Louisiana Department of Education, under the handpicked leadership of Governor Bobby Jindal, namely, Superintendent John White, is currently implementing state laws that make it very difficult for new education graduates of four year universities to get a teaching job in Louisiana, and much harder for existing public schoolteachers to maintain their hard earned tenure. Moreover, an education tool called Compass is being used to intimidate veteran and young public schoolteachers by using the scare tactic that classifies the latter as *effective or ineffective*. The contradiction here is Superintendent John White has no problem with teachers coming into public school classrooms with only five weeks of Teach for America Training; and yet, he, and his staff, including public

---

[217] Sentell, Will, "Teach For America aid sparks heated arguments," The Advocate, June 27, 2013, pp. 1 and 2.

school administrators at the local school district level, are continuously harassing public schoolteachers, by telling them they could lose their tenure, not receive tenure, or be outright terminated from their teaching appointments if their teacher evaluations, at the school level, shows they are ineffective. But, no one is complaining publicly about untrained Teach for America Teachers going into the Louisiana Public School Classroom to teach working class children. How hypocritical! At its core, Teach for America is nothing but a private business setup to receive Minimum Foundation Funds; educating Louisiana Children is just a convenient cover up for what is really happening. As we shall see later, many of Mr. John White's staff received Teach for America's five week training before they were appointed to high paying jobs to evaluate Louisiana Public School Teachers, who, unlike the TFA trained staff evaluators, have legitimate teaching certificates they earned, from four year accredited university professional education programs.

h. Louisiana Legislature, Charter Schools, Public School Failures, And Teacher Retirement

Furthermore. One would think that the protected K-12 budget would not contribute very much to the so-called Fiscal Year 2013 $1.2 billion shortfall created by the Jindal Administration on behalf of the Louisiana Ruling Class. However, Will Sentell's article tells a different story. Consider the following:

> "The state Department of Education's heavy reliance on contracts rather than doing the work in-house merits scrutiny, the chairman of the Louisiana House Appropriations Committee said Tuesday[April 1, 2013]. "I am wondering where the oversight comes," said state Rep. Jim Fannin, D-Jonesboro. The issue, which Fannin has raised in the past, surfaced during a budget review of the state Board of Elementary and Secondary Education, which sets policies for more than 700,000 public school students statewide... Department contracts totaled more than $60 million in one recent 12-month period and are

expected to be well over that this year, officials said... In 2010, amid questions by Fannin and others, officials said the department had executed more than 6,000 contracts in the past six years, including $342 million of agreements in that year... Fannin said the spending carries special significance amid budget problems, including a $1.3 billion shortfall to keep state spending at current levels."[218]

During Governor Bobby Jindal's first term in office, the Louisiana Department of Education executed an unheard-of 6,000 contracts, including vouchers. In 2010 alone, the mentioned department executed $342 million worth of contracts! Statistically, the latter amount represents 13. 68 percent of the Fiscal Year 2010 so-called shortfall of $2.5 billion. This is significant no matter what way the situation is viewed. While our governor gave lip-service to improving public education, he, and the Louisiana Legislature, played a key role in making it possible for this sum of money to flow out of the K-12 budget via the privatization channel. The evidence is irrefutable, and beginning April 8, 2013, new laws will be passed, by the Louisiana Legislature, aimed at extracting even more taxpayer dollars from the Louisiana State Budget. In order to temporarily get away with privatization voucher robbery, the Jindal Administration instituted a statewide attack on the dignity and professionalism of certified teachers, at both the elementary and secondary levels. The critical strike was leveled at teacher tenure, or job security. On April 10, 2010, a nightmare came true for Louisiana Public School Teachers. Education News reported the following:

> "Central parts of Governor Bobby Jindal's education reform program have received <u>final approval</u> from the Louisiana House of Representatives. They ratified the Senate versions of HB 974 and HB 976 by a margin of 60-43 and 60-42. As the Senate amendments didn't substantially alter the framework of the Governor's original proposals he is certain to sign the bills. This means that

---

[218] Sentell, Will, "Education contracts spark questions," <u>The Advocate</u>, April 03, 2013, pp. 1 and 2.

Louisiana will now curtail teacher tenure and link teacher pay to student performance. Louisiana will also advance the charter school movement by opening new paths to the creation of these independent public schools and create a statewide program to pay the private-school tuition for low income students using the public-school financing formula."[219]

In addition to the privatization voucher robbery plan that the Louisiana Legislature set in motion at the urging of the Jindal Administration, we see a vicious attack was included in the HB 976. The purpose was twofold: (1) To create a smoke and mirrors emotional roller coaster so that Louisiana Teachers would not be able to sort through the privatization voucher game. Teacher salary was linked to student performance, and as we have already seen, more than half of Louisiana Public School Students received free and reduced lunch. That meant Louisiana Teachers would not be able to successfully raise student academic performance scores, given the widespread poverty among a majority of Louisiana households, and, therefore, many would not receive pay increases as a result, and others with tenure would likely lose it, and it would be very difficult for new teachers to earn tenure for the first time. What Governor Bobby Jindal could not do because of his single-minded implementation of the Louisiana Ruling Class' neo-liberalism economic policies, the latter, hiding behind a so-called *reform of education in Louisiana, shifted the impossible burden onto the backs of Louisiana Teachers to do.* Moreover, throughout the 2012-2013 Academic School Year, increasing numbers of Louisiana Teachers-statewide-have been evaluated as being *ineffective, which is the first step toward their termination of employment.* All of this noise was purposefully orchestrated by Governor Jindal, and the Legislature, to destabilize Louisiana Teachers, and their unions, in order to create a veil behind which, similar to the Wizard of Oz, increasing privatization voucher robbery of the K-12 Public Education Budget could take place out of public view; while, publicly, Public School Teachers all across Louisiana enter their classrooms on a daily basis in a state of fear for their jobs and their sanity. It is this type of

---

[219]   _____ "Louisiana House Approves Jindal's Reforms," Education News, http://www.educationnews.org/k-12schools/louisiana, April 10, 2012.

atmosphere that the Atlanta Grade Changing Scandal grew out of; when expectations become so unrealistic, and academic goals are set so high-Common Core- they cannot be achieved. Consequently, the only avenue left open is cheating. Since the beginning of the 2012-2013 academic year, in Lafayette Parish alone, more than 200 teachers have decided to call it quits. This is one of the valued outcomes of the Jindal Administration's privatization voucher robbery scheme, namely, freeing up more money in the K-12 Public Education Budget that can be channeled to privately owned Charter Schools via vouchers.

Louisiana will, no doubt, continue to lead the nation in Charter School attendance, followed by Washington, D. C. in the number two spot with 36%. Even at 36%, Louisiana's Charter School attendance is nearly doubled. It is worth making note of the fact that Charters Schools originate in a social environment that has a long history of poverty.

For example, if we take a look at the percentage of students in America, who receive free or reduced lunch, the national total is roughly 44 percent; for Louisiana, the total is 65%.[220] And, the vast majority of public school students, who receive free and reduced lunch in Louisiana, are African-Americans. So, it is worth asking Governor Bobby Jindal can his HB 976 improve public education in Louisiana when the vast majority of the Louisiana Citizenry live in poverty? When charter school students go home at the end of the day, they will still live in poverty in their homes, although the voucher revenue that follows him or her to a charter school ends up in somebody's else's house, and, in many cases, they are located in other states! Although millions of taxpayer dollars have been transferred to charter schools via voucher robbery of the K-12 Louisiana State Budget, Louisiana Public Schools have not improved, and they are actually losing ground and becoming worse academically. Sentell stated "Despite some gains in recent years "chronic challenges" remain in improving Louisiana public schools, according to a report issued Tuesday morning. One key problem is the fact that roughly 250,000 students are performing below grade level, officials of the Council for a Better Louisiana, or CABL, said in its annual report on the state's education status...While three of four fourth-graders

---

[220] Ibid., p. 2.

have achieved "basic" in reading on a key state test, only one in five are rated as "proficient" on an exam called the nation's report card, the CABL review says."[221] Can a charter school bring a public school student, who has achieved a "basic" academic performance up to "proficient," or grade level in reading, math, and critical thinking, while privatization, or voucher robbery, is the underlying goal?

On the recent End of the School Year Exam, which is a replacement for the infamous Graduation Exit Exam, Millhollon stated "the lowest percentages of "good" or "excellent" scores were in Claiborne, East Feliciana, Franklin, Madison, St. Helena and Tensas parishes, the City of Baker School District and the Recovery School District."[222] The Recovery District in New Orleans and Baton Rouge Louisiana is where a large number of charter schools currently operate. On the recent End of the School Year Exam for the Academic Year 2012-2013, only 38 percent of the students in the Recovery School District in New Orleans, LA tested proficient on the exam, and just 17 percent tested proficient in the Recovery District-Baton Rouge, LA. Yet, millions of dollars are flowing into charter schools across Louisiana because Governor Bobby Jindal, and his political allies in the legislature, including the BESE, sold charter schools as the answer to reforming decaying educational attainment in Louisiana. The data, however, is proving otherwise.

Before we leave this charter school voucher scheme discussion, it is necessary to reiterate the impact it is having on certified Louisiana Public School Teachers. In order to get the charter school voucher scheme enacted as a Louisiana Law, Louisiana Public School Teachers were tormented daily, during Governor Bobby Jindal's First Term in office, with new teacher evaluation instruments to determine if a veteran Louisiana Teacher is an "effective" or "ineffective" classroom teacher. As a result of being unduly hounded and harassed, there is an upsurge of veteran teachers leaving the Louisiana Public School Classroom. Marsha Shuler provided the following insight:

[221] Sentell, Will, "La. schools get low marks," <u>The Advocate</u>, April 23, 2013, p. 1.
[222] Millhollon, Michelle, "Test results show some improvements," <u>The Advocate</u>, July 03, 2013, p. 2.

"Teachers are continuing to retire at higher-than-usual numbers — more than 7,500 in the last two years. The number of retirements in 2013 increased from the 24 percent increase last year. "We are up about 1,000 from what we would normally see," said Dana Vicknair, assistant director at Teachers Retirement System of Louisiana."These are people walking out the door. ... These people are actually gone.".... There are some 50,000 Louisiana public school teachers. TRSL registered 3,871 retirements in the fiscal year ending June 30. Of those, 3,415 worked in kindergarten through 12th grade...Last year, when the 24 percent jump occurred, there were 3,295 public school employees out of 3,724 Teachers'system retirements — more than 700 more than the prior year. About two-thirds of the public school employees who opted to retire had worked 20 or more years... The numbers rose 24 percent in the fiscal year that ended June 30, 2012, in the wake of legislative passage of Jindal's education system revamps and talk of pension system changes. In 2011, there were 2,994 retirements of which 2,581 were in K-12. Of them, 1,951 had 20 or more years with public schools. The number of retirements jumped to 3,724 in the following year, of which 3,295 were in K-12. Of them, 2,468 had 20-plus years. The new numbers show another jump to 3,871 retirements, 3,415 in public schools. Based on preliminary numbers 2,483 retirees had worked 20-plus years."[223]

Why are all these seasoned, veteran Louisiana Public School Teachers choosing to retire in the "prime of their teaching careers?" Shuler added the following:

"school superintendents...said the decision has a lot to do with changes occurring in the classroom, including new

---

[223] Shuler, Marsha, "Teachers retiring in high numbers," The Advocate, July 10, 2013, pp. 1,2 and 3.

teacher evaluations pushed by the Jindal administration, which one educator said created "a tipping point." ... The 2012 Legislature approved major changes in state education policy, including new rules making it harder to earn and keep a form of job security called tenure. The way teachers are evaluated will be linked partly to student performance... "For us this year has been particularly bad," Lafayette Parish School Superintendent Pat Cooper said. "We have some very talented teachers who have left out of frustration and were lucky enough to have other options." "Twenty years as a teacher you are just getting into your prime. We are losing some high-quality teachers," he said. "It's just the pressure on these people and the swiftness that it's all come about. ... It's just created a tipping point for our teachers."[224]

The interesting thing about the mass exodus of seasoned Louisiana Public School Teachers is the current Superintendent of Education, Mr. John White, attributes so many teachers leaving the classroom due to financial reasons. Shuler stated "State Superintendent of Education John White said the exodus should be looked at as primarily a financial decision on the part of more veteran employees... White noted the increase in retirements began as administration pension policy changes impacting benefits and retirement age were being debated for state employees."[225] Although veteran Louisiana Public School Teachers, in the prime of their work life, are filing out of the Louisiana Classroom in droves, as the foregoing data proves. Mr. John White added "... there is not an increase in the number of people leaving the classroom."[226] There are two reasons for Mr. John White's comments. First, he works for Governor Bobby Jindal, and this group, as we have already seen, is pushing the Louisiana Ruling Class agenda to privatize public education in Louisiana. Their charter school voucher gimmick is being used to siphon Minimum Foundation Program Funds from the constitutionally protected K-12 Budget. Second, Mr. John White, who is

[224] Ibid., pp. 1 and 2.
[225] Ibid., p. 1.
[226] Ibid., p. 1.

the head of the Louisiana State Department of Education, does not have a Ph.D. degree in education from an accredited graduate school in America. In Schools Matter article, " John White got his BA in English at UVA before he joined TFA [Teach for America]…Little John was quickly moved to the front of the line to replace Paul Vallas…as head of the Recovery School District in NOLA, despite the fact that White has never even been an assistant principal."[227] Moreover, Chiefs for Change reported "White received a B.A. in English…from the University of Virginia, and earned a Master's Degree in Public Administration from New York University."[228] Having never worked as an assistant principal anywhere in America, how could Mr. John White understand the underlying cause of the exodus of so many Public School Teachers, from the Louisiana Classroom?

As hundreds of seasoned, veteran Louisiana Public School Teachers make a mass exodus of the classroom during Superintendent of Education John White's tenure, hundreds of Teach for America Teachers file into the Louisiana Classroom, lacking the required Teacher Certification required by the state. Teach for America Teachers receive only a five week training before they enter the classroom to teach. According to Teach for America online home page, "corps members attend the five week institute…and help their students master critical content."[229] Moreover, "institute is an intensive five-week training program that prepares corps members for their teaching experience."[230] The Summer Training Institute consists of the following: (1) Teaching an average of two hours each day (2) Observation and Feedback where coaches observe trainees three times a week (3) Rehearsals and reflections where trainees meet in small groups and *practice teaching* (4) Lesson Planning Clinics where trainees receive lesson planning instructions from coaches and (5) Curriculum Sessions where trainees study the fundamentals of teaching.[231]

---

[227] _____ "Schools Matter," http://www.schoolsmatter.info/2011/05/john-white-english-major-oligarchs-boy.html.

[228] _____ "Chiefs For Change," Biography, http://chiefsforchange.org/members/john-white/#sthash.TywairkO.dpuf

[229] _____Teach   For   America,   http://www.teachforamerica.org/why-teach-for-america/

[230] Ibid.

[231] Ibid.

Why should Louisiana Parents send their children to a four year accredited university to study education when Teach for America and Superintendent John White are allowing non-certified individuals to teach in the Louisiana Classroom? Stop a moment to think, and ask oneself this simple question: Can a person learn how to become an effective teacher in five weeks? Yet, isn't it ironic that Teach for America trained individuals are observing veteran Louisiana Public School Teachers to determine whether they are *effective or ineffective*. No reputable business that is worth its salt would allow a public school teacher to become the CEO of it. Exxon would laugh at the idea, and find it most humorous and comical. Will Sentell stated "State Superintendent of Education John White, [is] a TFA alum..."[232] At Mr. John White's request, with Governor Bobby Jindal looking over his shoulders, Sentell added "The state Board of Elementary and Secondary Education in June [2013] approved $1.2 million for Teach For America..."[233] Not once since Mr. White was appointed as Superintendent of Education has he asked for any funds to support Louisiana Classroom Teachers; the vast majority of his time has been spent crafting ridiculously stringent evaluation measures to determine what is already known, and that is, whether a majority of Louisiana Public School Teachers are effective or ineffective, and other measures aimed at taking hard earned tenure away from the same. How can Superintendent John White determine if any Louisiana Teacher is effective or ineffective when he does not have the proper credentials to serve as the Superintendent of Education? At minimum, he would need a masters Degree in Education; at best, a Ph.D. degree. Mr. White has an undergraduate degree in English; he has never served a day as an assistant principal; and he only has a five week Teach For America Training to justify him being the top educational officer in the State of Louisiana. The Louisiana BESE Board in spite of Mr. White's inadequate educational credentials "...voted overwhelmingly in favor of making former head of the state's Recovery School District superintendent of schools. Despite only being in New Orleans for a few months..."[234]

---

[232] Sentell, Will, "Tulane state leader of Teach For America ranks," The Advocate, September 7, 2013, p. 1.

[233] Ibid., p. 2.

[234] _____ "John White Appointed as New Louisiana Superintendent," Education News, http://www.educationnews.org/education-policy-and-politics/

Remember, former Governor Mike Foster appointed Bobby Jindal as the head of the Louisiana Board of Trustees for Colleges and Universities.

D. John White, Superintendent of Education and his Executive Staff

The only member of the Louisiana BESE Board to vote against John White's political appointment was Mrs. Lottie Beebe. Education News reported the following:

> "[Beebe] questioned White's credentials and level of experience and called for a full national search, a position echoed by the state's two major teachers unions and the Coalition for Louisiana Public Education, an umbrella group that also includes school board members, superintendents and others..."[235]

So what is behind this game ? How did Mr. John White become a nearly unanimous selection as the top education chief for Louisiana despite his academic credentials being totally inadequate for t he job? The following explanation should not come as a surprise, given what we already know about the Jindal Administration, and what is behind it orchestrating its every move.

Mr. John White was handpicked by private business to open the door to the Louisiana K-12 Budget so millions of dollars could be drained out of it under the disguise of the Charter School Voucher Scheme Program, which was set in motion by the Jindal Administration, Louisiana Legislature, and their political backers. Thus, to get Mr. White looking like he might be qualified for the Louisiana Superintendent job, he was *given some high profile jobs beforehand to make him appear he has the credentials to be appointed to the position.* After graduating with his undergraduate degree in English from the University of Virginia, School Matters reported the following:

---

[235] Ibid.

"John White got his BA in English at UVA before he joined TFA and, in white missionary fashion, learned to teach on poor people's children in Newark. A stint as a TFA exec in Chicago followed, and then came five years as one of Klein's brigade of callous Corps members in NYC, trained to do what their "thought leaders" commanded. The positivized White impressed Bloomberg and Klein for his glassy-eyed devotion to shutting down city schools and running Klein's relocation war room on schools, and before you could say Martin Seligman, Little John was placed in charge of one of Bill Gates's self-serving plans to slash the number of required teachers by plugging children into computer screens for up to half of the school day. Called the Innovation Zone (iZone) (cute),it could spell twilight zone... Now freshly minted from Eli Broad's corporate training school (Class of 2010) for future superintendents who are trained how to use their power to hand over their systems to the Business Roundtable, Little John was quickly moved to the front of the line to replace Paul Vallas just weeks ago as head of theRecovery School District in NOLA, despite the fact that White has never even been an assistant principal. But don't unpack your positive psychology books so fast, John, for Bill, Eli, and Arne would like to put you in charge of your own state, or at least in charge of their own state: Louisiana. With the LEAP test in Louisiana newly-loaded with a set of fresh targets for the final bombing sorties on the state's struggling public schools, the Oligarchs figure they have as perfect an opportunity as they will ever get to use Little John to put into play... their portfolio school plan, with corporate welfare charters, public funding of private religious schools, schools with computers replacing half the teachers, and, of course, the greatest scam of all, the virtual charter schools, where children get virtually nothing for their education time."[236]

---

[236] Op. Cit., See Footnote Number 120.

As we see, Mr. John White was dressed up fairly well to assume his new starring role as the top education chief for Louisiana. He is "turtle on a telegram pole'; someone put him up there because a turtle cannot fly like a bird. The vast majority of Louisiana Educators have fallen for this well orchestrated Wizard of Oz phenomenon. Underlying it all is the *corporate welfare charter schools through which millions of dollars flow into the bank accounts of their private business owners.* For his part, Superintendent of Education John White is also getting paid well too. According to Will Sentell, Mr. White's executive staff is making six figure salaries. Consider the following:

> "State Superintendent of Education John white announced his executive staff…and said…even with the six figure salaries…department costs have dropped…The salaries on the superintendent's team range from $110,000 per year to $225,000 annually. Some of the 15 officials have been announced previously, including five "network leaders" who will oversee the efforts of 10 or so school districts each in setting up new teacher evaluations and tougher courses. White is paid $275,000 per year…"[237]

a. John White, Superintendent Of Education's Executive Staff

If Mr. John White's executive staff's credentials are inadequate as his own, these are astronomical salaries for individuals, who are overseeing the Louisiana Educational System, which is, as we have already seen, one of the worst in the nation, and probably just a little better than Mississippi's. The following Table 1.8 shows the six figure salaries for Mr. John White's executive staff.

---

[237] Sentell, Will, "La. superintendent reorganizes staff," The Advocate, October 12, 2012, p. 1.

Table 1.8
Six Figure Salaries of Superintendent of Education John White's Executive Staff, Including his Own, October 2012

NAME	TITLE	SALARY/YR
John White	Superintendent	$275,000
Patrick Dobard	RSD Superintendent	225,000
Mike Rounds	Deputy Superintendent for District Support	170,000
Warren Drake	Network Leader	160,000
Gayle Sloan	Network Leader	160,000
Kerry Caster	Network Leader	155,000
Dave Lefkowith	Asst. Superintendent Overseeing Vouchers, Charter Schools, etc.	145,000
Gary Jones	Policy Liaison with Local Superintendents	145,000
Erin Bendily	Asst. Superintendent for Policy and External Affairs	140,000
Melissa Stilley	Network Leader	135,000
Beth Scioneaux	Deputy Superintendent of Finance	132,000
Hannah Dietsch	Asst. Superintendent Overseeing Teacher Evaluations, etc.	130,000
Francis Touchet	Network Leader	130,000
Stephen Osborn	Asst. Superintendent for Student Programs	125,000
Joan Hunt	Executive Counsel	125,000
Ken Bradford	Asst. Superintendent for Content	110,000
TOTAL		**$2,462,000**

Source: Sentell, Will, "La. superintendent reorganizes staff," The Advocate, October 12, 2012, p. 2.

To highlight the disconnect between the titles and salaries shown in the above Table, let us focus in on Mr. Dave Lefkowith, who currently-October 2013-serves as the Assistant Superintendent Overseeing Vouchers, Charter Schools, etc. and Mrs. Hannah Dietsch, who currently-October 2013-serves as Assistant Superintendent Overseeing Teacher Evaluation, etc. Mr. Lefkowitch earns $140,000 annually, and Mrs. Dietsch $130,000. In Mr. Lefkowith Case, his resume states the following:

"Dave Lefty Lefkowith is a dynamic hands-on change agent, successful as an executive, a corporate consultant, an entrepreneur and a speaker/trainer. Dave provides leaders and organizations with the practical insights they need to be successful in the 21st Century. In today's business environment of unprecedented speed, turmoil and opportunity, Dave helps 21st Century Leaders with the right attitude, passion and guts to stay focused on prosperity. From Koosh Balls to Pampers, from power plants to pizzerias, Dave has worked with public and private organizations of every size to help them achieve unprecedented success...Dave started his career at Procter Gamble, where he helped launch six new national brands. He served as the COO of a national chain of retail stores in his late 20s, and for almost 20 years has worked as a corporate change agent specializing in growth-oriented initiatives, new product development, leadership skills development and cultural / organizational change."[238]

As we see, the great disconnect here is Mr. Dave Lefkowitch is not an educator, but a corporate executive by training! His resume does not include anything in it about having had any experience working directly in K-12 Education, at any level, either as a public school teacher, assistant principal, principal, and so forth. Yet, he earns $145,000 to oversee charter schools in Louisiana, which he, along with Mr. John White and Governor Bobby Jindal, profess to the Louisiana public as the answer for reversing some of the most difficult academic problems that African-American Public School Students present today, such as major difficulties with reading, writing, and comprehending two to three grade levels behind the grade they are currently enrolled in. Mr. Lefkowith is employed in the position he currently serves in because it is not about educating anyone; it is about *overseeing the corporate profits*

---

[238] _____ Dave Lefty Lefkowitch, Zoominfo, http://www.zoominfo.com/p/David-Lefkowitch/161434. Mr. Lefkowitch received a BA degree from Yale University and a MBA degree from Stanford University both in the business field.

that charter schools generate. So, in this regard, there is no disconnect; it is all about using African-Americans all over again, from their ancestors' brutal American slavery experience to the latter's descendants' ingenuous charter school experience. The common denominator is profit. In sum, and at the end of the day, the Louisiana Charter School-Voucher Scheme is, by its very nature, a business venture.

Similar to Mr. Dave Lefkowith, Mrs. Hannah Dietsch currently-October 2013-holds a position on Superintendent of Education John White's staff as Assistant Superintendent Overseeing Teacher Evaluation. Regarding her resume, there is nothing shown on it that indicates that Mrs. Dietsch has any direct experience with teacher evaluation at the K-12 Educational Level. In fact, ZoomInfo reported the following on her resume:

> "Hannah Dietsch is the director of strategy and achievement for the New York City Department of Education's empowerment support organization. In this role, she is directly responsible for supporting four networks of staff that serve a total of 89 schools and over 38,000 students. Previously, Dietsch served as a director on Teach For America's admissions team, where she led the overhaul of the organization's regional assignment and matriculation strategy and operations to effect the highest matriculation rates in the organization's history. She beganher career in education as a Teach For America corps member in Baltimore, where she taught language arts. Dietsch then started and managed a statewide, alternative-route certification program for special education teachers while working at the Maryland State Department of Education."[239]

Interestingly, Mrs. Hannah Dietsch began her "career in education as a Teach For America corp member in Baltimore." As we already

---

[239] _____ Hannah Dietsch, http://ZoomInfo.com/p/ Hannah-Dietsch/1486655256.

know, to become a classroom teacher with Teach For America, Mrs. Dietsch received a *five weeks training before she went into the public school classroom to teach language arts.* Therefore, what experience does Mrs. Dietsch have that qualifies her to oversee public school teacher evaluation in Louisiana. How can Mrs. Dietsch, who has a five week educational training, evaluate a seasoned veteran Louisiana Teacher, who has a 20 year career record in the public education field, and who has an education degree from an accredited four year university? Are we getting the point? Yet, all over Louisiana, Mrs. Dietsch is going about determining who is an *effective teacher and who is not.* We could possibly understand this if Mrs. Dietsch has a doctoral degree in education, and not a five week educational training as a Teach For America Corp member. It is long past the time when we need to wake up and stop letting this situation take our tenure and rob us of salary increases, and put an end to the charter school voucher-MFP robbery scheme. There are none so blind as those who refuse to see the truth. According to The Baltimore City Teachers' Trust, Inc., Mrs. Hannah Dietsch "... holds a Bachelor of Arts in English from Tulane University, a Master of Arts in Teaching from Johns Hopkins University, and a Master of Education from Harvard University."[240] These degrees do not indicate that Mrs. Dietsch received an education degree, during which time, she was required to do student teaching before graduating with her undergraduate English degree in education, from Tulane University. If you think things can't get worse, they do.

At this point, one question continues to surface in our consideration of K-12 Education in Louisiana. That is, if most of Mr. John White's Executive Staff, including himself, have very limited hands-on educational experience earned in the classroom, who is filling this void?

On July 9, 2012, the Department of Education's Louisiana Believes website published an article "State Superintendent Announces Team District Support Leaders," in which the answer to our question is clearly provided. According to the article, "State Superintendent of Education

---

[240] _____The Baltimore City teachers' Trust, Inc., http://www.bctt.org/aboutus. html.

John White announced today a new district support leadership team that will work directly with school districts and provide support in the transition to the new Compass evaluation system and implementation of the Common Core State Standards. Compass and the Common Core are the state's top instructional priorities..."[241] The new district support leadership team is a "...new network structure will serve as the primary support vehicle for districts as they implement new evaluation systems and standards. School districts will fall into one of five networks statewide that will assist in translating educational priorities into outcomes for students."[242] Since Superintendent John White, or any of his deputies, does not have any hands-on classroom experience, they will be at the total mercy of the newly formed network structure to provide them with information related to the new Compass Evaluation System, and the implementation of the Common Core State Standards. In short, anything the new network structure tells Mr. John White, he will have no choice but to accept it. Objectivity, balance, and student achievement assessments have-ALL-been compromised, and similar to partners in crime, one crook is no position to tell the other one to stop stealing. The network staff is as follows:

> "Each network will be supported by a team of instructional specialists who will be managed by a leader with education experience. These leaders will assess the unique needs and approaches of their districts and build upon those strengths to support implementation of instructional reforms. The network leaders announced today are Warren Drake, Superintendent of the Zachary Community School District; Kerry Laster, Deputy Superintendent of Literacy and former Superintendent for Concordia Parish; Gayle Sloan, District Support Officer in the Department of Education's Innovation Office and former Superintendent for St.Tammany Parish; Melissa

---

[241] _____ "STATE SUPERINTENDENT ANNOUNCES TEAM OF DISTRICT SUPPORT LEADERS," http://www.louisianabelieves.com/newsroom/news-releases/2012.07/09/state-superintende...
[242] Ibid.

> Stilley, Chief Academic Officer for the Tangipahoa Parish
> School Board, and Francis Touchet, Principal of Erath
> High School. The Department has paired each network
> leader with a network, and these pairings are available on
> a final network..."[243]

These individuals are not new to us; they are listed in Table 1.4, along with their unheard of high salaries. Together, the five listed network workers are paid $740,000 annually. To understand the charter school voucher robbery scam better than we already have, it is worthwhile taking a closer look at John White's Executive Staff. By doing so, we will see on one hand, who is responsible for keeping the Louisiana Masses ignorant to the extent many still believe our failing education system can be rescued by charter schools, and on the other, we uncover, and expose, who is responsible for cultivating, or growing charter schools, in the name of improving the academic performance of the vast majority of working class children, most of whom are African-Americans. To accomplish this aim, consider the organization chart below.

---

[243] Ibid.

b. Executive Staff Organizational Chart And Position Title

Table 1.9
Superintendent of Education John White's Executive Staff

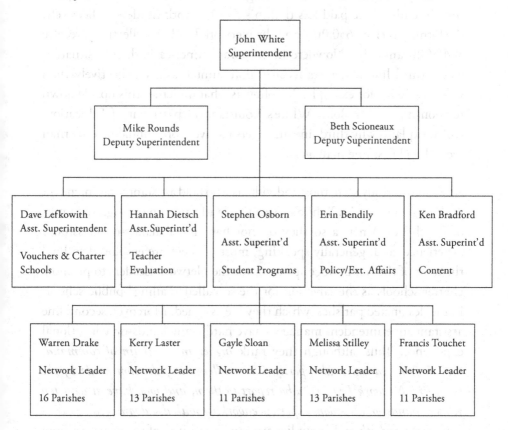

As we have seen thus far, every one of the members of John White's Executive Staff do not have any extensive hands-on experience with classroom teaching, including Mr. John White himself. From the Assistant Superintendent Level, in the above organization chart right up to the Superintendent, no one has extensive experience, or knowledge, about how to assess a child's academic progress beyond the obvious. This is far from being an oversight; the Louisiana Ruling Class, who elected Governor Bobby Jindal planned it this way by instructing Governor Bobby Jindal to appoint Assistant Superintendents who, collectively, have not served as an assistant principal in their individual educational careers. However, by giving them high sounding titles, and paying them disproportionately high salaries, each one of John White's assistant superintendent appointees, truly believe they know how to fix Louisiana's very low academic ranking nationally and statewide. Interestingly, Mr. John White's five assistant superintendents are paid less than his five Network Leaders; collectively, the former receive $650,000, and the Network Leaders, collectively, receive $740,000 annually. Nowhere in corporate America is there a situation where third line managers receive more annual salary collectively than vice presidents, for example. To follow is what underlies this upside down relationship in Mr. John White's Louisiana Department of Education, which explains why third line managers receive more annual income than second and first line managers.

As we have already seen, those individuals who hold assistant superintendent positions on Mr. John White's Executive Staff came up through the ranks of Teach For America so they do not have much hands-on classroom experience, and, generally speaking, most of them are employed to hold the door of the "chicken coup" open for the Network Leaders to promote charter schools as the salvation for the so-called "Failing" public schools in the designated parishes, which they are assigned. Moreover, second line assistant superintendent managers have hardly any hands-on educational experience. Thus, although they rank *higher in the chain of command, they have no educational experience to challenge any decision made by the third line Network Leaders, who report to them, and who have at least ten years of hands-on classroom experience working with disadvantaged African-Americans and others.* Herein lies the inner workings of the charter school voucher robbery scam.

Mr. Stephen Osborn, who is the assistant superintendent for student programs, is the trigger point for its implementation. Since he is responsible for student programs, each one of the Network Leaders report to Mr. Stephen Osborn about the status of the public schools located in the individual parishes, within the Network Structure, they are assigned to manage. For example, as the above organizational chart indicates, Mr. Warren Drake, for example, is responsible for 16 parishes located mainly in Northwest Louisiana, and stretching as far south as Vernon Parish in Central Louisiana. Each Network Leader is currently assigned to manage a minimum of ten parishes. When Mr. Stephen Osborn's resume is carefully observed, the part played by the Network Leaders in the charter school voucher robbery scam becomes clear.

Briefly, based on the foregoing information we quoted, taken from the Department of Education's Louisiana believes website, related to Mr. Stephen Osborn's work experience, the following information shows the charter school connection *embedded in Mr. John White's Executive Staff:*

> "Prior to joining the Department of Education, Stephen Osborn served as Chief Operating Officer (COO) for the Capital One - New Beginnings Charter Schools Network, which operates four charter schools in partnership with UNO and Capital One Bank. In this capacity, Osborn oversaw day-to-day school operations and the organization's finance…Osborn previously worked as the Compliance Manager for Excellent Education Development, a non-profit company that provides back office support to California's charter schools. He has also served as a consultant for Benjamin Franklin High School, KIPP (Los Angeles and New Orleans) and the National Association of Charter School Authorizers."[244]

Mr. Stephen Osborn is a corporate executive; he does not have any hands-on classroom experience, nor any as an assistant principal; yet, he is the Assistant Superintendent for the all important "Student Programs." What is a corporate executive doing managing student programs? In Logic 101, there is no connection; however, in this charter school voucher robbery scam, there is a crucial connection. That is, at Mr. Stephen Osborn level as Assistant Superintendent for Student Programs, he knows how to authorize charter schools based on his experience he obtained while working for the National Association of Charter School Authorizers, and what he learned from providing *back office support to California's charter schools.* Therefore,

---

[244] Op. Cit., http://www.louisianabelieves.com

when the Network Leaders get enough African-Americans in their region, who are attending "failing" public schools in it, the Network Leaders report to Mr. Stephen Osborn that the time is right to establish a charter school in this or that region, where the low academic achieving African-Americans can enroll, bringing with them, of course, the all important Minimum Foundation Funds-$9,000 annually. This scam is going-on as we write this. It is happening in broad daylight across the Louisiana Public School landscape, and the unsuspecting parents of each affected African-American Public Education Student, does not even have the slightest idea that they are being "Had," Bamboozled," and Hoodwinked." Lastly, if Capital One is involved in this charter school voucher robbery scheme bonanza, then there must be a lot of money to be made, literally billions of taxpayers' dollars could end up being taken from the Minimum Foundation Fund Program.

How much worse can the Louisiana K-12 situation be is borne out by Superintendent of Education John White's credentials and salary. We have already seen that Mr. John White, like many of his staff appointees, got his start in education with a *five week training through Teach For America*. Mr. White has an undergraduate degree in English and a Masters Degree in Public Administration; yet, if you or I went to one of the 70 local school districts in Louisiana and applied for a classroom teaching jobs with Superintendent of Education John White's credentials, or resume, we would be turned down flatly because we do not have any formal classroom teaching experience. Mr. John White does not have any either; however, he was appointed the chief education officer (CEO) for Louisiana by Governor Bobby Jindal, who former Governor Mike Foster appointed the CEO of the Board that oversees all Louisiana colleges and Universities except LSU and Southern University; he also called Governor Bobby Jindal the smartest man he ever met or knows. Like Governor Bobby Jindal, Superintendent John White was appointed without the qualifications necessary to do the job.

As a matter of fact, we researched the credentials of the persons who currently head-CEOs-the State Departments of Public Education in the MidSouth Region, consisting of Arkansas and Mississippi. The

Mississippi Department of Education is headed by Dr. Lynn House; Dr. Thomas Kimbrell is the head of the Arkansas Department of Education. In both cases, the mentioned CEOs of the Department of Education have a Doctoral Degree. To determine if this trend holds true outsiof the MidSouth Region, we researched Alabama and Georgia, two statess that are also located in the Deep South. We discovered Dr. Thomas R. Bice is the head of the State Department of Education in Alabama, and Dr. John Borge is the head of the State Department of Education in Georgia. As we see, in each case, the CEO of the State Department of Education has a Doctoral Degree in Education, qualifying them to make the best decisions for the parents and children of their respective state. Before closing our research, we checked to see if any high ranking staff persons, who reports directly to the identified CEOs, with Doctoral Degrees, have any Teach for America Five Weeks Training, and we could not find anyone.

However, State Superintendent of Education John White currently receives $275,00 annually; his salary is consistent with those CEOs with Doctoral Degrees previously mentioned; and, Mr. White's classroom experience is a five week training received from Teach for America. Even Mississippi knows better that it needs a highly trained CEO to lead public education. So, by now you may have this question in your mind: How did Mr. John White get appointed the CEO of education in Louisiana? According to the Education Reporter, "It's estimated that the newly expanded voucher program may remove as much as $3.3 billion annually from public schools — a fact that has public school officials worried..."[245] in Louisiana. This clearly explains Mr. John White's appointment as the CEO of public education in Louisiana. With limited credentials and hands-on classroom teaching experience, Mr. White's role is not to think critically about educational challenges and how to resolve them, but go along with the charter school voucher-robbery scheme discussed earlier. His method is the method he was given by private business, and that is, to implement their Charter School Voucher Scheme Program, which is aimed directly at siphoning billions of Louisiana taxpayer dollars out of the K-12 State Budget. Thus, Mr. White's $275,000 salary is a mere pawn in a much

---

[245] _____ "Louisiana Voucher Program Privatizes Education," Education Reporter, http://www.eagleforum.org/publications/educate/july12/1c, July 2012.

larger and more vastly lucrative Charter School Voucher Scheme Game. The latter makes casinos seem like small change, and the unfortunate pawn in the game are overrepresented Afro-American children; their ancestors labor power were stolen during the American Slavery Institution, and now, several centuries later, more than 90 percent of all the children enrolled in the Charter School Voucher Scheme are Afro-Americans, each one bringing with them roughly $9,000 annually when they enroll in a Charter School, which falsely tells them that they can bring their reading up to grade level or above in all academic subjects they are several grade levels behind in.

Later, we will take up the poverty issue in Louisiana. Currently, we will focus our attention on healthcare, another unprotected line item in the Louisiana State Budget, but one, similar to higher education, that is being drained of revenues by neo-liberalism privatization economic policy.

CHAPTER V

Healthcare Program Privatization and Staff Layoffs

A. Healthcare Budget Cuts, 2008 to 2013

Similar to the Louisiana Higher Education Budget, the Healthcare Budget is not protected from budget cuts by the Louisiana Constitution. Interestingly, the Louisiana Constitution *does not protect the two most vulnerable population segments in our society, namely, college students and children and the elderly.* Even though, on paper, the Louisiana Constitution prohibits any budget cuts to the K-12 Public Education Budget, Governor Bobby Jindal and the Louisiana Legislature, both operatives of the Louisiana Ruling Class[246] have used the latter's Privatization and Subsidization Economic Policies to achieve a common result, namely, to drain the Louisiana Citizenry's tax dollars from the public sector line items of the Louisiana State Budget, regardless of whether it is protected by the Louisiana Constitution or not. To begin this discussion, we examine what impact the mentioned policies have had on the Healthcare Budget since 2008, which was the first year of the first term of the Jindal Administration.

---

[246] Later, when we examine who pays the most taxes in Louisiana, we will, based on the tax and income data presented, define the Louisiana Ruling Class. It is common practice for the social media and politicians to talk about the middle class, but never do you hear any mention of the ruling class or working class. As far as the typical Louisiana resident is concerned, these classes do not exist; yet, they exist as surely as the oxygen we breathe on a moment-to-moment basis.

a. Louisiana Public Hospitals And Health Related Programs

The Neo-Liberalism Economic and Privatization Economic Policies of the Jindal Administration has, effectively December 11, 2013, closed every previously state-run, public hospital, and shifted-ALL-state government responsibility for running them to private business, along with taxpayer dollars. Why do we need a state government, or any government, that voluntarily abdicates its responsibility to serve the people? Michelle Millhollon stated "across Louisiana, the state is getting out of the business of running hospitals. Private hospitals are tackling patients' health care, either at the public hospitals themselves or in private hospitals such as the Lake."[247] To follow is a systematic documentation of the closure of all Louisiana Public Hospitals, by the Jindal Administration, and the impact public hospital closures have had on hospital employees and patients.

Governor Bobby Jindal is driving the privatization economic steamroller right over the most vulnerable people in Louisiana today-children and the elderly. Millhollon documented this fact in a recent article as follows:

> "Ten public hospitals in Louisiana provide care to the uninsured, either through the oversight of LSU Health Care Services or the LSU system. In a move that could eliminate thousands of state government jobs, Jindal is restructuring the state's public hospital and graduate medical education system. Management for most of that system would shift to the private sector, which would receive public dollars to care for patients and would pay the state lease payments for facilities under the plan... Patients and medical education programs at the LSU Earl K. Long Medical Center in Baton Rouge will move to Our Lady of the Lake Regional Medical Center. Leonard J. Chabert Hospital in Houma will partner with Ochsner Health System and Terrebonne General Medical Center.

---

[247] Millhollon, Michelle, "Jindal cuts ribbon on medical education center," The Advocate, December 10, 2013, p. 1.

Similar arrangements are planned for public hospitals in Lafayette, Lake Charles, Monroe, Pineville, New Orleans and Bogalusa."[248]

Millhollon hit the target because she noted "public dollars" will be used to care for patients. Aren't public dollars already being used to care for Louisiana patients before this privatization move? The difference is a *profit is going to be made by businesses.* Before privatization, it was illegal for a public run hospital to use public dollars to earn a profit. Millhollon added the following immoral commentary:

"In preparing his proposed budget for the fiscal year that starts July 1, the governor gutted funding *for the LSU Health Care Services Division, which is responsible for seven hospitals, including* Earl K. Long Medical Center in Baton Rouge. From a spending plan of $825 million Dec. 1, the division's budget would shrink to $45 million in the upcoming fiscal year, according to the budget documents. The budget for the LSU system, which has three public hospitals, would drop from $1.4 million on Dec. 1 to $827 million as Huey P. Long Medical Center in Pineville and E.A. Conway shift to private management... "Public hospitals are gone after this budget. Finished. Over. Do not exist. Nichols said public health services will be alive and present, just provided through a different model... state Department of Health and Hospitals Secretary Bruce Greenstein said he is counting on the agreements materializing.[249]

b. Impact of Neo-Liberal Economic Policy On The Louisiana Healthcare Budget, Fiscal Year 2013

Besides the tremendous added suffering existing Louisiana patients will

[248] Millhollon, Michelle, "Budgets for public hospitals depend on privatization agreements, " The Advocate, February 24, 2013, pp. 1 and 2.
[249] Ibid., pp. 2 and 3.

experience as a result of this privatization of statewide healthcare services, Millhollon noted the Louisiana Healthcare Budget consisted of a spending plan of $825 million on December 1, 2012; it will decrease to $45 million in the upcoming Fiscal Year 2013-a massive decline of -95 percent! We will show where the -95 percent decrease in the Louisiana Healthcare Budget went. To eliminate speculation about where this enormous decrease in Louisiana Taxpayers dollars' ended up, we will use the latest report published by the Public Affairs Research Council of Louisiana titled "A New Safety Net: The risk and reward of Louisiana's charity hospital privatizations, December 2013" to do so. This report shows where this large sum of money ended up during Fiscal Year 2013, and where it will end up five to fifty years from now.

b-1: Selecting Private Partners

The selection of private business partners to takeover Louisiana's public hospital system was done in private without any public discussion at the grassroots level. That is, the Louisiana Residents who have, and continue, to depend upon the charity hospital system for their healthcare were not ask if they were for or against the closure of the charity hospital that took care of their health needs. According to Gregory and Neustrom, "the process of selecting the public-private partnerships took place largely in private. The state did not use its usual contracting process and did not issue a Request for Proposals. LSU officials said they spoke to nonprofits and for-profits during the deliberations."[250] How could a state contract be awarded to a private business without following the usual contracting process? Why wasn't a Request for Proposal issued? The answer to these questions is the Jindal Administration was told by the Louisiana Ruling Class to put its head in the sand, and *give private business owners the contract without having to bid on them.* If you or I gave a multi-million dollar state contract to anyone without issuing a Request for Proposal, and if we were caught in the process, we would certainly end up in Angola State Prison on fraud and racketeering felony charges for a very long time.

---

[250] Gregory, Don and Neustrom, Alison, Ph.D., A New Safety Net: The risk and reward of Louisiana's charity hospital privatizations, Publication 333, Public Affairs Research Council of Louisiana, December 2013, p. 8.

Sensing there was significant underlying corruption taking place during the selection of private businesses to takeover Louisiana's Public Hospitals, the media made an effort to review the records related to the takeovers. Gregory and Neustrom stated "efforts by the media to review the records related to the budget cuts and privatization were rebuffed by LSU's legal counsel, which followed the advice of the governor's general counsel, as part of the "deliberative process privilege."[251] Too many questions related to state government corruption would require answering if the former was out front giving away state contracts without a Request for Proposal. In order to go around the "bidding process," the Louisiana State Government transferred the operation of its public hospitals to LSU in 1997. Gregory and Neustrom stated "Responsibility for managing the charity hospitals was transferred in 1997 from the Louisiana Health Care Authority to the Louisiana State University System..."[252]

Therefore, all questions about the privatization of Louisiana Public Hospitals were channeled through LSU's legal counsel, "which followed the advice of the governor's general counsel." Having silenced any dissenting voices, state contracts were given out to private businesses to takeover public hospitals without any competitive bidding. The next step in the "closed door process" involved the LSU Board of Supervisors approval of Memorandum of Understanding between selected private business and state government. Gregory and Neustrom explained this stage of the privatization process as follows: "Memorandums of Understanding were presented to the LSU Board of Supervisors for approval on December 14, 2012. These agreements specified immediate lease payments from the private partners..."[253] The last step involved the establishment of Cooperative Endeavor Agreements between state government and private business. Gregory and Neustrom stated "the board approved the memorandums unanimously...and said the other financing and operational details would be worked out in the Cooperative Endeavor Agreements, which are the formal contracts between the various state agencies and private partners."[254] Every department of

---

[251] Ibid., p. 8.
[252] Ibid., p. 4.
[253] Ibid., p. 9.
[254] Ibid., p. 9.

state government, under the direction of the Jindal Administration, gave its approval of the Cooperative Endeavor Agreements (CEA). Gregory and Neustrom wrote the following:

> "The Legislature must approve the closure of a public hospital. Both Earl K. Long Hospital in Baton Rouge and W. O. Moss Hospital in Lake Charles were slated to be closed. The Attorney General opined that the leasing of the state hospital facilities did not require legislative approval, although the Joint Legislative Committee on the Budget was required to review the Cooperative Endeavor Agreements. The partnership deals required – and received – funding through the 2013-14 state budget."[255]

With everyone on board, from the Governor's Office to the Attorney General's, including the Department of Health and Hospitals and the LSU Board of Supervisors, the road was paved for the implementation of the Louisiana Ruling Class' Neo-liberal Economic Policy, and in this case, the closure of nearly all of Louisiana Public Hospitals, and the subsequent transfer of their assets to the private business listed in the Cooperative Endeavor Agreement (CEA). The takeover of public hospitals by private business was not done as a gesture of "Good Will;" rather, the CEA is merely, in its exposed form, a process where the Jindal Administration "gives away" millions of Louisiana Taxpayer Dollars to private business. Profit is primary and healthcare is secondary at best. It is a bonanza for private business takeover of public hospitals. Gregory and Neustrom wrote the following:

> "The new operating partners will be compensated mainly with the same state and federal dollars that had been supporting the state-run charity hospitals. Adequate funding from the state to the private partner is one of the keys to a sustainable partnership. The CEAs stipulate that if adequate funding is not provided, the private partners may voluntarily withdraw from the agreements. All CEAs

---

[255] Ibid., p. 9.

have dispute resolution and wind-down clauses in case of cancellation of an agreement."[256]

Thus, what is the purpose of the takeover of a public hospital? As we see, it is the private business will be paid with the same state and federal dollars that formerly supported the operation of a privatized public hospital before a takeover. On top of this, the private business will be allowed, by the Jindal Administration, or state, to be reimbursed by Medicaid for any partner obligations such as leasing of closed public hospital infrastructure. Gregory and Neustrom stated "The operating partners will be paying the state for leases of LSU's assets…Significantly, a large portion of these dollars can be recovered by the private partners through the Medicaid reimbursement process. For partners who are guaranteed their costs, they can recover much of their rental lease payment. The administration says this arrangement will not require advance federal approval." [257] Similar to the no-bid manner in which state contracts were issued to private business, the latter will not incur any financial responsibility for the takeover of a Louisiana Public Hospital. To the contrary, private business will make, collectively, more than a billion dollars annually for the next 5 to 50 years. To follow is a lengthy quotation written by Gregory and Neustrom, which clearly verifies the substantial amount of taxpayer dollars, both state and federal, that private business will receive, for being allowed to takeover Louisiana's nine public hospitals.

> "The state's expenditures for fiscal year 2013 to run the entire charity hospital system were approximately $1.37 billion including administrative costs. The administration told the legislature in June 2013 that for fiscal year 2014, approximately $1.05 billion would be spent for support of the nine LSU partnership hospitals, of which about $400 million is state support. By September 2013, additional agreements had been made and PAR computes the 2014

---

[256] Ibid., p. 10.
[257] Ibid. p. 10 and 11.

expenditure amount to be approximately $1.09 billion for the nine LSU hospitals affected."[258]

For Fiscal Year 2014, the Jindal Administration will spend, or give, more accurately,-nine private businesses-$1.09 billion annually, for the affected Louisiana Public Hospitals. Now that all of Louisiana's nine Public Hospitals have been privatized, the "Daily Per Diem Rate," which formerly were paid to the state by the federal government, for Medicaid Reimbursements, are now paid directly to the private businesses that took them over. Gregory and Neustrom stated "the higher per diems for certain partners will cost the state about $31 million annually, by PAR's calculation. Taking both the savings from some lower per diems and expenditures from higher per diems into account, Louisiana will spend about $17.5 million more overall in per diem payments across all partners."[259] Another large pool of money that the nine private businesses will receive as income is called uncompensated care financing of hospital services.

In short, a significant amount of money is set-aside to cover "some of the cost borne by hospitals for treating the uninsured. UCC is the overall measure of hospital-provided care for which no payment is expected to be received from the patient or an insurer."[260] Again, Medicaid, and its "Medicaid Shortfall program," will reimburse each private business the difference between a service and its actual cost. Gregory and Neustrom explained the added source of money as follows:

> "A federal Disproportionate Share Hospital (DSH) supplemental Medicaid payment is used to cover these costs...The administration told the legislature in June 2013 that it had budgeted $659 million dollars in UCC payments for fiscal year 2014 for the nine partnership hospitals. This figure is a 1.4% increase over the LSU

---

[258] Ibid., p. 11.
[259] Ibid., p. 13.
[260] Ibid., p. 15.

reported UCC revenue for 2011 of $650 million for all 10 LSU hospitals."[261]

This is the Louisiana Ruling Class' Neo-Liberal Economic Policy at work, and Governor Bobby Jindal was s/elected to implement it flawlessly. Next, we will examine how much of the $1 billion plus annual bonanza each private business is receiving for its participation in the lucrative healthcare scandal currently taking place in Louisiana. This scandal is truly one of the biggest in Louisiana History to date. To keep us asleep to this reality, the mass media, continuously and subtly 24/7, feeds us mind-numbing trivia related to sports, sexual harassment scandals, weather events, mega-lotteries, crime dramas, comedies, and real life daily crime reports, among many others.

b-2: Earl K. Long Medical Center in Baton Rouge-Our Lady of the Lake (OLOL) Cooperative Endeavor Agreement, Fiscal Year 2013 and Beyond

Gregory and Neustrom stated "Earl K. Long Hospital located at 5825 Airline Highway, Baton Rouge, closed on April 15, 2013, and its services were taken over by Our Lady of the Lake (OLOL)... The private partner is Our Lady of the Lake Inc..."[262] With the stroke of a pen, Earl K. Long Hospital was closed, and-ALL-of its assets were given to a private partner-OLOL. The latter's obligation to the Louisiana State Government "...is leasing the former Earl K. Long outpatient clinics. The total rental due to the state is $3.8 million annually. It is important to note this lease expense will be treated as an allowable cost in the filing of the Medicaid cost report..."[263] Although OLOL will pay the state $3.8 million to lease the former Earl K. Long Hospital Outpatient clinic, "...OLOL is guaranteed a reimbursement of 100% of their UCC costs and 95% of their Medicaid costs, the hospital stands to be repaid by DHH for these rental costs."[264] In short, OLOL, on paper, is obligated to pay the state the mentioned sum of

---

[261] Ibid., p. 15.
[262] Ibid., p. A1.
[263] Ibid., p. A2.
[264] Ibid., p. A2.

money, the former will recover its lease payment to the state, along with its receipt of uncompensated care costs (UCC). OLOL is a big winner in this privatization sweepstakes; the big loser is the Louisiana Citizens; the Jindal Administration was s/elected to make sure the Louisiana Citizens are big losers by its willingness to transfer the Louisiana Citizens' tax dollars that were budgeted for Earl K. Long Hospital to OLOL.

The Louisiana State Government obligation to OLOL is a *financially massive one.* Gregory and Neustrom outlined it as follows:

> "The state's obligation is to pay OLOL 100% of their UCC cost for caring for patients who earn less than 200% of the federal poverty level and 95%of Medicaid costs. The CEA budget worksheet calls for an estimated total payment of $185.7 million for fiscal year 2014. There is no cost cap on this CEA, so if OLOL's expenses for care exceed this amount, the state is obligated to pay their costs. OLOL Hospital assumed additional financial risk by entering into the first private collaborative with Louisiana State University. A component of this public/private partnership was the closure of inpatient services at Earl K. Long (EKL) Hospital…During fiscal year 2011, Medicaid paid supplemental payments to OLOL in the amount of $129 million for inpatient and outpatient services."[265]

The $129 million was paid to OLOL in 2011 by Medicaid; during Fiscal Year 2014, OLOL is expecting to receive an estimated $185.7 million as part of the state obligation to it. Two hundred years ago, during American Slavery, the wealthy slave master profited off of the labor power of the African Slave; today, the former is profiting off of the basic health needs of the descendants of the African Slaves and others, whom the slave master profited off of two hundred years earlier. Nothing is new regarding this exploitation. Its just dressed up real nice in a modern day *Cooperative Endeavor Agreement.* What are the Terms of this agreement? Gregory and

---

[265] Ibid., p. A2.

Neustrom stated "the term of the agreement is 10 years with automatic renewal in one year increments after five years for a rolling five-year term."[266] The CEA will yield a steady avalanche of income/profits for OLOL well beyond 2020.

b-3:Interim LSU Public Hospital In New Orleans Cooperative Endeavor Agreement, Fiscal Year 2013 And Beyond

After Hurricane Katrina, the so-called "Big Charity" Hospital was closed in New Orleans, LA. Gregory and Neustrom stated "the Interim hospital replaced what was referred to as "Big Charity," which closed post-Katrina."[267] Moreover, the private partner is Louisiana Children's Medical Center, Inc…[and,] "the term of the agreement is 42 years with automatic renewal for three consecutive 15 year periods, for a total of 45 additional years."[268] Interestingly, the CEA gives Louisiana Children's Medical Center, Inc. the right to operate the above for nearly a century, and, during this time, the latter's obligation to the state, for leasing the Interim Hospital and the new hospital when it is completed, is $33.9 million annually. However, this payment will be recovered by Louisiana Children's Medical Center, Inc. because the Jindal Administration determined the former's lease payment is an allowable reimbursement cost. Gregory and Neustrom added "this lease expense will be treated as an allowable cost in the filing of the Medicaid cost report… Thus, the private partner stands to recover most if not all of these rental costs. Once the new hospital is open, the lease payments will increase to $69.4 million."[269] As we see, there is no risk involved, and any lease capital paid to the state will recovered by Louisiana Children's Medical Center, Inc. To show just how favorable this deal is, imagine person X goes to the local Mercedes Benz Dealership and buys an E Class Mercedes Benz that costs $60,000, and pays cash for it. Then, the state allows person X to be reimbursed for this cost via Medicaid. We see person X purchased a new Mercedes Benz E Class car without losing any money. Louisiana Children's Medical Center Inc.'s

---

[266] Ibid., p. A2.
[267] Ibid., p. A3.
[268] Ibid., pp. A3 and A4.
[269] Ibid., p. A4.

mentioned lease payment works the same way. In short, the latter has no real financial obligation to the state. To the contrary, the state has a huge one to Louisiana Children's Medical Center, Inc.

When we speak about the state obligation to Louisiana Children's Medical Center, Inc., we are talking about the amount of our tax dollars that are given to the latter. Gregory and Neustrom stated "the CEA budget worksheet calls for an initial UCC payment by the state of $184.5 million and additional supplemental payments of $44.1 million in fiscal year 2014. A total of $280.7 million is budgeted for the CEA in fiscal year 2014. There is no cost cap on this CEA."[270] This is hardly believable but it is true. Louisiana Public School Teachers are being harassed, intimidated, losing their hard earned tenure, and many seasoned veteran public school teachers, are being forced to prematurely retire. Other working class people are suffering from layoffs and other workplace uncertainties. Yet, the Jindal Administration has budgeted $280.7 million to cover uncompensated care payments. Worse of all, there is no "turn-off" switch because this budgeted amount for Fiscal Year 2014 can increase since there is no "no cost cap on the CEA." This is similar to being paid a salary to work a 9 to 5 job, and your salary has no cap; anytime you feel you need an increase in salary, you just ask for one, and it is budgeted with no questions ask by your employer. Where in Louisiana, or America, can we find a working class person with this kind of pay schedule? Every CEA is like a Christmas Stocking stuffed with Louisiana Taxpayers Cash.

b-4: University Medical Center In Lafayette, LA Cooperative Endeavor Agreement, Fiscal Year 2013 And Beyond

So far, the majority of the past revenue, for the closed public hospitals, came from Medicaid and Medicare. Through the Louisiana Ruling Class' Neo-Liberal Privatization Economic Policy, the Jindal Administration, overseeing its implementation, has opened the door for huge taxpayer dollars to flow out of these state government programs into the hands of Governor Bobby Jindal's benefactors. The same is true for the above CEA.

---

[270] Ibid., p. A4.

Specifically, the private business that took over the University Medical Center in Lafayette, LA "...is Lafayette General Health Systems, Inc.... [and,] The term of the agreement is five years with automatic renewal after the first year in one-year increments to create a rolling five-year term."[271] Written in each CEA, without exception, is an implied "bail-out" mechanism, which insures one main thing, and that is, the affected private business will not ever incur any *financial lost because they have a loophole to get out the CEA in the event something changes, which adversely affects their expected profits.* As it is, there are no financial risks involved behind the scenes, but publicly, state government mouthpieces manufactures dozens by the minute to keep us unaware and very confused about the truth.

That being so, private business financial liability, regarding the CEA, will be reimbursed. Gregory and Neustrom stated "the private partner is leasing the UMC hospital and affiliated clinics. The total rental payment is $15.8 million annually. This lease expense will be treated as an allowable cost in the filing of the Medicaid cost report... Thus, the private partner stands to recover most if not all of these rental costs."[272] When it comes to the state's obligation to Lafayette General Health Systems, Inc., the former has to pay the latter millions of taxpayer dollars. Gregory and Neustrom stated "The CEA budget worksheet calls for an initial UCC payment of $48.5 million and additional supplemental payments of $46.1 million in fiscal year 2014. A total of $125.4 million is budgeted for the CEA in fiscal year 2014. There is a cost cap of this amount."[273]

It is timely to point-out here that during Governor Bobby Jindal's campaign for governor in 2007, *nothing was mentioned about the privatization of Louisiana's nine Public Hospitals, especially their closures, and the amount of state government tax payers dollars that would be given to private business.* This was not an oversight because we were not ever suppose to learn about the CEA, or the giveaways of our public hospitals to private business. Can you remember anything today that was a major issue discussed during the 2007 Governor's Race? The privatization of our public hospitals, and if this

---

[271] Ibid., p. A4.
[272] Ibid., p. A4.
[273] Ibid., p. A5.

issue had been broadly discussed by the candidates statewide, and if the details of the CEA were repeatedly made known to the Louisiana people by the candidates, via the mass media and in other forums and so forth, it is highly unlikely that Governor Bobby Jindal would have ever been elected governor. After Governor Bobby Jindal was s/elected in 2007, the first Legislative Session took up the issue of ethics reform, which was an effort expressly designed to create the smoke and mirror impression that state government is being cleaned up of bribes, fraud, and corruption. While this ethic smoke and mirror illusion was being played out publicly, one of the biggest privatization scams was being planned behind the scenes, and quietly implemented publicly. The CEA's thus far examined bear this fact out.

b-5: Leonard J. Chabert Medical Center In Houma, LA Cooperative Endeavor Agreement, Fiscal Year 2013 And Beyond

The general trend remains consistent for the above. This Louisiana Public Hospital was closed by the Jindal Administration, and it was taken over by "...Southern Regional Medical Corporation ..."[274] As with all CEA's discussed so far, the majority of the past revenue of Leonard J. Chabert Medical Center in Houma was in the form of Medicaid and Medicare reimbursements. Gregory and Neustrom stated "Southern Regional is not required to pay rent. The Terrebonne Parish Hospital Service District No. 1 will make an annual intergovernmental transfer of $17.6 million in public funds to the Medicaid program for Southern Regional and its affiliates."[275] Although Southern Regional Medical Corporation does not have an obligation to pay the state rent, a combination of local and state public tax dollars are being placed in the Medicaid program to cover the rent for Southern Regional and its affiliates. On the other hand, the state, similar to the other CEAs, is financially obligated to Southern regional Medical Corporation. Gregory and Neustrom stated "The CEA calls for an initial UCC payment of $45.2 million. A total of $85 million is budgeted for fiscal year 2014, of which $45 million will be UCC and $9

---

[274] Ibid., p. A5.
[275] Ibid., p. A5.

million in Medicaid payments to the former Chabert, and $31 million in supplemental payments made directly to the private partner, Ochsner."[276]

The term of this CEA is the same as the others discussed regarding the inclusion of a "bail-out" loophole in the event it becomes financially unprofitable for Southern Regional Medical Corporation to operate the Leonard J. Chabert Medical Center in Houma, LA. Gregory and Neustrom stated "the term of the agreement is five years with automatic renewal after the first year in one-year increments to create a rolling five-year term."[277] After an initial five year period, there is a year to year renewal clause, which will allow Southern Regional Medical Corporation to end the CEA, if its profit margin is not sufficient. Every CEA is a spectacular financial deal.

b-6: W.O. Moss Regional Medical Center In Lake Charles, LA Cooperative Endeavor Agreement, Fiscal Year 2013 And Beyond

In 2013, the above public hospital was closed. Gregory and Neustrom stated "the hospital's operations were taken over by Lake Charles Memorial Hospital."[278] A majority of the public hospital's pre-takeover revenue came from Medicaid and Medicare reimbursements. Similar to the sunrise and sunset, such payments area sure thing because many of Louisiana residents are physically and mentally ill, and the numbers who require medical attention is not going down but on the rise. Lake Charles Memorial Hospital is obligated to make lease payments the state. Gregory and Neustrom stated "the private partner will operate a new outpatient clinic to serve the former Moss patients. The total rental payments to the state are $2.4[million] annually. This lease expense will be treated as an allowable cost in the filing of the Medicaid cost report... Thus, the private partner stands to recover most if not all of these rental costs."[279] So far, there is no financial risk taken. Imagine if every Louisiana resident who is paying on a home mortgage, or is paying rent to a landlord, could get reimbursed for these payments? Our bank accounts would certainly increase, and there

---

[276] Ibid., p. A5.
[277] Ibid., p. A5.
[278] Ibid., p. A6.
[279] Ibid., p. A6.

would be more money available to live and support our families. The problem here is we do not have a state-backed CEA.

As such, the state is obligated to pay Lake Charles Memorial Hospital a significant amount of Louisiana Taxpayer dollars. In fact, Gregory and Neustrom stated "since the legislature has approved closure of Moss... The CEA budget worksheet calls for an initial UCC payment of $42.2 million in fiscal year 2014. A total of $54 million is budgeted for the CEA in fiscal year 2014. There is a cost cap of this amount."[280] Even though there is a cost cap in place, the amount of Louisiana Residents' taxpayer dollars already budgeted for this CEA is very high to start. Moreover, this amount of money will flow to Lake Charles Memorial Hospital indefinitely under the terms of the CEA. Gregory and Neustrom stated "the term of the agreement is 10 years with automatic renewal after the first five years in one-year increments to create a rolling five-year term."[281] As in the case of other CEAs, the "bailout" clause is included here also.

Of the nine closed, or privatized Louisiana Public Hospitals, four of them will begin operation during Fiscal Year 2014. As previously done, we will provide details related to the CEAs that will govern their relationship with Louisiana State Government.

b-7: LSU Medical Center In Shreveport, LA Cooperative Endeavor Agreement, Fiscal Year 2014 And Beyond

The interesting thing about this CEA is all of LSU's hospitals located in Shreveport, LA, and associated medical facilities, have been privatized. The Louisiana people paid for the construction of the above, and the Jindal Administration, and the Louisiana Legislature, have, without any public discussion, turned them over to a private business as a profit-making tool. According to Gregory and Neustrom, the "...Biomedical Research Foundation of Northwest Louisiana, Inc..."[282] took over the Louisiana Medical Center in Shreveport, LA. Before its closure, the vast majority

---

[280] Ibid., p.A6.
[281] Ibid., p. A6.
[282] Ibid., p. A7.

of its past revenue came from Medicaid and Medicare reimbursements. It is worthwhile mentioning here that the primary reason Governor Bobby Jindal came out repeatedly in opposition to the so-called Obamacare-ACA-is the latter threatened to keep these money streams firmly in the hands of government control, thereby limiting how much money could be made off of them after their privatization. As it is, no longer are Medicaid and Medicare reimbursement accounting handled by state government; it is handled by the private business included in the CEA.

As such, Gregory and Neustrom stated Biomedical Research Foundation "...is leasing the LSU Shreveport hospital and affiliated clinics. The total rental payment is $44.6 million annually for both the Shreveport and E. A. Conway facilities. However, this lease expense will be treated as an allowable cost in the filing of the Medicaid cost report... Thus, the private partner stands to recover most if not all of these rental costs."[283] As a result of its lease payments being allowable reimbursement cost by the state, Biomedical Research Foundation, similar to the other private business with a CEA, will recover its lease payments paid to the state, free of any financial risks. On the other hand, the state obligation to Biomedical Research Foundation is economically substantial. Gregory and Neustrom stated "Funding details show a total of $242 million is budgeted for fiscal year 2014; of which $21.7 million will be UCC and $29 million in Medicaid payments to LSU, and $78.2 million in UCC and $113 million in Medicaid payments made directly to the private partner, Biomedical Research Foundation of Northwest Louisiana. There is a cost cap for this CEA for fiscal year 2014 of $197.2 million."[284] This amount of Louisiana Taxpayers' dollars will end up in the hands of Biomedical Research Foundation for years to come. Gregory and Neustrom wrote "the term of the agreement is five years with automatic renewal after the first year in one year increments to create a rolling five-year term."[285] As long as this large sum of money and more continues to flow into the bank account of Biomedical Research Foundation, the terms of the CEA will result in a rolling five-year term, free of any competition. This is like

---

[283] Ibid., p. A7.
[284] Ibid., p. A7.
[285] Ibid., p. A7.

an Alaskan grizzly bear feasting on salmon fish swimming upstream in shallow water. Similar to the privatization of healthcare in Northwest LA, or the conversion of Louisiana residents' basic health needs into a commodity, the same was done in Northeast LA.

b-8: E.A. Conway Medical Center In Monroe, LA Cooperative Endeavor Agreement, Fiscal Year 2014 And Beyond

The above privatized Louisiana Public Hospital is located at 4864 Jackson Street, Monroe, LA. As we have already seen, the privatization of healthcare stretches from New Orleans, LA to the farthest points in North Louisiana, including Shreveport and Monroe. Consistent with the other privatized public hospitals, Medicaid and Medicare contribute a substantial amount of revenue to the above CEA. Gregory and Neustrom stated the private businesses that took over E. A. Conway Medical Center in Monroe "…are Biomedical Research Foundation of Northwest Louisiana Inc…and BRF Hospital Holdings LLC. However, the partner has contracted with a firm, Alverez and Marsal, to manage and operate the hospitals."[286] As it is for the other CEAs already discussed, the two private businesses will recover the lease payment it is obligated to pay the state in the form of reimbursements. According to the CEA,

> "The private partner is leasing the Conway hospital and affiliated clinics. The total rental payment is $3 million annually and is included in the amount above for the Shreveport hospital. This lease expense will be treated as an allowable cost in the filing of the Medicaid cost report…Thus, the private partner stands to recover most if not all of these rental costs."[287]

In short, competition, and the financial risk that accompany it, has been eliminated by the CEA. However, the state's obligation to Biomedical Research Foundation of Northwest, LA, Inc. and BRF Hospital Holdings

---

[286] Ibid., p. A8.

[287] Ibid., p. A8.

LLC is a financially substantial one according to Gregory and Neustrom. The latter wrote the following:

> "LSU will operate the hospital for the first three months of the fiscal year and the partner for the remainder. Funding details show a total of $52.4 million is budgeted for fiscal year 2014; of which $6.8 million will be UCC and $3.7 million in Medicaid payments to LSU, and $22.8 million in UCC and $19 million in Medicaid payments made directly to the private partner. There is a cost cap for fiscal year 2014 of $43.4 million. Of special note: This private partner does not have prior history Operating a hospital. However, the partner has contracted with a firm to manage and operate the hospitals."[288]

Again, the private businesses will benefit directly from Medicaid and Medicare reimbursements. And, the other point worth noting is the two private businesses that took over the healthcare operation of E.A. Conway Medical Center "…does not have prior history operating a hospital."[289] This highlights the fact that privatization is a purely business venture, regardless of whether a private business has a previous history operating a hospital or not. It all comes down to making a profit off of the basic healthcare needs of the Louisiana Citizenry now into the future. Accordingly, the terms of the CEA "is a joint CEA for both the Shreveport and Monroe facilities… The term of the agreement is five years with automatic renewal after the first year in one year increments to create a rolling five-year term."[290] The pattern of making a profit off of the basic health needs of the Louisiana Citizenry today, and well into the future, holds true for the next CEA.

b-9: Huey P. Long Medical Center In Pineville, LA Cooperative Endeavor Agreement, Fiscal Year 2014 And Beyond

A state plan to relocate the above to the England Air Park changed on

---

[288] Ibid., p. A8.
[289] Ibid., p. A8.
[290] Ibid., p. A8.

September 6, 2013 "…when the LSU Board of Supervisors approved closure of Huey P. Long and the transfer of services to two private partners, Christus St. Francis Cabrini and Rapides Regional Medical Center"[291]…according to Gregory and Neustrom. Although the LSU Board of Supervisors closed Huey P. Long Medical Center in Pineville, LA in September 2013, Gregory and Neustrom stated "closure of the Huey P. Long hospital requires legislative approval, which will be sought in the 2014 legislative session. The transition is expected to occur by June 30, 2014…"[292] One thing is for sure, and that is, when the 2014 Legislative session takes place, the mass media will not publicly broadcast any news about this CEA. Only a homogenized group of Louisiana Legislators and media representatives will know what is taking place; the majority of Louisiana Residents will be watching the 2014 Winter Olympic Games in Russia and the NBA Playoffs. Any news coverage of the decision to approve this CEA will go noticed publicly. The only time most Louisiana Citizens will learn anything about this CEA is when they seek medical attention from it, and receive a hefty medical bill for some service provided. We are only consumers in the marketplace.

The majority of the past revenue Huey P. Long Medical Center in Pineville, LA received, before its closure, came from Medicaid and Medicare. Those capitalists, who are steering the privatization bus, realize the "win-win" profits they can make off of these healthcare programs. It is similar to going fishing in a bucket. Those private businesses, who have plans to fish in this CEA bucket by June 2014, "…are Christus Health Central Louisiana… and Rapides Healthcare System LLC, a for-profit Louisiana company owned in part by Hospital Corporation of America (HCA)."[293] As you might have guessed already, these are private businesses, and the latter are primarily in the privatization of healthcare business, to strictly make substantial profits. Gregory and Neustrom stated Christus Health System's headquarters is located in Dallas, TX, and it "…is one of the 10 largest Catholic health care systems in the country."[294]

---

[291] Ibid., p. A9.
[292] Ibid., p. A9.
[293] Ibid., p. A9.
[294] Ibid., p. A9.

Regarding the CEA these two corporations are a part of, there is no clause in it that obligates them to pay the state any lease payments. On the other hand, the state is heavily obligated to Christus Health Central Louisiana and Rapides Healthcare Systems LLC. The reason the latter is not obligated to pay the state any rental lease payments is Governor Bobby Jindal agreed "...the state will provide funding via capital outlay for the establishment of the new [outpatient] clinics...in the Alexandria region to serve the former Huey P. Long patients."[295] As we see, the private businesses have no competition, and they are fishing in a bucket, similar to the private businesses involved in the other CEAs we discussed already. On the other hand, the state is heavily obligated to Christus Health Central Louisiana and Rapides Healthcare Systems LLC. Gregory and Neustrom stated in the Louisiana State Budget for Fiscal Year 2014 "...but a total of $42.7 million is budgeted for fiscal year 2014, of which $5.9 million will be UCC and $1.4 million in Medicaid payments to LSU, and $33.4 million in UCC payments and $2 million in Medicaid payments to the private partners. However, going forward the two private hospital partners are guaranteed at least $49 million together per year under the terms of the CEA approved by the LSU Board of Supervisors on September 6, 2013."[296] This is a lot of Louisiana Taxpayers dollars set aside for the two private businesses annually. This is pure corporate welfare; the state is "giving money way" in the form of capital outlay for outpatient construction, and nearly $50 million per year, for the two private businesses, to provide *the same hospital services that the state operated public hospitals provided before they were privatized.* This "fishing in a bucket" is going-on while we are being told by Governor Bobby Jindal, and his Legislature allies, that there is a "budget shortfall," and many social and educational programs that serve the basic needs of the Louisiana Citizenry must be cut, resulting in thousands of lost jobs and rising crime daily. Under the terms of the CEA, Christus Health Central Louisiana and Rapides Healthcare Systems LLC will receive this financial windfall in profits from the state government for at least 25 years. Gregory and Neustrom stated "the term of the agreement is 10 years with three automatic five year extensions for a total of 25 years."[297]

[295] Ibid., p. A10.
[296] Ibid., p. A10.
[297] Ibid., p. A10.

By receiving $49 million annually for 25 years, this means Christus Health Central Louisiana and Rapides Healthcare Systems LLC will, collectively, be "given" $1,225,000,000 by the state. This is what we mean by "fishing in a bucket." The same is true for the Bogalusa Medical Center, Bogalusa, LA, the ninth Louisiana Public Hospital to go under the privatization closure knife since Governor Bobby Jindal took office in 2008.

b-10: Bogalusa Medical Center, Bogalusa, LA Cooperative Endeavor Agreement, Fiscal 2014 And Beyond

The above public hospital, before its closure, due to privatization, continuously served the Northshore Community, bordering Lake Ponchatrain, for more than 100 years. This rich history of experience was thrown to wind when the hospital was closed down by the Jindal Administration. What is interesting about this public hospital closure is a new private business did not take it over when it was closed by the state. Our Lady of the Lake, Inc., set up its own hospital-private business-to take advantage of this monetary affirmative action. Gregory and Neustrom stated "the private partner is Our Lady of the Angels Hospital, Inc… formed specifically for this endeavor by Our Lady of the Lake, Inc. St. Elizabeth Hospital, also a subsidiary of OLOL, will operate the hospital in Bogalusa. St. Elizabeth Hospital is located at 1125 W. Highway 30, Gonzales."[298] Does this ownership arrangement appear unethical, or has a strong odor of conflict of interest? Was this development discussed democratically during the 2007 Louisiana Governors Race? It wasn't because it was not supposed to be discussed, and we were not ever suppose to find out anything about it. Moreover, the closed Bogalusa Medical Center use to serve Louisiana Citizens within a 30-mile radius of its location on the Northshore. Beginning in June 2014, the latter will be operated by St. Elizabeth Hospital is located in Gonzalez, LA, which is over 70-miles west of the Northshore Community the public hospital use to serve.

Similar to the other previously discussed CEAs, the majority of the past revenue of Bogalusa Medical Center came from state government's

---

[298] Ibid., p. A10.

Medicaid and Medicare Programs. Consistent with the trend, St. Elizabeth Hospital is obligated to pay the state for leasing the Bogalusa Medical Center. Gregory and Neustrom stated "the private partner is leasing the Bogalusa Hospital and affiliated clinics. The total rental payment is $3.6 million annually. However, this lease expense will be treated as an allowable cost in the filing of the Medicaid cost report... Thus, the private partner stands to recover most if not all of these rental costs."[299] Again, this is affirmative action; set aside money; because St. Elizabeth Hospital will be allowed to reimburse the federal government for the lease payments. Unlike St. Elizabeth Hospital's obligation to the state, which is a $0.00 balance after reimbursement, the state is heavily indebted to St. Elizabeth Hospital, and its subsidiary, Our Lady of Angels Hospital.

As such, Gregory and Neustrom stated the Louisiana State Budget has "...a total of $34.7 million is budgeted for fiscal year 2014, including $10.6 million of UCC and $3.1 million in Medicaid payments to LSU. Also, there will be $15.6 million in UCC payments and $1.7 million in Medicaid payments to the former Bogalusa Hospital, with $3.7 million in supplemental payments made directly to St. Elizabeth Hospital."[300] This is privatization at work at its very best. Huge sums, well into the millions of dollars, will pour into the private business involved in this CEA for at least a decade. Gregory and Neustrom stated "the term of the draft agreement is 10 years with automatic renewal for five-year terms."[301] In ten years, the private businesses involved in this CEA will receive $316 million. This is enough state affirmative action money to build a brand new public hospital in Bogalusa, LA. Worse, because this CEA is owned by a Catholic Hospital Organization, women, who live in the Northshore Community, will no longer have access to birth control pills and so forth. Gregory and Neustrom added "Our Lady of Angels Hospital will not be providing women's services that are in conflict with the mission of the organization, such as dispensing birth control. Women needing these

[299] Ibid., p. A10.
[300] Ibid., p. A11.
[301] Ibid., p. A10.

services will access them through an alternate provider."[302] Who is the alternate provider? This seems to place women, who earn low incomes at a definite disadvantage, regarding transportation to an alternative provider clinic, and, imagine how many Louisiana Women are at risk of dying, including their unborn babies, because they no longer have access to timely birth control, nor abortion, services in their Northshore Community, which was available to them, within a 30-mile radius of Bogalusa Medical Center, before it was closed down by Governor Bobby Jindal's privatization of all of Louisiana's Public Hospitals, over the past three years.

To sum up just how much Louisiana Taxpayer Dollars will be consumed by the privatization of all of the Louisiana Public Hospitals discussed above, Table 1.10 shows the annual amount the Jindal Administration has set aside in the Fiscal 2013 and 2014 budgets for the private businesses involved in each of the Cooperative Endeavor Agreements.

Table 1.10
Total Annual Amount of Louisiana Taxpayer Dollars Given to Private Business as a result of the Privatization of All Louisiana Public Hospitals, Fiscal Years 2013 and 2014

Name of Hospital	Year Privatized	Private Business(s)	Annual State Obligation
Earl K. Long	2013	Our Lady of the Lake	$187,700, 000
Interim LSU Public Hospital	2013	Louisiana Children's Medical Center	280,700,000
University Medical Center	2013	Lafayette General Health Systems	125,400,000
Leonard J. Chabert Medical Center	2013	Southern Regional Medical Corporation	85,000,000
W. O. Moss Regional Medical Center	2013	Lake Charles Memorial Hospital	54.000,000
LSU Medical Center, Shreveport, LA	2014	Biomedical Research Foundation, NW, LA	242,000,000
E.A. Conway Medical Center	2014	Biomedical Research Foundation, NW, LA	52,400,000

---

[302] Ibid., p. 11.

Huey P. Long Medical Center	2014	Christus Health Central Louisiana & Rapides Healthcare Systems	42,700,000
Bogalusa Medical Center	2014	Our Lady of the Angels Hospital	34,700,000
		GRAND TOTAL	$1,103,900,000

Source: Gregory, Don and Neustrom, Alison, Ph.D., A New Safety Net: The risk and reward of Louisiana's charity hospital privatizations, Publication 333, December 2013, pp. A1 to A10.

Therefore, by the end of Fiscal Year 2014, Governor Bobby Jindal, and the Louisiana Legislature, both acting in concert, approved nine Cooperative Endeavor Agreements, which will result in a *net drain* of $1.1 billion of Louisiana Taxpayer Dollars, from the Louisiana State Budget, by the end of Fiscal Year 2014. This is money the state government, prior to the Jindal Administration, used to operate the nine Louisiana Public Hospitals before they were privatized. As part of this scam, the Jindal Administration came up with more deception to get the Louisiana Citizens to unknowingly believe that *a miraculous budget shortfall has occurred, causing the observed, magical disappearance of $1.1 billion from the Louisiana State Budget*. If you recall, beginning sometime in 2010 or 2011, most of what we heard coming through the Louisiana mass media was more and more bad news about this mysterious budget shortfall, and what would be needed to resolve it. As the above Table indicates, each of the private businesses listed will share in the outflow of this huge sum of Louisiana Taxpayers Dollars, which, like a spacecraft guided by GPS, is destined to end up in their hands. The gaping hole, or budget shortfall, left in the Louisiana State Budget, was patched up with a series of state government layoffs mixed together with millions of dollars of cuts to the higher education budget. So desperate was the Jindal Administration to find money to patch up this gaping hole left in the Louisiana State Budget that it forced all of the colleges and universities to cut their budgets sharply, by reducing state revenue to them. LSU was able to use its Foundation to offset some of its budget reductions in state revenue, while, across town, Southern University Baton Rouge Campus, for example, was forced to declare Financial Exigency, or bankruptcy in October 2011, to try to deal with sharply reduced state revenue. The impact privatization is having on the Louisiana Citizenry will be felt for generations well into the foreseeable and unforeseeable future. Many unborn Louisiana Children will be born into this socially backward and economic oppression. It is not necessary to recount the wide path of social and economic destruction that privatization is having on the people here, since we have already thoroughly documented the devastation going-on in a number of areas.

In order to move the Louisiana Ruling Class' Neo-Liberalism Economic Policy Agenda forward, especially keeping it outside of any serious Louisiana Public debate in the process, Governor Bobby Jindal gave this unwritten responsibility to Mr. Bruce Greenstein, who served as the Secretary of the Department of Health and Hospitals during Governor Bobby Jindal's first term in office. To advance privatization, and in this case, the closure of all of Louisiana Public Hospitals, it was critical to have someone working inside of the Department of Health and Hospitals, who had the final authority to develop, approve, and implement privatization policy. A chicken in the chicken coupe is not going to open the door at night and allow the wolves to come in unchallenged; a wolf dressed in chicken clothing is needed to open the chicken coupe door so the wolves could come in in the middle of the night and eat up all the chickens inside the chicken coupe. It is very important to get the majority of the chickens to think that one of them is always protecting the chicken coupe door. This deception causes the majority of the chicken in the chicken coupe to relax before they are awakened by the surprised arrival of the wolves in the middle of the night. By this time, it is much too late to do anything but accept their fate.

As such, Mr. Bruce Greenstein played this role at the Department of Health and Hospitals by working out the details required to obtain legislative approval for the closure of all nine Louisiana Public Hospitals. Any reports, data, legal documents, or terms needed to justify this end, were provided in a timely fashion to any legislative committee that requested them. Mr. Bruce Greenstein did an outstanding job preparing the way for the closure of all nine of the Louisiana Public Hospitals. He resigned from his job as head of the Department of Health and Hospitals, when he carelessly allowed himself to be exposed in a conflict of interest scam. To follow is what happened to Mr. Bruce Greenstein after he had worked to set up the closure of all nine of the Louisiana Public Hospitals. Before we move forward, keep in mind that Governor Bobby Jindal assured the Louisiana Citizens that his ethics reforms have wrung all of the corruption out of state government.

c. Bruce Greenstein: Privatization Architect Of The Louisiana Public Hospitals, 2008 to 2013

It is necessary to mention here that Mr. Bruce Greenstein was the architect, who worked in the trenches, to implement the neo-liberalism privatization plan, which diverted funds from the Louisiana Healthcare Budget into the coffers of private businesses, with the blessings of the Jindal Administration. He recently resigned his position as the Secretary of the Department of Health and Hospitals (DHH) because of a federal investigation into the role he played in making it possible for a business he formerly worked for to receive a large out-sourced contract with DHH, as a result of suspected bid-rigging. When a hunter does not need a Labrador Retriever to fetch his ducks anymore because they land two feet in front of him, the hunter becomes careless and arrogant, and he could make a major mistake of one kind or another. Mr. Bruce Greenstein engaged in corruption so often that it seemed normal. Marsha Shuler reported the following:

> "A federal grand jury is investigating the Jindal administration's award of a $185 million contract, according to a subpoena. The Baton Rouge-based federal grand jury subpoenaed documents related to the state's awarding of the contract for Medicaid claims processing to a company for which the state's health chief once worked. Client Network Services Inc., called CNSI and based in Gaithersburg, Md., was awarded the contract in 2011 amid some complaints that the company "low balled" the price and made erroneous assumptions in its proposal. The contract was awarded by the State Department of

Health and Hospitals and signed off on by the Jindal administration amid complaints from other vendors. At the time, State Health Secretary Bruce Greenstein, a one-time CNSI executive, said he took himself out of the contract dealings. Documents revealed Greenstein influenced a document change that allowed CNSI to compete. The CNSI contract has been amended once since it was signed, increasing its $185 million cost by about $9 million. CNSI takes over the processing of Medicaid claims from doctors, hospitals and others who provide health care services to the poor in 2014. At that time, the full conversion from current *vendor Molina would occur."* [303]

The Client Network Services Inc. contract with DHH is an arrogant privatization deal gone bad. If the other bidders on this contract had not vehemently complained, there would not have been any federal grand jury investigation, and Mr. Bruce Greenstien would not have resigned his post as Secretary of the Department of Health and Hospitals. As we have seen thus far, this CSNI Inc. conflict of interest deal is the tip of an iceberg. Melinda Deslatte reported on his departure after the evidence of corruption became transparent. She reported the following:

"Louisiana Gov. Bobby Jindal's health secretary and close ally, Bruce Greenstein, is resigning amid ongoing state and federal investigations into the awarding of a Medicaid contract to a company where Greenstein once worked, officials said Friday. The Jindal administration canceled the nearly $200 million contract with Maryland-based CNSI last week after details leaked of a federal grand jury subpoena involving the contract award. When the Medicaid contract was awarded two years ago, Greenstein denied any involvement in the selection. But he acknowledged under questioning from lawmakers

---

[303] Shuler, Marsha, "Federal grand jury looks at Jindal administration contract," The Advocate, March 21, 2013, pp. 1 and 2.

in his 2011 confirmation hearing that a change he pushed in the bid solicitation made CNSI eligible for the Medicaid contract. He also met with a top CNSI official within days of taking the health secretary's job. The state attorney general's office has said the 10-year contract for Medicaid claims processing and bill payment was improperly handled, and it is conducting its own criminal investigation into the contract award. David Caldwell, head of the attorney general's public corruption unit, said there was inappropriate contact between CNSI and DHH employees, among other issues. In a statement, Jindal praised Greenstein's tenure at the health department, during which he oversaw the privatization of many state-run health facilities and shifted much of the Medicaid program to private managed care. Greenstein also has been the architect of Jindal's ongoing push to privatize the LSU-run public hospitals that care for the poor and uninsured and that train many of Louisiana's medical students, an effort that has been criticized as poorly handled. Greenstein worked for CNSI from 2005 to 2006."[304]

In addition to the Mr. Bruce Greenstein unethical activity scandal (Recall, when Governor Bobby Jindal entered his first term in 2008, the first Legislative Session took up the ethic torch to cleanse Louisiana State Government of rampant corruption), and while he served as Secretary of DHH, one of his own staff members stole more than a million dollars of Louisiana Taxpayers' money. According to The Advocate staff report,

> "a former state Department of Health and Hospitals accountant was arrested Tuesday[June 4, 2013] on allegations she defrauded the state's Medicaid program out of more than $1 million — money she allegedly used for gambling at area casinos. Deborah Crowder Loper,

---

[304] Deslatte, Melinda, "Greenstein resigns post, " The Advocate, March 29, 2013, pp. 1 and 2.

46, 9642 Hardwood Drive, was booked into the East Baton Rouge Parish Prison on counts of theft by fraud, money laundering, and malfeasance in office for using her position to misappropriate public funds for personal use, authorities said in a news release. Attorney General Buddy Caldwell said Loper would be prosecuted "to the fullest extent of the law."[305]

Mrs. Loper's action must not be viewed separate from Mr. Bruce Greenstein's. The latter, carrying-out instructions from Governor Bobby Jindal, created a culture of corruption in the Louisiana Department of Health and Hospitals during the latter's first term. Mrs. Loper was just acting on what she felt was going-on all around her-stealing via fraudulent deals inspired by Mr. Bruce Greenstein. The latter made it possible for the multi-million dollar robbery of DHH's budget. Yet, Attorney General Buddy Caldwell said he plans to prosecute Mrs. Loper "to the fullest extent of the law." No word of prosecution was ever mentioned by Attorney General Buddy Caldwell, regarding the $185 million plus robbery of the DHH Budget, which was made possible by Mr. Bruce Greenstein. We are not saying, by any stretch of the imagination, that Mrs. Loper should not be prosecuted, but, more importantly, we are equally making note of the fact that some people have immunity from prosecution because their crimes are committed with prior knowledge of protection from prosecution by Attorney General Buddy Caldwell. This is a classic case of the small fish being sent to prison while the big fish continue to rob the Louisiana State Budget in broad daylight.

Before we show the tornado-like destruction of the Louisiana Public Healthcare System, which Mr. Bruce Greenstein is given the honor of being Governor Bobby Jindal's "hitman," it is noteworthy here to say that Mr. Greenstein's old employer, Client Network Services Inc., who he worked for before becoming Governor Bobby Jindal's Privatization "Hitman," has not gone away, although Governor Bobby Jindal ordered DHH to terminate the sweetheart deal gone bad with CNSI, Inc. to

---

[305] _____ "Former DHH employee accused of swindling $1 M in Medicaid funds," *The Advocate*, June 04, 2013, p. 1.

privatize a part of DHH's operation. As we have already seen, a hefty grant worth millions of dollars was involved. Today, CSNI, Inc. has filed a lawsuit against the Jindal Administration to recover the stolen Louisiana taxpayers' dollars it was *illegally awarded by the former in the first place.* This is a case of one thief becoming angry with the other. Marsha Shuler wrote the following:

> "Client Network Services Inc. filed a lawsuit Monday[May 6, 2013] over the Jindal administration's cancellation of a nearly $200 million contract for state Medicaid claims processing. The lawsuit, filed in 19th Judicial District Court, alleges "bad faith breach of contract" and seeks financial damages, including for harm to the Maryland-based company's reputation and business losses. Last week the administration rejected a settlement offer made by Client Network Services Inc., or CNSI, serving notice that an effort will be made to recover some of the $17 million the state paid the firm since it started work in 2012."[306]

Lastly, the CSNI, Inc. lawsuit reveals two symbolic things. First, it reveals the type of people the Jindal Administration has been dealing with since it came into office in 2008. Second, and more importantly, it reveals that CSNI, Inc. has no shame when it comes to money; it will do anything to get its hands on some, and it will demand money, publicly, that was illegally stolen as we have pointed-out already.

In short, Mr. Bruce Greestein, before his downfall as secretary of the Louisiana Department of Health and Hospitals, served as the architect that set in motion a privatization plan that, by the beginning of Governor Bobby Jindal's second term in office, led to the privatization of all of Louisiana's Public Hospital, and thousands of hospital workers were fired in the process. As we have already seen, this privatization plan has been achieved. One would think the Greenstein Conflict of Interest Scandal was enough to chase the ground hogs back into their holes; however, when

---

[306] Shuler, Marsha, "CSNI files suit against state," <u>The Advocate</u>, may 7, 2013, p. 1.

the kind of state government corruption we have seen taking place in Louisiana receives no serious attention from anyone, the latter only inspires a desire for more and more greed, or opportunities to rob the Louisiana State Budget.

For example, in early January 2014, Governor Bobby Jindal awarded a substantial government contract to a private business to look for ways to save the Louisiana Government more taxpayer dollars. Ironically, savings is a myth because rather than any identified taxpayer dollars that could be saved, which desperately need to be allocated to satisfy the basic needs shortfalls of the Louisiana Citizenry, a vast majority of any located taxpayer dollars, are, unfortunately, "given" to private businesses through the privatization process. According to Michelle Millhollon, the odor of corruption is impossible to overlook. She wrote the following:

> "Gov. Bobby Jindal wants to spend money to save money. The Jindal administration announced Friday [January 3, 2014] that a private consultant will receive $4 million to identify cost savings across state government. Tapped for the job was Alvarez and Marsal, the same New York-based global management firm that assessed the state's tax structure for the governor's failed tax overhaul last year…. Alvarez and Marsal and its subcontractors are tasked with brainstorming for improvements in the way the state delivers and manages health care, transportation, public safety and debt collection, among other areas. The administration emphasized that no net new taxes will be accepted as a workable idea."[307]

This is another excellent example of our "Fishing in a Bucket" metaphor, which, in short, demonstrates that the above $4 million contract awarded to Alvarez and Marsal is given to this private business to simply engage in a "Brainstorming Activity." Have you ever been given $4 million to do some brainstorming? Besides, to find better ways to make state government

---

[307] Millhollon, Michelle, "Jindal spending $4 million to find savings," The Advocate, January 3, 2014, P. 1.

operate more efficiently, and at lower costs, is the direct responsibility of the high paid department heads appointed by Governor Bobby Jindal when he took office in 2008. If Alvarez and Marsal is doing the jobs of Governor Bobby Jindal's department heads, why do we need the latter? This would obviously eliminate the duplication of effort, and save taxpayer dollars. But, this is not the goal; the latter is to waste as much Louisiana Taxpayer Dollars as possible.

Saving money is achieved via privatization based on massive layoffs. This occurred during the privatization of all of Louisiana Public Hospitals during Governor Bobby Jindal's second term in office.

d. Impact Of Privatization Of Louisiana Public Hospitals On Hospital Employees And Patients, 2013

Consider what Marsha Shuler recently reported on March 11, 2013.

"Much of the budget savings associated with the Jindal administration's privatization of LSU public hospitals comes from a $400 million reduction in funding for employee pay and benefits as hospital workers lose their state jobs across south Louisiana. Gov. Bobby Jindal's proposed $24.7 billion budget for the fiscal year beginning July 1, strips funding for hospitals in Baton Rouge, New Orleans, Lafayette, Houma, Bogalusa and Lake Charles, impacting potentially about 5,000 employee jobs. The hospitals are six of the seven medical facilities under the LSU Health Care Services Division that the Jindal administration wants to turn over to private operation. The initial current fiscal year budget included $439.2 million for employee salaries and benefits at the seven hospitals and for LSU Health Care Services Division central office staff, according to LSU HCSD records. Now all that's left is funding for Lallie Kemp Regional Medical

Center in Independence, including $18.66 million for salaries and benefits for employees."[308]

Close to one half billion dollars have been drained out of the Louisiana Health Care Budget during Governor Bobby Jindal's first term in office as a result of the privatization of Louisiana's Public Hospitals. One can easily ask an obvious question again, namely, why do the Louisiana Citizenry need a government when the majority of the money the Louisiana State Government is supposed to use to care for the health needs of its people has been transferred to private business? Is there a need for a Louisiana State Government beyond passing laws that subsidize and privatize nearly every critical component of the Louisiana State Budget? Shuler said "hospital privatization could impact thousands of state workers." There is no need to speculate any further because the "could" became "reality" by March 2013. Shuler substantiated this fact as follows:

> "Staff levels at LSU's Earl K. Long Medical Center and its clinics have declined so much that LSU officials have had to reduce both inpatient and outpatient clinic services to the poor and working uninsured in the Baton Rouge area. The number of employees leaving picked up in late January when LSU officials moved the Earl K. Long facility's closure date up to April 15 from its original November target and decided to turn over operation of its four free-standing clinics to Our Lady of the Lake Regional Medical Center, locally called the Lake, instead of keeping them under LSU. The Lake becomes home to LSU's inpatient hospital care and medical education programs on April 15. The state employees lose their state jobs with the privatization move."[309]

The most vulnerable segments of our Louisiana Citizenry are being

---

[308] Shuler, Marsha, "Hospital privatization could impact thousands of state employees," The Advocate, march 11, 2013, p. 1.
[309] Shuler, Marsha, "Loss of staff at EKL forces large reduction to activity," The Advocate, march 06, 2013,. 1.

heavily impacted, and that is not to say the least, that Louisiana families are suffering tremendously due to layoffs as a result of Governor Bobby Jindal's implementation of the Louisiana Ruling Class' Neo-Liberalism Privatization and Subsidization Economic Policies. As for people needing immediate hospital care, Shuler added the following:

"Dr. Kevin Reed is LSU's associate dean for Baton Rouge affairs and an associate professor of medicine. He said inpatient and outpatient capacity has to be based on staffing levels…"As we move closer and closer to the transition, our ability to staff beds has become increasingly difficult because of the attrition of staff," Reed said. The impact is being felt more dramatically on the outpatient side, where current patients are having difficulty scheduling appointments and new patients are on waiting lists, he said. Surgical clinic activity has also been negatively affected…. State Civil Service statistics show that there were 1,078 hospital and clinic employees as of June 29 at the Earl K. Long facility. As of March 1, there were 794 employees — a reduction of 284. Reed said there are particular shortages in primary care providers who are the key to providing medical services. The hospital, which had 76 staffed beds last fiscal year, downsized to 15 staffed beds this month. Ten staffed emergency room beds are stillavailable. Reed said the reduction in patients also will affect physicians in training and medical student experiences needed for graduate medical education and degree programs during the transition."[310]

As we have already seen, a majority of this social devastation was orchestrated during the Jindal Administration's first term by Mr. Bruce Greenstein, who, as we mentioned earlier, resigned due to conflict of interest corruption in the CSNI Inc. Medicaid Privatization deal. By the end of March 2013, the only thing left to seal the fate of Louisiana Public Hospitals was an awaited decision by the Louisiana Civil Service

[310] Ibid., pp. 1 and 2.

Commission, either to approve massive layoffs of healthcare workers or disapprove them. The decision was made in early April 2013, and it was not in favor of the Louisiana Citizenry in need of healthcare services, or in favor of the healthcare workers who provide such services to them. Shuler reported the effect of the Civil Service Commission action as follows:

> "More than 700 employees of the LSU Earl K. Long Medical Center and its clinics will lose their jobs in two weeks as a result of action taken Tuesday by the state Civil Service Commission. The seven-member commission voted 4-2 in favor of a public-private partnership deal, in which Our Lady of the Lake Regional Medical Center becomes home to the LSU public hospital's inpatient care and medical education programs, effective April 15. The Lake also takes over management of the LSU hospital's outpatient clinics the same day. Dr. Michael Kaiser, LSU Health Care Services Division chief executive officer, said all 777 employees of the hospital and its clinics located throughout the city will lose their jobs. About 215 Earl K. Long employees have been hired by the Lake, "and there's more in the pipeline," he said. Kaiser told the commission that the deal will produce a $110 million budget savings in the first year, rising to $117 million annually in year three of the 10-year initial agreement."[311]

In addition to this unheard-of sums that will be realized due to healthcare privatization, more taxpayer dollars will be realized by private-owned hospitals. In particular, prisoners, who formerly received healthcare from the EKL Medical Center, will now rely on such services provided by private hospitals. Shuler reported the following:

> "The state will rely on Baton Rouge-area hospitals to provide emergency care for prisoners with the closure of LSU's Earl K. Long Medical Center, according to plans

---

[311] Shuler, Marsha, "EKL layoffs of 700+ OK'd: Job losses effective April 15," The Advocate, April 02, 2013, p.1.

provided by state corrections officials... The Baton Rouge area is the highest demand area for state prisoner care with four institutions that have traditionally relied on LSU Earl K. Long hospital in north Baton Rouge. The prisons are Louisiana State Penitentiary at Angola; Elayn Hunt Correctional Center and the Louisiana Correctional Institute for Women, both at St. Gabriel; and Dixon Correctional Institute at Jackson... Last state fiscal year, $3.44 million was spent on in-patient inmate care at the north Baton Rouge hospital, according to statistics from the LSU System."[312]

As we see, besides the large sums of taxpayer dollars that will be generated by the 18,000 Louisiana Uninsured Residents, private business will receive another $3 million plus taxpayer dollars by providing prisoner healthcare. Similarly, if the money from Obamacare could be directed solely to private healthcare businesses, Governor Bobby Jindal would be highly in favor of approving the Affordable Care Act Program in Louisiana.

Done. This is a message we get when we request an action using the internet. In this case, DONE means the privatization deal, or the transfer of a vast majority of Louisiana Public Hospitals formerly managed by LSU to Our Lady of the Lake Regional Medical Center, was successful. Our Governor Bobby Jindal "...pushed the deal..."[313]and he said it will save the Louisiana taxpayer $400 million. A good algebra student in high school could figure out that this deal only helps Our Lady of the Lake Regional Medical Center. For example, as Marsha Shuler pointed-out, in the first year of the 10 year deal, $110 million will be transferred to Our Lady of

---

[312] Shuler, Marsha, "EKL closure will transfer prisoner care," The Advocate, April 13, 2013, p. 1. "Prisoners in Louisiana are being treated and screened for illness, injuries...at lockups rather than hospitals more than ever before...since the closure... of the Earl K. Long Medical Center...The state corrections department...saw an injection of millions of dollars previously allocated to inmate treatment at Louisiana's public hospitals, in 2013 were mostly turned over to private operators." Wallace, Ben, "Closure of public hospitals result in heavier price tag," The Advocate, November 29, 2014, p. 1.

[313] Ibid., p. 1.

the lake Regional Medical Center, rising to $117 million by the third year; the $117 million will be realized annually, from the third year of the deal to the tenth year. Our high school algebra student would have to simply add up the millions of dollars to understand total amount of taxpayer dollars that will be transferred to Our Lady of the Lake regional Medical Center, which use to be used to pay the salaries and benefits of Louisiana healthcare workers. The total amount is as follows: $1,156,000,000. Shuler quoted the vice chairman of the Civil Service Commission saying, "If I understand correctly, the savings occur because you no longer have the employees you have now," said John McLure, vice chairman of the Civil Service Commission. "You no longer have to pay those employees."[314] Interestingly, without the salaries of the laid-off healthcare workers, do you think Our Lady of the Lake Regional Medical Center would have come forward and put $1.2 billion on the table to improve healthcare provided by the Louisiana Public Hospitals? This is about business and healthcare for the Louisiana Citizenry is secondary. Shuler stated "Rene Torregrossa, a medical technician with the Earl K. Long facility, said the privatization is being pushed "in the name of politics and political ambition." What is being dismantled is "the safety net system in which everyone is eligible for care," she said."[315] With all of the Louisiana Public Hospitals now privatized statewide, there is no so-called safety net for the Louisiana Citizenry, especially the working class. State Representative Regina Barrow recently demonstrated just how dangerous it is now for the Louisiana Uninsured in her district to access healthcare services located at Woman's Hospital in South Baton Rouge. Mark Ballard put the dangerous journey in perspective as follows:

> "State Rep. Regina Barrow hiked Thursday morning on the shoulder of Airline Highway, as cars and trucks whizzed by, to demonstrate what poor and uninsured pregnant women have to go through since LSU closed its North Baton Rouge obstetrics clinic. Since September, the former obstetrics and gynecology, or OB-GYN, patients of the LSU clinic have to travel to the...Woman's Hospital

---

[314] Ibid., p. 1.
[315] Ibid., p. 2.

in south Baton Rouge... Barrow, D-Baton Rouge...walked
up the driveway off Pecue Lane in south Baton Rouge past
Canadian Geese swimming in a curving pond. She was
near the end of a mile-and-a-half trek from the nearest
bus stop, at South Sherwood Forest Boulevard and Airline
Highway. "It's just that you can't get here unless you drive.
It's something that the people in (Gov. Bobby Jindal's)
administration should have thought about. They're
absolutely clueless," Barrow said, adding that a low-cost
shuttle could alleviate much of the problem. "You know,
not everybody drives. Poor people, the people who relied
on clinic at Earl K. Long, a lot of them don't have cars.
They go to work, they go to the doctor on the bus." About
18,000 poor and uninsured patients a year were seen at
the North Baton Rouge clinic site, about 1,500 outpatient
visits per month. Many of those patients live in Barrow's
district, which stretches around the LSU Earl K. Long
Medical Center into West Baton Rouge Parish... For those
taking the bus, reaching the Woman's Hospital and the
attached doctor's offices require walking across the huge
Airline Highway intersection at Jefferson Highway; and
past luxury car dealers; and on the shoulder of a four-lane
highway without sidewalks and posted speed limits of 50-
to-55 miles per hour."[316]

So, the 18,000 Louisiana Uninsured residents, who live in North Baton
Rouge, and as a result of the privatization scheme we have already witnessed,
now have to make the long, dangerous journey to Woman's Hospital in
South Baton Rouge, many, by walking on the side of four lane highways
with fast moving vehicles passing by them as they walk on the side of the
highways. We wonder would any of the individuals, who are responsible
for the closure of the Earl K. Long Medical Center-Governor Bobby Jindal,
the Louisiana Legislature, Louisiana Ruling Class, and others, would
walk, or tell their own family members, they have to walk, from North

---

[316] Ballard, Mark, "Legislator takes walk to illustrate bus problem," The Advocate,
January 18, 2013, pp. 1 and 2.

Baton Rouge to South Baton Rouge, every time they need some type of medical assistance? The privatization of Louisiana's Public Hospitals deal was sealed during mid-April 2013. Koran Addo stated the "... LSU's Board of Supervisors approved agreements that would allow private companies to operate public hospitals in New Orleans and Lafayette."[317] There is only one conclusion any clear minded person can reach, namely, that it is heartless to put 18,000 decent human beings in this situation simply because of the privatization of Louisiana Healthcare Facilities. Moreover, backing up this point, Marsha Shuler added the latest information related to the privatization mania of public charity hospitals. She wrote

> "The LSU Board of Supervisors on Tuesday approved the private takeover of four more LSU hospitals with key financial and other details missing from the agreements... The LSU board action involved LSU hospitals in Houma, Lake Charles, Shreveport and Monroe... The documents before the LSU Board for all the four hospital deals had blanks where financial terms were missing and additions were noted but the attachments were blank pages...After the meeting, LSU Board Chairman Hank Danos said the board gave authority to LSU President William Jenkins to sign documents completing the deals "substantially in the form presented."[318]

This arrogance is stunning! The contracts mentioned above all have key financial data missing so the public-you and I-will never know just how much money was given to private business to takeover Louisiana Public Hospitals. Marsha Shuler stated "the documents the board used included a "cost-analysis" sheet filled with blank spaces as well as hospital and equipment leases with no numbers. The name of the legal entity with

[317] Addo, Koran, "State analyst defends Jindal policy," The Advocate, April 19, 2013, p. 1.
[318] Shuler, Marsha, "LSU board approves privatization for four more charity hospitals," The Advocate, May 28, 2013, pp. 1 and 2.

which LSU and the state is contracting is also missing. It is described elsewhere in the documents as NEWCO."[319] Moreover, Shuler added

"NEWCO is the placeholder name for what will become a newly formed affiliate of the Franciscan Missionaries of Our Lady Health System with which LSU and the state will partner. There are references to a master agreement, which was not provided. The Bogalusa pact marks the eighth out of 10 public hospitals for which the LSU board has voted to enter into public-private partnerships as the state moves away from a state-run "safety-net" system of health care for the poor and uninsured. At Bogalusa, 530 state employees will lose their jobs with the private takeover. The Franciscan Missionaries operates Our Lady of the Lake Regional Medical Center in Baton Rouge and St. Elizabeth's Hospital in Gonzales. The Lake took over LSU patient services and medical education programs when Earl K. Long Medical Center closed April 15."[320]

As recent as June 10, 2013, more Louisiana Public Hospitals were privatized by the Jindal Administration, and more hospital wage-workers were laid-off, adding to the thousands already laid-off due to privatization. Shuler reported the grim privatization news as follows:

"The state Civil Service Commission reversed course Monday approving privatization plans for four LSU south Louisiana hospitals... More than 3,000 state employees will lose their state jobs as a result of the move. Over half of the employees work at the Interim Hospital in New Orleans... Here's the breakdown by hospital of Civil Service employees facing layoffs:1,690 at the Interim Hospital in New Orleans; 487 at the University Medical Center in Lafayette; 556 at Leonard Chabert Medical

---

[319] Shuler, Marsha, "LSU approves blank contracts, " The Advocate. June 19, 2013, p. 1.
[320] Ibid., p. 1.

Center in Houma; and 220 at W.O. Moss Medical Center in Lake Charles... A Civil Service staff analysis done based on information provided indicated a $147 million savings when the four hospitals' operating budgets are eliminated and DHH costs to pay the new private providers are taken into account."[321]

Besides the loss of thousands of hospital jobs, including the devastation job loss will have on Louisiana Working Class families, it is also interesting to note here that Marsha Shuler makes note of the fact that the Jindal Administration will give private business $147 million to operate the privatized public hospitals mentioned above. It does not make business sense for us to believe that the costs to operate those privatized public hospitals will be covered by their new private business owners. The latter are in this game to make a profit anyway they can. Thus, the $147 million in Louisiana Taxpayers paid to operate the privatized public hospitals was given away to private business. To cover up the $147 million robbery, Governor Bobby Jindal, and his Louisiana Legislature allies, told the mass media that the Louisiana State Budget will realize a savings of $147 million. This is not how capitalism works; and, if there is such a savings, then, how is the $147 million currently being used? Was it given to LSU, the Southern University System, UL Lafayette and others to increase their operating budgets? As long as we do not ask any critical questions, the privatization deals are made; wage-workers are laid-off; and we are told anything by the mass media such as a cow jumped over the moon, or if the Miami Heat Basketball Team does not win this or that game, their chances of winning the NBA Finals' Trophy will end. So, we get together, eat and drink, and this is what we talk about over and over. If it is football season, we talk about football; if it is baseball season, we talk about baseball, car racing, horse racing, and whatever is in season at the time. While all of this trivia dance around in our heads, more privatization and subsidization deals are made without the vast majority of us knowing hardly anything about them ever. Yet, when election time rolls around, and all of the posters are strewn all over the side of the highways, we are repeatedly ask to get out

---

[321] Shuler, Marsha, "Panel approves hospital takeovers," The Advocate, June 10, 2013, pp. 1 and 2.

and vote so we can make a change about political deals we know nothing about, which never benefit us either.

This action by the LSU Board of Supervisors is consistent with the privatization mentality that is sweeping across Louisiana like a fast moving hurricane. The gutting of the Louisiana Healthcare Budget is a robbery of Louisiana Taxpayers' dollars in broad daylight. The LSU Board of Supervisors approved privatization contracts with private for-profit hospitals even though all of the financial data was left blank, concealing how much taxpayer dollars were being ripped-off. Shuler stated ""I've never seen a state board approve a contract that's incomplete," said Jackson, D-Monroe. About 50 pages of the Shreveport-Monroe hospital agreement were blank."[322] The only explanation for the missing pages in the privatization contracts is there is so much money being stolen that, if the amount actually being stolen was made public, it would unleash a political backlash, leading to the awakening of the Louisiana Citizenry. If a man or woman steals a loaf of bread from Wal-Mart, or rob a bank, he or she, no doubt, would spend several decades in prison; but, for privatization robbery of the Louisiana Healthcare Budget, nobody goes to prison. Many involved in making the privatization robbery possible are given medals and certificates for being good citizens.

The Jindal Administration, via privatization and subsidization economic policies, has provided businesses with a "bottom line safety net by transferring huge amounts of Louisiana taxpayer dollars to them, without the latter having to "compete" with one another. Marsha Shuler summed up the closure of Louisiana Public Hospitals as follows. Before we proceed, it is necessary to say nothing is sacred when it involves Neo-Liberalism Privatization Economic Policies of the Jindal Administration. Huey P. Long Medical Center, located in Pineville, LA, which has served the needs of the mentally insane for a half century or more, providing critical care for one of the most vulnerable segments of our Louisiana population, was privatized in September 2013. Marsha Shuler wrote the following obituary for the privatization of Louisiana Public hospitals:

[322] Ibid., p. 1.

"The LSU Board of Supervisors approved the closure of Huey P. Long Medical Center in Pineville on Friday[September 6, 2013] as the Jindal administration neared completion of its plan to get the state out of the business of operating hospitals... Under a cooperative endeavor agreement, ratified by the LSU Board, two private hospitals in Alexandria will assume patient care for the poor and uninsured in central Louisiana within their facilities. Involved are the companies that run Christus' St. Francis Cabrini and Rapides General Medical Center... Under the deal, the two private hospitals are guaranteed $49 million a year in reimbursement for patient care after the Huey P. Long facility closes. Huey P. Long makes the ninth out of LSU's 10 hospitals to be imp-acted by the privatization push. With completion of the deal, only Lallie Kemp Medical Center in Independence would remain under LSU operation. Two other LSU hospitals have closed: Earl K. Long Medical Center in Baton Rouge and W.O. Moss Medical Center in Lake Charles. The management of six other hospitals has been turned over to private entities, including those in New Orleans and Lafayette."[323]

The way privatization works is clear. The two private hospitals mentioned by Shuler above "are guaranteed $49 Million a year in reimbursement for patient care." Moreover, the privatization of healthcare scam involves several steps: First, the Louisiana Department of Health and Hospitals must create an erroneous justification for the privatization of a public hospital. Second, the Jindal Administration must publicly deceive Louisiana Residents to believe that they will get better healthcare from a privatized public hospital, which is taken over by a private hospital. Third, the money the former public hospital use to receive for the "reimbursement of patient care is now received by the private hospital, a significant portion of which becomes profit. And, Fourth, once the public hospital has been privatized,

---

[323] Shuler, Marsha, "LSU Board votes to close charity hospital in Pineville," The Advocate, September 7, 2013, pp. 1 and 2.

or operated by a private hospital, all hospital workers and doctors' salaries are paid to the latter the same way any private business meets its monthly payroll. Medical doctors are encouraged to recruit patients so the private run hospital can increase its "bottom line" via reimbursements for patient care. The medical doctor is given a significant amount of money for patient care services rendered; the more procedures a medical doctor request, the more reimbursement fees for patient care the private hospital receives, including the medical doctor. What a sweetheart deal! As a result of the privatization of public hospitals, the basic, human health needs of Louisiana Citizens have been converted into commodities, which are bought and sold in the so-called marketplace. Effective December 2013, all of Louisiana Public hospitals are privatized, and all of them are guaranteed millions of taxpayer dollars annually in the form of reimbursement for patient care and state government tax incentives. No such guarantee is possible in the so-called marketplace, if competition governs the daily behavior of decision-makers, who operate privatized public hospital services. Unfortunately, it does not; medical costs are at an all-time high today, and they continue to skyrocket.

Worse, the Jindal Administration has turned its back on Obamacare because the former feels too much federal money, in the form of Medicaid, would go to help improve the healthcare of thousands of Louisiana Citizens who currently do not have any health insurance at all. Before we take a closer look at some of the healthcare information for Louisiana, it is necessary to briefly show that Obamacare, or the Affordable care Act, is one of the biggest insurance scams in American History.

B. Obamacare: Its Authors, Who Benefits And What Is Insured?

In an article titled "Obamacare: the Biggest Insurance Scam in History," Kevin Zeese and Margaret Flowers wrote the following:

> "The Affordable Care Act (ACA), also called "Obamacare," may be the biggest insurance scam in history. The industries that profit from our current health care system wrote the legislation, heavily influenced the regulations and have

received waivers exempting them from provisions in the law. This has all been done to protect and enhance their profits."[324]

Because the American Healthcare System ranked as the worst one in the world among wealthy nations such as France, Japan, and Australia in 2008, healthcare took center stage during the 2008 Presidential Campaign. Realizing the pitiful state of healthcare in America, the giant pharmaceutical and health products companies gave a substantial amount of campaign donations to Candidate Barack Obama. During Candidate Barack Obama's run for president, the giant pharmaceutical and health products industry contributed a total of $5,075,153 to all of the candidates who ran for president. Of the $5,075,153, Candidate Barack Obama received $2,436,836, or 48.0 percent of the total. John McCain received $801,652, or 15.8 percent. Candidate Barack Obama's contribution was double the amount he received.[325] By 2008, the basic healthcare needs of the vast majority of Americans had been successfully turned into a commodity, and the human consequences are staggering. According to Zeese and Flowers, the huge sum of campaign donations was given to Candidate Barack Obama because he was the s/elected one to address the healthcare destruction in the American Healthcare Marketplace. They stated the healthcare condition of Americans as follows:

"In reality, the US health care system is the worst of the wealthy nations. We spend the most per person, have the lowest percentage of our population covered and have poor health outcomes. Forty-five thousand adults die each year merely because they do not have insurance, and 84,000 Americans die each year of preventable illnesses that would not die in the French, Japanese or Australian health systems. Even those with insurance find it to be

---

[324] Zeese, Kevin and Flowers, Margaret, "Obamacare: the Biggest Insurance Scam in History," http://www.truth-out.org/opinion/item/1962-obamacare-the-biggest-insurance-scam-in-hi...

[325] _____Presidential Candidates: Selected Industry Totals, 2008 Cycle, http://www.opensecrets.org/pres08/select.php?pnd=H04.

inadequate when they get seriously ill. Medical costs and illness are the greatest reasons for bankruptcy, and insurance does not prevent financial ruin. Every family is touched by the failures of US health care."[326]

The large campaign donation President Barack Obama received from the large pharmaceuticals and health products industry was given to him because the former did not want any "change you can believe in" to alter by a single hair the marketplace based manner in which healthcare is provided in America, regardless whether 45,000 Americans die each year simply because they do not have health insurance. This is purely heartless, and it shows to what extent the big health care providers are willing to go to make a profit. Life, and its improving quality, means absolutely nothing to them. Zeese and Flowers stated the following:

> "A fundamental problem with the ACA is that it is based on continuing our complicated private health insurance or market-based system. Despite their advertising slogans, private insurers primarily exist to create profit for their investors or, in the case of "nonprofit insurers," to pay exorbitant salaries to their executives. They care about health as much as Big Oil cares about the environment. Health insurers make their profits from charging the highest premiums they can and by restricting and denying payment for care. They want to take in as much money as they can, while paying out as little on health care as possible. They have many tools with which to do this, and they've successfully skirted regulations for decades. When they can't make a profit, they simply pull that product from the shelf and create new products."[327]

To make it perfectly sure that there would be no deviation from the above marketplace model, the Affordable Care Act was written by an insurance company executive. President Barack Obama did not write the

---

[326] Op.Cit. See Footnote 172.
[327] Op. Cit.

document to which his name has become attached-Obamacare. Zeese and Flowers stated "The ACA was written by an insurance company executive from Wellpoint, Liz Fowler, who went on to be hired by Obama's HHS to implement the law and now works for a pharmaceutical giant. So, all along the way, the insurance companies had someone protecting their interests."[328] Mrs. Liz Fowler was well compensated for writing the Affordable Care Act (ACA). The great millions of American Working Class people *did not have anyone protecting their interests when the ACA was written. Reminds us of one of Bob Marley's lyric that says, and we paraphrase, "we don't have no friends in high society."* To the contrary, Mrs. Liz Fowler put into the 2,000 or more pages of the ACA, one diversion after another to keep the average American totally clueless about how to understand the ACA. The fact is it is never suppose to be understood. Zeese and Flowers added "the public was ready for health care reform. Knowing that the majority of the public supports a Medicare-for-all system, it was going to take serious planning to silence that majority and enact a law that protected the interests of the health industries."[329] To protect the latter, Mrs. Liz Fowler threw in the smoke and mirrors to make sure we *thought we were getting healthcare insurance, through the ACA, but, in reality, we were nothing but diners seated at the table with no food on our plates to eat.*

For example, Zeese and Flowers says the first thing that had to be done was establish a foundation for the ACA healthcare scam. This was nicely done when the 2006 health law was passed by Massachusetts in 2006, under a Republican governor-Mitt Romney, who by the way, ran against Barack Obama in 2008 for president. This was the advanced groundwork that would be much needed by 2008 when President Obama was s/ elected president. According to Zeese and Flowers, "the foundation of a scam is the preparation done ahead of time to set up the scheme. In the case of the ACA, the foundation began with the health law passed by Massachusetts in 2006. The template was created by Stephen Butler of the Heritage Foundation, a conservative think tank. The law was passed under a Republican governor, Mitt Romney."[330] In short, the unwitting, average

---

[328] Op. Cit.
[329] Op. Cit.
[330] Op. Cit.

American concluded something to the effect that, if a conservative group developed a health law that helps the working class people in Massachusetts, then this health law must be good for everybody. When is the last time you heard a conservative came forward and helped working people with anything?! But, President Barack Obama was so smooth-talking about *change you can believe in* that we simply never ask the most important question, namely, can a conservative Massachusetts health law serve the public good? Your's and mine? So, we stayed asleep through it all, and now some of us are coming from under the health law novacaine, only to find that the healthcare nightmare that was in existence before 2006, is still wreaking havoc today. To keep us from demanding free healthcare such as what exists in England, Canada, and Russia for example, Liz Fowler wrote countless illusions in the ACA.

We will address only a few here, beginning with the Medicare-for-all concept. Using the latter, a new public insurance was modeled after Medicare to compete with private insurance. Zeese and Flowers stated "to further sell the ACA, Roger Hickey, a longtime Medicare-for-all advocate of the Campaign for America's Future (closely allied with the Democratic Party), took an idea from Jacob Hacker to create a new public insurance modeled after Medicare to 'compete' with private insurance. Hickey sold the model to progressive groups, and Hacker's proposal was used by the Obama campaign."[331] We already have a Medicare For All Healthcare System in America; by using the word Medicare For All, many Americans thought the ACA was going to work for them the same way Medicare For All works for Americans once they reach 65 years old. The ACA would allow Americans to receive "free" public insurance years before they reach 65 years old. Second, after President Barack Obama was s/elected, by December 2008, all across America, people were encouraged to meet in their neighbors and friends home to discuss the ACA. Obama's transition team provided them with booklets, including tightly scripted information, to build support for the continuation of the existing private insurance Marketplace Model, which, more than 45,000 Americans die annually due to a lack of insurance coverage. Zeese and Flowers stated, during these gatherings, nothing was ever done to "…elicit citizen input on what kind

[331] Op. Cit.

of health system was desired."[332] Again, Americans were getting together, on one hand, thinking they were developing a new public insurance for all Americans, when, in reality, they were discussing keeping the old private insurance model, which later became the ACA dressed-up in new flowery words. Third, by the Spring 2009, the Obama Administration held a White House Summit to discuss healthcare reform; Zeese and Flowers stated the summit "…representatives from health insurance corporations, hospitals and pharmaceutical companies. The only groups that were not included, until there was a threat of protest, were those who advocate for Medicare for all. The single-payer advocates did not speak, but the insurance spokesperson opened and closed the White House summit."[333] The private insurance representatives were invited to the White House to tell President Barack Obama to stay with the status quo, but make the ACA seem like it is a great departure from it.

Another key illusion used to sell Obamacare was the public option. For example, if you do not have any health insurance, you would have an option to choose a reasonably low cost plan that fit your needs. On the other hand, if you already have a health insurance plan, you could shop around and find one that offers you the same services, but at a lower cost. This all sounds good and dandy, if it were true. The fact is Zeese and flowers exposed this illusion as follows:

> "The convincer for many who supported real health reform was "the Public Option." The idea was that the law would force the uninsured to purchase insurance but would include the choice of a public health insurance plan. The public was told that this option would be more cost-effective than private insurance and, thus, less expensive, which would make it more attractive. Many were convinced that a public option would become a Medicare-for-all system, that it was a "back door" to single payer. They were told that going straight to a single-payer health care system would be too difficult and that the

---

[332] Op. Cit.
[333] Op. Cit.

public option was a first step. Health Care for America
Now organized grass-roots groups to put their energy
into fighting for a public option, and many responded."[334]

Everyone who enjoys fishing knows that you must use a good "hook."
The public option was the hook that "convinced' the vast majority of
working class people that the public option would become a Medicare-for-
all-system. Zeese and Flowers further exposed the illusion of the public
option. They stated "what most people did not understand at that point
was that the public option was not only a non-solution to the health care
crisis but that it was not even destined to be in the final legislation. Senator
Max Baucus reported in March 2009 that it was a "bargaining chip" to get
health insurers to accept regulations."[335] According to Glenn Greenwald,

> "I've argued since August that the evidence was clear that
> the White House had privately negotiated away the public
> option and didn't want it, even as the President claimed
> publicly (and repeatedly) that he did...No discussion of
> the public option is complete without noting how much
> the private health insurance industry despises it; the
> last thing they want, of course, is the beginning of real
> competition and choice."[336]

If you recall, most of 2012, and during early 2013, the Republicans in
Congress, led by House Speaker John Beohner, opposed every move
President Barack Obama, and the Democrats made, regarding getting
Obamacare-ACA-enacted into law. Thus, the illusion is unraveled as
follows: Publicly, President Barack Obama told the American People he
wanted the public option, yet privately the Wall Street Health Industry
capitalists already knew he would be privately opposed to it before he was
given the green light to run for president in 2007. On the other hand, while

---

[334] Op. Cit.
[335] Op. Cit.
[336] Greenwald, Glenn, "The 'Public Option': Democrats' Scam Becomes More
Transparent," http://www.commondreams.org/headline/2010/03/12-5, Tuesday,
December 17, 2013.

President Barack Obama publicly lied to the American People that he was for the public option, the Republicans opposed President Barack Obama's illusionary public support of the public option. *In short, President Barack Obama and Congressional Republicans both supported the non-inclusion of a public option in Obamacare-ACA.* To the unwitting American, suffering from the massive weight of healthcare cost, or having no healthcare insurance at all, watched months of partisan fighting between President Barack Obama and Congressional Republicans, although both agreed privately that both parties-Democrats and Republicans- 100% supported the *abortion of the beginning of real competition, a reality that the majority of the private health industry despises.* Zeese and flowers stated "The public option was just part of the con."[337]

Even though President Obama, and the Republicans, were both against "any real change" in the existing private marketplace driven healthcare system, it was essential, for both of them, to trick the American people to believe President Obama wanted a new healthcare system with a public option that would make health insurance *affordable and comprehensive.* To fool Americans en masse, in August 2009, the Tea Party, which is connected to the Right Wing Republican Party, and according to plan, intentionally attacked Obamacare publicly, calling it government-run and socialism among many others. It should be pointed-out here that the crisis was timed to occur after every possible aspect of the Obamacare, which would help the American Working Class, was vetted out of it, leaving only the status quo marketplace healthcare industry completely "unchanged." In August 2009, Zeese and Flowers wrote the following:

> "The Tea Party, backed by Americans for Prosperity (a Koch brothers front group), came out very aggressively against the ACA at local town halls. They called it "government-run" and opposed its fictional "Death Panels." This served to energize the progressive groups to rally around the president and come out strongly in favor of the law. Rallies in favor of health reform were organized across the country. Health reform advocates

---

[337] Op. Cit., Zeese and Flowers.

were activated further to support the law as the House and Senate struggled to come to consensus. As more aspects of the law that were important to health reform supporters were jettisoned, such as coverage for immigrants and inclusion of reproductive services, and the public option was whittled down to nothing, support for the law became a partisan statement of support for President Obama."[338]

At this point, the need for affordable healthcare was boil down, like collard greens cooking in a pot, to a mere support of President Obama's personality, being the so-called first black to be elected as president. The healthcare issue was forgotten. The American Ruling Class had, once again, succeeded *in getting the American Working Class to believe non-change is change we can believe in.* Put simply, like a hungry man or woman is conditioned to believe he or she is not hungry, we were, similarly convinced to believe the existing private marketplace driven healthcare industry is one in which we can obtain affordable healthcare. In a nutshell, Zeese and Flowers explained the scam this way:

> "Obama signed the ACA on March 23, 2010. Immediately the marketing began. The three words we heard the most to describe it were *universal, affordable* and *guaranteed.* Of course, the ACA is none of those…Progressive groups started the work of explaining the advantages of the new health law to the public. The few positive aspects of the law were promoted without explaining the big picture. Overall, the ACA is similar to other neoliberal economic policies; it defunds and destroys our public health insurances and further privatizes health care. The end goal of the ACA con, to make sure people do not realize they have been conned, is ongoing."[339]

---

[338] Op. Cit.
[339] OP. Cit.

In short, the health condition of millions of Americans is right where it was before President Barack Obama was s/elected the first African-American President of the United States. No surprise. Zeese and Flowers stated "a fundamental problem with the ACA is that it is based on continuing our complicated private health insurance or market-based system. Despite their advertising slogans, private insurers primarily exist to create profit for their investors or, in the case of "nonprofit insurers," to pay exorbitant salaries to their executives. They care about health as much as Big Oil cares about the environment."[340] It all comes down to this: The private healthcare industry, which is based on the private marketplace model, is not set up to serve the "Public Good," but, rather, it is meticulously designed to take health, a basic human need; convert it into a commodity; and then raise the cost of healthcare continuously; in order for the giant healthcare corporations, including hospitals, to realize larger and larger profits off of our illness and disease. Zeese and flowers stated "the public has been so hoodwinked by the partisan debate between Republicans and Democrats...similar to other neoliberal economic policies [already mentioned earlier]...[that] destroys our public health insurances and further privatizes health care."[341] Before we proceed, the con, scam, or trick, whatever someone want to call it, is operating fully out in the open, regarding the most recent *inability of the Obama Administration's White House to set up a functioning computer system, which Americans can log in to, and decide what health insurance coverage they desire.* We now know there is no public option. So, by keeping potential Americans from dropping an existing insurance policy, and choosing a cheaper one, the old, worn-out neo-liberal privatized healthcare industry marketplace keeps right on profiting off of the illness and diseases of millions of Americans daily. If NASA is considering sending a man or woman or both to Mars, then doesn't it make common sense that a website-Healthcare.gov, or whatever it is called, should be able to operate without a single glitch? It would do so, if it was not part of the healthcare con game.

---

[340] Op. Cit.

[341] Op. Cit.

C. Jindal Administration And Medicaid: No Expansion Of Coverage, 2013

The Public Affairs Research Council, a non-governmental research group, called upon Governor Bobby Jindal to provide any alternatives he might have for not agreeing to expand coverage of Medicaid to Louisiana's uninsured. Since the beginning, he has been totally against the federal Affordable Care Act, commonly known as Obamacare. Rather than agree to expand Obamacare, and provide a safety net of some kind for the growing pool of Louisiana uninsured-400,000 plus-, Governor Bobby Jindal has refused to expand Medicaid, and, to the contrary, provide millions of dollars to business in the form of subsidies and privatized deals that drain the Louisiana's uninsured tax dollars out of the state's healthcare budget. Shuler wrote the following:

> "The governor should explain his alternative path for health care coverage for Louisiana's uninsured if he chooses not to expand Medicaid, and the Legislature should play a role in shaping that policy," a new PAR report concludes... "If he has specific policy requests for flexibility under ACA and has not formally sought approval, he should make those requests to the U.S. Department of Health and Human Services. If an alternative plan to Medicaid expansion can be tailored to Louisiana, it deserves the public's consideration," according to the PAR report."[342]

In addition, the short form of this unwillingness to expand Medicaid coverage to 400,000 or more of Louisiana's Uninsured Citizens is the federal government spends roughly $1.1 billion annually[343] to provide medical care for the uninsured, and the Louisiana Ruling Class does not want an expanded amount of that money to bypass business in the form of federal government supported Medicaid coverage for Louisiana's Uninsured. The problem is business want to get its hands on the Obamacare dollars, and if

---

[342] Shuler, Marsha, "PAR seeks Jindal Medicaid explanation," The Advocate, march 12, 2013, p. 1.
[343] Ibid., p. 1.

they cannot, Governor Bobby Jindal has been coached to oppose Medicaid expansion in Louisiana. On April 24, 2013, the Louisiana Ruling Class got its wish. The Louisiana House of Representatives Committee killed HB 110, a bill that would have provided "free" Medicaid Healthcare to 400,000 uninsured Louisiana residents. Shuler wrote the following:

> "On a party-line vote, a Louisiana House committee Wednesday effectively killed legislation that would require state government to expand its Medicaid program to cover some 400,000 uninsured residents. The House Health and Welfare Committee voted 11-8 after five hours to involuntarily defer the legislation aimed at implementing a key provision of the federal Affordable Care Act, familiarly known as Obamacare. Involuntary deferral means the legislation cannot be brought up for reconsideration... Medicaid is the insurance program that provides medical services for the poor and is paid for mostly by the federal government, with some matching funds from state government. The Affordable Care Act would change, beginning in 2014, eligibility for Medicaid giving people with income of up to 138 percent of the federal poverty level to enroll. Today, that would mean individuals earning up to $1,285 a month. For a family of four, the earning level would be up to $2,651 a month."[344]

By 2014, the real damage Governor Bobby Jindal has done to many Louisiana Residents, as a result of his decision to not expand Medicaid, is more severe that previously thought. One group that is especially hard hit by not expanding Medicaid in Louisiana, is those residents with mental illnesses. Before we explain further, it is very hypocritical for politicians, scientists, college professors, and others to say the Americans who commit mass murders are usually those with mental illnesses; yet, Governor Bobby Jindal, for example, has refused to provide much needed healthcare to the mentally ill, when a decision was made for him to not agree to an expansion

---

[344] Shuler, Marsha, "house panel rejects Medicaid expansion, " The Advocate, April 24, 2013, p. 1.

of Medicaid in Louisiana. A recently published report, by the American Mental Health Counselors Association (AMHCA), provides data that shows how Neo-Liberalism Privatization Economic Policy is aggravating the distress of Louisiana Residents suffering with mental illness conditions. Dr. Joel E. Miller, Executive Director of AMHCA wrote the following:

> "Millions of uninsured Americans with mental health conditions find themselves living in the wrong place at the wrong time. That's because fully half of the states in the country have denied insurance coverage to eligible residents with mental health problems by refusing to participate in the federal government's New Medicaid Expansion Program. Health care coverage in the United States shouldn't be a Lottery based on a lucky location. But that's the current dismaying situation: 25 states have opted into Medicaid Expansion and 25 have opted out—including, disastrously, most of the states in the South."[345]

Overall, there are 6.7 million Americans who are eligible for health coverage under the Affordable Healthcare Act, or Obamacare. Interestingly, of this number, 4.0 million, or 60.0 percent, of the uninsured live in states that have opted out of making healthcare coverage available to them through an expansion of Medicaid. Louisiana is one of the 25 states in the South that have refused to provide healthcare coverage to its residents who are suffering "...with a serious mental illness [;] in serious psychological distress, or [;] who have a substance use disorder."[346] This is beyond cynicism, and borders on downright malicious intent, because "opting out" prolongs the suffering of Americans who are in so desperate need of mental healthcare, which an expansion of Medicaid could so easily provide them. Dr. Joel E. Miller explains there must be another reason the 25 states that opted out

---

[345] Miller, Joel E., Dashed Hopes; Broken Promises; More Despair: How the Lack of State Participation in the Medicaid Expansion Will Punish Americans with Mental Illness Report, http://www.amhca.org/assets/contents/AMHCA DashedHopes Report 2 21 14 final.pdf, Alexandria, Virginia, February 2014, p. 1.
[346] Ibid., p. 1.

of expanding Medicaid, including Louisiana, because these states do not have to use its own state tax dollars to fund the Medicaid expansion; the latter is covered by the federal government. He wrote the following:

> "With the federal government picking up most or all of the cost of Medicaid Expansion, the expense to individual states is low, making it even easier for states to opt in. These funds are already set aside in the federal budget. There is no practical or financial argument for governors and legislators in the 25 states that have rejected the Medicaid expansion to continue on their dangerous path that denies their citizens needed health care services. In this report, AMHCA details the drastic impact that living in a state without Medicaid Expansion has on health insurance coverage for adults who have mental health conditions.[347]

The invisible hand behind the 25 states' decision to opt out of expanding Medicaid, under the ACA, or Obamacare, is the continuation of privatization and the maintenance of a healthcare market in which our basic healthcare needs are packaged and sold to us as a commodity. We went into detail related to this fact during our discussion of the privatization of all of the charity, or public hospitals in Louisiana. Half of the 25 states that have opted out of expanding Medicaid are located in the South, namely, Alabama, Florida, Georgia, Louisiana, Mississippi, North Carolina, Oklahoma, South Carolina, Tennessee, Texas, and Virginia. According to Dr. Joel E. Miller, "nearly 8 in 10 of all uninsured persons with a mental health condition or substance use disorder who are eligible for coverage in the non-expansion states (3.7 million people), reside in the 11 Southern states that have rejected the Medicaid Expansion (2.7 million people)."[348] At this time, we shall examine what impact the Jindal Administration's decision to opt out of expanding Medicaid in Louisiana is having on its residents who are uninsured and who are suffering with a mental illness condition.

---

[347] Ibid., p. 1.
[348] Ibid., p. 2.

According to the American Mental Health Counselors Association Report, and in a February 26, 2014 Press release, Dr. Joel E. Miller painted a less than encouraging picture for more than 173,000 Louisiana Residents, who are suffering with a mental illness condition. These individuals will be denied health insurance because the Jindal Administration has refused to participate in the new Medicaid expansion program related to Obamacare, or the Affordable Care Act. Dr. Joel E. Miller explained the current situation this way:

> "... A new groundbreaking study shows that 173,000 Louisiana citizens are uninsured with a mental health condition, but eligible for health insurance under the New Medicaid Expansion Program. Unfortunately, Louisiana policymakers have refused to participate in the new health insurance initiative. Many of the eligible individuals have severe mental health conditions and currently have no coverage through any public or private health plan, but will be denied the opportunity to obtain coverage for treatment... The lack of coverage will deny people with mental illness affordable care."[349]

By February 2014, there were 382,000 Louisiana Residents eligible for healthcare insurance, if the Jindal Administration would have chosen to expand Medicaid in Louisiana under the ACA. Of this number, 173,000, or 45.3 percent suffer with serious mental health conditions. When the impact of the Jindal Administration's refusal to expand the new Medicaid Program in Louisiana is examined as a whole, it is absolutely amazing the numbers of people whose mental health needs will go unmet. Table 1.11 below includes the number of Louisiana Residents who suffer with a serious mental health condition, but who do not have any means of finding any relief due directly to the Jindal Administration's refusal to expand the new Medicaid Program in Louisiana.

---

[349] Miller, Joel, PRESS RELEASE, American Mental Health Counselors Association, http://www.amhca.org/assets/contents/dashedhopesLouisiana, February 26, 2014.

Table 1.11
Number of Uninsured Louisiana Residents Denied Health Insurance Due to the Jindal Administration's Non-Expansion of the New Obamacare Medicaid Program in Louisiana, By Mental Health Conditions, February 26, 2014

Age	Mental Health Illness	Not Insured By	Number Denied Medicaid Coverage
18-64	S, BD, MD*	Public or Private IP#	28,000
18-64	S, BD, MD	Public or Private IP	18,000
18-64	S, BD, MD	Public or Private IP	46,000
18-64	S, BD, MD	Public or Private IP	24,000
18=64	S, BD, MD	Public or Private IP	70,000
18-64	SP, A, MDisOrDr**	Public or Private IP	63,000
18-64	SP A. MDisOrDr	Public or Private IP	47,500
18-64	SP, A, MDisOrDr	Public or Private IP	110.000
18-64	SP, A, MDisOrDr	Public or Private IP	58,500
18-64	SP, A, MdisOrDr	Public or Private IP	168.500
18-64	D, A&D, S, AD***	Public or Private IP	72,000
18-64	D, A&D, S, AD	Public or Private IP	38,500
18-64	D, A&D, S, AD	Public or Private IP	110,500
18-64	D, A&D, S, AD	Public or Private IP	30,500
18-64	D, A&D, S, AD	Public or Private IP	141,000
		TOTAL	**1,026,000**

Sources: Miller, Joel, PRESS RELEASE, American Mental Health Counselors Association, http://www.amhca.org/assets/contents/dashedhopesLouisiana, February 2014.

*S (Schizophrenia), BD(Behavior Disorder), MD(Major Depression)

**SP(Severe Panic), A(Anxiety), MDisOrDr(Mood Disorder)

***D(Dependence), A&D(Alcohol &Drugs), S(Schizophrenia), AD(Anxiety Disorder)

#(Insurance Program)

Another **732, 500** uninsured Louisiana Residents with a serious mental health condition who are denied professional medical treatment due to the non-expansion of the new Medicaid Program in Louisiana.

The total Louisiana Population was an estimated 4,625,470 by the end of 2013. Using this number, it follows that the above 1,758,500 Louisiana Residents, who were suffering with a serious mental condition by February 2014, accounted for 38.0 percent of its adult population between 18 and 64 years old!! In addition, when we take a look at what racial group is most adversely affected by the non-expansion of Medicaid in Louisiana, we discovered that 34% of the total uninsured Louisiana population, which have a serious mental illness, and who are eligible for Medicaid under Obamacare, are African-American.[350] Miller added "over one-third of the uninsured population with a serious mental illness in the states of Mississippi and Louisiana are African-American residents, and eligible for health insurance coverage under New Medicaid Expansion Program."[351]

This massive human suffering would be understandable if the Jindal Administration did not have any way to address it; what is totally not understandable is Obamacare, or the Affordable Care Act, provides 100% federal government support for the Medicaid Program, beginning in 2014 to 2016; and, the federal government will cover 95% of the Medicaid Program cost in 2017; 94% in 2018; 93% in 2019; and 90% from 2020 on.[352] Unfortunately, the Jindal Administration has refused to take advantage of the Medicaid expansion, and knowingly, is allowing thousands of Louisiana residents to suffer, especially African-Americans, for no reason at all, except this is the kind of human suffering that must go on when Neo-Liberal Privatization Economic Policy is implemented. Corporate profits steadily rise, and working people suffer continually as a result. The non-expansion of Medicaid in Louisiana is a tactic used to by the healthcare capitalists to keep the basic health needs of the Louisiana Working People packaged as a commodity, which is bought and sold in the healthcare marketplace. Worse, Dr. Joel E. Miller reached the

[350] Miller, Op. Cit., Dashed Hopes; Broken Promises; More Despair…, p. 25.
[351] Ibid., p. 24.
[352] Miller, Op. Cit., Dashed Hopes; Broken Promises; More Despair…, p. 7.

conclusion that the 25 states, which have refused to expand the New Medicaid Program, under Obamacare-ACA-, have dashed the hopes and dreams of millions of working people, especially throughout the Deep South, including Louisiana, as we have already observed. We have included a rather long quote from Dr. Miller's research below because it shows clearly that, for millions of good, working class people, the *American Dream is nothing but dashed hopes, broken promises, and more despair and nightmares.* Dr. Miller wrote this powerful commentary on the current privatized American Healthcare System:

> "The decision by state officials to not participate in the Medicaid Expansion means that these 25 "Left Behind States" are going to commit millions of their fellow citizens who are suffering with a mental illness—as well as millions more with chronic or serious conditions—to poor health, more poverty, and more despair. The dream of receiving affordable health insurance and healthcare will be dashed...We believe the decisions of those 25 states to not participate in the Medicaid Expansion is misguided, alarming, and a dangerous stance on many policy levels—for health, budgetary and financial reasons. The health care reform law expands Medicaid eligibility and creates a way for lower-income and other uninsured individuals to purchase health insurance."[353]

In short, the Jindal Administration, and Governor Bobby Jindal's marriage to the Louisiana Ruling Class' Neo-Liberal Economic Policy, according to Dr. Joel E. Miller, is a gross mistake of irredeemable proportions. So, why have the 25 states, including Louisiana, refused to provide an opportunity for its working people, the masses who produce all value with their labor power, from which is the only source of corporate profits (Money, by itself, and no matter how much anyone has, it cannot create any new wealth; only working people's labor power can do so). Dr. Joel E. Miller sounded a loud warning, a very loud one indeed, regarding what it means today-2014-to have millions of Americans, including Louisiana, walking around with no

---

[353] Ibid., p. 30.

visible means of having their serious mental health disorders attended to by professional clinicians and doctors. He wrote,

> "There is no practical or financial argument for governors and legislators in the 25 states that have rejected the Medicaid expansion to continue on their dangerous path that denies their citizens needed health care and mental health services." [354]

This is more than dangerous; the denial of our citizens their birthright of basic healthcare is immoral, unethical, unworthy of human dignity, lacks any integrity, and it places this generation of Americans and the next at-risk to becoming a victim to aggression, crime, and a premature death. Later, we will provide information that demonstrates this reality is being acted out every day in every American city, both large and small. The theme for Louisiana is more dashed hopes, and in the Minnesota Case, an expansion of Medicaid in that state will benefit many of its citizens, who are in most need of healthcare.

D. Minnesota and Louisiana: Two States Apart On The Subject Of Medicaid Expansion

Minnesota ranks number one in the nation, regarding its healthcare programs for its elderly population. The primary reason Minnesota ranks number one in this regard is its legislature voted to expand Medicaid by approving the Affordable Care Act, or Obamacare.

Again, this is just another example of the heartlessness and lack of compassion that the Jindal Administration has toward the Louisiana Uninsured, and the Louisiana Citizenry in general. The only reason Governor Bobby Jindal was told by the Louisiana Ruling Class to reject passage of HB 110 is Medicaid would be paid for by the federal government, and many who have insurance already with private healthcare businesses, would have the choice to enroll under the "free" Medicaid Healthcare protection that would be provided by the federal government, or Obamacare. Shuler

---

[354] Ibid., p. 27.

stated" The Jindal administration puts the number of uninsured that would be covered at about 200,000, with others abandoning private insurance for the free program."[355] The average Louisiana resident does not even know what is going-on here. However, what the Jindal Administration is doing in the dark will soon come to the light, and then, the apologists will sing a common voice for the downtrodden Louisiana Uninsured, and others, to show compassion for the Jindal Administration and the Louisiana ruling Class.

In short, the only thing wrong with Obamacare, to the mind of business, is the latter cannot control the Obamacare dollars, thus, no Medicaid expansion in Louisiana. What the Louisiana Uninsured working people desire, in Louisiana's democracy, is of no real consequence. The bottom line is more important than *human pain and suffering*. On April 29, 2013, Marsha Shuler revealed the real reason Governor Bobby Jindal, and the Louisiana Legislature, do not want to expand Medicaid in Louisiana. If the Medicaid federal funds, commonly referred to as Obamacare, will help the Louisiana Uninsured, Governor Bobby Jindal instructed the Louisiana Department of Health and Hospitals to oppose any Medicaid expansion. The only part of Medicaid that the Jindal Administration has allowed to come to Louisiana is a portion that will benefit Our Lady Of the Lake Medical Center only. Shuler wrote the following:

> "In response to federal questions, state health officials scaled back their request for blanket approval of the supplemental Medicaid financing included in the private takeover of LSU hospitals. The state Department of Health and Hospitals has submitted only a request for approval of a deal involving Our Lady of the Lake Regional Medical Center in Baton Rouge."[356]

This is a calculated, egregious, and blatantly bad mistake made by Governor Bobby Jindal. In addition, the Mr. Bruce Greenstein fraud,

---

[355] Ibid., p. 2.
[356] Shuler, Marsha, "State scales back hospital request, " The Advocate, April 29, 2013, p. 1.

and everything else, is a part of a culture of greed that runs through every corner of Louisiana State Government, similar to a termite infested board. Just recently, several Louisiana medical doctors have been indicted for Medicare fraud. When Governor Jindal was first s/elected governor in 2008, his first order of business focused on *ethics reform*. However, by now, we know this was a diversionary tactic. Political and economic corruption has not come close to an end. Bill Lodge added the following:

> "two doctors in New Orleans and a third in Baton Rouge are among 11new defendants indicted as a result of investigations by the Baton Rouge Medicare Fraud Strike Force, federal officials announced Tuesday in Washington, D.C. Between $80 million and $100 million in fraudulent Medicare billings are alleged in two Strike Force indictments in Baton Rouge and New Orleans. Attorney General Eric Holder and Department of Health and Human Services Secretary Kathleen Sebelius said the 11 defendants in the Louisiana cases are among 89 announced nationwide as people who sent Medicare a combined total of $223 million in fraudulent billings."[357]

While Governor Bobby Jindal and Mr. Bruce Greenstein were privatizing the entire Louisiana Public Hospital System, and, within that same system simultaneously, millions of dollars of fraudulent Medicare claims were sent to the federal government for payment by Louisiana doctors. Worse, Governor Bobby Jindal refused to expand the Affordable Healthcare Act, or Obamacare in Louisiana, fearing, if he did, there would be less of a chance for a significant portion of those healthcare revenues to be stolen. Moreover, one of the saddest things about Governor Bobby Jindal's refusal to expand Medicaid Health coverage in Louisiana is the latter's elderly population ranks 48th in the nation, regarding their health indicators. As usual, Louisiana, once again, ranks near the bottom of the heap in another crucial social indicator, namely, the health status of its elderly population.

---

[357] Lodge, Bill, "3 La doctors indicted after nationwide Medicare probe," <u>The Advocate</u>, may 15, 2013, p. 1.

According to America's Health Rankings Senior Report, published by the United Health Foundation in 2013, Louisiana ranks 48th regarding the health status of its elderly population. Consider the following:

> *"America's Health Rankings® Senior Report* shows Minnesota at the top of the list of healthiest states for older adults. Vermont is ranked second and New Hampshire is third, followed by Massachusetts and Iowa. Mississippi is ranked 50th as the least healthy state for older adults. Oklahoma, Louisiana, West Virginia, and Arkansas complete the bottom 5 states."[358]

On one end of the age spectrum, a charter school gimmick is being used to pillage Minimum Foundation Funds out of the Louisiana K-12 Public Schools Budget. This gimmick now involves sending the MFP Funds to the General Fund line item in the Louisiana State Budget to get around the Louisiana Supreme Court Ruling, which says it is unconstitutional to use MFP Funds to pay for the tuition of public school student who formerly attended a failing public school. On the other, privatization of public hospitals has placed thousands of Louisiana's elderly population at risk because of a lack of healthcare insurance. As we have already witnessed, Minnesota voted to expand Medicaid in order to take full advantage of millions of available dollars of government funds included in the Affordable Care Act, or Obamacare. Governor Bobby Jindal refused to expand Medicaid in Louisiana, thus, causing thousands of elderly Louisianans to suffer and die premature deaths because of a lack of access to timely medical care, which could be provided to them by Obamacare at no cost to Louisiana State Government. Before we proceed, consider what Minnesota's expansion of Medicaid means for its senior citizens.

According to America's Health Rankings Senior Report,

---

[358] _____ AMERICA'S HEALTH RANKINGS SENIOR REPORT: A CALL TO ACTION FOR INDIVIDUALS AND THEIR COMMUNITIES, United Health Foundation, 2013 Edition, p. 11.

"Minnesota's strengths include ranking first for all health determinants combined, which includes ranking in the top 5 states for a high rate of annual dental visits, a high percentage of volunteerism, a low percentage of marginal food insecurity, a high percentage of creditable drug coverage, and ready availability of home health care workers. Minnesota also ranks first for all health outcomes combined, including ranking in the top 5 states for a low rate of hospitalization for hip fractures, a high percentage of seniors who report very good or excellent health, a high prevalence of able-bodied seniors, a low premature death rate, a low prevalence of full-mouth tooth extractions, and few poor mental health days per month."[359]

By expanding Medicaid, Minnesota's senior citizens will be able to maintain its national ranking of number 1 for healthcare provided to its elderly population. The latter's quality of life is high. However, on the other hand, as we have already seen, Governor Bobby Jindal opposed the approval of Medicaid expansion in Louisiana, insuring the state's senior citizens will continue to be ranked 48th overall, regarding the quality of life of its elderly population. In contrast to Minnesota's number one ranking, Louisiana had the following ranking for various healthcare indices by 2013: Overall rank-48th; Obesity (Seniors)-44th; Smoking (Senior)-48th; Diabetes (Senior)-34th; and physical inactivity-48th."[360] Given these serious health problems among Louisiana's senior citizens, what right minded person would not be in favor of expanding Medicaid, or any other program, which could potentially raise the life expectancy of thousands of elderly people, and for those who are approaching senior citizen status in a few years from now? We noted earlier that the *only reason Governor Bobby Jindal opposed the expansion of Medicaid in Louisiana is simply he was told not to by the Louisiana Ruling Class because Obamacare is federal funds, and this money cannot be easily stolen. When a way is figured out, which will allow a vast majority of the Medicaid federal dollars to be allocated by private business, then, Medicaid*

---

[359] Ibid., p. 11.

[360] _____ America's Health Rankings, State Overview, 2013, www.americashealthrankings.org/seniors/2013.

will be expanded in Louisiana. Meantime, thousands of Louisiana's senior citizens will suffer and die premature deaths.

We will see later how this action, and all of the others mentioned thus far, including many others to be discussed, combine to produce dangerously pathological behaviors among the Louisiana Citizenry. Who would deny a helpless baby, or anyone, their birthright to adequate, timely healthcare? By refusing to expand Medicaid, or the Affordable Care Act-Obamacare-in Louisiana, all Louisiana Working Class people, and their children, are suffering. One segment of the Louisiana Citizenry, the disabled, was thrown back to the dark ages when Governor Bobby Jindal recently vetoed funds in the Louisiana State Budget-HB 1-that would make it easier for Louisiana families with disabled children to receive more timely healthcare. As it is on June 25, 2013, thousands of affected disabled children will not receive quality care. Michelle Millhollon reported the situation this way:

> "funding for the disabled and arts programs fell out of the $25 billion state spending plan Friday [June 21, 2013] with the stroke of Gov. Bobby Jindal's veto pen. The governor deleted $4 million aimed at whittling down a waiting list for home-based services for the developmentally disabled. Parents of disabled children pleaded with legislators during the session to shorten the list. Some could wait 10 years before receiving services…Jindal also stripped money for children's clinics. Family violence programs [Later you will read about a grandson murder of his grandmother in New Roads, La] and an organization that helps the disabled become more independent through technological tools."[361]

Now that we know the real reason why Governor Jindal stripped the $4 million allocated to help the developmentally disabled from the Louisiana State Budget is to give private businesses millions of Louisiana taxpayers' dollars, it is laughable to read what the governor gives as an explanation for

---

[361] Millhollon, Michelle, "Jindal cuts budget items," The Advocate, June 22, 2013, p. 1A.

his heartless, cold, and calculated actions. At the core of his whining is he blames the Louisiana Legislature for not expanding Medicaid in Louisiana, yet, as we have already seen, it was Governor Bobby Jindal-himself-who instructed this body to reject any Medicaid expansion. Thus, unlike the previously discussed Minnesota Case, the funds that would have help our disabled citizens were simply refused because private business could not easily steal federal Medicaid Funds. Millhollon stated the following.

> "in his veto message, Jindal said the reduction in waiting time could not be accommodated because legislators removed too much funding for the routine increase in the number of patients being treated through Medicaid, the government program that pays for health care for the poor. The Jindal Administration contended the Legislature underfunded the state's health department by more than $20 million. "In light of the legislative reduction to Medicaid utilization, the program expansion cannot be funded," Jindal wrote again and again as he deleted lines in House Bill 1, the state operating budget for the fiscal year that starts July 1[,2013]."[362]

The disabled would have the Medicaid funds they need to live out their lives with quality and dignity if it were not for the greed of the Louisiana Ruling Class, and the willingness of politicians to act without morals or integrity who work for it. Millhollon's other article reporting on budget cuts to the developmentally disabled equally demonstrates Governor Bobby Jindal's lack of sincerity, and his "so-what' attitude toward the Louisiana working class generally. This statement is not made arbitrarily, but is flows from all of the foregoing information presented thus far showing that millions of dollars were given to private business in the form of tax breaks, leaving thousands of Louisiana residents' basic human rights needs, namely jobs, healthcare, housing, food, clothing and so forth, unaddressed. Not one legislative session has taken place since Governor Bobby Jindal became governor, whose goal was to address the mentioned social needs of Louisiana working class people. Millhollon wrote,

---

[362] Ibid., p. 1.

"In his first public comments since removing the dollars, Jindal blamed the decision on directives in the $25 billion state spending plan that legislators sent to his desk. He said the budget required him to cut $40 million, making it difficult to expand services for people with developmental disabilities. "Caring for people with developmental disabilities is important, and it is a responsibility we take seriously," Jindal wrote in a letter to newspaper editors. "We have worked hard over the last five and a half years to make things better for those who need care by implementing measures to help individuals who are ready to transition from institutional settings to more independent lives in their communities."[363]

The data presented shows just the opposite of a caring governor for the social needs of Louisiana residents. Even as Governor Bobby Jindal says he takes caring for the developmentally disabled seriously, Millhollon added "The governor's explanation is not enough for Jason Durham, of Clinton. Durham's 20-year-old daughter, Bailey, copes with severe neurological disorders. Her developmental level is similar to that of an infant. Twice, the children's health care program that the governor wants to shift to private providers saved Bailey's life through a coordinated structure of care, Durham said."[364] We have already seen the devastating toll privatization has on the Louisiana citizenry, and as we see, Governor Bobby Jindal has already tried twice to privatize the health care programs that serve the needs of children with developmental disabilities. Where will this falsehood stop? Because Governor Bobby Jindal, and his legislative allies, rejected the expansion of Medicaid-Obamacare-in Louisiana, thousands of pregnant women will no longer be eligible for healthcare through Medicaid. Marsha Shuler stated this fact as follows:

"Thousands of pregnant women will no longer be eligible for Louisiana Medicaid health insurance coverage after

---

[363] Millhollon, Michelle, "Gov. Jindal fires back on budget veto criticism, " The Advocate, June 25, 2013, pp. 1 and 2.
[364] Ibid., p.

Jan. 1 when Obamacare kicks in. Also, many of those
with disabilities will lose their Medicaid eligibility or face
a delay in receiving benefits as the Jindal administration
adjusts structures of three state health care programs
because of the federal Patient Protection and Affordable
Care Act, more commonly called Obamacare... The
Jindal Administration is changing the rules in three state
programs that will reduce the number of people eligible
for Medicaid. The state anticipates savings of $66.4
million from people moving off state Medicaid rolls...
The changes will shift about 6,200 pregnant women and
another 1,200 or so disabled to an insurance exchange
where, with the help of government subsidies, they get
policies. Medicaid provides health care insurance to low-
income people, and is paid for by the federal government,
mostly, and by state taxpayers. Medicaid pays doctors,
hospitals and others providing health care for the poor.
Medicaid covers about 1.2 million of the roughly 4.5
million people in Louisiana."[365]

In short, Governor Bobby Jindal's decision, which was crafted for him
by the Louisiana Ruling Class, to not expand Medicaid in Louisiana
was made to *throw thousands of Louisiana's Working Class poor off of the
Medicaid Rolls so they will be forced to find money to purchase a healthcare
insurance policy, of some kind, in the so-called marketplace.* Having few
dollars available to purchase such insurance, far too many Louisiana
Working Class Citizens will have no healthcare insurance at all, joining
the other nearly 50 million Americans who do have any. What is most
disturbing about this fact is, many pregnant women currently do not have
healthcare insurance to help them with prenatal care, hospital costs, and
postnatal care. Yet, Governor Bobby Jindal's Republican Party claim to
be anti-abortionists. How can, on one hand, medical care for the unborn
be taken away from pregnant women, and on the other, Governor Bobby
Jindal, and his Republican Party claim abortion is wrong and ungodly?

---

[365] Shuler, Marsha, "Changes to Medicaid expected, " <u>The Advocate</u>, July 01, 2013,
p. 1.

Making necessary healthcare unavailable to pregnant women is the same as an abortion; the risks are the same, and in many cases, the results are the same too. Moreover, what is worse is this. How can Governor Bobby Jindal say he has compassion for pregnant women in Louisiana, and at the same time, deny their unborn children healthcare, by refusing to expand Medicaid, or Obamacare, in Louisiana? Without adequate healthcare during childhoods, many Louisiana children grow up with serious behavioral problems; and yet, those mental health programs designed to address their mental health challenges have been eliminated, or their operating budgets were significantly cut.

D. Louisiana Mental Health Program, 2013

No better example of this fact is Governor Bobby Jindal did away with a mental health program that provides services to the Louisiana Citizenry with behavioral health problems. What hypocrisy!!! In the aftermath of the Sandy Hook Elementary School children murders, most of the politicians and academicians joined chorus and spoke in harmony that it is the behaviorally disturbed that commit heinous, violent crimes; and yet, Governor Bobby Jindal has stripped the above programs of funding in his FY 2013 state budget that provides medical help for the so-called mentally disturbed. We are beginning to wonder about who is mentally disturbed? Millhollon stated the following:

> "At the same time Gov. Bobby Jindal is launching a study committee on school safety, his administration is cutting a program that helps children with behavioral health problems. The Early Childhood Supports and Services program will stop providing assessment, counseling and case management to young children in low-income families at the end of the month. The program employs 76 people, who will lose their positions. The $2.8 million the program is slated to receive in federal funds over the next five months will be used elsewhere in the $25 billion state operating budget to supplant state dollars. Weak state tax

collections, coupled with education expenses, forced the governor to trim the operating budget by $166 million.[366]

There is enough confusion to go around several times or more. The early Childhood Support and Services program is ended. The $2.8 million, unlike Millhollon reported, is drained from the mentioned social program in an attempt to fill the enormous hole in Governor Bobby Jindal's FY 2013 Louisiana State Budget, which he created (!), as we have already seen, by "giving" millions of dollars of subsidies to business in the form of tax breaks. There is no such thing as any "weak tax collection" among others that are responsible for taking the $2.8 million out of the mental health line item in the budget. The preponderance of the data thus far continues to prove otherwise. Millhollon added "the Early Childhood Supports and Services program serves Orleans, East Baton Rouge, Terrebonne, Lafayette, St. Tammany and Ouachita parishes. The program is for children under the age of 6 who are considered at-risk of developing social, emotional or developmental problems...[There are]... 540 youth and families currently served through this program..."[367] We mentioned at the beginning of this discussion that the two most vulnerable segments of Louisiana society are those hardest hit by a lack of compassion demonstrated by the Jindal Administration. The termination of his program will, no doubt, have far-reaching consequences well into the future. Mentally unstable people walking around, with their behavioral needs not being served, are surely at-risk of carrying-out violent and aggressive acts later in life. Once again, Mr. Greenstein performed the budget-cutting surgery to remove the early Childhood Support and Services program from the Louisiana Department of Health and Hospitals' Budget. In fact, the architect of Governor Bobby Jindal's Healthcare Budget Cut Scheme was quoted by Millhollon as follows: "State Department of Health and Hospitals Secretary Bruce Greenstein said the program, which ends Feb. 1 [2013], was on the road map for elimination. The midyear budget cuts, he said, only accelerated the program's demise. "It's not necessarily the most efficient program," he said... He said Early Childhood Support and Services program costs, on average, $2,200 a year per child. He said the

---

[366] Millhollon, Michelle, "La. Mental health program to cease," The Advocate, January 18, 2013, p. 1.
[367] Ibid., p. 1.

Jindal administration is confident children can be treated for less money, although net savings have not been calculated."[368]

Former Senator Hubert H. Humphries was quoted earlier saying Louisiana economic policy planners for example, such as Misters Bruce Greenstein, Stephen Moret, Paul Rainwater and others, know that a decision to cut social services, which people need to remain human, such as in the case of mental health for children, will lead to pathological outcomes later. In a recent homicide case, a 24 year old male, who is mentally disturbed, murdered his grandmother in New Roads, LA. Terry Jones stated "...the Pointe Coupee Parish Sheriff's Office Thursday night named the 24-year-old grandson of fatally beaten Beulah Morris, 91, as her suspected killer. Sheriff Bud Torres said his office issued an arrest warrant on a count of first-degree murder for Brandon Battley, of New Roads."[369] It is ironic that Brandon Battley, the suspected murderer, voluntarily turned himself into the Acadia Vermillion Hospital in Lafayette, LA where he sought psychological assistance. Although this is a very tragic case, what is more tragic is the fact Governor Bobby Jindal, and his Legislative Allies, failed to provide mental health services for Brandon Battley during a time in his childhood, which could have prevented this young man from killing his own grandmother. Later, we will show exactly how the privatization and subsidization economic policies of the Jindal Administration are the ammunition that is the cause of criminal aggression and crime in Louisiana. The Brandon Battley Case is just one of hundreds of others. We noted earlier that government corruption in Louisiana is moving along at an unprecedented pace. Almost every state government department, ranging from public education to healthcare, has been adversely infected with the contagious disease of corruption known as privatization.

The Department of Health and Hospitals is a revolving door of government corruption. For instance, Michelle Millhollon turned our attention to a $363 million contract geared toward serving Louisiana Residents who have mental health and substance abuse issues. In this case,

---

[368] Ibid., p. 2.
[369] Jones, Terry L., "New Roads man accused of killing his grandmother," The Advocate, April 25, 2013, p. 1.

DHH allowed "...privately owned Magellan Health Services to handle paperwork and connect Medicaid patients with health care providers for 18 months without completing an external evaluation of the company's performance."[370] Similar to the $4 million contract awarded to Alverez and Marsal in January 2014, less than one month later, this $363 million contract awarded to Magellan Health Services has not been evaluated by the Louisiana Department of Health and Hospitals for the past 18 months. This has the odorous scent of corruption. The Louisiana legislative Auditor's Office wrote in "...an 11-page audit by the office concluded that the state Department of Health and Hospitals... will have allowed the program to operate ... without independent verification that Magellan has substantially complied with Medicaid regulations, state regulations, and contract requirements..." DHH has relied on the performance of Magellan without externally monitoring that performance."[371] Moreover, Millhollon added "the auditor's office warned that DHH could wind up renewing Magellan's contract without ever determining whether Gov. Bobby Jindal's idea of privatizing the management of 151,000 people's health care needs worked as planned."[372] What we can gather from this situation is two things: First, this is not an accident that Magellan Health Services is receiving such a large amount of Louisiana Taxpayer dollars essentially without any monitoring or evaluation. And second, the Louisiana Ruling Class has an aversion to government regulations, which is why, as we shall see later, Governor Bobby Jindal, called by Former Governor Mike Foster the smartest man he knows, is a Road Scholar. Governor Bobby Jindal has spent a disproportionate amount of time away from Louisiana engaged in fundraising, and making speeches on the behalf of other Republican Politicians. We will dig into this matter more in-depth later. Late Reggae Singer Bob Marley once sung a lyric that says "when the cats away, the mouse will play." All of the evidence thus far points to the fact that Neo Liberal Privatization Economic Policy has been playing a leading role in the absence of a democratically elected, and strong state government.

---

[370] Millhollon, Michelle, "Legislative Audit questions lack of performance review of $363M contract," The Advocate, December 16, 2013, p. 1.
[371] Ibid., p. 1.
[372] Ibid., p. 1.

Before we proceed to the next topic of discussion, it is timely to include some brief information that demonstrates that Neo Liberal Privatization Economic Policy is not adding any value to the improvement of the health condition of the vast majority of Louisiana working class people. Contrary to the belief this ideology can improve the social well-being of the Louisiana Working Class, a closer observation of material experience paints a totally different picture.

E. Inefficiencies Of Neo-Liberal Economic Policy, And Its Inability to Provide Practical Solutions to Social Problems

Given the closure and privatization of nine of Louisiana Public Hospitals previously discussed, a recent 2013 report done by the United Health Foundation contains data that ranks Louisiana's Health Condition one of the lowest in the nation. Specifically, "Louisiana ranked No. 48 among the 50 states in overall health... the report shows high percentages of Louisiana residents aren't exercising, and residents have high rates of obesity and diabetes. In 2013, 34.7 percent of Louisiana residents were obese, the worst rate in the country."[373] With more than one-third of Louisiana residents classified as obese, it follows that the private businesses that now operate the privatized public hospitals will, no doubt, make huge profits off of Louisiana's massive obese problem. It is not in the best interest of private business to try to solve Louisiana's obesity problem because that would mean a reduction in their profits. Thus, the obvious question is do private business have an economic incentive to help Louisiana residents get well? Another question that demands our attention is will prescribing prescription drugs lead to better health, or to increasing profits? Table 1.12 below shows the grossly poor health condition of Louisiana Residents by 2013, which corresponds to Fiscal Year during which all of Louisiana Public Hospitals were privatized.

---

[373] Advocate Staff Report, "La. improves one spot in health rankings to No. 48 out of 50," The Advocate, December 11, 2013, p. 1.

Table 1.12
Louisiana National Ranking Regarding
Selected Diseases, 2013

Diseases	Rank in order of Severity
Children in Poverty	50
Obesity	50
Low Birthweight	49
Cancer Deaths	48
Diabetes	48
Preventable Hospitalization	48
Infant Mortality	48
Physical Activity	47
Cardiovascular Deaths	46
High School Graduation	46
Lack of Health Insurance	46
Premature Deaths	46
Smoking	46
Violent Crime	44
All Determinants	**49**

Source: _____ America's Health Rankings, 2013 Annual Report, United Health Foundation, http://www.americashealthranking.org/LA-MS/2013.

It is interesting to note here that high school graduation and lack of health insurance are considered as disease promotion factors. What is particularly disturbing is Louisiana ranks 50th in children in poverty and obesity. Being cut-off from the satisfaction of their basic needs, many Louisiana Residents are forced to consume "junk foods," which inevitably leads to obesity and all of the other diseases show, including the previously mentioned "Diabetes Belt." Children are our most valuable human resource, and given the fact we are not caring for them, is a clear indicator that Neo-Liberal Privatization Economic Policy will only further worsen and already inoperable health condition among the vast majority of Louisiana working class people. Koran Addo added "...nearly half of all Louisiana children [are] classified as either overweight or obese..."[374]

---

[374] Addo, Koran, "Clinic opened to study childhood obesity," The Advocate, January 22, 2014, p. 1.

Moreover, it is not surprising that every day, during the 5 PM so-called news hour, one working class person's face after another is plastered on the television screen, showing who committed the most recent murders, robberies, and other violent assaults such as rape of women and children. It does not matter where you are in America, regardless of state, the real robbery of the Louisiana State Budget receives absolutely no attention, and to cover up the crime, poor, working class people, who are most affected by Neo-Liberal Privatization Economic Policy, are portrayed as senseless demons, who are, for no reason whatsoever, going around daily killing and robbing just for the fun of it. This thought recently led to the Mafia Style Execution of Michael Brown, an unarmed eighteen year old teenager, in Ferguson, Mo. As we have shown throughout this examination, this is as far from the truth as the moon is from the Earth. Later, we will discuss the poverty situation in Louisiana more thoroughly. At this point, now that we have observed the health ranking of Louisiana Youth-50th and lowest in the nation- when they embark on their life journeys, is the prospect any better for Louisiana seniors, or the elderly? The data in the following Table 1.13 demystifies any fantasies one may have.

Table 1.13
Louisiana National Ranking Regarding
Seniors Health Condition, 2013

Diseases	Rank in order of Severity
Community Environment/Macro	49
Health Status	49
Low-Care Nursing Home Residents	48
Physical Inactivity	48
Preventable Hospitalizations	48
Smoking	48
Volunteerism	48
Cognition	48
Able-bodied	46
Premature Deaths	46
Teeth Extractions	46
Obesity	44
Recommended Hospital Care	43
Multiple Chronic Condition	43
Overall Rank	**48**

Source: _____ America's Health rankings, 2013, Annual report, United Health Foundation, http://www.americashealthranking.org/seniors/ LA-LA/2013.

If we have any delusions that Louisiana Youth's life prospect would improve by the time one reach their senior golden years, then, the above data brings us right back down to Earth. As we see, Louisiana's Seniors overall health rank is 48th in the nation, or near the very bottom. Right below Louisiana's Senior ranking is Oklahoma ranked 49th, and Mississippi ranked 50th, at the very bottom. There is not any significant difference between a 48th and a 50th health ranking. In each case, Louisiana Seniors are suffering dearly. One other noteworthy factor shown in the above data is Louisiana Seniors ranked 49th, suggesting there is no community environment for our elderly citizens. This is beyond heart-breaking because as we grow deeper into our senior years of life, there is hardly nothing left to provide some form of nurturing support and appreciation for all of the long years of service many seniors provided to the development of Louisiana. Lastly, more worrisome than their high obesity rank, is Louisiana Seniors' higher 48th ranking related to cognition. In short, this means Alzheimer's Disease and dementia are commonplace among Louisiana elderly. To further verify this fact, an Advocate Staff Report includes the following information:

> "Louisiana nursing home care ranked second-worst in the nation, failing every staffing measure, according to a new report by Families For Better Care, a non-profit group whose goal is to improve long-term care. The group scored, ranked and graded states on eight different federal quality measures, such as the average number of hours of nursing care each resident received per day. The report gave Louisiana an "F" and said the state's nursing home residents receive "a paltry" 32 minutes of professional nursing care per day. The report also criticized Louisiana nursing homes for having the fewest facilities with above-average nurse staffing."[375]

[375] Advocate Staff Report, "Report: Louisiana nursing homes second worst in U.S.," The Advocate, August 15, 2013, p. 1.

This sums up the general condition of the nursing homes available in Louisiana to assist them at the most vulnerable stage of their lives.

Given these critical health challenges faced by Louisiana Youth and Seniors, we see the only thing that changes for the vast majority of Louisiana Working Class people is a generalized worsening of their overall health condition, as one moves from birth into their elderly years. Many do not make it to the latter because Louisiana was ranked 44th nationally regarding violent crime.

Presently, we will briefly examine another key Louisiana State Budget Line Item that went under Governor Bobby Jindal's Budget Cutting Machine, namely, the Department of Environmental Quality's Environmental Compliance Budget.

F. Department of Environmental Quality (DEQ) Budget, 2008 to 2014

The above agency, theoretically, is mandated by Louisiana Law to protect the environment from various types of pollution, both ground and airborne. How well this charge is being carried forward to maintain a safe, healthy, and green environment for the Louisiana Citizenry to live in can be measured by the amount of taxpayer dollars allocated to environmental compliance. According to the Sunshine Review's analysis of the Louisiana State Budget, the Obama Administration's Economic Stimulus Package allocated an "...estimated...$538,575,876 for infrastructure spending."[376] Overall, Louisiana is expected to receive approximately $4 billion. Of the $787,000,000,000 Economic Stimulus Package, Louisiana received $538,575,876, or .07 percent of it during Governor Bobby Jindal's first year in office in 2008. Moreover, the Sunshine Review provided a breakdown of the areas significant taxpayer dollars were made available to Governor Bobby Jindal to operate the state government:

---

[376] _____ Louisiana state budget (2008-2009), Sunshine Review, http://www. sunshinereview.org/index.php/Louisiana_sta, p. 1.

According to preliminary reports Louisiana is expected to receive:

- $1.7 billion for the state's Medicaid program
- $587 million in education dollars to help prevent layoffs and cutbacks
- $130 million in flexible dollars to help stave off budget cuts
- $455 million for road and bridge work
- $269 million for high-need schools
- $197 million for special education
- $77 million for transit projects
- $72 million for clean and drinking water projects
- $53 million for state and local law enforcement to hire officers and purchase equipment
- $27 million for homelessness prevention
- $16 million for the Head Start program[377]

Read more: http://www.sunshinereview.org/index.php/Louisiana_state_budget_(2008-2009)#ixzz2QAW67v3o

Based on the deep budget cuts already made to Louisiana Higher Education, how can anyone, preferably Governor Bobby Jindal, explain why the deep cuts higher education budget were made when the Economic Stimulus package provided " $587 million in education dollars to help prevent layoffs and cutbacks"? The foregoing information we provided, related to the consecutive higher education budget cuts, provides a clear answer where the Louisiana Citizenry's Economic Stimulus Package dollars ended up. If used properly, no higher education budget cuts would have been necessary, among many others made to fill the great holes left in the Louisiana State Budget as a result of privatization and subsidization economic policies designed to support business. There was even $130 million flexible dollars available to "...help stave off budget cuts."

The Louisiana DEQ Budget was chopped down too, although the Economic Stimulus Package provided $72 million to increase its care for the Louisiana Environment. Since 2008 to March 2013, there has been a

[377] Ibid., p. 1.

budget cutting party going-on in Louisiana with loudspeakers sounding words like shortfalls, deficits, fiscal cliffs, gaps, recession and many, many more. Regarding the Louisiana DEQ's Budget, Gov. Bobby Jindal unveiled his $24.7 billion FY2014 state spending plan on Feb. 21, 2013. The governor said the FY2014 budget will be...$1 billion smaller than the FY2013 state budget..."[378] In his FY2014 State Budget, Governor Bobby Jindal allocated $122.1 million for the Louisiana DEQ, which is a $5 million decrease from December 2012. This is a -3.9 percent budget cut during this time. Regarding the Office of Environmental Compliance Budget, in FY2010-2011, $3,708,696 were available to perform environmental compliance work; by FY 2012-2013, the number is $1,073,000[379]-a whopping -71.1 percent decrease! Statewide, the Office of Environmental Compliance's Budget has allocated $39,618,396 in FY2010-2011 to do environmental protection work; however, by FY2012-2013, the number was $36,744,790[380], which was a decrease of -7.3 percent. These figures demonstrate that there was a sharp reduction in funds available to conduct environmental protection work during the mentioned period due to budget cutting. Given the fact Louisiana has the most concentrated number of oil drilling rigs in the Gulf of Mexico relative to the number of active drilling rigs in other Gulf Coast State, it is shocking to discover that a meager $33,054[381] were allocated in DEQ's Environmental Compliance Statutory Dedications Budget for FY 2010-2011. As you may recall, it was on April 10, 2010 when BP's Deepwater Horizon Drilling Rig blew up, killing 11 oil rig workers, and psychologically injuring untold numbers of others. With so little funds allocated in the Oil Spill Contingency Fund, one has to laugh and conclude that no oil spill cleanup can be done with so little money.

It is worth taking a moment to show how various aspects of the Louisiana Environment are rapidly deteriorating as a result of the sustained budget cuts made to DEQ's Budget by the Jindal Administration.

---

[378] Ibid., p. 1.

[379] _____ Department of Environmental Quality, http://doa.louisiana.gov/ OPB/FY13/SupportingDocum, p. ENVQ-14.

[380] Ibid., p. ENVQ-15.

[381] Ibid., p. ENVQ-18.

Although BP has continuously filled the mass media with the message that Louisiana is back to normal, the evidence contradicts it. Harden wrote the following in a recent article. He stated,

> "BP is doing exactly what big corporations are expected to do, Muth said: Launch a massive public relations campaign to show that everything's back to normal on the Gulf Coast. Some things are, he said, but the extent of the damage remains an unknown...Almost three years after the Deepwater Horizon oil platform exploded, killing 11 men and spewing about 210 million gallons of oil into the Gulf of Mexico, Bay Jimmy is quiet. But the big questions still remain, said David Muth, director of Mississippi River Delta Restoration for the National Wildlife Federation. It is not known to what the extent the most toxic components of the oil have entered the eco-system, Muth said.... The suffocated marshes and oiled birds were obvious effects, but less observable is how much and how far the toxins — the lighter fractions of the oil — dissipated into the environment, he said.... Bamboo poles mark how much of the island's shoreline has receded since the oil hit, in places as much as 150 feet."[382]

Amy Wold's research supports Harden's. She concluded the BP deepwater Horizon Disaster continues to plague the Louisiana Gulf Coast Ecosystem, and the larger Gulf of Mexico Waters. As it is, Wold wrote the following:

> "Almost three years after the Deepwater Horizon rig exploded, killing 11 men and resulting in the country's largest oil spill, its impacts linger and the extent of the damage is unknown, according to a new report from the National Wildlife Federation. The report, "Restoring a Degraded Gulf of Mexico: Wildlife and Wetlands Three Years into the Gulf Oil Disaster," details high

---

[382] Harden, Kari Dequine, "Gulf health questions linger after oil leak," The Advocate, April 09, 2013, p. 1.

dolphin mortalities, sea turtle strandings, acceleration of coastal erosion and damaged deep sea coral, among other things… Of the handful of indicators the report examines, coastal wetlands, Atlantic blue fin tuna and sea turtles are rated as being in poor condition. …."Here on the ground in Louisiana, the disaster is ongoing," Muth said. Last year, he said, six million pounds of tar mats and other material from the leak were picked up from Louisiana's coast alone."[383]

In spite of the on-going land loss, sick and dying wildlife, and wetland general decay, the Louisiana DEQ's Environmental Compliance Budget had less than $40,000 (!) in it when the BP Deepwater Horizon oil drilling rig exploded on April 10, 2010. In April 2013, the National Wildlife Federation released a scientific report titled Restoring a Degraded Gulf of Mexico: Wildlife and Wetlands Three Years into the Gulf Oil Disaster. Particular attention was placed on the health of the dolphin by this report because the dolphin is at the top of the Gulf of Mexico's food chain. If dolphins are stranded, sick, and dying, this is a prime indicator of what is happening health-wise to other animals farther down the food chain. The report stated,

> "Ecosystem-wide effects of the oil are suggested by the poor health of dolphins, which are at the top of the Gulf's food chain. The same may be true of sea turtles, which also continue to die in alarmingly high numbers. More than 650 dolphins have been found stranded in the oil spill area since the Gulf oil disaster began. This is more than four times the historical average. Research shows that polycyclic aromatic hydrocarbon (PAH) components of oil from the Macondo well were found in plankton even after the well was capped…PAHs can have carcinogenic, physiological and genetic effects. Killifish residing in coastal marshes showed evidence of physiological impairment even

---

[383] Wold, Amy, "3 years later, oil leaks effects still unfolding," The Advocate, April 03, 2013, pp. 1 and 2.

at low levels of oil exposure, and corals hundreds of years old on the Gulf floor were killed by oil from the Gulf oil disaster. A recent study found that very low levels of PAH exposure reduced hatch rates and survival in fish such as mahi mahi, and resulted in impaired cardiac development and swimming performance in the fish that did survive... Furthermore, recent laboratory studies have found that the mixture of oil and the dispersant Corexit can prevent coral larvae from building new parts of a reef and was as much as 52 times more toxic than oil alone on rotifers, a microscopic grazing animal at the base of the Gulf's food web..."[384]

The above report also includes information that confirms that the Pacific herring population still has not recovered after "nearly a quarter-century after the Exxon Valdez spill in Prince William Sound..."[385] In addition to the poor quality of the dolphin's health, insects in the food chain have been seriously impacted. The BP Deepwater Horizon Rig Explosion has caused another silent spring regarding insects along the Louisiana Gulf Coast. Amy Wold reported the following:

> "Louisiana's coastal marshes can be noisy places with insects buzzing and chirping constantly, but that's no longer the case in some places "What happened after the Deepwater Horizon is when we came to marsh impacted by the oil, they were relatively silent," said Linda Hooper-Bui, associate professor in the Department of Entomology at LSU. Preliminary results from field work and lab experiments point to two oil components — naphthalene and methylnaphthlane — to be at least part of an explanation for large declines in insect populations within oiled or previously oiled areas of coastal marsh, she said...Hooper-Bui said the two compounds suspected as the cause for the decline in insect populations in the

---

[384] _____ Restoring a Degraded Gulf of Mexico: Wildlife and Wetlands Three Years Into the Gulf Oil Disaster, The National Wildlife Federation, April 2013, p. 1.
[385] Ibid., p. 1.

coastal marshes are known to be insecticides. She said they are widely used in mothballs because their toxicity to insects... She said they found symptoms of naphthalene poisoning match what some residents of south Louisiana have been complaining about including skin rashes, respiratory distress, digestive distress and more."[386]

The sharp reduction in the insect populations, along the Louisiana Coast affected by the BP Deepwater Horizon Rig Explosion, could be the reason the Purple Martins-migratory birds from South America-did not migrate to their normal inland habitats to raise their spring 2013 offsprings. Since they are airborne feeders only, many could have starved to death as a result of limited, or no available insects to feed on during their regular Spring 2013 migration cycle, which began February 1, 2013. For the past 15 years, we established a vibrant Purple Martins Colony in South Louisiana, consisting of as many as 20 Purple Martins during this period; however, since the BP Deepwater Horizon Rig Explosion in April 2010, and by April 2013, the number of Purple Martins in our established colony went from 20 to 0.

In short, how can the Louisiana DEQ, with its meager environmental compliance budget, on one hand, help the sick and dying Louisiana Ecosystem, and, on the other, hold BP, and other businesses, accountable for their actions? This is a question the Louisiana Citizenry must answer. Is Governor Jindal, DEQ Officials, and the Louisiana Legislature, aware that by the end of this century, or sooner, vast portions of the southeast corner of Louisiana, including New Orleans, LA, will be under 4.3 feet of water permanently? Bob Marshall, Advocate reporter, added the following:

> "New Orleans — Stunning new data not yet publicly released shows Louisiana losing its battle with rising seas much more quickly than even the most pessimistic studies have predicted to date... NOAA's Tim Osborne, an 18-year veteran of Louisiana coastal surveys, and Steve Gill, senior scientist at the agency's Center for Operational

---

[386] Wold, Amy, "Insects fall silent in oiled coastal marshes," The Advocate, April 23, 2012, pp. 1 and 3.

Oceanographic Products and Services, spelled out the grim
reality. When new data on the rate of coastal subsidence
is married with updated projections of sea-level rise, the
southeast corner of Louisiana looks likely to be under at
least 4.3 feet of Gulf water by the end of the century."[387]

Brian Handwerk, reporter for the national Geographic News, reported in
2006 "New Orleans may be sinking into the Gulf of Mexico even faster
than scientists realized. Satellite images reveal that some areas of the city
have been sinking at the rate of 1 inch (2.5 centimeters) a year."[388] This
information was a known fact two years before Mr. Bobby Jindal became
governor. If you recall, and throughout Mr. Jindal's 2008 campaign for
governor, not one word about the fact New Orleans, LA is sinking into the
Gulf of Mexico was ever mentioned. This reminds us of the frog in a pot
of water; like the frog, the Louisiana Citizenry will not become concerned,
or jump like the frog, until the water get waist high, or too hot for the frog
to continue to sit comfortably in water due to a steadily rising temperature.
The NOAA's prediction that Southeast Louisiana, and New Orleans,
LA in particular, will be under 4.3 feet of water permanently is a very
conservative prediction. NASA, USGS, and some other environmental
research organizations know that by 2030 most low-lying coastal cities
will be permanently under water by this time-no later than 2050. The
probability of New Orleans, LA becoming permanently flooded by this
time is great. According to The Advocate Newspaper, "Sen. David Vitter,
R-La., on Monday led a letter-writing effort to keep the federal government
from regulating greenhouse gas emissions under the 43-year-old National
Environmental Policy Act, called NEPA. Vitter, the ranking Republican on
the U.S. Senate Environmental and Public Works Committee, and 32 other
Republican senators, wrote to the White House Council on Environmental
Quality. Chairwoman Nancy Sutley asked the administration to withdraw

---

[387] Marshall, Bob, "La. Coast facing grim reality: Seas rising faster than predictions,"
The Advocate, February 27, 2013, p. 1.
[388] Handwerk, Brian, "New Orleans Sinking faster Than Thought, Satellites Find,"
National Geographic News, http://news.nationalgeographic.com/news/2006/0606(,
October 28, 2010, p. 1.

potential draft plans to expand the scope of NEPA."[389] All-in-all, Louisiana State Senator David Vitter, and his Republican U.S. Senate colleagues, are promoting the continued release of carbon dioxide, commonly known as greenhouse gas, in to the atmosphere, which, no doubt, will contribute significantly to sea level rise and the permanent flooding of New Orleans, LA by 2030, or shortly thereafter.

Yet, Governor Bobby Jindal is spending all of his time privatizing and subsidizing business with Louisiana Taxpayer dollars, and leaving the entire Southeastern part of the state vulnerable to catastrophic, permanent flooding in just a few generations from today. This is part of the legacy privatization and subsidization economic policies are passing on to the unborn generations of today's Louisiana Citizenry. If elected state government officials are aware of this inevitable flooding event in Louisiana's future, then can we ask this reasonable question: Do they care about human life?

At this point, we can make one generalization, namely, that the Louisiana Ruling Class' Privatization and Subsidization Economic Policies have *drained the Louisiana State Budget of available taxpayer dollars required to meet the basic needs of the Louisiana Citizenry.* Our next immediate concern is to show the social condition in which a majority of the Louisiana Citizenry currently live in. We will first take a look at how many people live in poverty during the Jindal Administration's tenure in office, from 2008 to date. Afterwards, we will return to Dr. M. Harvey Brenner's study of the long-term impact of unemployment n the creation of pathological behavior, and demonstrate how poverty and unemployment on the one hand, set the table for the development of violence and criminal aggression in Louisiana. In short, the latter is the kernel out of which violence and aggression germinate and evolve into what is commonly known as crime, suicide, health diseases, and prison admissions among other pathological effects.

---

[389] _____ "Vitter leads letter-writing campaign," The Advocate, April 23, 2013, p. 1.

CHAPTER VI

Poverty Among the Louisiana Citizenry During the Jindal Administration, 2008 to 2013

There is a common myth that is universally connected to the capitalist mode of production, namely, when business is in a cycle of prosperity, all boats rise. Since Governor Bobby Jindal became governor in 2008, billions of taxpayer dollars have been shifted continuously from social programs in the state budget to private business. If business production rose during this self-same time, as a result of this huge infusion of Louisiana taxpayer dollars in the business operations of those businesses identified earlier, then, we would expect the number of Louisiana Citizens, who live in poverty, to be small or nearly non-existent. However, the data paints a totally different, and gloomy picture for the vast majority of the Louisiana Citizenry. To put the poverty issue into perspective for Louisiana, take a look at the national situation for a moment.

A. Poverty In The United States, 2011

According to Hope Yen, "the ranks of the nation's poor have swelled to a record 46. 2 million-nearly 1 in 6 Americans...The overall poverty rate climbed to 15.1 percent...[By 2010,] ...the official poverty level was an annual income of $22,314 for a family of four."[390] The number without health insurance was 49.9 million. And, the states with the highest poverty rates coincided exactly with the regions of the country where

---

[390] Yen, Hope, "Poverty in U.S. increases: La. second in percentage of poor," <u>The Advocate</u>, September 14, 2011, p. 1A.

large concentrations of Blacks and Hispanics reside, namely the Deep South, Southeast, and the Southwest. It should be no surprise that the primary reason the Southeastern Conference, or SEC Football, includes Division I Universities located in states which have the highest percentages of poverty in the nation. Hope Yen pointed-out "broken down by state, Mississippi had the highest share of poor people, at 22.7 percent, according to calculations by the Census Bureau...It was followed by Louisiana..."[391] with the second highest percentage of people living in poverty.

B. Poverty In Louisiana During The Jindal Administration's First And Second Terms In Office, 2008 to 2013

Alemayehu Bishaw, Census Bureau Official, provided poverty statistics for each state, for the years 2010 and 2011. Regarding the number and percentage of people in poverty in Louisiana, Bishaw stated there were 825,144 people living below the poverty line in 2010.[392] That year, the poverty rate in Louisiana came to 18.7 percent, ranking it second in the nation in the number of its people living below the poverty line, which was defined by Hope Yen earlier. Keep in mind, this number of people was living in poverty at a time when Governor Bobby Jindal was approving million dollar tax breaks and subsidization deals for business at an unprecedented rapid rate. By 2011, the number of Louisiana Citizens, who lived in poverty, did not decrease, but rose significantly. In fact, by 2011, the number jumped to 908,375-an increase of 10.1 percent during the twelve month period identified. Yet, the state's higher education budget was cut, all of its public hospitals were privatized. Advantage was taken of many Louisiana families living in poverty when Governor Jindal told them that the answer to their problem was a voucher that they could use to send their impoverished children to a Charter School of their choice. To the contrary, we now know better what the voucher is really used for: To

---

[391] Ibid., p. 1A.
[392] Bishaw, Alemayehu, Poverty: 2010 and 2011: American Community Survey Briefs, Issued September 2012, ACSBR/11-01, p. 3.

siphon taxpayer dollars out of the K-12 public Education Budget without violating Louisiana Constitution, which protects this budget from cuts.

Moreover, Louisiana's poverty rate went from 18.7 percent in 2010 to 20.4 percent by 2011. As a result of this rise in the number of Louisiana Citizenry who live in poverty, their levels of anger have also increased simultaneously. A research study conducted by a team of researchers at the University of Vermont concluded that Louisiana is the saddest state in the country. Steven Ward reported the following:

> "Louisiana, according to some math researchers, is the saddest state in the country. And, they claim, the saddest city in the saddest state is Shreveport. Those are among the conclusions of "The Geography of Happiness," a study released Wednesday by University of Vermont math researchers who determined the happiness and sadness of the states and cities by linking key words and geographic locations in tweets on the Twitter social media site... So how did Louisiana wind up as the saddest state in the study? The researchers looked at more than 10 million geotagged tweets from 2011 as well as lists of words that they deemed either "happy" or "sad." As an example, "rainbow" is a happy word while "earthquake" is a sad word, according to the study. The answer is as profane as it is mundane: Louisianans like to curse. "Louisiana is revealed as the saddest state primarily as a result of an abundance of profanity relative to the other states," the researchers said in the study...Key words such as "McDonald's," "wings," "heartburn" and "ham" in tweets were considered a negative correlation to obesity while words such as "apple," "sushi," "tofu" and "grill" were considered a positive correlation to obesity...Blanchard said some of the words coming out of the tweets are a reflection of culture. "And the culture in Louisiana is rich

but the culture also involves food that is not considered super healthy," he said."[393]

Of course, the Jindal Administration denied the above findings. No surprise because the easiest thing to do is to deny the *truth, especially when one has not lived in poverty one day of his or her life.* In addition, Ward added the following information:

> "Louisiana experienced a significant increase from 2009 to 2010 in the number of residents living in poverty, according to new data released by the U.S. Census Bureau. The state's percentage of the population living in poverty grew from 17.3 percent in 2009 to 18.7 percent in 2010... Poverty for Louisiana's children-those under 18-increased from 24.2 percent in 2009 to 27.3 percent in 2010... Louisiana had the...sixth-highest rate of child poverty. In 2010, 75,000 more Louisiana residents lived in poverty than in 2009."[394]

As a way to gloss over this ridiculous increase in poverty that more of the Louisiana Citizenry currently live in, and in an effort to mislead the Louisiana people away from taking a look at the impact privatization and subsidization of business by the Jindal Administration had, and continue to have, on worsening the overall poverty condition statewide, the Jindal Administration has attempted to use the BP Deepwater Horizon Rig Explosion, which occurred on April 10, 2010, as the primary cause of the observed poverty upsurge during Governor Bobby Jindal's first and second term in office.

---

[393] Ward, Steven, "Study: Louisiana is saddest state in the U. S., The Advocate, February 20, 2013, pp. 1 and 2.
[394] Ward, Steven, "Poverty rises in Louisiana: Poor Louisianan ranks grew 75,000 between 2009 and 2010," The Advocate, September 25, 2011, p. 1.

a. Jindal Administration's Explanation For Rising Poverty In Louisiana, 2008 to 2013

In politics, there is a tactic often used called *smoke and mirrors*. It is employed to create an illusion, or make believe, of reality, while the truth underlying the illusion of reality remains hidden in plain sight for a while. This is how BP's Deepwater Horizon Rig Explosion has been used. In short, the latter says the Jindal Administration, the latter has caused mass layoffs, and increased poverty is the result. Ward documented the Jindal Administration's smoke and mirror tactic as follows:

> "Governor Bobby Jindal and State Department of Economic Development Secretary Stephen Moret both attributed the jump to the deepwater oil drilling moratorium installed by the federal government following the April 2010 oil rig explosion in the Gulf of Mexico. "The from 2009 to 2010 data is largely a result of President Obama's shutdown of offshore drilling, which even a federal judge ruled was 'arbitrary and capricious.' Just a s we told the White House and argued in federal court, bad federal policy that stops offshore drilling has a direct, negative impact on our economy," Jindal said in a written statement in response to the data. Moret said that when the moratorium went into effect, there was a large impact on thousands of oil drilling-related jobs, leading to layoffs, lost overtime and shorter work schedules."[395]

This is the Jindal Administration's smoke and mirrors aimed at keeping the true cause of the upsurge in poverty in Louisiana a secret. The over-simplification of increasing statewide poverty began to give off a rotten egg smell as Louisiana's poverty numbers continued to go up. A political analyst, based in Shreveport, LA, sounded an early alarm and raised growing suspicion. Ward stated,

[395] Ibid., p. 1.

"Shreveport political analyst Elliott Stonecipher said
the 2010 poverty increase seems at odds with Jindal's
continued message stressing Louisiana's economic
prosperity. "The picture the Jindal Administration paints
has as its main objective the promotion of his political
career, not an open and honest discussion of all the facts
available," Stonecipher said. "When those at or below the
poverty level are increasing, his case is very difficult to
accept as fact."[396]

Baton Rouge, LA, the State Capitol, and Louisiana State Government
Headquarters, ranked 10th among the 100 largest metropolitan areas
in the nation, regarding poverty by 2009, which was the end of the
Jindal Administration's first year in office. The Brookings Institution's,
a Washington, D. C. Conservative Think Tank, data demonstrated that
by 2009, there were 740,111 people living in Baton Rouge, LA. Of this
number, 115,641 people lived in 15 "poor poverty tracts," or 15.6 percent
of the total Baton Rouge, LA population. And, of the total number who
lived in poor poverty tracts, 56,285, or 49 percent, lived in "Extreme
Poverty."[397] Steven Ward added the following information based on the
Brookings Institution's data:

"The Baton Rouge metro area ranked No. 11 in
"concentrated poverty" among the nation's 100 largest
metro areas from 2005 to 2009, according to a new study
released Thursday by the Brookings Institution. The city
of Baton Rouge, meanwhile, ranked No. 5 out of the
primary cities located in those same metro areas and time
period. The report also reflected that the concentrated
poverty rate in the Baton Rouge metro area increased by
13.5 percent from 2000 to the 2005-2009 study period

[396] Ibid., p. 2.
[397] Kneebone, Elizabeth, Nadeau, Carey, and Alan Berube, The Re-Emergence of
Concentrated Poverty: Metropolitan Trends in the 200s Report, Metropolitan Policy
Program at Brookings, Brookings Institutions, Washington, D.C., November 2011,
p. 20.

and that the increase for the city of Baton Rouge was 22 percent. The 13.5 percent increase caused the Baton Rouge metro area to rank No. 4 in rate of change out of the 100 largest metro areas... The report measures the concentrated poverty rate — defined as the share of poor people living in extremely poor neighborhoods. An extremely poor neighborhood is a Census tract with a poverty rate of 40 percent or higher."[398]

Poverty among children is very extreme as well. Former "Parish School Superintendent John Dilworth said the numbers do not surprise him... He said Louisiana ranked 49th in the country in the 2011 Kids Count report which looks at well-being issues such as children born prematurely and children living in poverty."[399] When the poverty data for African-American families is considered, the numbers are startling. Jordan Blum stated " the median net worth — not income — of black families in the U.S. is less than $5,000 compared with more than $110,000 for comparable white families, said small business officials."[400] Therefore, in one *prepared statement after another, Governor Bobby Jindal stated Prosperity is strong in Louisiana, and business is doing well.* But wait one minute. The prosperity parroted by Governor Bobby Jindal appears one-sided by the poverty data thus far presented.

Moreover, the economic prosperity repeatedly mentioned by Governor Bobby Jindal refers to the economic prosperity he has facilitated via the Louisiana Ruling Class' Privatization and Subsidization Economic Policies. When a closer look at the economic impact of the BP Deepwater Horizon Rig Explosion, including the oil-drilling moratorium that followed, had on the Louisiana economy, it was discovered that the Jindal Administration's smoke and mirrors tactic fell apart like the man behind the screen in the Wizard of Oz movie. It has no credibility whatsoever. In short, Governor

[398] Ward, Steven, "Report: Poverty high in BR," The Advocate, November 3, 2011, p. 1.
[399] Ibid., p. 3. By January 2014, Louisiana ranked 50th in children living in poverty.
[400] Blum, Jordan, "Wealth gap hits black families in U.S., La," The Advocate, September 24, 2012, p. 1.

Bobby Jindal would like us to believe that the extreme poverty in Louisiana is solely due to the federal government's oil-drilling moratorium. But, the data proves differently.

b. Economic Impact Of The Federal Government's Oil-Drilling Moratorium On The Louisiana Economy, 2008 to 2013

On the surface, it appears plausible that the federal government's oil-drilling moratorium would have a significant economic impact on the Louisiana economy. However, to the contrary, there was not any according to the available data. In the Estimating the Economic Effects of the Deepwater Drilling Moratorium on the Gulf Coast Economy: Inter-Agency Economic Report, published September 16, 2010, Barry Leonard, editor, concluded the following:

> "Evidence on employment, unemployment and unemployment insurance (UI) claims in the parishes most affected by the deepwater drilling moratorium indicates that there have not been large increases in unemployment or decreases in employment in these parishes. These data do not indicate that there has been no unemployment impact associated with the drilling moratorium, but they do suggest that any losses have not been large to date, since significant losses would have shown up in the employment and UI claim activity data."[401]

The data in Table 1.14 below proves the federal government oil-drilling moratorium did not have a significant economic impact on the Louisiana economy.

---

[401] Leonard, Barry (Editor), Estimating the Economic Effects of the Deepwater drilling Moratorium on the Gulf Coast Economy: Inter-Agency Economic Report, September 16, 2010, p. iii.

Table 1.14
Employment Changes from April 2010 to July 2010 for
Five oil Industry Intensive Parishes in Louisiana

	Employment Level(In thousands)				Unemployment Rate		
	April	July	Change	% Change	April	July	Change
U.S. total	139,302	140,134	8.32	0.6%	9.5	9.7	0.2
Louisiana	1,958.6	1,971.9	13.3	0.7%	6.2	7.6	1.4
Total for 5 parishes	259.5	261.2	1.7	0.7%	5.2	6.1	0.9
Iberia	31.4	31.9	0.5	1.6%	6.8	7.7	0.9
Lafayette	107.2	108.1	0.9	0.8%	4.7	5.7	1.0
Lafourche	46.8	47	0.2	0.3%	4.4	5.0	0.6
Saint Mary	21.4	21.5	0.1	0.5%	8.0	9.3	1.3
Terrebonne	52.6	52.8	0.2	0.4%	4.8	5.3	0.5

Source: Author's calculations using data from the Bureau of Statistics, Current Population Survey (U.S. total) and Local area Unemployment Statistics program (statewide and parish).[402]

In addition, Barry Leonard noted that the federal government oil-drilling moratorium did not shutdown deepwater oil-drilling rigs operating in the Gulf of Mexico.

In fact, he provided the following evidence:

"according to the Mid-Continent Oil and Gas Association, the moratorium does not affect the 591producing deepwater wells or the over 4,500 shallow water wells in the Gulf of Mexico. The Department of the Interior estimates that there are a total of 80,000 offshore oil and gas production, construction, and drilling workers in the

---

[402] Ibid., p. 7.

Gulf of Mexico...fewer than 10,000 of these workers were employed on rigs affected by the moratorium."[403]

In view of this information, Governor Bobby Jindal and Mr. Stephen Moret's claim that the extreme poverty in which a large segment of the Louisiana Citizenry currently live in is humorous to say the least, and preposterous at worse. As we have already seen, the real cause of the extreme poverty in Louisiana, and its perpetuation, is the Privatization and Subsidization Economic Policies that have been put into affect during the Jindal Administration. These economic policies, as we shall see shortly, are the soil out of which *violence and criminal aggression originate.*

Meantime, if the Privatization and Subsidization Economic Policies of the Jindal Administration delivers an extreme poverty "left jab" to the emotional stability and well-being of the Louisiana Citizenry, then the "amount of taxes paid" by it delivers a deafening knock-out punch.

---

[403] Ibid. p. 3.

CHAPTER VII

Louisiana Ruling Class and Taxes Paid During the Jindal Administration

A. Louisiana Ruling Class Definition

Earlier, we deferred the necessity to provide a definition of the ruling class until now. The mass media repeatedly talk freely about the middle class and lower class, but seldom, if ever, is there any mention of the ruling class in Louisiana, and in America in general. If we always mention a snake has a tail, and a body, and never mention it has a head, eventually, this conditioning will lead us to this point: When we see the entire snake, we will not be able to recognize its type because we never were taught-beforehand-to identify its type by the characteristics of its head. In our Louisiana society, we are taught about who is at the bottom, or tail-end of it; we are taught who is at the middle, or stomach; but we are intentionally not taught who is at the top of Louisiana society. This is done to keep everyone who is in the middle class and the lower class, or working class, from knowing there is a ruling class, and who is a part of it. Before we address the latter, let us define the meaning of ruling class.

The Louisiana Ruling Class consists of a small, tightly knitted group of Louisiana Families, usually no more than one-half of one percent of the total population, who exert control and dominance over the *political, economic, judicial, social, and environmental affairs of state government, through its control of at least 90 percent of the wealth and means of production in Louisiana.* Nationwide, the top 10 percent of U. S. households control "nearly two-thirds of the increase in household wealth since 2009 [,which] is due to rising stock prices... Stock indexes reached record highs this month. Those gains disproportionately benefit affluent households: About 80 percent of stocks are held by the wealthiest 10 percent of the population."[404]

To verify the existence of the Louisiana Ruling Class, we will use taxpayer data to show how much taxes was paid by the Louisiana Ruling Class, and how much was paid by the middle and lower class, or working class.

B. Taxes Paid by the Louisiana Ruling Class, January 2013

The Institute on Taxation & Economic Policy (ITEP), which is "...a non-profit, non-partisan research organization that works on federal, state, and local tax policy issues..."[405] published an extensive report-See Footnote 120-on which classes in Louisiana pay more and less taxes. The class with the greatest authority, power, and control of the state government apparatus *always pays less taxes, and the class with the least power and authority always pays the most.* The following tax data for Louisiana consistently supports this fact.

The top 1%, those few Louisiana Residents that makeup the ruling class, who earned $979,700 or more by 2013, paid only 1.3% in sales and excise taxes; 1.4% in property taxes; and 2.9% in income taxes. Overall, the top 1% of Louisiana residents only paid 4.6% of their earnings in taxes by 2013.[406] Jordan Blum summed up just what these low taxes paid by the Louisiana ruling Class means. He stated "...Louisiana has the fourth-lowest

---

[404] Rugaber, Christopher S., "Average U.S. household far from regaining its wealth," The Advocate, May 30, 2013, p. 1.

[405] Davis, Karl, Davis, Kelly, Gardner, Matthew, Heimovitz, Harley, Mcintyre, Robert S, Phillips, Richard, Sapozhnikova, Alla and Meg Wiehe, Who Pays?: A Distributional Analysis of the Tax Systems in All 50 States, 4th Edition, January 2013, p. 2. "This study was made possible by grants from the Annie E. Casey Foundation, the Ford Foundation, the Popplestone Foundation, the Stephen M. Silberstein Foundation, the Stoneman Family Foundation, and other anonymous donors," p. 2.

[406] Ibid., p. 62.

tax burden in the nation for its residents with an average "burden" of 7.8 percent in state and local taxes of an individual's income, according..."[407] to the ITEP During the Jindal Administration's second year in office in 2009, Blum added "Using the latest full statistics from 2010...Louisiana had the second biggest dip in its average tax burden, dropping from 8.2 percent in 2009 to 7.8 percent."[408]

In short, the top 1 percent of Louisiana residents pay far less of their income than the working class, which consists of the middle and lower class.

C. Taxes Paid By The Louisiana Ruling Class, 2013

One of the interesting features associated with the top 1 percent of the Louisiana Ruling Class is its members are non-producers. In order for a product to be produced, a certain amount of socially necessary labor must be transferred to it by the worker during production. Thus, the Louisiana Working Class is the one that actually produce products that have a value based on the amount of socially necessary labor embodied in them. Yet, the vast majority of Louisiana residents, which make up the working class, earn far less of the value they produce, and they *pay far more taxes than the non-producing Louisiana Ruling Class.* Jordan Blum added "Low taxes for wealthy Louisianans have done nothing to help the state's poor...and, as such, Louisiana has one of the nation's highest income inequality ratings... [Governor Bobby Jindal said in an e-mail] 'this is great news for our state...'"[409] Governor Bobby Jindal was elected by some Louisiana voters, but he is employed by the Louisiana Ruling Class to carry-out one central goal, namely, to insure that all economic policies, as we have already seen, generate huge profits for it, and to reject any ideas that may surface that aims to allow the Louisiana Working Class to equitably share in the great wealth that it produces.

---

[407] Blum, Jordan, "La. among lowest tax-burden states: But state has 'incredibly high' sales taxes that affect poor, working class," The Advocate, October 24, 2012, p. 1.
[408] Ibid., p. 1.
[409] Ibid., p. 2.

Moreover, on January 31, 2013, the Capitol News Bureau wrote the following:

> "Louisiana's tax system takes a much-larger share from middle-and-low income residents than the wealthy just like most states... The [ITEP] [410]study showed Louisiana households earning less than $16,000 annually pay nearly 11 percent of their income in state and local taxes. Households earning up to $85,000 pay 10 percent. Meanwhile, households in the top 5 percent pay less than 5 percent of their incomes in taxes. Currently, the bottom 20 percent of Louisiana households pay seven times as much of their income on sales taxes compared to the wealthiest households, the study found."[411]

As we see, the top 1 percent of Louisiana residents pay far less taxes than the vast majority of working class Louisiana residents, or wage-workers, who are the actual producers of value. Non-producers, or the top1percent of the Louisiana ruling Class do not produce value in a product, but their members receive the greatest portion of the produced product by the Louisiana Working Class, and on top of this, they pay far less taxes. The following ITEP data provides a stark contrast between who pays more taxes in Louisiana.

D. Taxes Paid by the Louisiana Working Class, 2013

The Louisiana Working Class paid more in taxes during Governor Bobby Jindal's first term in office than the Louisiana Ruling Class. Of the taxes paid, as a share of family income for non-elderly taxpayers, the Louisiana Working Class paid an amazing and disproportionate 47.7 percent compared to the 4.6 percent paid by the Louisiana Ruling Class in

---

[410]

[411] _____ "Low-income taxpayers pay larger share in La.," The Advocate, January 31, 2013, pp. 1 and 2.

2010.[412] Worse, that year, the lowest 20 percent of the Louisiana Working Class paid 10.6 percent of its family income in taxes, which is more than doubled the 4.6 percent paid by the Louisiana Ruling Class. To further highlight this gross disparity, the ITEP data reveals, for taxes paid on family income, that the lowest 20% of Louisiana Working Class residents paid 10.6 percent of their earnings in taxes, or 130.4 percent more (!) than the top 1 percent of the Louisiana Ruling Class in 2010. Taking the Louisiana Working Class as whole, the amount of personal family income paid in taxes skyrocketed to 937.0 percent more than the 4.6 percent paid by the top 1 percent of the Louisiana Ruling Class. Since Governor Bobby Jindal was s/elected governor in 2007, the number of Louisiana millionaires increased sharply by January 2014.

On the front page of The Wall Street Journal, the latter published a U. S. Map on January 17, 2014 titled "Newly Minted Millionaires." It is interesting to note here that Louisiana, which ranks near the bottom nationally in nearly every health and social index, experienced a sharp increase in "newly minted millionaires" by 2013. As this map indicates, Louisiana experienced a "0.35 change in percentage of households with investable assets of $1 million from 2012 to 2013."[413] Although Louisiana ranks near the bottom in most social indices as we have already seen, Eric Morath stated "Louisiana jumped 10 spots to No. 32,"[414] regarding "newly minted millionaires." At the end of Governor Bobby Jindal's first term in 2012, Louisiana ranked 41th in millionaire households; by 2013, this rank changed in one year to No. 32. They are given this label because of the tremendous outflow of Louisiana Taxpayer Dollars flowing, from the Louisiana State Budget like an irreparable broken water pipe, to private businesses, as a result of the Jindal Administration's implementation of the Louisiana Ruling Class' Neo-Liberal Privatization Economic Policy. Earlier, we saw the Louisiana Ruling Class, as a whole, pays far less in taxes than the vast majority of the Louisiana Working Class.

---

[412] Davis, Davis, et. al., Op. Cit., p. 61.
[413] _____ "Newly Minted Millionaires," The Wall Street Journal, Vol. CCLXIII, No. 14, January 17, 2014, p. A1.
[414] Morath, Eric, "Where to Go If You Want To Marry a Millionaire," The Wall Street Journal, Vol. CCLXIII, No. 14, January 17, 2014, p. A2.

Generally speaking, for every tax dollar collected by the Louisiana State Government in 2010, the Louisiana Working Class paid significantly more of its earnings in taxes. This is particularly true for members of the lowest 20 percent. For example, the latter paid 1.7 percent of its family income in property taxes, while, at the self-same time, the top 1 percent of the Louisiana Ruling Class paid 1.4 percent. It seems this figure is in-line with the taxes paid by the lowest 20 percent. However, when we take into consideration the millions of dollars of value of property owned by the top 1 percent of the Louisiana Ruling Class, it follows that the 1.4 percent in property taxes paid on it, by the latter, is insignificant. Thus, the Louisiana Working Class, which produces the greatest product value, earns the least from its production; however, its members consistently pay the greatest amount of taxes. Moreover, Governor Bobby Jindal has repeatedly held one inflexible position, namely, while serving as governor, there will not be any increases in taxes, of any kind. Given the fact the Louisiana Ruling Class pay less of its income in taxes than the Louisiana Working Class, one does not need to be a rocket scientist to understand what is underlying Governor Bobby Jindal's call for no tax increases. For example, who would have to pay more taxes? A person who has an income of $1 million per year would have to pay more taxes on it than one who has an annual income of $25,000. Yet, as we have already witnessed, Louisiana Working Class people pay far more of their income in taxes than someone with a $1 million income. This is why Governor Bobby Jindal refuses to call for a tax increase, which is sorely needed for road repairs, education, and healthcare among many others. It is necessary to remind the reader here that the payment of significantly more federal and state taxes by the Louisiana Working Class is not an accident, but, historically speaking, the higher tax payment grew out of the Louisiana Ruling Class', including the collective action of the American Ruling Class nationwide, to weaken and destroy the New Deal put in place during the Franklin D, Roosevelt Era following the Great 1929 Depression.

CHAPTER VIII

Dismantling of the New Deal Regulations, and Paving the Road for the 2008 Depression

A. End Of New Deal Regulations Insuring Another 1929 Great Depression

As it was, Wolf stated the following:

> "After 1945...capitalists were increasingly able to evade, weaken, or repeal New Deal laws and regulations. From 1945 to the 1970s, the rightist attacks took their tolls. The rightist coalition grew, winning more adherents especially among business and upper-income groups in response to such victories as the Taft-Hartley restrictions on labor unions and the shift in the burden of federal taxation from corporations to individuals and from upper-income groups."[415]

Therefore, the disproportionate payment of higher, much higher federal and state taxes, by the Louisiana Working Class is not new. It is the effect of the rollback of the New Deal programs designed to help the workingman and woman. In short, the "game" is to take as much from human labor as it is possible without starving the wage-worker to death. It is more economically beneficial to work the wage-workers to death than

---

[415] Wolff, Op. Cit., pp. 35 and 36.

starve them to death; the former is less dramatic but, in the end, the same goal is achieved. The "game" was replayed once again in 2008 with the Wall Street engineered collapse of the American economy into the worst economic depression since the 1929 Great Depression.

For eighty years, the last protection against financial depression, and prevention of higher taxes paid by the Louisiana Working Class, and working class people nationwide, was the Glass-Steagall Act, legislation approved by the U.S. Congress to prevent huge Wall Street Investment Banks from engaging in fraudulent securities activity, namely subprime housing mortgages and so forth. However, by 1999, the die was cast, and the wheels of greed rolled steadily to the devastating 2008 Depression. Connie Crawford's research article points-out that former President Bill Clinton was elected to approve the repeal of the Glass-Steagall Act. With a single stroke of a pen in 1999 former President Bill Clinton set in motion an $850 billion bailout package-working class tax increase-, which is nothing but a higher tax the Louisiana and Working Class people across America are forced to pay, including their unborn children generations to come. Crawford stated,

> *"The Glass-Steagall Act forced banks to choose between being a commercial bank or an investment bank, in effect constructing a wall between commercial banking and investing banking activities. The Glass- Steagall Act was the first law signed by President Franklin D. Roosevelt upon taking the oath of office. Almost immediately upon enactment, the financial community lobbied to have the Act repealed. Over the years, this persistent lobbying led to a continual reinterpretation and liberalization of the Glass-Steagall Act, until the Act was repealed in 1999. On the dawn of repeal, the late Senator Paul Wellstone made an impassioned plea on the Senate floor. He said the repeal of Glass-Steagall would enable the creation of financial conglomerates which would be too big to fail. Furthermore, he believed that the regulatory structure would not be able to monitor the activities of these financial conglomerates and they would eventually fail due to engaging*

in excessively risky financial transactions. Ultimately, he said, prophetically, that the taxpayers would be forced to bail out these too-big-to-fail financial institutions. Clearly, Senator Wellstone was in the minority as the legislation repealing the Glass-Steagall Act was passed in both the House and the Senate with large majorities. President Bill Clinton signed the legislation into law in late November, 1999. It has now been over ten years since the repeal of Glass-Steagall and the United States is in the grip of the largest financial crisis since the Great Depression."[416]

And, make no mistake about it. This means inflation, which is nothing but a *$850 billion bail-out package of higher taxes that the Louisiana and Working Class, as a whole, will be saddled with paying for generations to come, or until we wake up and, collectively, demand some concrete answers.* To keep Former Bill Clinton hidden from public sight regarding his signing of the repeal of the Glass-Steagall Act, Monica Lewinsky, so-called White House Intern, was set up in the Oval Office to engage in fornication behavior with him. The latter dominated the last years of Bill Clinton's Presidency; impeachment was even considered while the huge Wall Street Investment Banks turned their Greed wheels faster and faster toward the coming depression, which occurred nine years after former President Bill Clinton repealed the Glass-Steagall Act, unleashing the beast that eventually devoured the life force of millions of innocent Americans.

B. Post-Glass-Steagall Act Repeal And Rise Of Neo-Liberal Privatization Economic Policy

American Presidents, since the Ronald Reagan era, beginning with the early 1980s to date, have been selected, packaged for public consumption, and then they are elected by the American public. Since the Reagan era,

---

[416] Crawford, Corinne, "The Repeal Of The Glass-Steagall Act And The Current Financial Crisis, " Journal of Business & Economic Research, Volume 9, Number 1, January 2011, p. 127.

the American Ruling Class has selected weak, egotistical, wealthy, and incompetent men to run for President of the United States. In order to hide this generalized trend in plain daylight, a diversionary tactic is used by the American Ruling Class to achieve a twofold purpose: (1) To use the selected president to request congressional legislation that results in billions of dollars of profits gained by deregulation or declarations of wars, and (2) To divert the attention of the American public away from cause and effect, by creating and carrying-out a significant emotional event that keep the American Working Class in a state of shock, fear, and depression.

For example, beginning with former President Ronald Reagan, a massive de-regulation and military buildup campaign was carried-out, which resulted in billions of dollars of profit for the American Ruling Class, and, at the same time, Working Class Americans suffered one of the greatest budget cutting assaults on social programs in American history. To hide this fact, former President Ronald Reagan spent his entire Presidency talking about the lack of freedom of people in the Soviet Union and East Germany, and referring to the former as an Evil Empire. Former President George H.W. Bush took over the reins from Ronald Reagan, and he immediately mobilized for war, namely, Desert Storm. Billions of dollars of profit were realized by big business, and the American public was fed a steady diet of Saadam Hussein's murder of his own people with Sarin gas. Former President Bill Clinton was selected next to repeal the Glass-Steagall Act, deregulating the only safeguard that served to keep large investment bank conglomerates from engaging in fraudulent schemes since the 1929 Great Depression. His repeal of the Glass-Steagall Act in 1999 set in motion the next Great Depression, which occurred in 2008. To cover up the repeal of the Glass-Steagall Act, Monica Lewinsky was brought into the White House to engage in oral sex with former President Bill Clinton. This sex scandal dominated the last years of the Clinton Presidency, and it kept the sheep-American people-blindly walking toward the 2008 financial cliff. After former President Clinton completed his script, former President George W. Bush was selected to oversee the Iraq-American War and the bombing of the World Trade Twin Towers in Lower Manhattan, New York, which is now known famously as 9/11.

The 9/11 bombing of the World Trade Twin Towers completely dominated both terms of former President George Bush; after the bombing, war was expanded to Afghanistan. To hide in plain daylight the enormous profits rolling in from the Iraq-American War, Afghanistan War, and the $40 plus billion given to business immediately after 9/11, George W. Bush set in motion a Terrorism Campaign that continues to hold the American people in the grip of a McCarthyism-Type fear today. The trend remained unbroken with the election of Barack Obama President in 2008. He was elected to advocate for the approval of the greatest Wall Street Bailout Package, or tax hike for working class people, in American history. His first action taken during the first months in office was his approval of the $850 billion Wall Street Bailout Package. The latter, and the 2008 Great Depression, were caused by former President Clinton's repeal of the Glass-Steagall Act in 1999. To distract the American people's attention from these tragic events, President Obama's entire Presidency has been bogged-down in partisan politics related to healthcare. While the American people listen to this or that argument, either for or against approval of a national healthcare bill, little, if any attention, is focused on how the $850 billion Wall Street bailout Package was spent.

This entire political development always, in the end, resulted in the American people, and the Working Class in particular, having to pay more and higher taxes; the $850 billion dollar Wall Street Bailout Package is a tax on the American Working Class. The foregoing information is included to demonstrate it matters not if a governor or president tell you he or she is against a tax increase; the fact is he or she was selected to office to enrich the American Ruling Class, and subtly force the American Working Class to pay higher taxes. Wolff added "...businesses...pay less in taxes to fund local, state, and federal governments...In the simplest terms, corporations and the rich partly utilized the explosion in profits that began in the late 1970s to wield enough political power...to shift the [state and] federal tax burden from themselves onto the "middle classes."[417] For clarification, the latter refers to the Working Class.

Due to the repeal of the Glass-Steagall Act in 1999 by former President

---

[417] Wolff, Op.Cit., pp. 23 and 60.

Bill Clinton, Wall Street, or the American Class, which consist of a half-of-one percent of the total U. S. Population, unleashed one of the greatest economic scandals in American History. By 2008, less than one decade, the greed of the American Ruling Class froze, or shutdown their American Capitalist System. Paul Davidson stated the "...financial system...virtually froze as mortgage-related losses mounted at top banks."[418] The American Financial Market Crash in 2008 has been described as a wreckage, similar to a head-on collision between two 18 wheeler trucks, moving at 80 miles per hour! However, within five years since the 2008 Great depression, the half-of-one-percent American Ruling Class is back thanks to President Barack Obama's 2008 $700 billion bail-out of the former's Wall Street Investment banks, and to his indifference to taking a strong stand to help the majority of working class people who voted for him based on the "Yes We Can" illusion. Moreover, while President Barack Obama delivered his State of the Union Address on January 21, 2014, The Wall Street Journal published an article, on January 17, 2014, which shows the half-of-one percent American Ruling Class' profits are astronomically high, and in many cases, higher than they were before the 2008 Great Depression. Two-The Wall Street Journal-reporters provided the profit details in their published article, which President Barack Obama completely overlooked mentioning during his State of the Union Address. For the less than one-half percent of Americans, the State of the Union could not be any financially rosier. Fitzpatrick and Rapoport wrote the following:

> "Large U. S. banks are finally emerging from the wreckage of the financial crisis, on the back of rising profits...and drastic cost cutting. After a five year stretch in which J.P.. Morgan Chase & Co, Bank of America Corp., Citigroup Inc., Wells Fargo & Co., Goldman Sachs Group Inc. And Morgan Stanley have been buffeted by sluggish growth... and a spate of new regulations, executives and analysts say the worst is behind them. As a group, the six earned $76 billion in 2013. That is $6 billion shy of the collective all-time high achieved in 2006, a year U.S. housing prices

---

[418] Davidson, Paul, "BERNANKE DOWNPLAYS COST OF STIMULUS," USA TODAY, Section B, Money, January 17, 2014, p. 1B,

peaked amid a torrid economic expansion. "The industry is back," said Gerard Cassidy, an analyst at RBC Capital Markets. Banks "should break all records" for earnings in 2014, he said."[419]

The "torrid economic expansion" Fitzpatrick and Rapoport refers to is the unbridled greed that swept across the American landscape during the first decade of the 21th Century, sucking innocent working class Americans into its bottomless stomach like a giant unstoppable vacuum cleaner. Having screeched to a terrifying halt for millions of working class Americans, and, rather than assist the wounded and dying on the battlefield, President Barack Obama held up the head of the dying American Capitalist System, and poured $700 billion plus down its throat, heading off temporarily its inevitable death. With this financial transfusion, the dying American Capitalist System came out of its brief coma, and the financial beast leapt to its feet like a temporarily dazed and disoriented professional football player, flexing its muscles and snorting to get back on the playing field. To achieve the above return to extreme profitability mentioned above, the half-of-one percent American Ruling Class embraced a tactic of self-cannibalism in the form of layoffs. This is a by-product of Neo-Liberal Privatization Economic Policy.

For example, thousands of American Working Class people have lost their jobs since the 2008 Great Depression to 2013. Yet, President Barack Obama instead chose to highlight an injured military soldier, who suffered gross injuries after 10 deployments, and remain silent about the plight of the unemployed. Fitzpatrick and Rapoport identified one of the ways Wall Street Banks increased their profits after the 2008 Great Depression. They stated the following:

> "One way for banks to improve their standing with investors is to cut compensation, jobs, and business lines. This past week, Goldman Sachs announced its 2013 payroll was 3% lower than 2012s, while Bank of America

---

[419] Fitzpatrick, Dan and Rapoport, Michael, "Profits show Biggest Banks Are Back From Brink," The Wall Street Journal, January 17-19, 2014, p. A1.

disclosed it eliminated 25,000 positions during the year... The six biggest banks [have] reduced their workforce by more than 44,000 positions in the past year...Goldman Sachs's 2013 pay reduction brings compensation expenses down to 36.9% of total revenue, the lowest percentage since 2009."[420]

The capitalist juggernaut has an insatiable thirst for more and more profits. No job is safe from the cannibalizing Neo-Liberal Privatization Economic Policy that continues to sweep across the American landscape like a Category 5 Hurricane Storm Surge does when it sweeps across the coastal landscape when it makes landfall. The 2008 Great Depression is our most recent devastating experience. Corporate profits are not only breaking through the ceiling at the six largest Wall Street banks, it is skyrocketing across the nation at all of the commercial banks. Fitzpatrick and Rapopart stated "smaller banks are recovering, as well... together, all 6,900 commercial banks in the U.S. are on pace to match or exceed the industry's all-time earnings peak of $145.2 billion in 2006, according to an analysis by The Wall Street Journal of federal Deposit Insurance Corp. Data."[421] Where does a vast majority of this profit originate? In short, it comes from layoffs, and surplus value, which is wrung out of the labor power of the American Working Class. The surplus value is the profit the capitalist realizes after the worker earns his or her wages during a part of the day; the remaining hours of the day each worker work in a day becomes surplus value, or profit. Table 1.15 shows the sharp income inequality present in American Class Society by 2014.

[420] Ibid., p. A2.
[421] Ibid., p. A2.

Table 1.15
Income Inequality in American Class Society
For Selected Corporations, 2014

CEO	CEO PAY	Corporation	Corp. Employee Pay	CEO-to-Worker Pay Ratio
Joel Gemunder	$98.3 million	Omnicare	$38,600	2,546-to-1
John Hammergren	$145.3 million	McKesson	$60,500	2,401-to-1
Ralph Lauren	$66.7 million	Polo Ralph Laure	$50,200	1,328-to-1
Thomas Ryan	$68 million	CVS	$36,300	1,875-to-1
John Plant	$76.8 million	TRW Automotiv	$69,400	1,107-to-1
Frank Coyne	$69.4 million	Verisk Analytics	$50,100	1,386-to-1
Adam Metz	$66.7 million	Gen. Growth Properties	$53,800	1,240-to-1

Source: MSN Money, http://money.msn.com/investing/7-ceos-pulling-in-outsized-p.

In addition, many CEOs not shown have a salary equal to more than one-half billion dollars or more annually. For example, according to MSN Money, John Hammergren's company net income is $1.2 billion; Ralph Lauren, $630 million; Robert Iger, $4.6 billion; George Paz, $1.29 billion; Jeffrey Boyd, $720 million; Lew Frankfort, $800 million, Stephen Hemsley, $4.9 billion; John Wren, $900 million; John C. Martin, $2.73 billion; James Dimon, $18.6 billion; Leslie Moonves, $1.2 billion; Richard Adkerson, $5.59 billion; John Chambers, $6.49 billion; Louis C. Camilleri, $7.9 billion; and John Tucci; $2.12 billion.[422] As we have already seen, the income gap between non-producers-CEOs and producers of value with their labor power-American Working Class-is steadily widening with no sign of slowing down. Ironically, American Working Class children are taught everyday in public schools all across America they can achieve the "mythical-American Dream. However, the data, as have seen, paints a whole different picture contrary to this message. Wall Street's return to extreme profitability by 2013 is far from a mystery; similar to former President Bill Clinton's repeal of the Glass Steagall Act, after the 2008 Depression began

[422] _____ "America's 25 Highest Paid CEOs, Forbes, http://www.forbes.com/pictures/mef45eghm/ and http://money.msn.com/investing/7-ceos-pulling-in-outsized-p.

in September 2008, the U.S. Congress passed legislation, in the form of the Dodd-Frank Bill, which was supposed to tighten regulations governing how Wall Street Investment Banks conduct their business investments. However, we shall see below that, like the Glass-Steagall Act, Dodd-Frank was completely co-opted, and compromised. The information is eye-opening.

C. Post 2008 Depression And The Wall Street Compromise Of The Dodd-Frank Bill's Investment Bank Regulations

The subject of Time Magazine's September 23, 2013 issue is could another American Capitalist System financial meltdown occur again? Few political economists, and so-called political scientists, felt another American Capitalist System meltdown could not occur again because of the safeguards put in place after the 1929 Depression, namely in the form of congressional legislation known as the Glass-Steagall Act. The latter prevented another Wall Street induced financial meltdown for seventy-nine years. The Glass-Steagall Act established an impenetrable Firewall of Regulations that could not be penetrated from the outside by Wall Street. However, a private Wall Street Plan was hatched and implemented, which led to the s/election of former President Bill Clinton. Underlying his election as President, and away from the "presidential campaign mudslinging," Bill Clinton agreed to advocate, on behalf of Wall Street, for the repeal, or rollback, of all of the regulatory measures, or Firewall Safeguards, which, before 2008, had collectively prevented another financial meltdown, similar to the one that became known as the Great 1929 Depression. In short, the Glass-Steagall Act was torpedoed from within the American Government itself during the Bill Clinton Administration. Utilizing this playbook that led to the downfall of the Glass-Steagall Act, the Dodd-Frank Bill experienced a similar fate during the Obama Administration. The masses got their first Black President while, behind the scenes of the first Black President smoke and mirrors, President Barak Obama "turned the other cheek," and allowed private business regulators to dismantle the Dodd-Frank Bill regulatory measures one-by-one, which on one hand, has rendered Dodd-Frank impotent, and on the other, this has allowed Wall Street to return to extreme profitability by 2013, as we have already seen. To follow is the way in which Wall Street undermined Dodd-Frank, which, has set the table for another financial meltdown of the American Capitalist System in the near future, and, unimaginable new hardships for the American Working Class to bear.

Rana Foroohar called the Dodd-Frank Act, at best, a myth of financial reform, or stated in another way, it is a "glass that is half empty." Rana Foroohar wrote the following:

> "Five years after the crisis, growth is back...The financialization of the American economy, a process by which we've become inexorably embedded in Wall Street, just keeps rolling on. The biggest banks in the country are larger and more powerful than they were before the [2008] crisis, and finance is a greater percentage of our economy than ever...U.S. financial institutions remains free to gamble billions on risky derivatives around the world. We're relying on the banks' good intentions and self-interests, a strategy that didn't work out so well before. The truth is, Washington did a great job saving the banking system in '08 and '09 with swift bailouts that averted even worse damage to the economy. But swayed too much by aggressive bank lobbying, it has done a terrible job of regulating the financial industry and reconnecting it to the real economy."[423]

Lobbying has turned the Dodd-Frank Act into something much, much less than a bird with two broken wings. Because of intense Wall Street lobbying, the Dodd-Frank Act does not have a bee sting, or any lion's teeth. It is harmless regarding having power to regulate Wall Street investment banks. Since the 2008 Depression began that year, and after Wall Street investment banks brought the American Capitalist System to its knees, "... Foroohar stated "...only 40% of the new rules called for by Dodd-Frank

---

[423] Foroohar, Rana, "The Myth Of Financial Reform," Time, Vol. 182, NO. 13, September 23, 2013, pp. 31 and 32.

have been written. No wonder banks have bucked the regulation..."[424] This arrogance has some history underlying it, and in order to grasp the pointlessness of the Dodd-Frank Act, we must understand the enabling role former President Clinton played in creating the conditions that ultimately rendered it a paper lion.

In 1993, former President Bill Clinton appointed Eugene Ludwig to head the Office of the Comptroller of the Currency (OCC), which is "...the primary regulator for many big [Wall Street Investment] banks..."[425] Former President Bill Clinton's appointment of Eugene Ludwig to run the OCC was one of the first steps leading toward the privatization of the regulation of large Wall Street Investment Banks. In short, we shall see shortly that Eugene Ludwig is a private business owner, who was brought in by Former President Bill Clinton to oversee the regulation of the financial activities of Wall Street Investment Banks. Stated simply, the federal government is allowing private business to regulate Wall Street for it.

By 2011, three years after the 2008 Depression, the federal government, during the Obama Administration's first term in office, accused "the nation's biggest banks...of wrongly foreclosing on vast numbers of Americans...4.4 million borrowers were potentially affected...Billions in payouts from titans Bank of America, Wells Fargo and Citibank were at stake...[and] up to $125,000 for each affected homeowner..."[426] Rather than aggressively pursue this case on behalf of the millions of Americans who had lost their homes and savings after the mentioned banks, and others, collapsed the American Capitalist System, the federal government regulators, in the Office of the Comptroller of the Currency, refused to aggressive prosecute the Wall Street Investment Bank violators of the public trust, and, by 2013, the federal government's case ended in failure. Calabresi stated "... it collapsed in failure. By January of this year[2014], the OCC canceled the program as complaints from borrowers mounted."[427] Remember, we

---

[424] Ibid., p. 32.
[425] Calabresi, Massimo, "Oversight for Hire: The rise, and downsides, of private bank examiners," Time, Vol. 182, No. 13, September 23, 2013, p. 36.
[426] Ibid., p. 36.
[427] Ibid., p. 36.

mentioned earlier that former President Bill Clinton appointed Eugene Ludwig to run the OCC in 1993, which, by 2013, was the same federal government office that refused to pursue its corruption case against the large Wall Street Investment Banks. What is the significance of Mr. Eugene Ludwig appointment to run the OCC in 1993?

The Office of the Comptroller of the Currency (OCC) is the door to the American Chicken Coup. Mr. Eugene Ludwig learned how its regulatory process works, and by 2013, his private business was able to exert massive influence on the federal government's inability to prosecute Wall Street Investment banks for corruption. Mr. Eugene Ludwig's private business called "...Promontory Financial, a Washington-based firm...emerged as something of a shadow regulator."[428] Calabresi offered a detail description of Promontory Financial:

> "Promontory is arguably the most powerful of these regulators-for-hire. The expertise of former watchdogs, including founder and CEO Eugene Ludwig, is at the heart of the company's business model. The 450-person firm boasts two former SEC heads, two former top Federal Reserve enforcers and a former leading official from the newly formed Consumer Financial Protection Bureau. Last year[2013], Ludwig was among the highest-paid executives in the financial world, reportedly making more than $30 million-more than JP Morgan Chase CEO Jamie Dimon of Goldman Sachs chief Lloyd Blankenfein. Ludwig oversees the enterprise from a 13,000-sq.ft. mansion in northwest D.C., the 19th most expensive home in the city according to *Washingtonian* magazine. Promomtory occupies the top floor of a new steel-and-glass office building two blocks from the White House."[429]

Promontory Financial influenced the outcome of the OCC's case-Obama Administration- against Wall Street Investment Banks in 2011, which led

---

[428] Ibid., p. 38.
[429] Ibid., p. 38.

to the latter's avoidance of prosecution by the federal government. Calabresi stated "the episode ended well for some: private consultants made huge profits. Half of the fees the banks paid them-nearly $1 billion-went to a single company: Promontory financial..."[430] Using its money, and by 2014, the entire Office of the Comptroller and the Currency, which is the so-called federal government watchdog agency charged with regulating Wall Street Investment Banks, has been privatized. That is, during the Obama Administration. private business consultants have become the watchdogs watching Wall Street. In a chicken coup, the chickens do not need any chicken to watch out for the best interest of all of the chickens; however, if a wolf is in the chicken coup that is dressed up in chicken feathers, the wolf dressed up like a chicken is the able to explain to all of the other chickens the reason real chickens are being eaten up. Private business consultants make sure private Wall Street businesses are not held accountable for any of its corrupt activities such as its collapse of the American Financial System in 2008, which led to the widespread destruction of the social and economic well-being of millions of the American people's livelihoods, especially when job loss and housing foreclosures are concerned. This is how privatization of regulations of Wall Street works.

By 2013, Calabresi stated "Julie Williams, chief counsel for the Office of the Comptroller of the Currency (OCC)...was forced out of the OCC"[431] as a result of the $1 billion Wall Street Banks paid private consultants such as Promontory Financial, and others, to derail the Obama Administration's legal case, which was geared toward helping more than 4 million Americans receive compensation for their personal losses caused by the 2008 Depression. At the beginning of 2013, Julie Williams, who was supposed to help millions of Americans, regardless of race, receive justice, "...was hired as a managing director at Promontory, a position that has previously paid more than $1 million in salary and bonuses."[432] Knowing how the OCC works, Mrs. Julie Williams brought her knowledge of federal government regulations to Promontory Financial, which used it, among others, to prevent Wall Street Investment Banks from being

---

[430] Ibid., p. 38.
[431] Ibid., p. 36.
[432] Ibid., p. 38.

sued, by the federal government, for wrongdoings related to the 2008 Depression, during which time, millions of Americans lost their homes and jobs. Moreover, Amy Friend, a former employee of Promontory Financial, is a key author of the Dodd-Frank Act itself. Calabresi stated "government has also hired from Promontory's ranks. Amy Friend, Williams' eventual replacement at the OCC and a key author of Dodd-Frank when she worked on Capitol Hill, worked at the firm from 2011 to early 2013."[433] Senator Chris Dodd, Senate Banking Committee Chairman, set up a committee to study the causes of the 2008 Depression immediately after its occurrence. Calabresi stated "the month after September 2008 global run on U.S. money markets nearly brought low the world economy, Senate Banking Committee chairman Chris Dodd empaneled his first hearing of outside experts on the crisis and on potential responses by lawmakers to ensure it never happens again. Two of the five panelists were from Promontory-former SEC chair Arthur Levitt, a board member, and Ludwig."[434] From inside the chicken coup, Mr. Eugene Ludwig, and Mr. Arthur Levitt instructed Senator Chris Dodd on ways to prevent another Wall Street induced economic depression from reoccurring. How can one heroin addict help another one quit the habit? If Because Promontory Financial is a Wall Street consultant, Mr. Eugene Ludwig at the table and helped Senator Chris Dodd develop new regulations that he will use to insure that another Wall Street induced economic depression will occur. Mr. Eugene Ludwig helped write the new government regulations aimed at policing wall Street. Calabresi stated "...it was Dodd-Frank regulatory overhaul in the wake of the crash that solidified an important line of business for the firm: shaping the rules themselves. The bill laid out broad goals but left crucial rulemaking to regulators."[435] There are more wolves, dressed up like chickens, in the chicken coup, than chickens, following the 2008 Depression. Calabresi wrote the following:

> "At the OCC alone, one-third of legal actions taken against banks since 2008 have required the aid of outside consultants. Most are staffed with former regulators, who

[433] Ibid., p. 38.
[434] Ibid., p. 38.
[435] Ibid., p. 38.

now implement the rules theyhelped write. Consultants have become so indispensable to the system, they have started to shape it...And because so much banking regulation has been pushed out of government agencies and into the private sector, even private regulators find themselves stretched to capacity and have outsourced the work to still other contractors. In its review of millions of dollars' worth of foreclosures by Bank of America, for instance, Promontory outsourced the hiring and management of hundreds of reviewers to staffing company Solomon Edwards Group...Former FDIC chair Bair [stated] ...regulators are not independent of the banks they regulate, and that is undermining their authority as regulators."[436]

Thus, as we see, all roads lead directly to the inevitable re-occurrence of another catastrophic depression in the near future. Americans, to a large extent, are at-risk and they do not even know it. Privatization of regulations, which means private business is regulating private business equals no Wall Street regulation at all. For all of our colleagues, who are constantly chattering about the widening income gap between the American Ruling Class and the American Working Class, we highly recommend that they spend some time studying the history of the American Capitalist System so they can begin to grasp the one simple idea, namely, that public democracy in America is political consumption of illusions, and, in private, a whole other world of politics shapes the daily American Economic Agenda. A look inside the American Chicken Coup is very revealing and disturbing.

Therefore, the $76 billion the capitalist realized by 2013 has widened the income gap between the "haves and the have nots," namely the class income inequity that exist between the one-half-of-one percent American Ruling Class and the vast majority of the American Working Class. According to Karl Marx: A Biography, 1973, the income gap differential is described as follows:

---

[436] Ibid., pp. 38 and 39.

"Consequently, as capital is accumulated there is a growth at the one pole of bourgeois society of vast wealth, luxury, parasitism and extravagant spending by the exploiting classes, and at the other, ever-increasing oppression, exploitation, unemployment

and an insecure existence for the working people."[437]

Moreover, the income gap mentioned above has become such a concern among the American Ruling Class by 2014, that one of its members compared it to fascist Nazi Germany. Tom Perkins, multi-billionaire and founder of Kleiner Perkins Caufield & Byers, published an article in The Wall Street Journal that includes the following information:

"...I would call attention to the parallels of fascist Nazi Germany to its war on its "one percent," namely its Jews, to the progressive war on the American one percent, namely the "rich." From the Occupy movement to the demonization of the rich embedded in virtually every word of our local newspaper, the San Francisco Chronicle, I perceive a rising tide of hatred of the successful one percent...This is a very dangerous drift in our American thinking. Kristallnacht was unthinkable in 1930; is its descendent "progressive" radicalism unthinkable now?"[438]

Mr. Tom Perkins has a good point. Once the public emotionalism is removed from his public disclosure about the Grand Canyon size, widening of the American income gap, it is no longer fairytale that the American Working Class, a sleeping progressive giant, will soon awaken to an understanding of what is driving this income gap, namely, the capitalist exploitation of their collective labor power, both nationally and at the state government level.

---

[437] Fedoseyev, P. N., Bakh, Irene, et. al, *Karl Marx: A Biography*, Progress Publishers, Moscow, 1973, p. 383.

[438] Perkins, Tom, "Progressive Kristallnacht Coming?, http://www.wsj.com/news/articles

This is the direct outcome of Neo-Liberal Privatization Economic Policy; the latter inevitably promotes a widening gulf between the wealthiest one-half-of one percent of Americans and the remaining 99 percent of the American Working Class, including the middle class. As we have already witnessed, there was a spike in new Louisiana millionaires by 2013, a development that neatly parallels the Jindal Administration's implementation of the Louisiana Ruling Class' Neo-Liberal Privatization Economic Policy in the state. This was achieved in part by the Louisiana Working Class payment of more taxes. And lost of their labor power through their production of surplus value for the capitalist as wage-earners.

Finally, in the Executive Summary of the Institute on Taxation & Economic Policy Report 2013, Davis, Davis, et. al. stated "the main finding of this report is that virtually every state's tax system is fundamentally unfair, taking a much greater share of income from middle- and low-income families than from wealthy families."[439] What does this mean?

That the vast majority of the Louisiana Working Class, regarding their social and economic well-being, have experienced tremendous, sustained stress since the Jindal Administration's first term in office, which began in 2008. One of the surest ways to document this stress is to examine the unemployment situation in Louisiana during Governor Bobby Jindal's implementation of the Louisiana Ruling Class' Neo-Liberal Privatization and Subsidization Economic Policies. According to Governor Bobby Jindal, the latter is supposed to increase employment; however, the unemployment statistics paint a totally different picture.

---

[439] Davis, Davis, et. al., Op. Cit., p. 1.

CHAPTER IX

Louisiana Unemployment During the Jindal Administration, 2008 to 2013

A. Neo-Liberal Privatization Economic Policy And Rising Unemployment

To make this carnage of privatization and subsidization economic policies smell odorless and, as indigestible as it is with extreme stomach pains, Governor Bobby Jindal's prepared script required him to focus on how many "good Louisiana jobs" will be created by the unheard-of Louisiana Taxpayer Dollars Giveaways. Affirmative Action was killed years ago because large business owners thought too much money was being set-aside for minorities: African-Americans, Hispanics, Asians, Native Americans and many others, whose ancestors built America from scratch with their labor power. Ironically, the Louisiana Ruling Class, which is the direct beneficiary of the trillions of dollars of *unpaid slave labor,* from the Sixteenth to the Twenty-First Century, has resurrected Affirmative Action from its grave, and gave it a new name: Privatization and Subsidization Action. There is no need to restate here the vast amount of taxpayer dollars that have been shifted from the Louisiana State Budget to the private sector. Moreover, Louisiana's infrastructure, including roads, bridges, and so forth, is crumbling. Yet, this raises a question: Why are businesses choosing to relocate their operations in Louisiana, a state which has the worst roads in the nation? Will Sentell wrote the following:

"Louisiana's infrastructure needs immediate attention." Kam Movassaghi, executive director of the study group and former secretary for the state Department of Transportation and Development. Louisiana's roads, bridges and other infrastructure are in dire need of improvements, officials of the state branch of the American Society of Civil Engineers...The report gave letter grades in nine areas, with the state's roads getting a "D" and its bridges a "D-plus." Both grades mean "crumbling infrastructure..."[440]

With a crumbling infrastructure, the main carrot handed-out to business, as an incentive to come to Louisiana, is *unheard-of tax breaks*. The other incentive is a relatively uneducated workforce. By 2010, Louisiana ranked 50th in the nation, regarding the number of its residents with a high school diploma or higher. Only 78.7[441] percent were classified in this category. In short, this is considered an excellent environment in which to do business-large unskilled workforce, unheard-of tax breaks and subsidies-Affirmative Action for business-low business tax rate, and crumbling infrastructure.

B. Rising Tide Of Louisiana Unemployment

Presently, the need is to follow up on Governor Bobby Jindal's prepared script, where he is always sounding the horn about jobs. What exactly has been the case with employment since 2008, the year Governor Bobby Jindal started talking big about job creation in Louisiana? During Governor Bobby Jindal's address to the Second Special Session of the Louisiana Legislature, given on March 9, 2008, he made the following statement:

> "We will revamp our workforce training programs to cultivate the highest-trained, most skilled workforce in the world right here in Louisiana. These are all critical

---

[440] Sentell, Will, "Will Sentell stated Engineers say improvements needed, " The Advocate, January 19, 2012, p. 1.

[441] _____ High school diploma or higher, by percentage (most recent) by state, Statemaster, http://statemaster.com.

steps toward greater business growth, more jobs, and more opportunities for our young people so our children and our grandchildren no longer have to move away to pursue their dreams."[442]

Were jobs created as the Governor mentioned in his speech? On March 9, 2008, when Governor Bobby Jindal made the above statement, the Louisiana unemployment rate was 3.8 percent.[443] There were 78,216 people unemployed that year. Here is the contradiction, or misleading untruth, spoken by Governor Bobby Jindal in his mentioned speech. By December 2008, the number of Louisiana residents unemployed rose to 113,147-an increase of 44.7 percent. Simultaneously, based on the tax break and subsidization information provided earlier, Governor Bobby Jindal approved the removal of $113,225,000 out of the Louisiana State Budget for business, while unemployment rate rose 44.7 percent at the same time. Why does the Louisiana State Government have to interfere in the so-called *marketplace*? This is the story of the chef and a hungry man; the chef tells the hungry man "I will cook your dinner for you but you-hungry man-have to *give* me all of the ingredients I need first, before I cook you any food."

By March 2009, the Louisiana unemployment rate skyrocketed to 6.8 percent.[444] This was a 63.2 percent increase; yet, earlier, Governor Bobby Jindal told the Louisiana legislature on March 9, 2008 that "we will revamp our workforce training program..." One year after Governor Bobby Jindal made this claim, there were 128,638 Louisiana residents unemployed, which was 64.5 percent more unemployed than the 78,216 unemployed on March 9, 2008, when he gave his speech before the Louisiana Legislature. Keep in mind too that the whole idea behind the promotion of the so-called privatization and subsidization economic policies of the Louisiana

---

[442] _____ Revamp our workforce training programs, http://www.onthe issues. org/GovernorBobby_Jindal_jobs.

[443] _____ Databases, Tables & Calculators by Subject, Bureau Of Labor Statistics, United States Department Of Labor, http://data.bls.gov/ timeseries/?ASST220000003, 2003 to 2013.

[444] Ibid.

ruling Class is job creation. This job reduction trend continued by March 2010, at which time, 144,390 Louisiana residents were unemployed. The unemployment rate went from 6.2 percent in March 2009 to 7.0 percent by March 2010-an increase of 12.9 percent. Midway through Governor Bobby Jindal's first term in office, the unemployment rate steadily increased. Did the latter continue to increase by March 2011?

Yes. By this date, 153,779 Louisiana residents were unemployed, which was an increase of 6.5 percent over the number unemployed on March 2010. By the end of Governor Bobby Jindal's first term, and by March 2012, the unemployment rate stood at 6.8 percent, and 142,554 Louisiana residents were still unemployed. This was 65,429 more Louisiana residents unemployed than the 77,125 unemployed the day Governor Bobby Jindal stepped into the Governor Mansion on January 2008.

All-in-all, unemployment steadily rose during the Jindal Administration's first four years in office. More importantly, and referring back to Dr. M. Harvey Brenner's Distributed Lag Relationship, which says a sustained 1.4 percent unemployment rate over five year period will have a significant pathological effect on the affected population by the fifth year. In short, the accumulated economic and emotional stress and distress will cumulatively take its toll by the fifth year.

Governor Bobby Jindal first day on the job, in January 2008, the unemployment rate was 3.8 percent; by December 2012, the last day of his first term in office, the unemployment rate was 5.6 percent, and during this period, there was a sustained unemployment rate of 1.8 percent. Given this fact, we are now in position to show what cumulative impact Neo-Liberal Privatization and Subsidization Economic Policies, and the sustained 1.8 percent unemployment rate, had on a vast majority of the Louisiana Citizenry, and its working class in particular.

C. Cumulative Impact Of The Sustained 1.8 Percent Rise In Unemployment During The Jindal Administration's First Five Years In Office, 2008 To 2013

Sustained, massive tax breaks, privatization, and subsidization economic policies, along with their effects of unemployment, falling real wages, and inflation, or tax increases, have-all-contributed simultaneously to the production of high levels of economic stress and emotional distress among the vast majority of Louisiana Working Class People during the first five years of the Jindal Administration. Anger among this population is at an all-time high. Given the sustained 1.8 percent rise in unemployment in Louisiana during this time, our intent is to determine whether there has been a simultaneous increase in pathological behavior among Louisiana Citizens, including its working class in particular.

To refresh our memory of Dr. Harvey Brenner's Distributed Lag Relationship Theory, we will restate it again briefly here. It is very important that we connect the dots relationship that exists between the Louisiana Ruling Class Neo-Liberal Privatization Economic Policy; sustained unemployment that it produces; and both creation of increased pathological behavior among the Louisiana Citizenry. The Louisiana Ruling Class, and its paid appointees, would like nothing better than for us to continue to shuffle around believing that we are innately degenerate, and our aggressive, self-destructive behavior towards self and others, is due to a chemical imbalance in our brain, which cause us to become "bullies," and kill one another indiscriminately, for no reason at all. Dr. Harvey Brenner's pioneer work provides a realistic explanation for the human carnage sweeping across America today, similar to repeated storm surges pushed onshore by an endless Category 5 Hurricane.

a. Brief Review Of The Distributed Lag Relationship Theory

In his study prepared for the Joint Economic Committee of the Congress of the United States titled "Estimating the Social Costs Of national

Economic Policy: Implications For Mental And Physical Health And Criminal Aggression," Paper No. 5, October 26, 1976, Dr. Harvey Brenner discovered that a sustained 1.4 percent increase in unemployment, from 1970 to 1975, "... is directly responsible for some 51,570 total deaths, including 1,740 additional homicides, for 1,540 additional suicides, and for 5,520 additional mental hospitalizations."[445] Moreover, regarding sustained unemployment, Dr. Harvey Brenner wrote the following:

> "...pathological reactions will follow increased unemployment, increased inflation, and decreased per capita income...In the case of each of these three economic sources of distress, we expect what is referred to as a "distributed lag" relationship. This means that the relationship to economic stress are dispersed over time so that during each of several years, a certain proportion of the economic stress initiated during the first year takes its toll."[446]

Since the Jindal Administration took office in 2008, Louisiana unemployment data, previously discussed, showed a 1.8 percent sustained unemployment rate by December 2012. Moreover, President Barack Obama, at the national level, signed a $700 billion-plus interest- Wall Street bail-out, which is a double edge sword for American Working Class people, including Louisiana's. On one hand, the bail-out is a hidden tax increase the unborn babies of working people currently owe before their birth, and on the other, the bail-out is inflationary because working class people will be forced to pay higher prices for goods and services due to the fact the $700 billion plus bail-out has artificially placed more money in the economy, thereby causing consumer prices to rise. And, with unemployment, the per capita income for Louisiana Citizens has decreased. According to the Department Of Numbers, "...the median per capita income for Louisiana was $23,800 in 2012,"[447] by the end of the

---

[445] Brenner, Harvey, Ph. D., Op. Cit., pp. Vi and Vii.

[446] Ibid., pp. 22 and 23.

[447] _____ Louisiana Per Capita Income Trends since 2005, Department Of Numbers, http://www.depofnumbers.com/income/louisiana/

Jindal Administrations' first term in office. In fact, when Governor Bobby Jindal took office in 2008, the Louisiana per capita income was $24,853, which, by 2012, was equal to a -7.5 percent decrease!

b. Distributed Lag Relationship And Neo-Liberal Privatization Economic Policy

In view of Dr. Brenner's Distributed Lag relationship, Louisiana's sustained 1.8 percent unemployment rate, inflation caused by President Barack Obama's Wall Street Bail-out, and its decreased per capita income-All-took a pathological toll on the Louisiana Working Class by 2012, the fourth year these economic distress factors were in effect since 2008. More importantly, each of these economic distress factors do not function independently of economic policy, but, to the contrary, economic policy generate them. In Louisiana's case, and as we have witnessed all along, Louisiana Neo-Liberal Economic Policy has been the catalyst underlying the vast majority of economic distress experienced by the Louisiana Working Class since the Jindal Administration began implementing this economic policy. In sum, Dr. Harvey Brenner's came to the following conclusion:

> "This study indicated that action which influence national [and state] economic activity-have a substantial bearing on physical health, mental health, and criminal aggression.. In any event, it would be imprudent to disregard the implications of substantial social costs associated with factors that stem from economic policy...To the extent, therefore, that economic policy has acted to influence economic activity[-Neo-Liberal Privatization Economic Policy in Louisiana], it has always been related to the nation's [and state's] social health. It would appear that on a day-to-day basis, nearly all political and deliberate economic policy decisions which affect the national, regional, and local economic situation also are associated with many aspects of the nation's [and state's] well-being."[448]

---

[448] Brenner, Harvey, Dr., Op. Cit., p. 7.

Given this fact, we have already presented foregoing information that verifies Neo-Liberal Privatization Economic Policy has had a great unsettling social impact on the day-to-day social well-being of the Louisiana Working Class. At this time, we are in a position to demonstrates the pathological toll Louisiana Neo-Liberal Economic Policy has historically had on the Louisiana Working Class. We will examine the impacts the following have has on the latter since 2008 to 2012: (1) Suicide (2) State Prison Admissions (3) Homicides (4) Cardiovascular-Renal Disease (5) Violence Against Women (7) Drug Offenses and (8)Total Mortality.

D. Pathological Impact Of Neo-Liberal Privatization Economic Policy On The Health Of The Louisiana Working Class, 2008 to 2012

Thus far, we have provided various data that demonstrates Louisiana ranks at or near the bottom nationally in every major social index, including obesity, premature deaths, low birth weight, children in poverty, cardiovascular deaths, cancer deaths, and infant mortality to name only a few. Each one of these social indicators have worsened since Governor Bobby Jindal was s/elected governor in 2008. Rather speculate about this worrisome trend, we will provide information that verifies there has been an upsurge in the quantity of social decay among the Louisiana Working Class since the Jindal Administration took office. We will begin our task with suicide because it represents an individual's inability to find any hope, meaning, or purpose in life, and, therefore, one escapes his or her *hell by committing suicide.*

a. Suicide In Louisiana During The Jindal Administration

In 2002, there were 18 reported suicides in Louisiana; from 2002 to 2007, there were a total of 177 new suicides. A total of 200 new suicides occurred between 2008 and 2013[449]. This change represents a 13.0 percent increase. The median age of those Louisiana Residents who committed suicide is consistent with Dr. Harvey Brenner's Distributed Lag Relationship. In particular, of the 55 new females who committed suicide between 2008 and 2013, their median age ranged from 45.1 years old to 52.3 years old. What makes this interesting is rather than older Louisiana residents becoming more socially stable in their older years, a significant number of those who committed suicide fell in the identified age group. One would imagine younger age people would commit suicide in larger numbers because they are living their lives, to a large extent, in a state of flux and uncertainty. Of course, we see the opposite is true. The other fascinating thing here is the vast majority of older age females, who committed suicide between 2008 and 2013, were Caucasian. Specifically, Of the 84 females who committed suicide between 2002 and 2013, 55, or 66.0 percent took their own lives during this time. In contrast, from 2002 to 2007, one year before Governor Bobby Jindal was s/elected governor, 32. or 38.1 percent committed suicide during this period. Moreover, the 55 new suicides represent a 72.0 percent increase relative to the number of suicides committed, from 2002 to 2007. Male suicides followed a similar trend.

Of the 304 total male suicides committed between 2002 and 2013, 148, or 49.0 percent occurred between 2002 and 2007. During the 2008 to 2013 period, 146, or 48.0 percent new male suicides occurred. Males, who committed suicide between 2008 and 2013, ranged in median age, from 43 years old to 51. Similar to females, we see older male Louisiana residents committed suicide more frequently than younger ones. Since 2002 to 2013, 304 Caucasian males committed suicide; from 2008 to 2013, 135, or 44.4 percent committed suicide during the Jindal administration's first term in office. Overall, 177 new suicide cases were recorded during this time. Another indicator that shows suicides deaths worsened by the first year of Governor Bobby Jindal's second term in office, is the suicide rate, or "number of deaths due to intentional self-harm per 100,000 population."

---

[449] _____Recap Of suicides May 2002 through 2013, St Tammany Outreach for the Prevention of Suicide, http://www.stops-la.org/Stats.asp

By 2012, the Louisiana suicide rate was 11.1 per 100,000 population.[450] By 2013, the latter rose to 12.4 per 100,000 population, which represents a 1.3 increase in the Louisiana suicide rate. Next, we turn our attention to state prison admissions.

b. State Prison Admissions During The Jindal Administration

For many Louisiana Residents, including the thousands who travel here each year to experience the state's creole, cajun, and jazz culture, most, unfortunately, do not realize that "Louisiana is the world's prison capital,"[451] according to Cindy Chang, reporter for The Times-Picayune. Just as the Ole Mississippi River flows lazily through the state on its way to its Gulf of Mexico destination, thousands of Louisiana Residents flow unnoticed, and quietly, into the jaws of the state's criminal justice system. Many remained locked up for life. What makes Louisiana's distinction being the world's prison capital so interesting, is the state incarcerates more of its residents, behind iron bars and razor wires, than any other state, or country worldwide. Accordingly, Cindy Chang added "the state imprisons more of its people, per head, than any of its U.S. counterparts. First among Americans means first in the world. Louisiana's incarceration rate is nearly five times Iran's, 13 times China's and 20 times Germany's."[452] And, we remind you, if any foreign government, or so-called terrorist groups, was holding this many Louisiana Residents hostage, this, without doubt, would be a justification for declaring war against that government or group. Instead, the American Ruling Class, operating through its s/elected Jindal Administration, is pursuing a "scorched Earth" incarceration policy against Louisiana Working Class people, especially African-Americans.

Currently, "Louisiana imprisons more people than any nation in the

---

[450] _____2013 Annual Report, AMERICA'S HEALTH RANKINGS, http://www.americashealthranking.org/LA/Suicide/2008-2008

[451] Chang, Cindy, "Louisiana is the world's prison capital," The Times-Picayune, http://www.nola.com/crime/index.ssf/2012/05/Louisiana_is_the, May 29, 2012.

[452] Ibid.

world...”[453] As it is, Louisiana imprisons 1,619 people per 100,000 residents.[454] This is more than the 730 per 100,000 for the United States; 525 per 100,000 for Russia; 450 per 100,000 for Rwanda; 333 per 100,000 for Iran; 122 per 100,000 for China; and the 62 per 100,000 population for Afghanistan. To make this point even more clear, Louisiana imprisons 2,844.0 percent more people than Japan, which imprisons the fewest people, in the world, at 55 per 100,000! When the United States is considered, Louisiana imprisons 867 people per 100,000 population, which is more than any other state. Mississippi ranks second in the nation with 686 per 100,000. The states that incarcerates the most of its residents are geographically located in the South, inclusive mainly of the states that make up the Southeastern Football Conference (SEC). It is not surprising this football conference has won most of the Bowl Championship Series (BCS) during the past decade. The latter also is inclusive of the Black Belt, which has an historical reference to the American Slavery institution. Given this background, we shall take a closer look at how many Louisiana residents are incarcerated in its criminal justice system.

c. Louisiana Residents Incarcerated Since The Jindal Administration Took Office, 2008 to 2013

During 2007, Governor Bobby Jindal campaigned for governor, and he was s/elected that year. When the votes were counted, there were simultaneously 37,496 Louisiana Residents incarcerated in state prison.[455] This number did not decrease once Governor Bobby Jindal took office in 2008. As he, along with his Louisiana Legislative allies, began to implement the Louisiana Ruling Class' Neo-Liberal Privatization Economic Policy, the total number of Louisiana Residents increased sharply. In fact, by 2007, there were 37,496 Louisiana Residents in state prison; at the end of Governor Bobby Jindal's first year in office in 2008, this number jumped to 38,228, an increase of 2.0 percent. Specifically, another 732 people were sent to state

---

[453] Ibid.

[454] Ibid.

[455] _____ Statistical Briefing Book, Louisiana Department of Public Safety and Corrections: Corrections Services, http://www.doc.la.gov/pages/contact-us/headquarters/.

prison. By 2009, the total number of Louisiana residents locked up in state prison rose to 39,780; the latter decrease slightly to 39,391 at the end of 2010; over the next twelve months ending in 2011, the total number rose again to 39,709; at the end of Governor Bobby Jindal's first term in office in 2012, the total number of Louisiana Residents rose to 40,170; and by the end of the first year of his second term in 2013, the total number of increase to 41,295. Overall, between 2008 and 2013, the total number of Louisiana Residents incarcerated in state prison increased 8.0 percent! Later, we will examine the underlying cause of this large increase. Meantime, what segments of the Louisiana population make up the large majority of the individuals incarcerated in state prison?

By June 13, 2013, 68.3 percent of the 39,926 Louisiana Residents incarcerated in state prison were Black; 94.4 percent were males; and their average age was 35.7 years old. The majority of the Black Males incarcerated by then were between 20 and 50 years old.[456] Whites accounted for 31.3 percent of the total adult incarcerated population by June 13, 2013. As we see, the total number of Black Males incarcerated in Louisiana Adult Prisons is more than doubled the number of Whites. Regardless of what many scientists say about this disproportionate number of Black Males incarcerated in Louisiana State Prison, the large number is having an unbelievable socially destructive impact on the Black Family and Community generally. Currently-February 2014-a significant number of black females are unable to find life-long partners because of this great number of African-American males incarcerated today. Equally distressing is the total number of youth who are incarcerated in Louisiana Prisons today also.

According to James M. Le Blanc, Secretary of the Louisiana Department of Public safety and Corrections, "presently there are 477 offenders who are youthful offenders housed in state prisons. The youthful offender population is composed of offenders who are currently 16, 17, 18, and 19

---

[456] Le Blanc, James M., Secretary, Demographic Profiles of the Adult Correctional Population: Fact Sheet, Louisiana Department of Public Safety and Corrections. http://www.doc.la.gov/wp-content/uploads/stats/2apdf, June 30, 2013, p. 31.

years of age and who were convicted in criminal court...[457] Of the 477 youthful offenders currently incarcerated in Louisiana State Prisons, 80.9 percent are Black; males make up 97.1 percent of the youthful offender population; and the current average is 18.6 years old."[458] Whites make up only 19.1 percent of the 477 youthful offenders, which means there are 408 percent more African-American youth incarcerated in Louisiana State Prison than Whites! Moreover, of the 477 youthful offenders, 313, or 66.0 percent are 19 years old. In addition, the vast majority of African-Americans incarcerated in Louisiana State Prison are currently serving a sentence between 2 and 20 years.

Similar to African-American adult males, who are also serving a sentence between 2 and 20 years, including 4, 674 who are serving life sentences, the youthful offender population indicates that the latter is a feeder population that maintains, as we have already seen, a steady increase in the total number of Louisiana residents, who are incarcerated in Louisiana State Prison. Interestingly, all across Louisiana, the local 5 PM News hour continuously report, everyday without exception, the latest crimes committed in this or that city. Generally, it is the faces of African-Americans that are shown on your television screen, and many of them, as the data proves, eventually end up incarcerated in the Louisiana State Prison System.

Let us proceed to a discussion of the driving force, or cause, Louisiana incarcerates more of its citizens, per 100,000 population, in state prisons today than any other country in the world, including the United States. Before we begin this discussion, it is necessary to state here that since the Jindal Administration took office in 2008, 4,188 new Louisiana Residents were admitted to state prison.

---

[457] Le Blanc, James M., Demographic Profiles of the Youthful Offender Population, Louisiana Department of Public Safety and Corrections: Fact Sheet, http://www.doc.la.gov/wp-content/uploads/stats/2g.pdf, June 30, 2013, p. 43.

[458] Ibid., p. 43.

d. Origin Of The Louisiana State Prison Population And The Part Played By Neo-Liberal Privatization Economic Policy In The Modern Era

Many Louisiana Residents, save the very small percentage who have given some attention to the driver of the "massive upsurge" in incarcerated African-American Males, do not know that the current day Louisiana Criminal "Justice" System has its roots solidly planted in the American Slavery Institution, which dates back 400 years or more. The academic community has glided over this question similar to a car attempting to move forward on a highway that is covered with a layer of frozen ice and snow. All the driver of the car is able to do is spin his wheels and slide one way or another. At best, the question has been studiously written and spoken about in a descriptive manner, rather than it being addressed using an historical, dialectical approach in which change is viewed within the material context of social, economic, political, and class development. As it is, the majority of Louisiana Residents are left thinking quite one-sided that the current, vast pool of incarcerated Afro-American Males are generally delinquent individually, and that hardly nothing else is driving them to make a choice to spend the best years of their lives, or a lifetime, in the Louisiana State Prison System. A closer examination of the Louisiana State Prison Plantation paints a quite different picture.

The roots of the modern day Louisiana State Prison System Plantation dates back to the early 1840s, when Alexandre Mouton served as Louisiana's Sixth Governor, from 1843 to 1846. It was during former Governor Alexandre Mouton Administration that the latter first introduced Privatization Economic Policy, which initiated the leasing of convicted prison population labor to private business. While serving as governor, Alexanadre Mouton, according to Jeff Forret, stated as governor, Mouton approved the leasing out of convict labor from the state penitentiary, then located in Baton Rouge, LA.[459] By 1865, private businesses thirst for cheap labor, especially that of the so-called freed African Slaves,' spread across the South like an out-of-control forest fire.

---

[459] Forret, Jeff, "Before Angola: Enslaved Prisoners in the Louisiana State Penitentiary," Louisiana History, 54 (2013), p. 142.

Specifically, since former Governor Alexandre Mouton, who owned a 20,000 plus acre sugar plantation in St. Martin Parish called Ille Copal, ignited the leasing of convicted prison population labor by 1846, Douglas A. Blackmon wrote in his book *Slavery By Another Name*, 2008, the following:

> "...the concept of reintroducing the forced labor of blacks as a means of funding government services was viewed by whites as an inherently practical method of eliminating the cost of building prisons and returning blacks to their appropriate position in society. Forcing convicts to work as part of punishment for an ostensible crime was clearly legal too; the Thirteenth Amendment to the Constitution, adopted in 1865 to formerly abolish slavery, specifically permitted involuntary servitude as punishment for "duly convicted" criminals. Beginning in the late 1860s, and accelerating after the return of white political control in 1877, every southern state enacted an array of interlocking laws essentially intended to criminalize black life...Every southern states...had passed laws by the end of 1865 outlawing vagrancy and so vaguely defining it that virtually any freed slave not under the protection of a white man could be arrested for the crime."[460]

Thus, millions of African-Americans today are not aware of the fact that the Thirteenth Amendment to the U.S. Constitution contains language that permits involuntary servitude as a punishment for a convicted criminal. By 1865, vagrancy was made a crime, and thousands of so-called freed African Slave were convicted of this crime; sent to prison; and then leased to private businesses to work for "nothing" like they did during the centuries of slavery itself. No American History book used in any school district nationwide contains any information of depth that address this re-enslavement of African Slaves, although a Lincoln Monument was built in Washington, D.C. to indefinitely honor former President Abraham Lincoln for "freeing" the African Slaves in 1865 via his Emancipation Proclamation. The Thirteenth Amendment to the U.S. Constitution reads as follows:

---

[460] Blackmon, Douglas A., *Slavery By Another Name*, Doubleday, 2008, p. 53.

"Neither slavery nor involuntary servitude, except as a punishment for crime whereof the party shall have been duly convicted, shall exist within the United States, or any place subject to their jurisdiction."[461]

Here it is written in plain sight for us to see, but only a few people, regardless of color, have taken any time to discern, or grasp, the fact that the Thirteenth Amendment to the U.S. Constitution actually re-established American Slavery; the latter was ended on paper only. As we have already seen, every southern state after this amendment was approved passed laws making vagrancy a crime, thereby allowing for the roundup of so-called freed African Slaves, and then justly returning them to slavery through the southern states criminal justice system. Blackmon stated,

"...an exponentially larger number of African Americans [were] compelled into servitude through the most informal- and tainted-local courts. The laws passed to intimidate black men away from political participation were enforced by sending dissidents into slave mines for forced labor camps. The judges and sheriffs who sold convicts to giant corporate prison mines also leased even larger numbers of African Americans to local farmers, and allowed their neighbors and political supporters to acquire still more black laborers directly from their courtrooms."[462]

As we see, the Thirteenth Amendment, approved by the U.S. Congress in 1865, set in motion the leasing of convicted criminals, especially former African Slaves, to private business to work for them for nothing. By 1900, the "Involuntary Servitude Seed Thought" hidden in the Thirteenth Amendment, which supposedly formally abolished slavery in America, evolved into the Neo-Liberal Privatization Economic Policy today, which has taken root, and is being applied throughout the Louisiana Economy, and the American Capitalist Economy generally. Before we pass to a

---

[461] Woll Peter and Binstock Robert H., *America's Political System*, Fourth Edition, Random House, New York, p. 569.
[462] Blackmon, Op. Cit., p. 6.

consideration of how the Thirteenth Amendment's Involuntary Servitude clause is working in the Louisiana Economy today, it is worth showing the deep roots Neo-Liberal Privatization Economic Policy had taken by 1900. According to Blackmon,

> "by 1900, the South's judicial system had been wholly reconfigured to make one of its primary purposes the coercion of African-Americans to comply with the social customs and labor demands of Whites. It was not coincidental that 1901 also marked the final full disenfranchisement of nearly all blacks throughout the South. Sentences were handed down by provincial judges, local mayors, and justices of the peace-often men in the employ of the white business owners who relied on the forced labor produced by the judgments...The same men who built railroads with thousands of slaves and proselytized for the use of slaves in southern factories and mines in the 1850s were also the first to employ forced African-American labor in the 1870s.The South's highly evolved system and customs of leasing slaves from one farm or factory to the next, bartering for cost of slaves, and wholesaling and retaining of slaves regenerated itself around convict leasing in the 1870s and 1880s. The brutal forms of physical punishment employed against "prisoners" in 1910 were the same as those used against "slaves" in 1840."[463]

Moreover, Vicky Pelaez added the following:

> "prison labor has its roots in slavery. After the 1861-1865 Civil War, a system of "hiring out prisoners" was introduced in order to continue the slavery tradition. Freed slaves were charged with not carrying out their sharecropping commitments (Cultivating someone else's land in exchange for part of the harvest) or petty

---

[463] Ibid., pp. 7 and 8.

thievery-which were almost never proven-and were then "hired-out" for cotton picking, working in mines and building railroads. From 1870 until 1910 in the state of Georgia, 88% of hired-out convicts were black. In Alabama, 93% of the "hired-" miners were black. In Mississippi, a huge prison farm similar to the old slave plantations replaced the system of hiring out convicts. The notorious Parchman plantation existed until 1972."[464]

From 1865 to the present, involuntary servitude has grown into a multi-billion dollar business by 2014. Blackmon stated the Thirteenth Amendment to the U.S. Constitution gave rise to the following:

"...a system in which armies of free men, guilty of no crimes and entitled by law to freedom, were compelled to labor without compensation, were repeatedly bought and sold, and were forced to do the bidding of white masters through the regular application of extraordinary physical coercion...Indeed, nearly all of the early industrial locations of the South were constructed by such slaves, thousands of whom became skilled masons, miners, blacksmiths, pattern makers, and furnace workers. Slaves performed the overwhelming majority of the raw labor of such operations... "[465]

Of importance for us to remember is two facts. First, the Thirteenth Amendment to the U.S. Constitution was added to re-enslave the recently so-called freed African Slave Population of the South immediately after the Civil War. This amendment was advocated for by private business, which were desperately in need of figuring out a way to re-capture the *free labor power of the African Slaves, who, on paper, were granted their freedom, but, in reality, they were re-enslaved to provide the labor power*

---

[464] Pelaez, Vicky, "The Prison Industry in the United States: Big Business or a New Form of Slavery?" Global Research, http://www.globalresearch.ca/the -prison-industry-in-the-united.

[465] Blackmon, Op. Cit., pp. 4 and 47.

necessary for private businesses to carry on their business operations, without having to pay one dime, as they had done before the Civil War. And, Second, Neo-Liberal Privatization Economic Policy was set in motion with the approval of the Thirteen Amendment in 1865, and by 2014, it application in the American Capitalist System has created wide class divide between the "haves and have-nots." By now, it should be plain to see that the vast pool of incarcerated Louisiana residents is an outgrowth of the growing need for labor power at the cheapest cost over time.

e. Prison Privatization Boom: A Perfect Marriage Between The Availability Of Incarcerated Labor Power Of African-Americans And Private Business Interests

After the Civil War in 1865, Jim Crow Laws imposed segregation among the black and white races, including separation in the areas of housing, public schools, higher education, retail stores, entertainment outlets, recreation, government, transportation, marriage, and even religions to name just a few. This was the norm in American History through the March On Washington in August 1963. After the Civil Rights Bill was passed by the U.S. Congress in 1964, yet, again, Jim Crow refused to die of old age, and gained a new life, after 1970, in the form of economic segregation. Earlier, we noted that Louisiana incarcerates more of its residents than any other country in the world, including the United States which is a part. By no means is this an accident, rather, it is a calculated result of re-establishing a majority African-American modern day slave population within Louisiana's Criminal Justice System, and the nation's as a whole. Vicky Pelaez stated "today, a new set of markedly racist laws is imposing slave labor and sweatshops on the criminal justice system, now known as the prison industry complex," comments the Left Business Observer."[466]

In order to continue to cast a wide net in which to capture huge, and increasing numbers of African-American males in the U.S. Criminal Justice System, new laws have been passed by the U.S. Congress and the states to entrap the valuable labor power within the physical bodies of the

---

[466] Pelaez, Op. Cit.

so-called criminal. As we have already seen, right after the Civil War in 1865, all of the southern states used the Thirteenth Amendment to the U.S. Constitution, which was suppose to abolish human slavery, but, rather, it actually established a new form of slavery on the American Judicial Plantation. Once convicted of any baseless and groundless crime, former African Slaves were re-enslaved via the Convict Leasing System. Over the last fifty years, new laws were enacted that has extended the workings of the American Judicial Plantation through today-2014.

f. Racist Laws And The Criminal Justice System Plantation

The Code Noir laws passed during American Slavery were designed to keep African Slaves under the strictest social control on plantations throughout the South. After former President Abraham Lincoln signed the Emancipation Proclamation supposedly freeing African Slaves, by 1865, the U.S. Congress passed the Thirteen Amendment to the U.S. Constitution, which made it legal to return former African Slaves back to southern plantations as a result of the involuntary servitude clause. To implement the latter, southern states passed many laws aimed at re-capturing the so-called freed African Slaves. As we indicated earlier, any former African Slaves could be thrown in jail for any petty crime such as vagrancy, walking on the wrong side of the street, idleness, and more. Many of the re-enslaved Africans were coerced by the American Criminal Justice System to work for private businesses, without any compensation, for the rest of their lives. One would think this general pattern of racial oppression ended during the Civil Rights Era? To the contrary, it has gained increased momentum spurred on by the passage of new laws, which have, collectively, transformed the southern plantation into the Criminal Justice System Plantation. Later, we will see how many African-Americans, who are descendants of African Slaves, are presently incarcerated on the Criminal Justice System Plantation. Some of the laws that maintain the latter are addressed first.

Ronald Weich and Carlos Angulo wrote the following about the Criminal Justice system Plantation:

"...in one critical arena — criminal justice — racial inequality is growing, not receding. Our criminal laws, while facially neutral, are enforced in a manner that is massively and pervasively biased...today, racial profiling and police brutality make...travel hazardous to the dignity and health of law-abiding black and Hispanic citizens...Today...Blacks, Hispanics and other minorities are victimized by disproportionate targeting and unfair treatment by police and other front-line law enforcement officials; by racially skewed charging and plea bargaining decisions of prosecutors; by discriminatory sentencing practices; and by the failure of judges, elected officials, and other criminal justice policymakers to redress the inequities that become more glaring every day."[467]

No matter how much time has elapsed since the Thirteenth Amendment was passed by the U.S. Congress in 1865, the pattern remains unbroken, namely, racist laws were passed to increase the number of African-Americans incarcerated on the Criminal Justice System Plantation. The above are examples. Racial profiling is another racist law that continues to roundup a large number of African-Americans, who labor power is eventually turned into "cheap labor" on the American Criminal Justice System Plantation. Weich and Angulo added "a growing body of statistical evidence demonstrates that black motorists are disproportionately stopped for minor traffic offenses because the police assume that they are more likely to be engaged in more serious criminal activity."[468] This racial profiling allows law enforcement officials to book African-Americans into jail, and many end up on the American Criminal Justice System Plantation-oftentimes-for minor infractions. Some studies done in Florida and New Jersey found between 40.0 percent and 70 percent of all traffic stops made by highway patrolmen/women involved blacks and Hispanics.

---

[467] Weich, Ronald and Angulo Carlos, "Racial Disparities in the American Criminal Justice System," *Justice on Trial: Racial Disparities in the American Criminal Justice System* Report, 2000, pp. 185 and 186.
[468] Ibid., p. 187.

In addition to Racial Profiling, another law that continues to roundup hundreds of African-American Males is called *Mandatory Minimum Sentencing*.

As it was back during the American Slavery Institution period, the most important thing to the productive operation of a plantation was maintaining an available supply of African Slaves, whose labor power could be transformed into a commodity, and eventually exchanged for a profit. The objective still holds true by February 2014. Before 1980, a judge had the authority to impose sentences in criminal cases that came before his or her court. This usually allowed some individuals to receive shorter sentences, if the judge felt the person would likely not commit another crime. However, by the mid-1980s, this humanism was wrung out of the American Criminal Justice System Plantation. Weich and Angulo stated the following:

> "Sentencing is arguably the most important stage of the criminal justice system...prosecutorial choices help determine who will be granted leniency from the full force of the law...At several points in this century, most recently in the mid-1980s, Congress and many state legislatures have enacted laws to deny judges sentencing discretion. These laws establish a minimum penalty that the judge must impose if the defendant is convicted under particular provisions of the criminal code... Mandatory sentencing laws...deprive judges of their traditional authority to impose just sentences...Mandatory minimum laws embody a dangerous combination. They provide the government with unreviewable discretion to target particular defendants or classes of defendants for harsh punishment. But they provide no opportunity for judges to exercise discretion on behalf of defendants in order to check prosecutorial discretion."[469]

Immediately after the Civil War, southern states passed laws to re-enslave African Slaves. Today, with Mandatory Minimum Sentencing Laws,

---

[469] Ibid., p. 196.

African-American Males are being disproportionately sentenced to "hard labor" on the American Criminal Justice System Plantation. Later, we will see how long African-American Males are being sentenced to "hard Labor," and exactly for what specific reasons. Their so-called criminal act is similar to the *hook that a fisherperson uses to catch a fish; once caught, the fish seldom is thrown back in the water save if it's size is too small to keep.* Based on Mandatory Minimum Sentencing laws, many African-American Males are snared by the American Criminal Justice System Plantation, and they remain incarcerated doing "hard Labor" for many years, often for a lifetime. To further highlight just how much in demand the labor power of African-American Males is on the American Criminal Justice System Plantation, and similar to the large numbers of former African Slaves who were arbitrarily rounded up for vagrancy law violations right after 1865, today, the mandatory Minimum Sentencing Law called "three Strikes, you're out" is sweeping the streets clean of petty drug users. For instance, Weich and Angulo wrote the following:

> "Mandatory minimums such as "three strikes" laws result in the extended incarceration of nonviolent offenders, who, in many cases, are merely drug addicts or low-level functionaries in the drug trade. Indeed, in the first two years after enactment of California's "three strikes, you're out" law, more life sentences had been imposed under that law for marijuana users than for murderers, rapists, and kidnappers combined. An Urban Institute study examining 150,000 drug offenders incarcerated in state prisons in 1991 determined that127,000 of these individuals — 84% — had no history of violent criminal activity, and half of the individuals had no criminal record at all.[470]

Life sentences, for drug convictions, insured that a supply of cheap, African-American labor power would be available on the American Criminal Justice System Plantation for a long time. Weich and Argulo stated "drug arrests are easier to accomplish in impoverished inner-city neighborhoods

---

[470] Ibid., p. 199.

than in stable middle-class neighborhoods, so the insistence of politicians on more arrests results in vastly more arrests of poor, inner-city blacks..."[471] Weich and Angulo provided data that shows just how easy it has been to roundup African-American Males on drug charges, which has had the overall effect of causing their total numbers to outstrip all other racial groups even though the Black Race in America makes up only 13.0 percent of the total population. Weich and Argulo wrote the following:

> "Between 1980 and 1995, the number of state prisoners locked up for drug crimes increased by more than 1000%. Whereas only1 out of every 16 state inmates was a drug offender in 1980, 1 out of every 4 in 1995 was a drug offender. By the middle of the 1990s, 60% of federal prison inmates had been convicted of a drug offense, as opposed to 25% in 1980. If local and county jail inmate populations are included in the calculation, there are now some 400,000 federal and state prison inmates — almost a quarter of the overall inmate population — serving time or awaiting trial for drug offenses. Drug offenders accounted for more than 80% of the total growth in the federal inmate population— and 50% of the growth of the state prison population — from 1985 to 1995.[472]

As we see, African-American males are "fish in a bucket." They continue to be arrested in large numbers because, as we have mentioned before, their labor power is incredibly valuable to the operators of the American Criminal Justice System Plantation in Louisiana, and the nation as a whole. One excellent example of how African-Americans Males are being warehoused on this plantation is the sentencing disparity related to powder and crack cocaine. According to the Political Research Associates Organization, anyone arrested in 2014, for possession of crack cocaine, will served a significantly longer sentence than if arrested for possession of powder cocaine. This organization wrote the following:

---

[471] Ibid., p. 199.
[472] Ibid., pp. 197 and 198.

"Although crack and cocaine are virtually the same thing, Congress has assigned far harsher penalties to crimes involving crack, a drug primarily associated with people of color. In 1988, Congress passed a law that created a 100:1 quantity ratio between the amount of crack and powder cocaine needed to produce certain mandatory minimum sentences for trafficking and created mandatory minimum penalties for simple possession. In order to receive a five-year sentence for possession with intent to distribute for powder cocaine, a person must possess 500 grams or more. To receive a five-year sentence with crack cocaine, a person need only have 5 grams in their possession."[473]

Given this gap between sentencing for powder cocaine and crack cocaine, it is the latest in a long history of laws passed by the American Ruling Class' controlled federal, state, and local government aimed at an on-going roundup of African-American Males; once arrested, thousands are locked up on the American Criminal Justice System Plantation; and then their labor power is exploited similar to the way it was taken advantage of before and after 1865. By 2014, so many African-American Males are serving "long sentences" on the American Criminal Justice System Plantation.

g. Doing Time In Louisiana During The Jindal Administration

In its Briefing Book, updated in July 2013, and submitted to Bobby Jindal, Governor, the Louisiana Department of Public Safety and Corrections reported there were 39,926 Louisiana Residents locked up on the Louisiana Criminal Justice System Plantation by July 2013. Of the 39,926 total prison population, 94.4 percent were males, and 68.3 percent were Black.[474] According to the United States Census, by 2012,

---

[473] _____ Political Research Associates, DEFENDING JUSTICE: AN ACTIVIST RESOURCE KIT, Factsheet, http://defendingjustice.org/factsheets, p. 3.
[474] Leblanc, James M., Secretary, *Briefing Book: Louisiana Corrections*, July 2013 Update, p. 31.

Louisiana's total population was 4,602,134.[475] Interestingly, of this total, African-Americans accounted for 32.4 percent of the total population; yet, 68.3 percent of the 39,926 total Louisiana prison Population was African-American by July 2013; and, the vast majority of this total were African-American Males. Moreover, the average maximum sentence in the 39,926 total Louisiana Prison Population is 15.4 years. In addition, 4,674, or 11.7 percent of the total prison population are serving a life sentence, which means they will never leave the Louisiana Criminal justice System Plantation similar to their African Slave ancestors during the American Slavery Period. In short, their labor power will be available for exploitation during their entire lifetime.

Beginning in 1865, the easiest way for the slave masters to re-capture the so-called freed African Slaves was to get the legal system to arrest the latter on such charges as vagrancy, and other misdemeanors. Thousands were re-enslaved. By 2014, the easiest way to capture the labor power of African-American Males is to arrest them on drug charges such as the powder and crack cocaine sentencing disparity mentioned earlier. The result of this is apparent because the second largest percentage of Louisiana Residents, who were serving time by 2014, were sentenced to the Louisiana Criminal Justice System Plantation for drug offenses. Of the 39,926 Total Louisiana Prison Population by July 2013, 10,300, or 25.7 percent are serving time for drug offenses.[476]

Overall, so many African-American Males are currently serving "Big Time" on the Louisiana Criminal Justice System Plantation that an entire generation in the African-American Community has been lost. According to Weich and Angulo stated "Black…America ha[s] lost a generation of young men to the criminal justice system."[477] In addition, so many African-American Males are currently serving time on the Louisiana Criminal Justice System Plantation that the *availability of male partners are far less*

---

[475] _____ State & County QuickFacts, United States Census, http://quickfacts. census.gov/qfd/states/22000.html

[476] Leblanc, Op. Cit., p. 32.

[477] Weich and Angulo, Op. Cit., p. 205.

than the number of African-American Females who are looking for partner. Weich and Angulo described the social problem as follows:

> "The massive incarceration of black…males also has a destabilizing effect on their communities. It skews the male-female ratio in those communities, increases the likelihood that children will not be raised by both parents, and contributes to the fragmentation of inner-city neighborhoods that renders the crime-race linkage a self-fulfilling prophecy."[478]

The only thing left to do now is go inside the Louisiana Criminal Justice System Plantation and take a closer look at what is going-on. We will, most likely, all find it very shocking, but not surprising, to learn that a giant Prison Industrial Complex, consisting of numerous private businesses, has been established on this plantation for the primary purpose of exploiting the labor power of a vast majority of the current prison population, which, as we already know, are African-American Males.

h. Louisiana Criminal Justice System Plantation And The Prison Industrial Complex (PIC)

Since the enactment of the Thirteenth Amendment to the U. S. Constitution, which gave slavery a new meaning through involuntary servitude, the total number of Americans, especially Afro-Americans, who are locked up on the Louisiana Criminal Justice System Plantation, including the Prison Industrial Complex (PIC), which operates inside it, has grown to more than two million. Weich and Angulo stated "two million people are housed in American prisons. Although they comprise less than a quarter of the U.S. population, black…Americans make up approximately two-thirds of the total U.S. prison population. The percentage of prisoners who are black is four times that of the percentage of blacks in the U.S. population (49% to12%)… [479] To highlight the growth of the total U. S. Prison Population, Weich and Angulo added "in 1972, the population

---

[478] Ibid., p. 205.
[479] Ibid., p. 204.

of federal and state prisons combined was approximately 200,000. By 1997, the prison population approached 1.2 million, an increase of almost 500%."[480] Since 1972, the total prison population increased 900.0 percent. "...the legacies of colonialism, slavery and racism still affect our policies and practices today. Of the nearly 2.1 million adult men and women imprisoned in the United States, roughly 70% are persons of color."[481] Vicky Pelaez's research supports the existence of this massive buildup of prisoners in the United States. She wrote recently,

> "there are approximately 2 million inmates in state, federal and private prisons throughout the country. According to California Prison Focus, "no other society in human history has imprisoned so many of its own citizens." The figures show that the United States has locked up more people than any other country: a half million more than China, which has a population five times greater than the U.S. Statistics reveal that the United States holds 25% of the world's prison population, but only 5% of the world's people. From less than 300,000 inmates in 1972, the jail population grew to 2 million by the year 2000. In 1990 it was one million."[482]

Given the enormous number of African-American Males locked down on the Louisiana Criminal Justice System Plantation, and nationwide, Pelaez raised an important question: Is this a new form of slavery? Based on the evidence we have presented so far, the answer is positive. There must be some purpose underlying the massive buildup of prisoners in Louisiana and the nation? When we looked beneath the surface of the crimes committed by the people incarcerated, we discovered the true purpose of today's Louisiana Criminal Justice System Plantation is the same as it was during the American Slavery Institution, namely, to exploit cheap labor to make a large profit. African Slaves worked for 400 plus years, and not one

---

[480] Ibid., p. 197.
[481] _____Political Research Associates, Op. Cit.
[482] Pelaez, Vicky, "The Prison industry in the United States: Big Business or a New Form of Slavery?." http://www.globalresearch.ca/the-prison-industry-in-the-united

became a millionaire; prisoners make pennies a day today, and not one leaves prison a millionaire at the end of his or her sentence. Usually, when a prisoner leaves the Louisiana Criminal Justice System Plantation, he or she returns to society having been stripped of their civil and human rights. Simultaneously, as a result of Neo-Liberal Privatization Economic Policy, there has been an upsurge in privately owned prisons; inmates are the free labor used by them to realize unheard-of profits because everything an employer pays a wage worker outside of the prison industrial complex, those who operate the latter do not pay anything approaching a federal minimum wage of $10.10 per hour; an inmate is lucky if he or she earns 10 cents per hour!! The prison industrial complex is unmasked below.

The Louisiana Criminal Justice System Plantation, both state and nationwide, conveniently remove various social problems "out of sight" and "out of mind." They're like closets stuffed with bones. Angela Davis stated "homelessness, unemployment, drug addiction, mental illness, and illiteracy are only a few of the problems that disappear from public view when the human beings contending with them are relegated to cages. Prisons thus perform a feat of magic…prisons do not disappear problems, they disappear human beings. And the practice of disappearing vast numbers of people from poor, immigrant, and racially marginalized communities has literally become big business."[483] Mrs. Angela Davis provides an excellent description of the inner workings of the prison industrial complex; she wrote,

> "…penal infrastructures must be created to accommodate a rapidly swelling population of caged people. Goods and services must be provided to keep imprisoned populations alive…Vast numbers of handcuffed and shackled people are moved across state borders as they are transferred from one state or federal prison to another. All this work, which used to be the primary province of government, is now also performed by private corporations, whose links

[483] Davis, Angela, "Masked Racism: reflections on the Prison Industrial Complex," http://colorlines.com/archives/1998/09/masked_racism_reflections, September 10, 1998.

to government in the field of what is euphemistically called "corrections" resonate dangerously with the military industrial complex. The dividends that accrue from investment in the punishment industry, like those that accrue from investment in weapons production, only amount to social destruction. Taking into account the structural similarities and profitability of business-government linkages in the realms of military production and public punishment, the expanding penal system can now be characterized as a "prison industrial complex."[484]

The linkage between "the realms of military production and public punishment" referred to by Mrs. Angela Davis is an excellent example of Neo-Liberal Privatization Economic Policy at work. Without the implementation of this policy, a prison industrial complex could not exist. Therefore, the roughly 40,000 Louisiana Residents who are incarcerated on the Louisiana Criminal Justice System Plantation, and the other million or more incarcerated by other states and the federal government, are, in fact, the infrastructure that constitute the prison industrial complex. In short, the latter involves the direct, day-to-day operation of a privatized state prison, which is operated like a private business for the sole purpose of realizing a profit off of the exploited labor power of an affected inmate population. Earlier we saw how various racist laws have greatly influenced the buildup of the total prison population in the United States. Overtime, the American Criminal Justice System transformed itself, as a result of racist laws, into the American Criminal Justice System Plantation. Pelaez stated "during the post-Civil War period, Jim Crow racial segregation laws were imposed on every state, with legal segregation in schools, housing, marriages and many other aspects of daily life. "Today, a new set of markedly racist laws is imposing slave labor and sweatshops on the criminal justice system, now known as the prison industry complex..."[485] The prison industrial complex gained its ascendancy during the early 1980s when former President Ronald Reagan unleashed the beast of Neo-Liberal Privatization Economic Policy. Pelaez wrote "the prison privatization boom

---

[484] Ibid.
[485] Pelaez, Op. Cit.

began in the 1980s, under the governments of Ronald Reagan and Bush Sr., but reached its height in 1990 under William Clinton, when Wall Street stocks were selling like hotcakes."[486] As we have seen, more than 2 million Americans have been sucked into the jaws of the beast of the prison industrial complex since that time.

During its early infancy, only a handful of private prisons existed during the Reagan Era. But, the Gulag gained quick momentum. Pelaez stated "ten years ago there were only five private prisons in the country, with a population of 2,000 inmates; now, there are 100, with 62,000 inmates. It is expected that by the coming decade, the number will hit 360,000, according to reports."[487] Furthermore. She added "thanks to prison labor, the United States is once again an attractive location for investment in work that was designed for Third World labor markets."[488] As we mentioned earlier, former President Ronald Reagan swung the privatization door wide-open for private businesses to continue its history of making profits off of the labor power of prisoners, which began in 1865 and continues today.

Before we show how the prison industry complex works, it is necessary to re-state here that prisons lock people up, and their labor power is then utilized by private businesses to make profits. Pelaez wrote the following about privatizing prisons for the exploitation of prisoners' labor power:

> "The prison industry complex is one of the fastest-growing industries in the United States and its investors are on Wall Street. "This multi-million-dollar industry has its own trade exhibitions, conventions, web-sites, and mail-order/Internet catalogs. It also has direct advertising campaigns, architecture companies, construction companies, investment houses on Wall Street, plumbing supply companies, food supply companies, armed security, and padded cells in a large variety of colors." "The private

[486] Ibid.
[487] Ibid.
[488] Ibid.

contracting of prisoners for work fosters incentives to lock people up. Prisons depend on this income. Corporate stockholders who make money off prisoners' work lobby for longer sentences, in order to expand their workforce. The system feeds itself," says a study by the Progressive Labor Party, which accuses the prison industry of being "an imitation of Nazi Germany with respect to forced slave labor and concentration camps."[489]

The prison industry complex stretches from Wall Street to Main Street, and it has some of America's largest Fortune 500 Corporations invested in it. As we stated earlier, prison labor power is very attractive and profitable in the eyes of investors-capitalists. In a lengthy quote below, Pelaez identifies the latter:

> "Who is investing? At least 37 states have legalized the contracting of prison labor by private corporations that mount their operations inside state prisons. The list of such companies contains the cream of U.S. corporate society: IBM, Boeing, Motorola, Microsoft, AT&T, Wireless, Texas Instrument, Dell, Compaq, Honeywell, Hewlett-Packard, Nortel, Lucent Technologies, 3Com, Intel, Northern Telecom, TWA, Nordstrom's, Revlon, Macy's, Pierre Cardin, Target Stores, and many more. All of these businesses are excited about the economic boom generation by prison labor. Just between 1980 and 1994, profits went up from $392 million to $1.31 billion. Inmates in state penitentiaries generally receive the minimum wage for their work, but not all; in Colorado, they get about $2 per hour, well under the minimum. And in privately-run prisons, they receive as little as 17 cents per hour for a maximum of six hours a day, the equivalent of $20 per month. The highest-paying private prison is

---

[489] Pelaez, Vicky, "The prison Industry in the United States: Big Business or a New Form of Slavery, " http://www.globalresearch.ca/the-prison-industry-in-the-united, March 2008.

CCA in Tennessee, where prisoners receive 50 cents per hour for what they call "highly skilled positions." At those rates, it is no surprise that inmates find the pay in federal prisons to be very generous. There, they can earn $1.25 an hour and work eight hours a day, and sometimes overtime. They can send home $200-$300 per month."[490]

The prison industry complex is a billion dollar operation, and no matter how some try to glorify the wages prisoners earn in it, it is still, in its most naked form, modern day slavery. In a federal prison, $1.25 an hour is said to be a good wage, and $300 a month a great salary. This is nothing compared to the millions of dollars private business make off of the exploitation of prisoners' labor power. This is Wall Street exploitation of prisoners. There is another form of privatization going-on in the prison industry complex, which is known as private prisons.

Former Presidents Reagan, Bush Sr., and Bill Clinton were all s/elected presidents by capitalists supporters, who, in return for their financial campaign contributions, were rewarded with opportunities to operate their own private prisons, or privatize the operations of state-run publicly-owned prisons. Pelaez added,

> "private prisons are the biggest business in the prison industry complex. About 18 corporations guard 10,000 prisoners in 27 states. The two largest are Correctional Corporation of America (CCA) and Wackenhut, which together control 75%. Private prisons receive a guaranteed amount of money for each prisoner, independent of what it costs to maintain each one. According to Russell Boraas, a private prison administrator in Virginia, "the secret to low operating costs is having a minimal number of guards for the maximum number of prisoners." The CCA has an ultra-modern prison in Lawrenceville, Virginia, where five guards on dayshift and two at night watch over 750 prisoners. In these prisons, inmates may get their sentences

---

[490] Ibid.

reduced for "good behavior," but for any infraction, they get 30 days added – which means more profits for CCA. According to a study of New Mexico prisons, it was found that CCA inmates lost "good behavior time" at a rate eight times higher than those in state prisons."[491]

Two of the largest private prisons in the United States are Correctional Corporation of America (CCA) and Wackenhut. Both of these private industries are listed on Wall Street, in which millions of dollars are invested in them by so-called stockholders. As Pelaez mentioned in the above quotation hat 18 private corporations run their own prisons in 27 states. And, to insure that profits will remain high at all times, the roundup of African-Americans in particular is necessary and desired by private prison owners. As we already know, Louisiana incarcerates more of its people than any other state in the nation, and more than any other country worldwide. As a result, the private prison business on the Louisiana Criminal Justice system Plantation is booming during the Jindal Administration.

From 1843 to 1846, Former Governor Alexandre Mouton, Sixth Louisiana Governor, popularized the leasing of prison labor inasmuch as he leased the latter out to private business, which, then, constituted the infamous Convict Labor System. The latter has not gone away; it has simply changed form overtime. Today, Cindy Chang, who wrote a series of articles for The Times-Picayune, on the Louisiana crime problem, stated "each inmate is worth $24.39 a day in state money, and sheriffs trade them like horses, unloading a few extras on a colleague who has openings. A prison system that leased its convicts as plantation labor in the 1800s has come full circle and is again a nexus for profit."[492] So, from Wall Street to the Louisiana swamps, home to Cajun and Creole Cultures, is also home to the largest prison industry complex, regarding total population per 100,000 incarcerated. Of course, this industry kept far out-of –the-sight of Louisiana residents and its tourists. However, when one leaves the tourist track, and ventures into the backwoods of Louisiana, and even

---

[491] Ibid.
[492] Chang, Cindy, "Louisiana is the world's prison capital," The times-Picayune, http://www.nola.com/crime/index.ssf/2012/05/Louisiana_is_the_, May 29, 2012.

in some large cities, he or she will be shocked to learn that there exists today, as it did before the Civil War, a Louisiana Criminal Justice System Plantation, on which thousands of African-American males, at least 70.0 percent, are using their labor power to create huge profits for sheriffs, other private prison owners and capitalist investors. Before we go deeper into the exploitation of prison labor power for profits, a few words about the way the private prisons operate in Louisiana requires some attention at this moment.

In the 1990s, Cindy Chang stated "...a prison-building boom swept north Louisiana..."[493] It actually began when Richard Stalder became the Secretary of the Louisiana department of Corrections in 1992. According to Chang, the Louisiana Prison Boom took off when Richard Stalder increased the per diem payment to house a prisoner. She described the Stalder Financial deal as follows:

> "Richard Stalder, who took over the Department of Corrections in 1992, saw a solution. Sweeten the financial incentives, he reasoned, and sheriffs would change their tune. Sure enough, an increased per diem payment and a guarantee of 40 percent occupancy was enough to spark an incarceration gold rush. Sheriffs, seeing jobs for their constituents and new equipment for their deputies, volunteered to build the new prisons the state could not afford. The once-recalcitrant Foti expanded his prison to more than 7,000 beds. In rural, impoverished north Louisiana, the deal was particularly alluring, not only for sheriffs but for private investtors, who knocked on sheriffs' doors, dangling financing and profit-sharing deals. Low, cinder-block buildings ringed with barbed wire sprouted along country highways across the state... Another Louisiana company, LCS Corrections, developed a similar profile, with three prisons in Louisiana and three

---

[493] Chang, Cindy, "North Louisiana family is a major force in the state's vast prison industry," http://www.nola.com/crime/index.ssf/2012/05/jonesboro_family, May 14, 2012.

in Texas. Louisiana's private prison industry is mostly home-grown: The national chains CCA and GEO each operate a state prison but no local prisons.[494]

After Richard Stalder made it most profitable for sheriffs, and private business, to build and operate private prisons in Louisiana, the expansion of the Louisiana Criminal Justice System Plantation gained unbridled momentum, because great profits could now be made by stuffing more and more people, especially African-American Males, into prisons so that the occupancy rate would remain at a guaranteed 40 percent level. Adding to this a per diem-$24.39-for each prisoner incarcerated on the plantation, everyone would make a profit off of mostly African-American Males the same way slave owners did during the American Slavery Period a few centuries earlier. In fact, Chang reminds us that the sheriffs, who operate most of the private prisons in rural areas of Louisiana, actually do so the same way slave owners operated their plantations. She stated "sheriffs compete with each other for the catch of the day. They trade inmates as they please -- shipping some to a colleague with beds to fill, unloading a guy who complains too much or asking around for a skilled mechanic."[495] As a result of the Richard Stalder privatization deal handed-out to sheriffs and private business, by 2011, there were more prisoners locked up in local, privatized prisons than state-run ones. In fact, in privatized, local prisons, there were 20,866 prisoners incarcerated in them statewide, and 18,843 were warehoused in state prisons. Since 1990, the number of prisoners incarcerated in Local, privatized prisons went from 4,720 that year to 20,866-a 299.2 percent increase! The number of prisoners held in state-operated prisons went from 14,079 in 1990 to 18,843 by 2011-a 33.8 percent increase. It should be noticed here that while there was an increase in the number of prisoners incarcerated in state-operated prisons during this time, the percentage increase was more than eight times less than the percentage of prisoners incarcerated in local, privatized prison facilities. Therefore, local prisons, though part of the massive Louisiana Criminal Justice System Plantation, is where the bulk of the privatization action is. Sheriffs are the modern day slave owners profiting off of mostly African-

---

[494] Ibid.
[495] Ibid.

American Male prisoners. Chang commented "in rural, impoverished north Louisiana, the deal was particularly alluring...for sheriffs [and] for private investors...South Louisiana's crime problems fuel north Louisiana's incarceration industry. The dollars that might have been scraped together to pay for inmate rehabilitation go instead to upgrading a rural sheriff's vehicle fleet."[496] To make it all happen, sheriffs ban together with private business, and together, they provide campaign contributions to political candidates who can deliver the human prisoner cargo today.

The vast majority of Louisiana Citizens, including many tenured professors working in-and-out of its major universities, believe, especially our esteemed political scientists professors, who hold this or that endowed chair of distinctions, there is no correlation between the great upsurge in the Louisiana prison industry complex ; its upsurge in locked up African-American Males and political campaign contributions. This is the same as saying there is no correlation between the great winter storms of 2013-2014 and global warming. Once the dust settles, and all of the lowery words have been spoken, Chang brought a sense of reason to this question when she wrote the following:

> "A drop in the incarceration rate could spell doom for both LaSalle Corrections and the sheriffs. The Louisiana Sheriffs' Association lobbies extensively on its members' behalf and funds campaigns through a related political action committee. Private prison companies have the resources to be major political donors themselves. With strategically placed contributions, they can influence legislation as well as potentially steer inmates to their own prisons. In the past decade, LaSalle and the McConnells have donated about $31,000 to campaigns, including $10,000 to Gov. Bobby Jindal and numerous contributions to north Louisiana state legislators. LCS and its owners have thrown much more cash at politicians -- about $120,000 since 1999."[497]

---

[496] Ibid.
[497] Ibid.

This is, for better or worse, the way the "behind the scenes game" is played; the surface of this same game is the "smoke and mirrors'" superficial layers, which hare electronically fed to us, via the social media, justifying the great re-enslavement of thousands of African-Americans on the Louisiana Criminal Justice System Plantation (LCJSP). The "behind the scenes" aspect of the "campaign contribution for favors" game has had one result, namely, the indisputable buildup of local privatized prisons across Louisiana by 2014, or by the sixth year of Governor Bobby Jindal's second term in the Governor's Office. Chang added "so many prisons were built in the boom times of the 1990s that sheriffs are having trouble keeping their beds full, in a business where less than 100 percent occupancy means going in the red."[498] As we have seen already, the LCJSP is not "going in the red," it is "going in the black." An answer to how widespread is the LCJSP is considered below.

At the forefront of the LCJSP, is the privatized LaSalle Corrections Prison. Clay McConnell, an ordained minister, and his father, Billy, created LaSalle Corrections, which represents a major force in Louisiana's vast prison industry complex. Chang wrote the following:

> "Today, the McConnells are a major force in Louisiana's vast prison industry, playing a role in the incarceration of one in seven prisoners. The family's fortunes have risen hand in hand with those of rural sheriffs who are the best-known face of Louisiana Incarceration-for-Profit Inc. More than half of the state's 40,000 inmates are housed in local prisons run by sheriffs or private companies like LaSalle for the express purpose of making a buck."[499]

The LaSalle Corrections Prison's component of the LCJSP stretches across several North Louisiana Parishes. Chang wrote,

> "...Jackson Parish Correctional Center...gets about a quarter of its inmates from the New Orleans metro

---

[498] Ibid.
[499] Ibid.

area, with more than 200 typically hailing from Jefferson Parish. LaSalle houses many more south Louisiana natives at its other prisons, which form a swath roughly paralleling Interstate 20 -- Catahoula, Claiborne, LaSalle, Richwood, Lincoln, Concordia. In Richland Parish, the company has a financial stake in the prison but does not manage it. Few Louisianians have heard of LaSalle Corrections, but its reach is broad: A quarter of local prison inmates are incarcerated in a LaSalle-affiliated facility."[500]

This is a wide network. Is it any wonder anymore, at this point, what is the real reason underlying the fact, as we have previously mentioned, Louisiana holds the distinction of having the highest per capita incarceration rate in, one, the United States, and two, the entire world? When we add in the geography of the privatized prisons operated on the LCJSP, the geographical expanse of the latter becomes even more formidable. Chang stated "several homegrown private prison companies command a slice of the market. But in a uniquely Louisiana twist, most prison entrepreneurs are rural sheriffs, who hold tremendous sway in remote parishes like Madison, Avoyelles, East Carroll and Concordia. A good portion of Louisiana law enforcement is financed with dollars legally skimmed off the top of prison operations."[501] The privatized LCJSP, or Louisiana Prison Industry Complex, covers twelve parishes. Chang added there is no chance thee will be a drop in the inmate count; she stated "if the inmate count dips, sheriffs bleed money. Their constituents lose jobs. The prison lobby ensures this does not happen by thwarting nearly every reform that could result in fewer people behind bars."[502] If there is no benefit to our research at all, it must stand as a direct warning to every African-American adult, who is married, thinking about getting married, their born and unborn children, and any other Louisiana ethnic group, that there is a privatized spider web, Louisiana Criminal Justice System Plantation already built; operating; and ready to lockup you, your child, or anyone, regardless of

[500] Ibid.
[501] Chang, Cindy, "Louisiana is the world's prison capital," http://www.nola.com/crime/indexssf/2012/05/Louisiana_is_the, may 29, 2012.
[502] Ibid.

race, in order, for private business owners-modern day slave owners-to keep their prison beds at 100% occupancy so they can easily take advantage of what each inmate is worth to them financially. We mentioned earlier that each one incarcerated in a local privatized prison was worth $24.39 per head, and just over $55.00 per head if one is incarcerated in a state-run prison. A third grade student knows what dollar amount is larger so the thinking of the Jindal administration is "let's privatize the state prison system, to the greatest degree that we can, and this will save us some taxpayer money." We know what you're thinking: "Maybe if any taxpayer dollars are freed up by privatization of a major portion of the LCJSP, then there will be money available to repair Louisiana roads, its unsafe bridges, build new schools, open up new daycare centers, provide money for public and higher education, giving teachers in both cases, long overdue pay raises, provide free healthcare to the millions of Louisiana people who do not have healthcare insurance, extend greater support our disabled and handicap people and much more. This is not a fantasy! This is our birthright, and we deserve it because our labor power has created the wealth for us to enjoy our basic needs on Earth, and not somewhere else, as we are taught. Every social index, where data is tracked related to the social well-being of Americans, we have, based on the data, shown that Louisiana ranks at or near the bottom in nearly every category. Chang's research echoes our point. She added "every dollar spent on prisons is a dollar not spent on schools, hospitals and highways."[503] Even the much beneficial healthcare services that would be available to thousands of Louisiana residents are being denied them, for no good reason, because Governor Bobby Jindal has been told to deny the new Medicaid Expansion associated with Obamacare. The famous 1960s soul group called the O'Jays sung a lyric in one of its songs saying "people will do anything for a dollar; a woman will sell her precious body."

It is appropriate now to spend a moment discussing exactly how much money is being generated off of the per diems being received by sheriffs and private business owners of the Louisiana Criminal Justice System Plantation (LCJSP).

---

[503] Ibid.

Everybody is making money except the incarcerated modern day African-American Male Slaves, who constitute roughly 70.0 percent of the inmate population locked up on the LCJSP. The Richland Parish Detention Center is an excellent example of how local privatized prisons, throughout Louisiana, by 2012, were making a profit off of their locked up prisoners, who, as we now know, are primarily African-American Males. This prison currently has behind its bars, chains, and razor wire 782 prisoners[504], "... bringing with them the $24.39 a day the state pays the Richland Parish sheriff to house them. Anything left over is profit for the sheriff."[505] Chang quoted Sherriff Charles McDonald saying ""I hate to make money off the back of some unfortunate person," Sheriff Charles McDonald said. "The fact is, somebody's going to keep them, and it might as well be Richland Parish."[506] If we do the simple math, the 179 prisoners, who were incarcerated at the mentioned prison by 2012, had a value of $19,073 per day; one week of lock up was valued at $133,511; a month's incarceration had a value of $534,043.4; and for one year's imprisonment, the value was $6,408,512.30. Once the cost of housing the 782 prisoners is deducted from this bounty, Chang stated "anything left over is profit for the sheriff. Other than a 1/2-cent sales tax, the prison is the sheriff's biggest revenue generator, underwriting the purchase of new squad cars, shotguns and bulletproof vests."[507] Moreover, Chang added "more than a decade since a prison-building boom swept the state, Louisiana's corrections system is a sprawling, for-profit enterprise. Private companies got in on the spoils, but the primary beneficiaries have been local sheriffs, who use the per-diem payments from the state to finance their departments and to pump jobs into moribund rural economies."[508] This is what African Slaves did for plantations during the American Slavery Period, which lasted for more than 400 years. How long will the exploitation of African-American Male and Female labor power go on is a question a majority of privatized

---

[504] Ibid.

[505] Chang, Cindy, "In world of prisons, some rural parishes' economies hinge on keeping their jails full," http://nola.com/crime/index.ssf/2012/05/ in world of prison, May 13, 2012.

[506] Ibid.

[507] Ibid.

[508] Ibid.

prison owners would rather see go unanswered for another 400 years? There are more prisoners locked up in the Richland Parish Detention Center than the total population of the small town of Mangham, which had a total population of 672 in 2010. Chang stated "indeed, the 2010 census has Mangham's population at 672, while the prison is 782 at full capacity."[509] A closer look at the overall economic picture shows privatized local prisons generate multimillion dollars in revenue for privatized prisons that constitute the Louisiana Criminal Justice System Plantation.

According to Cindy Chang's research, "the hidden engine behind the state's well-oiled prison machine is cold, hard cash. A majority of Louisiana inmates are housed in for-profit facilities, which must be supplied with a constant influx of human beings or a $182 million industry will go bankrupt...If the inmate count dips, sheriffs bleed money. Their constituents lose jobs. The prison lobby ensures this does not happen by thwarting nearly every reform that could result in fewer people behind bars."[510] Chang added "The state spends $182 million a year to house inmates in local prisons...Annual profits in good years range from about $200,000 for an average-sized operation to as much as $1 million for parishes with several prisons."[511] The Louisiana Prison Industry Complex is what Cindy Chang termed an "incarceration gold rush." Every day, during the 5 PM so-called local news, photos of Louisiana residents, who have committed this or that criminal offense, is flashed across your fancy flat screen television. Unknowing to the viewer-us-that a majority of these new crime reports will eventually end up as part of the "incarceration gold rush." We really need to wake up an understand soon that the daily reporting of a crime blotter is really not news; its one, a social effect of a failing capitalist system, and two, the Louisiana Residents' households, which exists within this exploitative economic system, is a potential feeder of the "incarceration gold rush." That is, a vast majority of African-American Households, in particular,

---

[509] Ibid.

[510] Chang, Cindy, "Louisiana is the world's prison capital," http://www.nola.com/crime/indexssf/2012/05/Louisiana_is_the, May 29, 2012.

[511] Chang, Cindy, "North Louisiana family is a major force in the state's vast prison industry," http://www.nola.com/crime/index.ssf/2012/05/jonesboro_family, May 14, 2012.

and many Caucasian Households, to a lesser degree, constitute thousands of good working class families, whose children are at-risk of getting caught up in the incarceration gold rush. The reason is not important; what is critical is a steady stream of our children become new head counts, who continuously receive long prison sentences, and equally important, they flow right before our very eyes while we standby looking at the procession, feeling powerless there is nothing we can do. Once we wake up, there are ways to stop the "incarceration gold rush." However, until then the beat will go on, namely, "in Louisiana... Locking up as many people as possible for as long as possible has enriched a few while making everyone else poorer. Public safety comes second to profits."[512]

Since we have been addressing the number of Louisiana residents who have been admitted to state prisons since Governor Bobby Jindal was s/ elected to serve as governor in 2008, we shall continue our investigation of Dr. Harvey Brenner's Distributed Lag relationship Theory to show how many homicides have occurred in Louisiana, from 2008, the year Governor Bobby Jindal took office to 2013. Recall, Dr. Harvey Brenner's mentioned theory states the full, pathological toll of a sustained 1.4 percent unemployment, in the first year, will reveal its great social impact on the affected population by the fifth year.

i. Homicides Reported In Louisiana During The Jindal Administration, 2008 to 2013

In order to understand the social impact the Neo-Liberal Privatization Economic Policy is having on the social well-being of the vast majority of the Louisiana people, who are mostly working class, homicide, or murder, is an excellent indicator of the breakdown in the social fabric of Louisiana Society. In the jungle, for example, there is an orderly relationship that exist among predators and prey. Once an animal's basic need for food, water, and shelter is satisfied, aggression cease in the jungle. However, in Louisiana, in our so-called civilization, and among people who are supposed to be at the top of the food chain, murders occur in large numbers year round without stopping. To get a clear perspective on homicide in Louisiana during the

[512] Chang, Cindy, Op. Cit., "Louisiana is the world's prison capital."

Jindal Administration, it is useful to show the homicide situation for the United States as whole first. Within this context, we will then show the extent to which murders are tearing apart the lives of thousands of Louisiana Families.

In 2008, the national murder rate was 5.4 per 100,000.[513] By the end of Governor Bobby Jindal's first term as governor in 2012, it was 4.7 per 100,000 people. From a regional perspective, during this same period, the South's murder rate per 100,000 people was 6.6 and 5.5 respectively. It is noteworthy to mention two facts here. One, the South's murder rate was higher than the national murder rate, and two, it was higher than the Midwest, West, and Northeast Regions during the identified years. Interestingly, between 2008 and 2012, the South's murder rate was higher than the mentioned regions in which such large cities such as New York City, Washington, D. C., Philadelphia, Baltimore, Los Angeles, Oakland, CA, and Chicago are located. Overall, by 2013, 2,106 homicides were reported in the Northeast, and 6,466 were reported in the South. Strikingly, 207.0 percent more homicides occurred in the South compared to the Northeast in 2013. Given this irony, we shall examine the murder/homicide situation in Louisiana against this backdrop.

When the states were ranked, regarding murder rates per 100,000 people, from highest to lowest, between 2008 and 2012, Louisiana led the nation with a higher murder rate per 100,000 people than any other state. In fact, Louisiana was the only state with a double digit murder rate per 100,000 people. As it was, in 2008, its murder rate per 100,000 people was 11.9; in 2009, it was 11.8; 11.0 in 2010; 11.1 in 2011; and 10.8 in 2012.[514] During this time, Mississippi was ranked behind Louisiana with the second highest murder rate per 100,000 people. As such, for the years shown, its murder rate was 8.1, 6.6, 6.9, 7.8, and 7.4 respectively. Although Mississippi's murder rate per 100,000 people were high, they, nonetheless, were noticeably lower than Louisiana's during Governor Bobby Jindal's first term in office. Excluding Michigan, Delaware, and Maryland, eight

---

[513] _____ DEATH PENALTY INFORMATION CENTER, http://www. deathpenaltyinfo.org/murder-rates-nationally-
[514] Ibid.

out-of-ten states with the highest murder rates per 100, 000 people, in the nation, were located in the South. It is worth repeating here that Louisiana had the highest murder rate per 100,000 people in the nation between 2008 and 2012. Table 1.16 below shows the relationship between all violent crimes and the proportion and percent, which were murders.

Table 1.16
Violent Crimes and Murders/Homicides In Louisiana
During the Jindal Administration, 2008 to 2012

Year	Violent Crime Total	Murder/Homicide	Percent of Total
2008	29,613	544	1.8
2009	28,878	529	1,8
2010	25,241	500	2.0
2011	25,373	506	2.0
2012	22,868	495	2.2
		Percent Increase	**22.2**

Source: Uniform Crime Reporting Statistics, Federal Bureau of Investigation, http://www.ucrdatatool.gov/Search/crime/Runcrimestat, Query date: March 17, 2014.

On the surface, the above Table shows an increase and decrease in the total number of new murders/homicides between 2008 and 2012. However, beneath the surface, we see murder/homicides, as a percent of the total violent crime by year, actually increased 22.2 percent during Governor Bobby Jindal's first term in office. This increase occurred during the sustained 1.8 percent increase in unemployment between 2008 and 2013. In any case, these annual violent crime and murder/homicide total are a direct outcome of the pathological consequence of the Neo-Liberal Privatization Economic Policy, which guides the purpose of existence of the Jindal Administration. As we have already seen, these murder/homicide totals are the foundation upon which Louisiana is distinguished as the state with the highest murder rate per 100,000 people nationwide. Next, we will examine the homicide situation in a few of Louisiana's largest cities.

By 2012, Baton Rouge, La's homicide rate per 100,000 people was higher than most major American cities. Vetter wrote the following:

> "Baton Rouge's homicide rate exceeds the rates in New York, Los Angeles and Washington D.C… Baton Rouge's homicide rate last year[2011] surpassed the rates in many American cities — including Houston, Los Angeles, New York, Washington D.C., Chicago, Cleveland and Boston — and was the second-highest in Louisiana, next to New Orleans… Using the recently revised U.S. Census population estimate of 229,493, the city of Baton Rouge had a per-capita homicide rate of 28 per 100,000 people in 2011 — a 40 percent jump from a decade ago when the rate was 20 per 100,000…Based on available data, the homicide rate in Baton Rouge has fluctuated between 20 and 34 per 100,000…reaching a high of 34 in 2009… That picture in Baton Rouge is grim…"[515]

By 2011, which was six years after Hurricane Katrina, and three years into Governor Bobby Jindal's first term in office, Dr. Harvey Brenner's Distributed Lag Relationship Theory continues hold true inasmuch as Baton Rouge, LA's homicide rate has shown a steady increase in tandem with sustained unemployment. Vetter stated "Using the recently revised U.S. Census population estimate of 229,493, the city of Baton Rouge had a per-capita homicide rate of 28 per 100,000 people in 2011 — a 40 percent jump from a decade ago when the rate was 20 per 100,000."[516] She added "the number of people killed and the rate at which people were slain in the city has generally been on the rise since 2005 and peaked in 2009, when 75 people were slain."[517] In the southwestern region of the state, commonly known as Acadiana, Gunn stated in Lafayette. LA "the number of homicides in the city shot up… in 2012… The number of

---

[515] Vetter, Kimberly, "High homicide rate plague Baton Rouge, The Advocate, February 26, 2012, pp. 1 and 2.
[516] Ibid., p. 2.
[517] Ibid., p. 3.

homicides doubled to 12 in 2012...[518] That year, New Orleans, LA had the second highest murder rate in the United States, which was 53.2 per 100,000 people. New Orleans, LA murder rate was higher than St. Louis, Baltimore, Oakland, Kansas City, Philadelphia, Cleveland, Memphis, Atlanta, Chicago...[and]Miami.[519]

All-in-all, Erin Fuchs summed up the homicide situation during Governor Bobby Jindal's first term in office as follows: "One state in the heart of the Deep South-Louisiana-is...the murder capital of the United States."[520] Within the Louisiana Murder Capital, it is necessary give attention to the worsening plight of women, who, unfortunately, are murdered in increasing numbers. Before we conclude our discussion of the Women Question, we will spend some time bringing to light the rising sexual assault against women in Louisiana and in the United States Military.

j. Murder of Women In Louisiana And Sexual Assault During The Jindal Administration, 2008 to 2013

The most decisive indicator that a society has lost its moral compass of human decency and humanity, is the way in which it treats its women, who, in the long course of human history, have, hitherto, served as the seed bearers of nations. Anywhere it is seen that the murder of women is rising, it can be objectively concluded, and in the case of Louisiana in particular, that the heart, or love center, which makes human beings human, is rapidly declining. The data presented below supports this viewpoint.

Consistent with Louisiana's rank at the very bottom of nearly every social index, the trend is unchanged when the socio-economic well-being of women is considered. According to the Center for American Progress, Louisiana ranked 50th regarding overall well-being of women, and the

[518] Gunn, Billy, "Homicides in Lafayette up, other crimes down," The Advocate, February 8, 2013, p. 1.
[519] _____ Highest Murder rate US cities, http://shareranks. com/994.highest-Murder-Rate-US-Cities
[520] Fuchs, Erin, "WHY LOUISIANA IS THE MURDER CAPITAL OF AMERICA," http://www.businessInsider.com/Why-is-the-murder-rate-high-

state earned an overall grade of "F." The overall ranking score assigned to Louisiana was based on an analysis of data in three categories: (1) Economic Security (2) Health and (3) Leadership.[521] Moreover, 22.2 percent of women and girls lived in poverty by September 25, 2013, or the first year of Governor Bobby Jindal's second term in office. In addition, 62.4 percent of Louisiana Women and Girls held jobs that paid them a minimum wage at the same time. 36.1 percent of African-American Women and Girls lived in poverty by this time, and this percentage was higher than the 27.0 percent of Hispanic Women who lived in poverty, and higher than the 25.6 percent of Asian American Women and Girls, as well as the 25.6 percent of Native American Women and Girls, who lived in poverty respectively. The significant percentage of Louisiana Women and Girls, who lived in poverty by 2013, is not surprising, given the earlier fact 62.4 percent earned minimum wages. By any estimation, the state of women and girls' well-being in Louisiana, during Governor Bobby Jindal's first term in office, was devastatingly poor; for African-American Women and Girls, family decay is even more devastating inasmuch as 70.0 percent of African-American Males were simultaneously incarcerated on the Louisiana Criminal Justice System Plantation by 2013. Jordan Blum added "The median net worth...of black families in the U.S. is less than $5,000 compared with more than $110,000 for comparable white families... In 2010, the net worth for black families was $4,995."[522] Yet, Governor Bobby Jindal, and his Legislative accomplices, together, passed legislation that, in a nutshell, says the problem in Louisiana Education is there are too many "ineffective teachers' in the classroom, and the solution is: allow Louisiana girls to leave "Failing (D and F) public Schools, and enroll in a Charter School. How much smarter must we become to realize the simple fact that every public school will be given a grade of "F," by the BESE Board, which has an enrollment of a significant number of children who live in black families that have a net worth of $4,995. Given the economically depressed social environment in which the majority of Louisiana Women and Girls

---

[521] _____ Explore the Data: The State of Women in America, http://www.americanprogress.org/issues/women/news/2013/0

[522] Blum, Jordan, "Wealth gap hits families in U.S., La.," The Advocate, September 24, 2012, p. 1.

currently live in, one critical question surfaced, namely, what is the health rank for women and girls who live in Louisiana today?

Of the 50 states in 2013, Louisiana held the distinction of being ranked 49th regarding the health of Louisiana Women and Girls.[523] Regarding Louisiana Women's personal well-being, the state is ranked in the top ten, regarding women who are killed by men.

Throughout human history, the hearth, tribe, or home, has been the safest place for women and girls to live. However, by the commencement of civilization, roughly 3,000 years ago, which corresponds to the fall of feudalism and the rise of capitalism, the home, a former source of protection against bodily harm, has-today-become a place in which Louisiana women are being killed by men, largely intimate partners, at an alarming and unprecedented rate. In September 2013, the Violence Policy Center wrote the following:

> "Intimate partner violence against women is all too common…The most serious is homicide by an intimate partner…A study by Harvard School of Public Health researchers analyzed gun use at home and concluded that "hostile gun displays against family members may be more common than gun use in self-defense, and that hostile gun displays are often acts of domestic violence directed against women…" The U.S. Department of Justice has found that women are far more likely to be the victims of violent crimes committed by intimate partners than men…two thirds of women who own guns acquired them "primarily for protection against crime," the results of a California analysis show that "purchasing a handgun provides no protection against homicide among women

---

[523] _____ Explore the Data: The State of Women in America, http://www. Americanprogress.org/issues/women/news/2013/0

and is associated with an increase in their risk for intimate partner homicide."[524]

Referring to The Center for American Progress' Report titled "America Under the Gun", Robert Stewart stated "Louisiana ranks first among all states for gun violence rates in the United States... Louisiana ranked No. 1 or No. 2 in six of the 10 categories...[such as] overall firearms deaths in 2010 to aggravated assaults with a firearm in 2011. Louisiana's average ranking in the 10 factors was 5.0..."[525] Although Louisiana ranks at, or near the bottom of every social index, and at the top of the list in gun violence, our Governor Bobby Jindal, in his usual avoidance of reality, "...in a statement... [he] denounced the study... Jindal said his office is working to have more mental health records put into the National Instant Criminal Background Check System to prevent guns from falling into wrong hands."[526] Earlier, we provided detailed information that showed thousands of Louisiana Residents, who are currently in need of mental health treatment, will not receive any services because Governor Bobby Jindal refused to expand the new Medicaid Expansion Program in Louisiana, which is made possible by the Affordable Care Act, or Obamacare. That being so, it is not surprising that Louisiana currently leads the nation in gun violence because thousands of Louisiana Residents are walking around every day with some form of untreated mental health problem. It is impossible for Governor Bobby Jindal's staff to place ten of thousands of mental health records in database, capable of stopping deadly gun violence. A significant portion of deadly gun violence is acted out against Louisiana Women and Girls; many of their lives could have been saved, if their intimate partner could have obtained some form of mental health treatment in advance of his commission of a homicide. A gun does not kill anyone; it is an instrument used by a mentally unstable person, whose basic human needs since birth have not been satisfactorily met due to limited opportunities available for self-expression and self-determination. When we examined

---

[524] _____ When Men Murder Women: An Analysis of 2011 Homicide Data, Violence Policy Center, http://vpc.org/when-men-murder-women/, p. 1.
[525] Stewart, Robert, "Study: Louisiana has highest rate of gun violence in U.S.," The Advocate, April 3, 2013, p. 1.
[526] Ibid., p. 2.

the deadly violence committed by Louisiana Men against Women and Girls, once again, Louisiana ranks very high.

In its Report, When Men Murder Women: An Analysis of 2011 Homicide Data, the Violence Policy Center, as part of its analysis, ranked the 50 states regarding the number of females murdered by males by states and rate per 100,000 people in 2011. Louisiana was ranked number nine among the ten states with the highest number of women and girls murdered by men. By the third year Governor Bobby Jindal was in office in 2011, 39 females were murdered by Louisiana Men, which was equivalent to a 1.67 per 100,000 Females Homicide Rate.[527] In 2011, Louisiana was ranked number one in the nation in gun violence, and number nine in female homicides committed by Louisiana Men. All of this social destruction continues to go on unabated, and unresolved, beneath the Jindal Administration's implementation of the Louisiana Ruling Class' Neo-Liberal Privatization Economic Policy, which as we have already seen, caused Louisiana to be ranked Number twelve in the nation in newly minted millionaires. South Carolina was ranked number one in the nation, regarding females and girls murdered by men with a female homicide rate of 61 per 100,000 people. One other critical point need to be made about Louisiana Men who murdered Women and Girls.

We mentioned earlier that Louisiana Women and Girls are most at risk of being murdered in their own homes. A Louisiana Woman or Girl is more likely to be killed in her own home than if she was a "deployed American Soldier" serving in the Iraq or Afghanistan Wars. Of the 39 Louisiana Women and Girls murdered in 2011, the Violence Policy Center stated "for homicides in which the victim to offender relationship could be identified, 94 percent of female victims (31 out of 33) were murdered by someone they knew...Of the victims who knew their offenders, 61 percent (19 victims) were wives, common law wives, ex-wives, or girlfriends of the offenders."[528] What can we say about a household in which there is a high probability that the women and girls, who live in them, are at risk of being murdered

---

[527] _____When Men Murder Women: An Analysis of 2011 Homicide Data, Violence Poli8cy Center, http://vpc/when-men-murder-women/, p. 5.
[528] Ibid., p. 23.

by their intimate partner? Could this have anything to do with the upsurge in "same sex" marriages that are sweeping the country? Are women and girls in desperate need of love and safety? Many Louisiana Women on one hand, live in fear of losing their lives at the hand of an intimate partner, and on the other, they do not have a significant political voice that could serve them as an instrument of change. Currently, according to the Center for American Progress, Louisiana has 0.0% women elected to executive seats statewide; 11.8% elected to a state legislative seat; and 5.0% of all elected seats held by minority women.[529] One of the reasons the American Revolutionary War was fought against England in 1776 was "Taxation Without Representation." We all were spoon fed this in our American History Classes, both statewide and nationwide. Furthermore, as we see, more than two centuries later, the same situation exist in Louisiana today, namely, Taxation Without Representation. However, there is one striking, and most obvious difference, from Colonial Times, and that is, the majority of women in Colonial America, excluding African Slaves, were not being murdered by their own intimate partners. Such an occurrence was rare. It is commonplace today in Louisiana, and all across America. Before we move on to a discussion of cardiovascular deaths during the Jindal Administration, we shall include additional information related to sexual assaults against women in the American Military. The latter is included to further emphasize that violence against women is not limited to their intimate partners, but it is rampant in the American Military, an organization advertised as the defender of human rights at home and abroad such as in Iraq and Afghanistan.

k. Sexual Assault Against Women In The American Military, 2008 to 2013

In most cartoons seen by children all across America on a daily basis, there is one common central theme in all of them, namely, *a Bad Guy and a Good Guy*. We had the opportunity to be around children, ranging in ages from 5 years to 6 years old. What was interesting is during their dialogue during the day, we heard them refer to each other as either the "Good Guy" or

---

[529] _____ Explore the data: The State of Women in America, http://www. Americanprogress.org/issues/women/news/2013/0

the "Bad Guy." If you are wondering what does this have to do with sexual assault of women in the American Military, the latter's mission is to defend the *human rights of American Citizens, and those of peoples globally.* One recent television commercial stated the American Military is a "Force For Good." If this is as the television commercial hope we believe is so, then, we ask: Why are an increasing number of enlisted female soldiers being sexually assaulted every year? Sexual Assault of females in the American Military tells the real truth about a "Force For Good," because it cuts at the heart of what a real "Force For Good" is all about. That is, to uphold, and defend, the human rights and dignity of women and all people, regardless of race and gender. So, the question we leave you to answer as we proceed is as follows: Is it possible to defend the human rights of people in Iraq, Afghanistan, or anywhere else in the world, when, at the same time, right here in America, an increasing number of enlisted female soldiers' human rights are violated every year? What is the American Military's definition of sexual assault?

According to the U.S. Commission On Civil Rights Report published in September 2013, titled Sexual Assault In The Military, Castro, Thernstrom, et. al., wrote the Department of Defense (DoD) defined sexual assault as follows:

> "Intentional sexual contact characterized by use of force, threats, or cannot consent. The term includes a broad category of sexual offenses consisting of the following specific UCMJ offenses: rape, sexual assault, aggravated sexual contact, abusive sexual contact, forcible sodomy (forced oral or anal sex), or attempts to commit these acts..."[530]

As we see, this is one of the main reasons any military action is justified against another nation, if women and children are the recipients of this

---

[530] Castro, Martin, Thernstrom, Abigail, et. al., Sexual Assault In The Military, U.S. commission On Civil Rights, http://www.uscr.gov/pubs/09242013 Statutory Enforcement Report Sexual Assault in the Military, September 2013, pp. 3 and 4.

type of treatment from their own political leaders, regardless of the form of the abuse. From an historical perspective, sexual assault of female soldiers in the American Military has been worsening problem for quite a long time.

Specifically, by 2012, the Service Women's Action Network-SWAN- stated "despite over 25 years of Pentagon studies, task force recommendations, and congressional hearings; rape, sexual assault and sexual harassment continue to occur at alarming rates year after year."[531] Sexual assault of female soldiers in the American Military dates back to the Navy's Tailhook Scandal. Castro and Thernstrom, et. al. outlined the history of sexual assault against females in the military as follows:

> "The issue of sexual assault among Service members first garnered national attention during the Navy Tailhook scandal in 1991. Ninety Service members alleged that they were sexually assaulted or harassed by 119 Naval officers and 21 Marine Corps officers during a convention in Las Vegas.6 Reports of sexual assault at Aberdeen Proving Ground in 1996 and the Air Force Academy in 2003 created more public awareness of the issue.7 Most recently, the scandal at Lackland Air Force Base resulted in six drill sergeants being convicted of sexual misconduct..."[532]

Although these incidences of sexual assault brought early attention to the gross violation of the human rights of women soldiers in the American Military, they are only the tip of a vastly large iceberg that lies just beneath the water's surface. In fact, the U.S. Commission On Civil Rights provided sexual assault frequency data that shows just how extensive this problem is. It stated the following:

> "since DoD began maintaining data on reported sexual assaults, the number of reported sexual assaults has

[531] _____ Service Women's Action Network: quick Facts, policy@servicewomen.org, July 2012.
[532] Castro, Martin, Thernstrom, et. al., Op. Cit., p. 2.

increased from 1,700 in calendar year 2004 to 3,374 in fiscal year (FY) 2012…The majority (61 percent in 2012, 68 percent in 2011) of the reported sexual offenses involved a completed, penetration-type offense—rape, aggravated sexual assault, and forcible sodomy. Over a third (39 percent in 2012, 32 percent in 2011) involved sexual contact offenses (i.e., non-penetration type sexual offenses)…"[533]

In 2011, there were "…3,192 reported sexual assaults…[in the] military…"[534] According to the Department of Defense's Sexual Assault Prevention and Response Strategic Plan dated April 30, 2013, there were 26,000 service members, a majority of whom were females, who experienced "… unwanted sexual contact."[535] It is interesting to note here that half of these sexual assaults were committed by enlisted soldiers with a rank, from E1 to E4. Castro and Thernstrom stated "Approximately half of those accused of sexual assault were junior enlisted Service members (grades E-1 to E-4); approximately a quarter were enlisted members with supervisory duties (grades E-5 to E-9); and four percent were officers…"[536] Moreover, to keep their recruiting numbers high, young Americans, right out of high school, who come from poor working class family backgrounds, are recruited in the military, and they are thrown on the frontlines of war. When their lives are fodder for the killing machines of war, sexual assaults against female soldiers is consistent with their own feelings of devaluation and purposelessness. No matter what any of our experts say, using all of their flowery words and theories to rationalize war, cannot change the fact that killing another human being is insanity. Sexual assaults against women will not stop until we stop using imperialist and aggressive wars as a means of human destruction. Sexual assault and imperialist war are

---

[533] Ibid., pp. 5 and 6.

[534] _____ Service Women's Action Network: Quick Facts, policy @ servicewomen .org, July 2012.

[535] Hagel, Chuck, Department Of defense Annual Report on Sexual Assault in the Military, http://www.sapr.mil/, April 30, 2013, p. 28.

[536] Castro and Thernstrom, et. al., Op. Cit., p. 5.

inseparable, and its toxic energy has permeated, or spread to the highest levels of command in the American Military.

For example, recently Brigadier General Jeffrey A. Sinclair was given a "slap on the wrist" for his unwanted sexual assault of female soldiers under his command over a three year period. The Associate Press reported the verdict of the Sinclair Trial, and, not surprising, Brigadier general Jeffrey A. Sinclair was basically given a free pass. It stated the following:

> "U.S. Army Brigadier General Jeffrey Sinclair admitted he mistreated a captain during an adulterous sexual affair and had inappropriate relationships with other junior female officers…An Army general who carried on a three-year affair with a captain and had two other inappropriate relationships with subordinates was reprimanded and docked $20,000 in pay… avoiding jail time…Sinclair, the former deputy commander of the storied 82nd Airborne Division, was believed to be the highest-ranking U.S. military officer ever court-martialed on sexual assault charges, but earlier this week those charges were dropped… In closing arguments, prosecutors argued Sinclair should be thrown out of the Army and lose his military benefits, while the defense said that would harm his innocent wife and children the most."[537]

An American Court Martial Trial failed to hold Brigadier General Jeffrey A. Sinclair accountable for his sexual assault against women in the military, although the court knew he was long-time violator of the human rights of women. Botelho and Baldacci stated,

> "prosecutors said Sinclair broke military law through sexual relationships -- including threats to some women involved who held lower ranks -- between 2009 and 2012 in Iraq, Afghanistan and Germany, as well as Fort Bragg, North

---

[537] _____ "Army general avoids jail time, fined $20,000 in sexual assault case," New York Daily News.Com, March 20, 2014.

Carolina, and Fort Hood, Texas...Retired Rear Adm. Jamie Barnett, a partner with a law firm that represented one of Sinclair's accusers, called Thursday's sentencing a "slap on the wrist" that is "beyond disappointing. It is a travesty and a serious misstep for the Army." He said the ordeal shows remaining "challenges" in the military when it comes to sexual abuse and assault..."[538]

The hypocrisy that arises here is: As the American Government sends its military to the far reaches of the world to stamp out injustice, yet, at the same time, the same soldiers, oftentimes, high ranking officers, who are assigned the task to go after the so-called "Bad Guys," are the very "Bad Guys"-themselves- who are committing horrendous sexual assault crimes against the women soldiers under their command. In Louisiana recently, a high ranking military commander was released from his military Command for committing a crime against a woman soldier. Paul Purpura added "the Louisiana National Guard's adjutant general fired his senior enlisted adviser... after investigators substantiated allegations of sexual harassment involving another member of the Guard...Sgt. Maj. Tommy Caillier has committed a sexual assault, said Lt. Col. Michael Kazmierzak, the state's public affairs officer...He was the highest-ranking enlisted soldier in the state's military force"[539] This is not a private but the highest ranking enlisted soldier in the Louisiana Military Force. We can imagine what is going-on at the lower ranks in this organization?

As we see, women in America, and in Louisiana, are suffering from continuous sexual assault initiated by their supervising commanding officers. Obviously, there is a sexual maladjustment and abuse of power going-on. Underneath this failure in the male-female social relationship is an assault on the American Heart. Where love exists, sexual assaults against women, regardless of whether they serve in the military or civilian

---

[538] Botelho, Greg and Baldacci, Marlena, "Brigadier general accused of sexual assault must pay over $20,000; no jail time," CNN Justice, http://www.cnn.com/201403/20/justice/jeffrey-sinclair-court, March 20, 2014.

[539] Purpura, Paul, Louisiana National Guard's top enlisted adviser fired amid sexual harassment allegations," The Times-Picayune, NOLA.com, June 15, 2013.

society, cannot exist; where love does not flow from the human heart, it is attacked by stress and hypertension. It is recorded in a category known as cardiovascular deaths, and the disease is commonly referred to as a heart attack.

I. Cardiovascular Deaths In Louisiana During The Jindal Administration, 2008 to 2013

Ironically, as we have already seen, Governor Bobby Jindal, and his Louisiana Legislative Allies, have made deep cuts in the higher education budget; closed all of the public-charity-hospitals; refused to expand the new Medicaid Program under the Affordable Care Act; overseen the highest incarceration rate in the United States, including the world, and while all of this social decay is taking place, there has been a sharp increase in the number of millionaires in Louisiana thanks primarily to Governor Bobby Jindal's implementation of the Louisiana Ruling Class' neo-liberalism economic policy. The latter has greatly influenced the buildup of stress among the Louisiana People, manifested by a growing number of cardiovascular deaths. Before we examined the latter, from 2008 to 2013, which coincides with the Jindal Administration's first term in office, it is timely to recall that Louisiana, regarding the social well-being of its people, rank at or near the bottom in every social index-nationwide.

As we have already witnessed, from an earlier discussion, by 2013, Louisiana ranked 50th in the nation in obesity; 48th in diabetes; 47th in physical activity; 46th in smoking; and 46th in cardiovascular deaths. Regarding the social well-being of its elderly population at the same time, Louisiana ranked 44th in obesity; 48th in smoking; 48th in physical inactivity; and 49th in health status. These ranking, as a whole, are a devil's brew, which, ultimately lead to catastrophic health outcomes for thousands of Louisiana Citizens every year. As we provide more detail information related to cardiovascular deaths below, remember, for this social index by 2013, Louisiana ranked 46th in the nation. No doubt, all of its other social index rankings identified earlier combine to create an erosion of the healthy functioning of the human heart, which, for many end in premature deaths.

Moreover, Louisiana ranked 46th in the nation in premature deaths by 2013.

1. America's Least Healthy States, 2013

Of the ten most unhealthy states ranked by the Huffington Post, Louisiana was ranked Number 3 based on the following factors: (1) Percent obese: 34.7% (the highest in the nation) (2) Children living in poverty: 31% (the highest in the nation) (3) Cardiovascular deaths per 100,000: 318.5 (5th highest) and (4) "Louisiana residents also were more likely than most Americans to die of cardiovascular disease or cancer."[540] Mississippi was ranked the Number 1 least healthy state and Arkansas was ranked Number 2. Alexander, et.al. added "in 2011 and 2012, nearly one-fifth of the state's population lacked health coverage. Obesity has skyrocketed in Louisiana, nearly tripling from 12.3% of the adult population in 1990 to 34.7% last year, the highest rate of any state."[541] While Governor Bobby Jindal has tirelessly submitted himself to the advancement of the neo-liberalism economic Policy of the Louisiana ruling Class, the mentioned social decay is having a cancerous affect on the lives of thousands of Louisiana Citizens. There is hardly any sustained consideration of the health problems faced by the Louisiana people, either in social media, or mainstream Louisiana news broadcast on a daily basis. What is mentioned is the effect of neo-liberalism economic policy in the form of a daily social media-streaming of crimes; hardly any news is ever presented related to the underlying causes that make Louisiana the third most unhealthy state in America today. A few health indicators further verify Louisiana's status as the third most unhealthy state in America.

2. Additional Indicators That Make Louisiana The Number 3 Most Unhealthy State In America, 2013

According to America's Health Rankings 2013 Annual Report, in 2008,

---

[540] Hess, Alexander E.M., Sauter, Michael B., and Thomas C. Frohlich, "America's Least Healthy States: 24/7 Wall St.," http://huffingtonpost.com/2013/12/21/least-healthy-state, January 23, 2014.

[541] Ibid. http://24/7wallst.com/special-report/2013/12/17/america-most.

Louisiana's cancer death rate was 223.8 per 100,000 people.[542] This cancer death rate falls in the cancer death rate category of 214.1-233.1, which was the highest in the nation in 2008. Also, that year, 32.1% of the Louisiana people were diagnosed with high blood pressure. By 2012, Louisiana's cancer death rate was 217.5 per 100,000, which still placed it in the highest cancer death rate category in the nation. Regarding high blood pressure, a tell-tale sign of advancing heart disease, 38.4% of the Louisiana population was diagnosed with it. This was a 19.6 percent increase in four years, or during the Jindal Administration's first term in office. As we pointed out earlier, it does not matter which social index you choose to consider, in the end, we discover Louisiana has a solid distinction of being ranked at the bottom of every social index, or in the category that has the highest percentage or rate of a particular disease. With this background, we are prepared to examine changes in the total number of cardiovascular deaths during the Jindal Administration's first term in office, from 2008 to 2013.

To carry-out this examination of cardiovascular deaths in Louisiana between 2008 and 2013, we will make use of the Final Death Data provided by the Centers For Disease Control.

By 2010, or the third year of Governor Bobby Jindal first term in office, the American Heart Association stated "Louisiana has the 5th highest death rate from cardiovascular disease in the country."[543] According to the National Vital Statistics Report published by the Center for Disease Control in 2008, 10, 347 Louisiana Residents died, that year, from all forms of cardiovascular disease. This was equivalent to 234.6 deaths per 100,000 people.[544] This is more than the number of American Soldiers who died in the Iraq and Afghanistan Wars combined. During 2009, another 10,169 Louisiana Residents perished from cardiovascular disease with a

---

[542] _____America's Health Rankings: 2013 Annual Report, America'shealthranking.org/LA/cvdDeaths/2008

[543] _____ Louisiana State fact Sheet, American Heart Association, http://www.heart.org/idc/groups/heart-public/@wcm/@adv/d, 2010.

[544] Minino, Arialdi M., Murphy, Sherry L. B.S., Xu, Jiaquan M.D., and Kenneth D. Kochanek, M.A., National Vital Statistics Reports: Deaths: Final Data for 2008, Volume 59, Number 10, December 7, 2011, p. 94.

death rate of 226.4 per 100,000 people.[545] Another 10,282 Louisianans died in 2010 with a death rate of 226.8 per 100,000 people.[546] The Center for Disease Control released preliminary data for 2011 and 2012; however, it does not include the total number of cardiovascular deaths by state. To provide an idea of how many Louisiana Residents died as a result of cardiovascular disease, from 2011 to 2013, the latter is taken from Americas Health Ranking.

Between 2011 and 2013, 318.9, 318.2, and 318.5 Louisiana Residents died from cardiovascular disease respectively.[547] Only Mississippi had more cardiovascular deaths than Louisiana, during this time, with 366.4 in 2011; 357.4 in 2012; and 358.6 in 2013. Mississippi and Louisiana rank Number 2 and 3, in the nation, regarding the number of people who are overweight, and classified as being obese. 68.9% of Mississippi's adult population is overweight and obese, and 67.6% of Louisiana's. It follows that for Mississippi, its heart disease death rate per 100,000 people is 265.98, and Louisiana's death rate for the same is 225.42.[548] Both states death rates were ranked among the top ten in the nation by 2013. In Louisiana in particular, the incidence of cardiovascular disease has gotten so bad that an entirely new medical procedure was devised in attempt to address the heart problem.

As the numbers of annual heart disease crises remain high in Louisiana, more and more heart surgeons are resorting to Percutaneous Coronary Intervention (PCI). Bloomberg stated "When doctors opt for stents, they prop open coronary arteries in a procedure called Percutaneous Coronary

---

[545] Kochanek, Kenneth D. M.A., Xu, Jiaquan, M.D., Murphy, Sherry L B.S.., Minino, Ariaaldi, M. M.P.H., and Hsiang-Ching Kung, Ph.D., National Vital Statistics Reports: Deaths: Final Data for 2009, Volume 60, Number 3, December 29, 2011, p. 84.

[546] Murphy, Sherry L., B.S., Xu, Jiaquan, M.D., and Kochanek, Kenneth D., M.A., National Vital Statistics: Deaths: Final Data for 2010, Volume 61, Number 4, May 8, 2013, p. 86.

[547] _____ Cardiovascular Deaths, AMERICA'S HEALTH RANKING, http://www.americashealthranking.org/LA/cvdDeaths/2008

[548] _____Louisiana Life Expectancy: live longer live better, http://www.worldlifeexpectancy.com/USA/louisiana-heart-disease

Intervention, or PCI. More than 90 percent of PCIs include stenting."[549] Waldman, Armstrong, and Freedberg added there are "...700,000 stent procedures [performed] in the U.S. annually...Two out of three elective stents, or more than 200,000 procedures a year, are unnecessary. According to David Brown, a cardiologist at Stony Brook University School of Medicine in New York, that works out to about a third of all stents. Unnecessary stents cost the U.S. health care system $2.4 billion a year, according to Sanjay Kaul, a cardiologist and researcher at Cedars-Sinai Medical Center in Los Angeles"[550]

Louisiana performs an above average to high use of stents in an attempt to address the growing number of cardiovascular disease cases. Most of the stents are placed in the coronary arteries of patients who have Medicare Insurance. As we already know, all of Louisiana's public-charity-hospitals were privatized during Governor Bobby Jindal's first term in office. Waldman, Armstrong, et. al., stated "Hospitals receive an average payment of about $25,000 per stent case from private insurers, according to Healthcare Blue Book, a website that tracks reimbursements."[551]As a result of the large sum of money hospitals receive per stent implanted into a patient's coronary artery, the rate of Percutaneous Coronary Intervention (PCI) performed by Louisiana Hospitals is, generally speaking, higher than the national average throughout the state, save Baton Rouge, LA and New Orleans, LA. Table 1.17 below shows the PCI rate per 1,000 patients.

[549] Whiteaker, Chloe and Kuntz, Phil, Mapping America's Coronary Stent Hot Spots, Bloomberg View, http://go.bloomberg.com/multimedia/mapping-coronary-stent, September 26, 2013.

[550] Waldman, Peter, Armstrong, Daniel, and Sydney P. Freedberg, "Deaths Linked to Cardiac Stents Rise as Overuse Seen," http://www.bloomberg.com/news/2013-09-26/deaths-linked-to, September 26, 2013.

[551] Ibid.

Table 1.17
Percutaneous Coronary Intervention Rate Per 1,000
Louisiana Residents For Selected Cities, 2013

City	PCI Rate per 1,000	U. S. Average
Covington	19	7.6
Monroe	13	7.6
West Monroe	12	7.6
Ruston	11	7.6
Lafayette	9	7.6
Shreveport	7.3	7.6
New Orleans	6.7	7.6
Baton Rouge	4.3	7.6

Source: Waldman, Peter, Armstrong, Daniel, and Syndney Freedberg, "Deaths Linked to Cardiac Stents Rise as Overuse Seen," http://www. bloomberg.com/2013-09-26/

Deaths-linked-to, September 26, 2013.

Why Baton Rouge and New Orleans, LA's PCI per 1,000 Louisiana Residents is below the national average is worth further examination in another study. Meantime, all other cities shown, and the privatized hospitals that serve them, are performing stent procedures above the national average. The patient, who receives a PCI, is the pawn on the chessboard. Manufacturers of stents received several billion dollars in 2012. "...stent makers **Abbott Laboratories (ABT)** Inc., **Boston Scientific Corp. (BSX)**, Cordis Corp. and **Medtronic Inc. (MDT)**...sales of cardiac stents were about $5.5 billion globally last year...according to the Health Research International consulting firm.[552] Even though PCI medical procedures are the norm in Louisiana, the total number of cardiovascular deaths remain high.

This brings us to a close of our discussion of the attendant pathology associated with the Jindal Administration's implementation of the Louisiana Ruling Class' Neo-Liberal Economic Policy. As we have already witnessed from everything that has been mentioned, from suicides to cardiovascular

---

[552] Ibid.

deaths, hardly anything-nothing-is being done to reverse the worsening social plight of thousands of Louisiana Citizens. Instead, during his first term, from 2008 to 2012, when a majority of the social decay was occurring in our state, Governor Bobby Jindal has spent a significant amount of his time "out-of-state" campaigning for other republican politicians, and supposedly preparing to make a run for the 2016 Campaign for President of the United States. While people in Louisiana are suffering every day just to make enough money to satisfy their minimum basic needs such as shelter, healthcare, employment, food, and recreation among others, Governor Bobby Jindal has been absent as governor. We provide some available information below that substantiates on paper, Louisiana has a governor, but, in reality, the majority of the Louisiana people are governor less. When anything is ever heard from Governor Bobby Jindal, it is in a so-called "Prepared Statement." We can quickly train a high school student, who attends a "D" public school to write a prepared statement. Table 1.18 below provides information that shows the worsening impact sustained unemployment had on the Louisiana Working Class by the beginning of Governor Bobby Jindal's second term as governor.

Table 1.18
Cumulative Impact Of The Sustained 1.8
Percent Rise in Unemployment During The
Jindal Administration: 2008 to 2013

Social Stress indicator	Stress Incidence-2013	Increase in New Cases
Suicide	200	177
State Prison Admission	41,295	4,188
Homicides	2,574	2,574
Cardiovascular Deaths	10,347	1,417*

Source: See Footnotes 449, 450, 455, 513, and 547. *The Center for Disease Control Final Data shows 17,007 cardiovascular deaths occurred between 2003 and 2010. It is projected that there will be slightly less than 1,500 new cases by the end of 2015. Center for Disease Control, 2003 to 2010 Final Data, www.Cardiovascular%20Deaths%20by%20 ParishBARGRAPHLouisiana%20Heart%20Disease.htm

CHAPTER X

Governor Bobby Jindal: A Louisiana Road Scholar

The average Louisiana Resident does not know Governor Bobby Jindal, and the latter does not know them, nor represent their working class interests. Yet, in October 2007, Gilbert Cruz stated "Bobby Jindal, a 36-year-old Republican Congressman, won the Louisiana gubernatorial election, becoming the nation's first governor of Indian-American descent and the youngest chief executive of any state. Jindal took 54% of the vote..."[553] The 54% of the vote was reported throughout the social media a mandate. Cruz quoted Governor-S/Elect Bobby Jindal stating "there has never been a clearer mandate for our state."[554] Regarding which class s/elected Governor Bobby Jindal is apparent when the amount of money spent on his gubernatorial campaign is considered. Specifically, "the race was one of the highest-spending in Louisiana history. Jindal alone raised $11 million..."[555] Overall, $35,117,604 was spent by the candidates during the 2007 Gubernatorial Campaign. "...Republican Gov. Jindal, who won handily, raised $13.7 million..."[556] of the total. At this point,

---

[553] Cruz, Gilbert, "Jindal Triumphant in Louisiana," Time, http://content.time.com/nation/article/0,8599,1674122,oc, October 21, 2007.

[554] Ibid.

[555] _____ "GOP Congressman Bobby Jindal Wins Louisiana Governor's Race," Associated Press, http://www.foxnews.com/story/2007/10/21/gop-congressman, October 21, 2007.

[556] _____Legislative Committee Analysis Tool (L-CAT), http://www.followthe money.org/press/ReportView.phtml?=42

three facts have emerged. One, the Oxford educated Governor Bobby Jindal was s/elected the youngest governor in Louisiana History, two, the 2007 Gubernatorial Campaign was the most expensive in Louisiana History, and three, Governor Bobby Jindal's s/election, with 54.0 percent of the votes, was considered a mandate. A closer examination of the 54.0 percent of the votes received by Governor Bobby Jindal paints a picture of inaccurate mathematics rather than a mandate.

In 2007, there were "...2,884,453 Registered Voters..."[557] in Louisiana. That year, 1,297, 840 Louisiana Registered Voters casted a vote in the Gubernatorial Race. Of this total, Governor Bobby Jindal received 699,275 votes. If the 1,297,840 votes are used to calculate the percent of the vote received by Governor Bobby Jindal, we see he received 53.88 percent of this total.[558] However, when the 2,884,453 Louisiana Registered Voters is used to make the same calculation, Governor Bobby Jindal received only 24.2 percent of the votes casted by registered voters. And, when the 699,275 votes Governor Bobby Jindal received are subtracted from the 2,884,453 total Louisiana Registered Voters, the remainder is 2,185,178! The elephant in the room is this big question: Who s/elected Governor Bobby Jindal, and who does he represent? The 2,185,178 Louisiana Registered Voters, who did not vote for Governor Bobby Jindal, are, generally speaking, working class people. The 699,275 Louisiana Registered Voters, who voted for Governor Bobby Jindal, consists of the Louisiana Ruling Class, and upper class people who earn an annual income well in excess of $60,000. Included in the 699,275 Louisiana Registered Voters, who voted for Governor Bobby Jindal, are middle class people, who are working class, but aspire to join the Louisiana Ruling Class, an American Dream that will likely never become a reality. To determine if this view is correct, we proceeded to examine age and household income in Louisiana to see if the total number of people, who earn an annual salary of $60,000 or more came close to the 699,275 votes Governor Bobby Jindal received during the 2007 Gubernatorial S/Election?

---

[557] _____ "How many registered voters in Louisiana,? Answers, http://wiki. answers.com/Q/How_many_registered_voters_in_Louisiana, 2007.
[558] _____ 2007 Gubernatorial general Election Results-Louisiana, http://useelectionatlas.org/RESULTS/state.php?fips=22&year=2

Using U.S. Census Pathfinder Data for Age of Louisiana householder by household income, 2008 to 2012, and adding the total numbers for 25 years old and under to 65 years old and over, we discovered there were 644,527 Louisiana Residents, who earned $60,000 or more by 2008. As we see, the latter, comes very close to the total number of Louisiana Registered Voters, who voted for Governor Bobby Jindal in October 2007. Therefore, now that we have straightened out the percent of the registered voters, who voted for Governor Bobby Jindal in 2007, we can answer the question we raised from the outset, namely, who does Governor Bobby Jindal represent?

A. TURTLE ON A POLE

This metaphor sums up Governor Bobby Jindal rise to Governor of Louisiana. Operating under the best of conditions, it takes time to develop the skill sets and experience to be an effective leader in any chosen profession. However, to short circuit the learning curve, it is possible to dress someone up with job titles, which, in the real world of the workplace, would take years to achieve. After graduating from Brown University at the age of 20, Governor Bobby Jindal "…chose to attend Oxford as a Rhodes Scholar where earned a Masters degree in… health-related public policy."[559] As we see, Governor Bobby Jindal did not study political science at Oxford University to prepare himself for the multiple-tasks of operating a state government. Governor Bobby Jindal's rise to various positions was nothing short of *magical.* Hawkins stated his meteoric rise to the Governor's Office as follows:

> "at the age of 25, Bobby Jindal was appointed as the Secretary the Department of Health and Hospitals in Louisiana, one of the largest government agencies in the state…By 1999, and at the age of 28, Jindal became president of the University of Louisiana system. From there, he worked for two years in the Bush administration as an Assistant Secretary of Health and Human Services. He then returned to Louisiana to run for public office. In

---

[559] Hawkins, Dustin, "Profile of Louisiana Governor Bobby Jindal," About.com: US Conservative Politics, http://usconservatives.about.com/od/thinkersanddoers/p/profi

2004, Jindal was elected to the US House of Representatives, where he served for two terms until running for Governor. In 2007, Jindal became the first non-incumbent Governor to win outright election in Louisiana history, locking up an unprecedented 54% of the vote in first round voting. In 2011, he won again in first round balloting, with an impressive 66% of the vote."[560]

Amazing is an understatement. Between 25 and 28 years old, Governor Bobby Jindal rose to secretary of a major government office and to president of the University of Louisiana System. No doubt, many individuals with doctoral degrees and medical degrees were confused about why they were overlooked for these positions, given the numerous years of experience they had already acquired when Governor Bobby Jindal was appointed to them. The smartest man or woman on the planet would be seriously challenged to do the mentioned jobs at such a young age. People all over America are turned down daily, that is, they are not hired to do a job, because they are too young, and they do not have enough practical experience. Governor Bobby Jindal continued to soar unstopped by his youth, lack of political education training, and lack of on-the-job experience. Similar to the so-called 2007 s/election landslide, in which Governor Bobby Jindal received 699,275 of the registered votes casted, which, as we have already seen, turned out to be 24.0 percent of the vote, rather than 54.0 percent, a number the media prefers that we believe.

By 2011, 1,023,163 Louisiana Registered Voters voted in the general gubernatorial s/election.[561] Governor Bobby Jindal received 673,239, or 65.80 percent of this voter turnout statewide. However, as it was in 2008, there were 2,884,453 Registered voters in Louisiana. Using this total as the accurate base, Governor Bobby Jindal received, once again, only 23.34 percent of the Louisiana Registered Voter's vote statewide. This is far, very far, from any so-called mandate to change anything. Returning to our earlier question, namely, who, in fact, is responsible for placing

---

[560] Ibid.

[561] _____2011 Gubernatorial General Election Results, http://uselectionatlas. org/RESULTS/ state.php?year=2011&off

the turtle on a pole? As we know, turtles cannot climb a pole, therefore, someone has to pick the turtle up; give it some high ranking positions at a very young age; and make the turtle appear to defy gravity and place its own self at the top of the pole. If we see a turtle on top of a tall pole, the only conclusion we can reasonably come to is, the turtle is brilliant, smart, creative, intelligent, and resourceful because unlike all other masses of turtles, one of them figured out a way to climb to the top of the pole, and the rest of us still have not figured out how to climb to the top of the pole like Governor Bobby Jindal did. So, how did Governor Bobby Jindal reach the top of the pole at such a young age? Who lifted him up to the top of it? And, who, in the end, is he completely dependent upon, and for whom, is his every government action taken to benefit financially?

The answers to all of these questions are the same: The Louisiana Ruling Class. Earlier, we provided data published by The Wall Street Journal, which showed a sharp increase in the number of Louisiana Millionaires during Governor Bobby Jindal's first term in office. The neo-liberalism economic policy platform is not new; it was popularized by the Reagan Administration. For the latter policy to work, that is, for millions of dollars to be stolen from the state government treasury legally, the Louisiana Ruling Class created for itself a "Turtle On A Pole." We have seen Governor Bobby Jindal rise quickly to the status of a Rhodes Scholar, and in short order, rise magically into positions of authority that make many experienced politicians at best suspicious, and at worst-very envious. At the heart of this creationism, lies a hidden desire to *eliminate any government accountability.* This is the best political environment in which to privatize as many government social services as possible, which ultimately, transfers billions of dollars of taxpayer dollars to private business. Regarding Louisiana Working People, we are told that this move will save government money, and make government operations more efficient. We know this is happening right now in 2014 because, generally speaking, very seldom do we see Governor Bobby Jindal leading state government as a *Statesman*; what we actually see, in reality, is Governor Bobby Jindal responding to government problems through the *Mode of Prepared Statements, either read to the media by a staff-person, or it is, oftentimes, published in a newspaper.* To insure that Governor Bobby Jindal does not get in the way of the privatization tidal wave, the Louisiana Ruling Class has sent him out of the State of Louisiana to campaign for President; to make speeches supporting other republican candidates; to raise money for his 2016 Presidential campaign; and to attack President Barack Obama's Affordable Care Act every chance he gets. While Governor Bobby Jindal is traveling all over America doing these and other things, Louisiana Private Businesses are feeding at the trough, and their snouts are buried in greed up to their ears. Therefore, Governor Bobby Jindal, as we will see shortly, should, more accurately, be called a *Road Scholar.*

B. Road Scholar, 2008 to 2014

While Louisiana is buried at the bottom of nearly every social index, Governor Bobby Jindal, being a former Rhodes Scholar, is apparently detached and unaware of this reality, given the fact he spends a disproportionate amount of time traveling out of state, leaving the former to be run by the private business owners, who placed him in the Governor's Office. Nothing at the Governor's Level of government is left to chance or arbitrary. There must be a precise, continuation of continuity required to shape Louisiana's political culture. According to an Opinion Editorial published by The Advocate Newspaper, it stated the following:

> "During his days as Louisiana governor, Mike Foster did at least two things that continue to shape the state's political culture. Foster brought a young Bobby Jindal into his cabinet as a health secretary, and Foster also enrolled as a part-time law school student while still in office."[562]

Governor Bobby Jindal was just 25 years old when he was appointed Secretary of the Department of Health and Hospitals, which was an unprecedented move, given the fact 25 year olds just do not have enough work experience to be appointed a cabinet member. This is how the turtle was being groomed to sit on top of the pole a few years later when Mr. Bobby Jindal was s/elected Governor of Louisiana in 2007. "Foster's appointment of Jindal helped advance the young cabinet secretary's

---

[562] _____ "Our Views: Mr. Jindal, road scholar," The Advocate, March 3, 2013.

political career, and Jindal eventually became governor himself."[563] The other thing former Governor Mike Foster did was enroll in the Southern University Law School while serving simultaneously as Governor. With Louisiana being bogged-down at the bottom of nearly every social index, former Governor Mike Foster enrollment in law school made it seem like being Governor of Louisiana is a part-time job, or a pastime, and it does not require much thought or effort to run state government. Accordingly, "... in signing up for law school while still serving as governor, Foster created the impression that leading Louisiana is a part-time job — a pastime that leaves plenty of hours open for sideline interests."[564] Impression is another word for "smoke and mirrors or illusion. By enrolling in law school, former Governor Mike Foster *turned the operation of Louisiana State Government over to private business to do as it pleased.* Without a leader, Louisiana State Government became a tool that served the financial needs of private business, and, simultaneously, became a tool of dissatisfaction and disservice to the Louisiana Working Class, and the public sector that is suppose to satisfy their basic human needs. When Mr. Bobby Jindal was s/ elected Governor in 2007, he followed the same governor-less path; the tag he was given, by the Louisiana Ruling Class, was that of a Road Scholar, spending significant amounts of time traveling around the country, while the important business of governing the state to satisfy the basic needs of the Louisiana Working Class people-obviously-would go unattended to by calculated design. As we noted earlier, this is not arbitrary but it has been a political tactic since the early 1960s when a "singing governor," namely, Jimmy Davis was s/elected as governor. Former Governor Jimmy Davis spent his years in office singing old-time spirituals, which were broadcasted on the radio for everyone statewide to hear and make them *dream of better and brighter days somewhere in a faraway, unknown life.* Some of us are old enough to remember this during our childhoods. We do.

Former Governor Mike Foster was not ask to leave the state; Governor Bobby Jindal was told to leave frequently by his neo-liberalism backers.

---

[563] Ibid.
[564] Ibid.

a. Governor Bobby Jindal: A Frequent Flyer

The Advocate reported during 2012, "Jindal spent almost one day of every four traveling outside the state, mostly speaking, campaigning for GOP candidates and fundraising around the nation."[565] Millhollon added "during 2012, Gov. Bobby Jindal spent almost one day of every four — at least 86 of 365 days — out of the state, mostly campaigning for Republican candidates around the nation and speaking to conservative political groups." [566] Governor Bobby Jindal frequently flies out-of-state laying the groundwork he needs to make a run for president in 2016. With all the social problems the people of Louisiana are facing every day, Governor Bobby Jindal, like former Governor Mike Foster, treats his governor job "…merely [as] a title on a résumé."[567] Louisiana did not hold any statewide elections in 2012; however, several such elections were held in other states, and Governor Bobby Jindal spent much of his time, away from governing the state, on campaigning for other Republican presidential candidates. Millhollon wrote the following:

> "On many of his trips out of the state, Jindal campaigned fo Republican candidates: North Dakota Gov. Jack Dalrymple; Wisconsin Gov. Scott Walker; U.S. Sen. Dean Heller, of Nevada;U.S. Rep. Mike Coffman, of Colorado; and Bill Maloney, the GOP candidate for governor in West Virginia, among others. He dressed state Republican party organizations in Oklahoma, Arkansas and Alabama and helped raise money for Virginia Gov. Bob McDonnell's Opportunity Virginia PAC. Jindal spoke to the American Federation for Children, a national group pushing legislation to allow public tax dollars to help pay tuition for private schools. He also spoke to the Conservative Political Action Conference and attended several Republican Governors Association events and the annual Red State Gathering, as well as other events.

---

[565] Ibid.
[566] Millhollon, Michelle, "Jindal on the road," The Advocate, April 10, 2013.
[567] Ibid.

He was out of Louisiana at least 86 days, making stops in more than half of the 50 states, according to State Police records and statements from the Governor's Press Office."[568]

Was Governor Bobby Jindal s/elected as governor to campaign for other Republicans running for office? The 86 days he was out-of-state means 24.0 percent of his time was spent addressing the business of another state, and *ignoring or neglecting the welfare of the vast majority of the Louisiana People.* As we have already shown, Governor Bobyy Jindal was traveling out-of-state when a majority of critical decisions required his presence related to higher education budget cuts and privatization of Louisiana Public Hospitals among many others. The Associated Press stated "since Jindal took office in 2008, he has traveled out of state 110 different times, to more than 30 different states and Washington, D.C...more than two-thirds of those trips have been for fundraisers, Republican candidate events and interviews promoting Jindal's book "Leadership and Crisis."[569] Melinda Deslatte added,

> "When Gov. Bobby Jindal was named leader of the Republican Governors Association, he... has traveled out of state at least 69 days this year, much of it to meet with RGA donors, fundraise for the organization and work on strategy for Republican gubernatorial races... The governor was on the road and away from Louisiana at least 1 out of every 5 days of the year so far, AP found, using the information provided to the media by Jindal's office when he leaves the state."[570]

Table 1.19 provides a list of a few of Governor Bobby Jindal's out-of-state travel destinations.

---

[568] Ibid.

[569] _____ "Gov. Bobby Jindal's out-of-state travel costs the state $175,000," The Associated Press, March 7, 2012.

[570] Deslatte, Melinda, "Jindal out of state more than 2 months this year," The Advocate, November 11, 2013, p. 1.

Table 1.19
Governor Bobby Jindal's Out-Of –State Travels
On Non-Louisiana State Government Business
During His First And Second Terms In Office

Year	Location	Purpose	Source
2013	Washington, DC	Three-day CPAC Rally	The Advocate-3/15/13
2013	Aspen, Colorado	Republican Governors Assoc.	The Advocate-7/24/13
2014	Austin, TX	Texas Public Policy Foundation Address	The Advocate-1/9/14
2014	New Hampshire	NE Republican Leadership Conf.	The Advocate-2/6/14
2014	California	Ronal Reagan Presidential Library	2/14/14
2014	National Harbor, Md	Political Action Conference	The Advocate-3/6/14
2014	New Hampshire	Wild Irish Breakfast	The Advocate-3/14/14
2014	Miami, FL	Promote NewRepublican.org	The Advocate-4/6/14

As the above Table indicates, the purpose of Governor Bobby Jindal's travels out-of-state had absolutely nothing to do with solving the massive social, economic, and political problems currently faced by the vast majority of Louisiana Working Class people. How can any of the identified travels transform more than 300 of Louisiana Public Schools, from a Report Card "F" Grade to an "A" Grade?

Moreover, our Road Scholar reminds us of the Titanic just before it sunk to the bottom of the North Atlantic Ocean. As the Titanic was taking on more and more water, and the bow raised higher and higher into the air, *the fiddlers sat calmly playing their music seemingly completely unaware of the fact that in a matter of a few hours, the Titanic was destined to sink to the ocean floor forever.* As much as Governor Bobby Jindal has traveled out-of-state during his first and second terms in office, it seems he is also completely unaware of the fact that Louisiana is sunk at, or near the bottom of every social index, ranging from obesity, education, cardiovascular deaths to rate of incarceration of Louisiana Citizens among many others previously discussed. Who was responsible for paying the travel expenses of Governor Bobby Jindal, as he traveled to more than 25 different states taking care of his personal political business, while allowing the political business he was s/elected to take care of, for the masses as Governor of Louisiana, to go unattended?

b. Road Scholar Travel Expenses Paid For By The Louisiana Taxpayers

Because Governor Bobby Jindal's out-of-state travel had nothing to do with solving the problems facing the vast majority of Louisiana Working Class People, ethically speaking, he, like anyone else, need to be held accountable for paying his own travel costs. However, it was the Louisiana Taxpayers who ended up paying for Governor Bobby Jindal's travel expenses. Melinda Deslatte wrote the following:

> "Gov. **Bobby Jindal** solidified his place in the national GOP over four years of traveling to fundraise for his re-election and Republican colleagues, pitch his book and mingle with hefty donors and well-connected political organizations... Jindal's out-of-state travel cost taxpayers more than $175,000 since he took office in 2008, and more than 57 percent of that spending for flights, hotel rooms, meals and taxis for the Louisiana State Police security guards traveling with Jindal covered trips that had less to do with his job as governor than with his political aspirations. None of the money has been reimbursed by the governor's campaign, which raised $13 million for his 2011 re-election and still has nearly $4 million in his campaign account, even after wrapping up his election costs and tallying much of his inauguration ceremony spending."[571]

Two points can be readily discerned from the $175,000 bill charged to the Louisiana Taxpayers and the $13 million given to Governor Bobby Jindal for

---

[571] Deslatte, Melinda, "Gov. Bobby Jindal's out-of –stsate travel costs the state $175,000," The Times-Picayune, http://www.nola.com/politics/index.ssf/2012/03/gov_bobby_jin, March 7, 2012.

his 2011 re-s/election Gubernatorial Campaign. First, as Melinda Deslatte indicated, "had less to do with his job as governor than with his political aspirations." This is a violation of the so-called ethics reforms Governor Bobby Jindal ask the Louisiana Legislature to enact, during a Special Legislative Session, back in 2008. In short, it is "down home" Louisiana Corruption. If you or I took a trip out-of-state on state government time, as is Governor Bobby Jindal's custom, we would be fired from our job based on some ethical law we violated. Ironically, they do not apply to the governor. Second, if we follow the money trail of the $13 million, we would discover that the majority of it was given to him by members of the Louisiana Ruling Class; yet, during Governor Bobby Jindal's 2011 re-s/ election campaign, the vast majority of Louisiana's Working Class people were constantly encouraged to come out and exercise their vote, during the 2011 Gubernatorial Campaign, although the $13 million given to Governor Bobby Jindal to run for re-s/election, by the Louisiana Ruling Class, had already purchased the governor position, which, in reality, creates an illusion of pseudo-democracy. However, as we have already seen, more of Louisiana's Working Class are waking up because, contrary to any so-called landslide voter turnout for Governor Bobby Jindal, he actually only received 24 percent of the votes casted, while thousands of Louisiana Voters did not even bother to go to the polls to take part in *pseudo-democracy.*

Governor Bobby Jindal's Road Scholar Travels to promote his own personal political aspirations could not happen in a political environment in which the vast majority of the Louisiana people are politically conscious. To the mind of Governor Bobby Jindal, Road Scholar, he thinks he can travel all over the nation on personal business, and, at the same time, still conduct state government business effectively. Melinda Deslatte quoted him saying, "I do think it's possible to chew gum and walk at the same time," Jindal said in an interview. He added, "With today's technology, certainly when I'm not in the state, it's possible to stay in contact with my staff when we make decisions on important issues."[572] The Louisiana Ruling Class sent the Road Scholar out-of-state so every major political decision we have

---

[572] Melinda Deslatte, Jindal out of state more than 2 months this year," The Advocate, November 11, 2013, p. 1.

discussed thus far, could be made with the least intervention by Governor Bobby Jindal. In short, while the Louisiana Public Hospitals, for example, were being shutdown by the Louisiana Ruling Class' neo-liberalism economic policy, Governor Bobby Jindal was likely traveling taking care of his personal political aspirations. In short, Governor Bobby Jindal used texting, and other forms of technology, to run state government. In short, for neo-liberalism economic policy to take root, and spread like a cancer throughout the state government operation, Louisiana, or any state, must have in place a governor who feels the governors job is part-time, or its serious business can be conducted using a smart phone. In the conclusion below, we point out a few areas of state government that have gotten worse as a result of a lack of political leadership.

CHAPTER XI

Conclusion

Shortly after Governor Bobby Jindal began his first term in office in 2008, his promotion of neo-liberalism economic policies were in full swing. As much as $1 billion dollars in tax breaks were given to private business right from the start, which was circulated across Louisiana, by social media, including print and electronic, as a so-called budget shortfall. This is easy to understand; if you need ten pencils to live, and I convince you to give me eight of them, you have a shortfall of eight. Every dollar taken from one state budget and given to private business creates a rolling, cumulative shortfall. Louisiana's State Budget, and especially the public sector, continues to be the target of increasing privatization, tax breaks and tax incentives activity, which has proceeded unabated into Governor Bobby Jindal's second term in office. Due to an erosion of funds to conduct state business, most of the state's social services continues to be severely impacted by cutbacks and layoffs, which manifest itself in worsening state government problems across the board. We will select a few examples to highlight the deteriorating affects tax breaks and privatization neo-liberalism economic policies continues to have on Louisiana State Government's inability to solve pressing budget, health, and environmental problems among many others. This ideology promotes a massive indifference to any human concerns other than using humans as a means of "getting" what their labor power produces in the form of commodities, and "getting" as much of the state taxes paid by the same working class producers when they buy them at the store. We begin with a look at the Louisiana State Budget.

A. Louisiana State Budget, 2014

When out-going Democratic Governor Kathleen Blanco left office at the end of 2007, Louisiana had a budget surplus, which was mostly the result of a surge in post-Hurricane Katrina re-building activity, federal recovery dollars, and sky-high energy prices. Jan Moller summed up the Louisiana Budget situation at that time as follows:

> "The news follows three consecutive years of record surpluses, as a surge of post-hurricane economic activity combined with and influx of federal recovery dollars and sky-high energy prices to give the state government more money than it could spend. Last year, lawmakers had $866 million left over from the 2007-08 fiscal year, and the previous year the surplus was $1.1 billion. Even in the 2005-06 fiscal year, when Hurricane Katrina devastated much of south Louisiana's economy, the state managed to generate an $827 million surplus."[573]

When Governor Bobby Jindal served his first day in office in January 2008, Louisiana had a budget surplus roughly equal to $1billion. This was not a poor way to start his tenure as governor with a state treasury bulging in excess cash to spend on the social needs of the Louisiana people. Adam Nossiter added "...it was springtime in <u>Louisiana</u>, dollars were raining in from high oil prices, and the tax cuts and highway spending couldn't come fast enough in the euphoric Legislature...Mr. Jindal entered office this year with the happy duty of spending a $1 billion surplus — and he and the legislators promptly did so, appropriating millions of dollars for...tax breaks, including one to parents of private school students."[574] The newly s/elected Governor Bobby Jindal wasted no time carrying out his neo-liberalism economic policy Mandate. The millions given to him to run for

[573] Moller, Jan, "Louisiana has a budget surplus after all," <u>The Times-Picayune</u>, http://www.nola.com/politics,index.ssf/2009/10/louisiana_has_, October 17, 2009.
[574] Nossitier, Adam, "For Louisiana, Bons Temps Proved All Too Brief," <u>The New York Times</u>, http://www.nytimes.com/2008/12/19/us/19louisiana.html?_r=0, December 18, 2008.

governor was returned to his Louisiana Ruling Class backers a hundredfold and over. At this point, the more than $1 billion state budget surplus on hand when Governor Bobby Jindal entered the first year of his first term in office, was quietly transferred to private business in the form of massive tax breaks, which were discussed earlier. Jeremy Alford wrote the following:

> "When Gov. Bobby Jindal took office in January 2008, he inherited a state budget that included a $1 billion surplus... What did Jindal do with all that money? In the hip-hop vernacular, he made it rain. He rolled back income taxes that *voters approved* under the so-called Stelly Plan in 2002, plowed $245 million into lawmakers' pet projects and created a slew of tax breaks, including one with a price tag of $360 million. Jindal called it "terrific news."[575]

So, between giving massive tax breaks to private business, dumping huge surplus dollars into some legislators' pet projects, and rolling back the income tax, this neo-Liberalism economic policy set the stage for Governor Bobby Jindal to bankrupt the Louisiana State Treasury. He referred to doing this as "terrific news!" By Christmas 2008 the "chickens had started to come home to roast." Alford stated "Jindal's first Christmas in the governor's mansion brought news of a $341 million midyear budget shortfall. The young governor, an avowed fiscal conservative, somehow had allowed the state to spend more money than it took in. Complicating matters, revenue forecasters warned of a possible $2 billion deficit for the 2009-2010 budget year."[576] By 2010, the budget deficit swelled to $580 million, and it was projected by economists that it would further worsen to $1.6 billion by 2011. The 2008 budget surplus did not suddenly evaporate; even liquid water when it evaporates does not disappear; it turns into a gas in the Earth's atmosphere. However, the Jindal Administration would prefer we believe the $1billion plus budget surplus Governor Bobby Jindal inherited, when he took office in 2008, completely disappeared in the

[575] Alford, Jeremy, "Bobby Jindal's Bad Math: The republican wunderkind has failed Louisiana as a fiscal steward," gambit, http://www.bestofneworleans.com/gambit/bobby-jindal-bad
[576] Ibid.

form of a budget shortfall. This is pure nonsense; we have already seen the $1billion budget surplus was given to private business in the form of private business tax breaks and so forth. And, having repealed the Louisiana Income Tax Law, via the Stelly Plan, Louisiana had no way of raising any funds to meet its financial obligations save those protected by Constitutional Law. Governor Bobby Jindal even found a way around Constitutional Law that protects the K-12 Public Education Budget, by devising a Voucher Scheme Plan, which allows protected K-12 Public Education Taxpayers' Dollars to follow a public education student, from a failing public school, to a Charter School operated by a private business. Many of them are currently owned and operated by private businesses as far away as New York and California.

As the financial problems worsened causing public hospital closures, layoffs, social service cancellations, and financial exigency at Southern University Baton Rouge Campus among many others, Governor Bobby Jindal, road scholar, after giving away the 2008 budget surplus to private businesses, resorted to the gross manipulation of the Louisiana Budget Process, by resorting to "accounting gimmicks" as a means of attempting to balance the Louisiana State Budget, which is required by law.

John Kennedy, State Treasurer, compared Governor Bobby Jindal's Louisiana Budget to a worn-out shoe with a big hole in the sole. As a gimmick to repair the shoe, he said duct tape can be wrapped around it, but the budget problem inevitably must get worse. Millhollon stated "State Treasurer John Kennedy compares the current state budget situation with a worn-out pair of boots with a hole in the sole. In the short term, he said, tape can be wrapped around the sole, but eventually a major repair will be needed. "What we've done about the budget for the past five or six years is just wrap duct tape around it. We've been balancing the budget with smoke and mirrors and accounting tricks," Kennedy said."[577] Because of massive tax cuts, and private business tax breaks associated with neo-Liberalism economic policy, state government revenues have dwindled in-kind.

---

[577] Millhollon, Michelle, "Critics say Jindal's budget strategies amount to 'accounting gimmicks,' The Advocate, March 1, 2014, p. 1.

Millhollon described Governor Bobby Jindal's accounting gimmicks, or smoke and mirrors, to raise revenue to operate state government as follows:

> "For the past four years, the Jindal administration has counted on iffy dollars. The governor sold property, tried to sell prisons, accelerated revenue through advance hospital rent payments and banked on savings yet to materialize. The strategy gets the state through a single year, but offers little guidance on how the bills will be paid the following year... What legislators and the governor have settled upon to make ends seem to meet — with a lot of gnashing of teeth by Republicans who pride themselves on being fiscal conservatives — is to sell unneeded state property and to raid funds. The funds were created through legislation and parked in the state treasury. Their purposes range from paying for a gambling hotline or landscaping at New Orleans' City Park to funding probation and parole officers' retirements... The reliance on nontraditional revenue in the current year's $25.6 billion state budget approaches $500 million."[578]

Any real Rhodes Scholar would recognize wrapping duct tape around the Louisiana State Budget to plug-up its gaping revenue hole, or budget deficit, is at best synonymous to using a doughnut spare car tire in place of a standard one required for long-term, safe vehicle operation. Extended use of the doughnut spare tire will inevitably result in a "blow-out." The Louisiana State Budget is similar to a doughnut with a hole in the center in which Governor Bobby Jindal is throwing one-time non-recurring dollars into, which is only delaying an inevitable blow-out. Millhollon added "Jindal acknowledges he gave costly tax breaks...[579] that caused this fiscal nightmare for the vast majority of Louisiana Working Class people.

Moreover, Millhollon and Addo have provided additional information that demonstrates Governor Bobby Jindal's proposed Fiscal 2014 state budget

---

[578] Ibid., pp. 1 and 4.
[579] Ibid., p. 5.

is full of new accounting gimicks and smoke and mirrors. They accurately point out the following:

> "The problem is the governor's proposed $25 billion state operating budget for the fiscal year that starts in July. Legislators found several surprises when they started unraveling the mammoth spending plan. State Rep. Brett Geymann, R-Lake Charles, said the governor's budget is littered with accounting tricks to make the numbers work. He said legislators are not going to back taking $50 million from New Orleans' Morial Convention Center or shuffling around coastal funding... A trust fund for the elderly that helps with nursing home expenses is hovering on empty. The state's number crunchers made a $40 million mistake in tax amnesty program calculations... Legislators are especially concerned about a line in a report by the Legislative Fiscal Office. The office — staffed by financial experts — looked at the governor's budget and concluded that "$982.5 (million) may require another source of revenue in FY 16." In other words, nearly $1 billion in fiscal obligations could need a new funding source in a year's time. "It looks like all we're doing is kicking the can down the road, and now it looks like the can might be getting bigger," said state Rep. Eddie Lambert, R-Prairieville."[580]

The accounting gimmicks used to put the Fiscal 2014-2015 Louisiana State Budget together has so much "Rob Peter To Pay Paul" in it that by Fiscal Year 2016, the year Governor Bobby Jindal leaves the Governor Office, it is estimated that he will leave Louisiana with a whopping $1 billion budget deficit. Our Road Scholar entered the Governor Office with a budget surplus of $1 billion, and he is expected to leave behind an in-kind deficit. However, in the meantime, given the revenue loopholes in the proposed Fiscal Year 2014-2015 State Budget, Governor Bobby Jindal, seeing the

---

[580] Millhollon, Michelle and Addo, Koran, "Funding questions surround Jinal's budget," The Advocate, April 13, 2014, pp. 1 and 2.

writing on the wall caused by his use of accounting gimmicks and smoke and mirrors used to balance his proposed budget, issued a spending freeze on Friday, April 14, 2014. According to The Advocate, the following action was taken:

> "Gov. Bobby Jindal issued a spending freeze late Friday to ward off a possible state budget shortfall. "Whereas, to ensure that the State of Louisiana will not suffer a budget deficit due to fiscal year 2013-2014 appropriations exceeding actual revenues and that the budget challenges in the ensuing fiscal year are met, prudent money management practice dictate that the best interests of the citizens of the State of Louisiana will be served by implementing an expenditure freeze throughout the executive branch of state government," the governor wrote in his order."[581]

This spending freeze, in short order, was put into affect to counteract the accounting gimmicks that were used to balance the Fiscal Year 2013-2014 Budget. When real estate property did not sale, or other accounting gimmicks failed to generate dollars anticipated to balance the mentioned budget, the spending freeze serves as a last ditch effort to hold back the coming deficit storm surge, which threatens to wreck the lives of thousands of innocent Louisiana Working Class people. As recent as November 11, 2014, Marsha Shuler reported Louisiana is in the worst deficit spending it has been in in many years. Specifically, she wrote the following:

> "Through the first third of the state budget year — July through October — $925 million has been borrowed from treasury funds to pay bills. Last year at this point the number stood at $656.7 million and the year ended with a $141 million deficit comparing revenues to expenditures... But... [Treasurer John] Kennedy said the stepped up pace in the current fiscal year is troublesome.

---

[581] _____ "Jindal orders spending freeze to avoid shortfall," The Advocate, April 4, 2014, p. 1.

"This is the worse shape we have been in by far" since fiscal year 2010, Kennedy said. In 2010, there was $181 million in borrowing, he said. "It's clear to me we are deficit spending," said Kennedy. He noted that the state health agency reported last week its Medicaid spending was at a pace that could lead to a $171 million deficit... The bond rating agency, Fitch, stated the state's financial situation in its latest analysis. "Fitch believes that it is clear that the state's revenues in fiscal 2014 were insufficient to fund operations in that year and the state's application of cash balance to solve the revenue shortfall lowers direct GF (general fund) cash resources and is likely, in Fitch's opinion to contribute to increased interfund-borrowing in fiscal 2015."[582]

As we see, since Governor Bobby Jindal became governor in 2008, he has presided over a Louisiana State Budget characterized by on-going deficits. The budget deficit problem will not be solved during Fiscal Year 2015, given the fact Fitch remarked in order for Louisiana State Government to meet its fiscal responsibilities during 2015, it will have to increase its reliance on shifting money from one budget line item to another, similar to a mountaineer, who has run out of food on the way to the summit, and, as a result, his or her body's cells begin cannibalizing, or preying on one another in their desperate attempt to keep one bodily organ of the mountaineer functioning at the catastrophic expense of another.

Moving forward, the environment is worth giving some attention, given the fact the BP Gulf of Mexico Oil Spill, which occurred on April 10, 2010, is another clear example of an area suffering from gross neglect and indifference by our traveling governor due to the previously discussed budget cutting trend since 2008.

---

[582] Shuler, Marsha, "Treasurer John Kennedy: Louisiana in deficit spending; it's worse than past years," <u>The Advocate</u>, November 11, 2014, pp. 1 and 2.

B. Environmental Deprivation, 2014

A significant, growing body of scientific research is constantly demonstrating to anyone who will heed the truth that the April 20, 2010 BP Gulf of Mexico Oil Spill continues to wreak havoc and massive devastation on the Gulf of Mexico ecosystem. Yet, Governor Bobby Jindal obviously must be unaware of this fact because on April 8, 2014, the National Wildlife Federation released a report that includes data that unequivocally proves there is *on-going devastation on the Gulf of Mexico wildlife four years after the BP Oil Spill occurred.* On the other hand, Amy Wold reported on April 15, 2014 that the U.S. Coast Guard says that the active search for oil along the Louisiana Gulf Coast came to an end on April 15, 2014. This is a question that requires the highest level of state government intervention to address.

As mentioned earlier, Amy Wold reported the following:

> "The active search for Deepwater Horizon oil along the Gulf Coast ended Tuesday [April 15, 2014], when the final three miles of shoreline in Louisiana were removed from active cleanup status, according to the U.S. Coast Guard... As of April, 91 million pounds of oily material have been taken out of Louisiana shorelines since the April 2010 Deepwater Horizon drill rig explosion, the U.S. Coast Guard reported... The disparity continues this year where so far a total of 29,000 pounds of oiled material has been collected in the four states with about 26,000 of that coming from Louisiana shores... Earlier in the year, the U.S. Coast Guard used augers to dig thousands of holes in Louisiana beaches to look for additional submerged oil. The effort helped find and remove about 2.6 million pounds of oily material between Jan. 5 and June 30 last year..."[583]

Even though the U.S. Coast Guard has removed the Louisiana Coast from

---

[583] Wold, Amy, "Final stretch of Gulf coast removed from active cleanup status," The Advocate, April 15, 2014, pp.1 and 2.

any further active search for Deepwater Horizon oil, Amy Wold's research indicates that as late as 2013, large amounts of oil was still found along the mentioned coast. Governor Bobby Jindal has not made any public appearance to inform the Louisiana Public that he is actively working to protect the Louisiana Gulf Coast from the deadly devastation hydrocarbons have on vegetation, wildlife, and human health. More than anyone, the U.S. Coast Guard knows from firsthand experience what lasting affects the Bp Oil Spill will have on the Louisiana Gulf of Mexico Ecosystem many decades from April 2014. Yet, the latter has shutdown the active search for Deepwater Horizon oil along the Gulf Coast. In her groundbreaking book titled *Sound Truth And Corporate Myths: The Legacy of the Exxon Valdez Oil Spill, 2005,* Dr. Riki Ott stated the following:

> "On 24 March 1989 the *Exxon Valdez* gutted her hull on Bligh Reef, spilling about 30 million gallons of crude oil-56 percent of her cargo into Prince William Sound... Ultimately over 3,200 miles of Alaska's shorelines were oiled from the Sound, past the Kenai Peninsula and Kodiak Island, to parts of the Alaska Peninsula some 1,200 miles distant from Bligh Reef...By 2004, fifteen years after the *Exxon Valdez* spill, scientists developed a new oil toxicity paradigm to explain the persistent and harmful effects to sea-life...Scientists discovered oil can retain its toxicity for decades when buried in areas with little disturbance...The new paradigm holds that oil causes delayed and indirect effects by unraveling bits of the complex tapestry of life that we simply call "ecosystem."[584]

Moreover, the National Wildlife Federation stated "given the huge quantity of oil that remains unaccounted for, the fact that even small amounts of oil can have significant biological effects, some of which may manifest themselves over time, and the unprecedented use of dispersants, the full scope of the Deepwater Horizon disaster on the Gulf ecosystem will likely

---

[584] Ott, Riki, *Sound Truth And Corporate Myths: The Legacy of the Exxon Valdez Oil Spill,* Dragonfly Sisters Press, Cordova, Alaska, 2005, pp. 393 and 395.

unfold for years or even decades to come."[585] The prophetic wisdom in this statement is demonstrated by the illustration of the on-going effects that Bp's Deepwater Horizon Oil Spill Disaster is still having on the Gulf of Mexico's Ecosystem four years after the oil spill disaster occurred in 2010. Table 1.20 below provides the names of various key Gulf of Mexico wildlife, and the effects polycyclic aromatic hydrocarbons-oil-is having on them.

Table 1.20
Gulf of Mexico And Louisiana Wildlife Affected by the BP Deepwater Horizon Oil Spill Disaster Four Years Later-April 2014

Name	Impact of oil on Wildlife
Bottlenose Dolphin	"900 plus bottlenose dolphins found dead or stranded in the oil spill area since April 2010, the month the Deepwater Horizon rig exploded. In 2013, dolphins were still stranding at more than three times average annual rates before the spill." P. 1
Sea Turtles	"Roughly 500 stranded sea turtles have been found in the area affected by the spill every year from 2011 to 2013. This is a dramatic increase over the numbers found before the disaster." P. 1
Atlantic Bluefin Tuna	"Atlantic bluefin Tuna breed in only two places in the world: the Mediterranean Sea and the Gulf of Mexico. The Deepwater Horizon rig exploded while the April-May breeding season in the northern Gulf was underway. In 2011, NOAA researchers estimated that as many as 20% of laval fish could have been exposed to oil, with a potential reduction in future populations of about 4%." P. 4
Blue Crab	"The Deepwater Horizon spill occurred during the blue crab spawning season, when female crabs were migrating out of estuaries into deeper waters of the Gulf to release their eggs…Oiled marshes may be continuing to affect blue crab populations and distribution." P. 4

[585] _____Report: Oil Is Not Gone; Impacts to Wildlife On-going,' National Wildlife Federation, http://www.nwf.org/~/media/PDFs/water/2014/ NWF deepwater, 2014

Brown Pelican	"As of May 2011, some 826 brown pelicans were exposed t oil and collected from the spill area. 577 of these pelicans died. More than 40% of all pelicans collected were visibly oiled and the oiling status of another 29% wasn't." P. 6
Brown Pelican	"As of May 2011, some 826 brown pelicans were exposed t oil and collected from the spill area. 577 of these pelicans died. More than 40% of all pelicans collected were visibly oiled and the oiling status of another 29% wasn't." P. 6
Common Loon	"Many common loons migrate more than a thousand miles to the Gulf coast fort he winter...Scientists discovered that the frequency and concentrations of PAHs[polycyclic aromatic hydrocarbons]in common loons increased between 2011 and 2012...oil compounds are making their way up the food chain." P. 7
Coral	"Deep sea coral colonies provide a foundation for diverse assortment of marine life, including many invertebrates and fish. After the Deepwater Horizon spill, a survey of...a coral colony seven miles away was heavily impacted. Marine life associated with the deep sea corals also showed visible signs of impact from the oil...coral larvae that had been exposed to oil...and oil/dispersant mixture all had lower survival rates than control larvae in clean seawater." P. 7
Eastern Oyster	"Oysters...play an essential role in the ecology of the Gulf. An adult oyster can filter as much as 50 gallons of water per day, and oyster reefs provide important foraging and refuge habitat for...shrimp and blue crabs...oyster eggs, sperm and larvae were exposed to oil and dispersants during the 2010 oil spill. Oil compounds known as...(PAHs) can be lethal to oyster... larvae, juveniles and adults...In portions of Louisiana, oysters have experienced...high mortality...related to oil..." P. 8

Foraminifera	"There are nearly 1,000 known species of foraminifera in the Gulf of Mexico. These small marine creatures form part of the base of the marine food web, serving a s food source for marine snails, sand dollars and fish...Rapid accumulation of oiled sediments on parts of the Gulf between 2010 and 2011 contributed to a dramatic die-off of foraminifera. Researchers found a significant difference in community structure and abundance during and after the Deepwater Horizon event at sites located from 100-1200 meters deep in the Desoto canyon...Deep sea foraminifera had not recovered in diversity a year and a half after the spill." P. 9
Gulf Killifish	"Killifish...play an important role in the Gulf food web...These large minnows are preyed upon by many sport fish, such as flounder, speckled trout and red snapper...In 2011, Louisiana State University researchers compared the gill tissue of killifish in an oiled marsh to those in an oiled-free marsh. Killifish residing in oiled marshes showed evidence of effects even at low levels of oil exposure..." P. 9
Red Snapper	"Red snapper spend most of their lives offshore and congregate around hard structures such as natural and artificial reefs. They breed offshore, and the fertilized eggs float on the ocean surface and hatch within a day. Oil was on the water surface during red snapper spawning season, and much of the red snapper's range in the northern Gulf overlaps the area of surface oil distribution from the blowout. In the aftermath of the spill, a number of fish, including red snapper, caught in Gulf waters between eastern Louisiana and western Florida had unusual lesions or rotting fins. University of South Florida researchers examined red snapper and other fish and determined that their livers contained oil compounds that had a strong "pattern coherence" to oil from the Deepwater Horizon spill." P. 10
Sea Turtle	"A recent federal report reveals that large-scale aerial surveys conducted during 2010 indicated that tens of thousands of sea turtles were exposed to oil within the surface oiling...Sea turtle strandings remain far above normal. In 2011, 2012, and 2013, approximately 500 turtle carcasses per year were found in Alabama, Louisiana, Mississippi and the upper Texas coast." P. 12

Sperm Whale	"Roughly 700 sperm whales live year-round in the Gulf's deep waters off the continental shelf…The preferred range of northern Gulf sperm whales largely overlaps the area of surface oil contamination…A researcher at the University of Southern Maine has found higher levels of DNA-damaging metals such as chromium and nickel in sperm whales in the Gulf of Mexico compared to sperm whales elsewhere in the world. These metals are present in oil from the spill. Whales closest to the well's blowout showed the highest levels." P. 13
White Pelican	"American white pelicans nest in colonies…on the Pacific and Gulf of Mexico coasts. Most white pelicans were in their northern breeding grounds at the time of the spill. Two years after the spill, researchers found evidence of oil and dispersants in the eggs of white pelicans nesting in Minnesota…Petroleum compounds were present in 90 percent of the first batch of eggs tested. Nearly 80 percent of the eggs contained the chemical dispersants used in the Gulf oil disaster…these compounds… have been known to cause cancer, birth defects and to disrupt embryo development in other species." P. 14
Seaside Sparrow	"Seaside sparrows live only in coastal marshes, where they are common year-round residents…In 2012 and 2013, seaside sparrows in Louisiana salt marshes were found to have reductions in both overall abundance and likelihood to fledge from the nest." P. 11

Source: FOUR YEARS INTO THE GULF OIL DISASTER: STILL WAITING FOR RESORATION, National Wildlife Federation, http://www.nwf.org/~/media/PDFs/water/2014/nwf_deepwater, April 2014.

In order for Governor Bobby Jindal to hold BP Oil accountable, and in order to protect the Louisiana Ecosystem from decades of further decay, he would have to confront the same businesses, who placed him in the Governor's Office to implement its neo-liberalism economic policy. Those businesses, including the Louisiana Oil Industry, is the same one, among others, that turned Governor Bobby Jindal into a Road Scholar so he would not be around to advocate for environmental protection and social issues critical to the lives of the vast majority of Louisiana Working Class people. Consistent with Dr. Rike Ott's research, the National Wildlife Federation recently released a report that shows, four years after the BP

Deepwater Horizon Oil Spill, significant devastation is on-going related to sea life in the Gulf of Mexico Ecosystem.

As we see, the effects of BP's Deepwater Horizon Oil Spill Disaster has placed the so-called Louisiana Sportsman's Paradise at great risk of losing many, if not all, of its outdoor activities associated with the Louisiana Wetlands and the Gulf of Mexico, including, but not limited to, fishing and land loss. More importantly, Governor Bobby Jindal has taken a hands-off approach to dealing with the ill-health of many of the wildlife that depend on the Gulf of Mexico for survival. What is striking too is the food chain that humans depend on is compromised, and, this could lead to the extinction of many other species of fish that currently make the Gulf of Mexico Ecosystem home. The Jindal Administration's indifference to this growing threat is also filled with silence related to the impact polycyclic aromatic hydrocarbons are having on the health of BP Oil Spill Cleanup workers. As we have already seen, during Governor Bobby Jindal's first term in office, he spent a significant amount of time traveling around the country advancing his own personal agenda while the health of the Louisiana environment continues to undergo freefall deterioration, including the health of the BP Oil Spill Cleanup Workers.

Thousands of Exxon Valdez Cleanup Workers suffered lasting ill-health effects after being exposed to polycyclic aromatic hydrocarbons during their attempt to cleanup oil spilled along the shoreline of Prince William Sound. Dr. Riki Ott wrote the following about the impact of the oil cleanup operation on human health:

> "Within the first week of the spill, some 800 people were hired for the cleanup response. Within one month, there were some 3,000 people hired. As Exxon geared up for shoreline treatment, the number surged to 9,000, then over 11,000...Mestas was president of the Alaska Chapter of Trial Lawyers for Public Justice...He found a graphic summary of the [Exxon}clinical data, which showed 300 to 500 workers were treated every week of the cleanup from late May through mid-September for "URI"-upper

respiratory infections with cough and flu-like symptoms...
He tallied the columns and found *a total of 6,722 reported
cases of URIs,* yet during the cleanup, Exxon had claimed
a near zero work-related illness rate..."[586]

In addition to URIs, many Exxon Valdez Cleanup Workers contracted many other diseases such as leukemia, kidney ailments, neurologic disorders, migraine headaches, and skin rashes among many others. Similar to the experience of the Exxon Valdez Cleanup Workers' health problems, which manifested in them four years after the event, many cleanup workers exposed to polycyclic aromatic hydrocarbons during the BP Oil Spill cleanup, along the Louisiana Coast, experienced lasting health effects four years after the Deepwater Horizon Oil Rig Explosion in April 2010.

Two years after the 2010 Deepwater Horizon disaster, hundreds of cleanup workers were exposed to polycyclic aromatic hydrocarbons during cleanup operations along the Louisiana Coast. Bob Marshall wrote the following:

"According to the U.S. Coast Guard, in the past few weeks this one spot has yielded 1.5 million pounds of "oily material" – a designation that includes oil products as well as associated shell, sand and water. And that's in addition to 1.79 million pounds already collected from Fourchon, by far the largest share of the 8.9 million pounds recovered from all Louisiana beaches in the past two years. The heavy ongoing cleanup is emblematic of the problems spill experts say Louisiana can expect due to the rapid erosion of its coastline, especially along the beaches between Grand Isle and Port Fourchon...These are more than mere eyesores. The weathered oil contains toxic hydrocarbon components than can remain a threat to fish, wildlife and human health for 50 years."[587]

---

[586] Ott, Op. Cit., pp. 29, 56, and 58.

[587] Marshall, Bob, "More massive tar mats from BP oil spill discovered on Louisiana braches," The lens: Focused On New Orleans And The Gulf Coast, http://the lensnola.org/2013/12/18/more-massiv-tar-mats-from, December 18, 2013.

During the Deepwater Horizon Disaster, more than 200 million gallons of corexit, a chemical dispersant that was used to hide the millions of gallons of oil that spilled into the Gulf of Mexico, less than 50 miles off of the Louisiana Coast. Corexit was used to hide the 50 million gallons of oil spilled into Prince William Sound by the Exxon Valdez Super Tanker. In both cases-Exxon and BP's-corexit merely breakup the spilled oil into a smaller size, and sink it beneath the Gulf of Mexico's surface so it cannot be seen by the public but, nevertheless, there in droplet size form. According to Richard Thompson,

> "...many questions remain unanswered about the potential long-term impacts of exposure to the millions of gallons of sweet crude and large quantities of dispersants that were used to break up the oil as it poured into the Gulf of Mexico, into wetlands and onto beaches along the Gulf Coast...Based on witness interviews, the Government Accountability Project, a whistleblower advocacy group, released a report last year that said coming into contact with Corexit...lead to a host of ailments, including abdominal pain, hypertension, kidney and liver damage, inability to withstand exposure to the sun, memory loss and respiratory problems. The report urged a federal ban on the chemical. Now, doctors and scientists are beginning to understand the short-term consequences faced by the potentially more than 200,000 cleanup workers and Gulf Coast residents who may face health problems related to the spill."[588]

Thompson added "preliminary observations from initial health exams found an approximately 30 percent increase in anxiety and depression among cleanup workers. Many workers also say they've experienced physical symptoms, such as respiratory problems, skin rashes and neurological issues."[589] These are the same ailments that manifested in the

---

[588] Thompson, Richard, "4 years after spill questions remain about health impacts," http://www.theneworleansadvocate.com/home/8950601-172/f, April 24, 2014.
[589] Ibid.

health status of Exxon Valdez Cleanup workers more than twenty years ago. These, and other health problems, will affect the lives of Louisiana Citizens, who participated in the BP Oil Spill Cleanup, for the next 50 years or more. Corexit is a deadly poison, and so is polycyclic aromatic hydrocarbons-PAHs.

While the worst environmental disaster-Deepwater Horizon Oil Rig Explosion-was unfolding 50 miles off of the Louisiana Coast in 2010, Governor Bobby Jindal was not engaged, but, to the contrary, he spent a significant amount of time, at the Louisiana Taxpayers expense, traveling out-of-state, either campaigning for Republican politicians in other states, or raising money for his possible 2016 presidential campaign. Given the growing health concerns presented by thousands of BP Oil Spill Cleanup Workers and Louisiana Gulf Coast Residents, Governor Bobby Jindal sat idly by, and gave his approval to the closure and subsequent privatization of every Louisiana Public-Charity-Hospital. As it is, currently, many Louisiana Residents, thousands and thousands, do not have a healthcare alternative where they can go to get their health problems treated and corrected. Making matters even worse, Governor Bobby Jindal, as we have already seen, refused to expand Medicaid in Louisiana, leaving other thousands of its residents without any healthcare options! Governor Bobby Jindal, and his Legislative allies, both of whom worked for the Louisiana Ruling Class under the disguise of democracy and market efficiency, effectively killed the last hope of expanding Medicaid in Louisiana on April 23, 2014. Marsha Shuler stated the following:

> "An attempt to go around Gov. Bobby Jindal and put the issue of Medicaid expansion to Louisiana voters failed to clear its first legislative hurdle Wednesday. After more than four hours of testimony, most of it from supporters, including leading Democratic Party elected officials, the Senate Health and Welfare Committee voted 6-2 to defer action on the proposed constitutional amendment, effectively killing it."[590]

---

[590] Shuler, Marsha, "Medicaid expansion bill fails in Senate committee," The Advocate, April 23, 2014, p. 1.

Medicaid expansion was rejected, not because it would be too costly for
Louisiana Residents, as Governor Bobby Jindal want us to believe; rather, it
was not approved because Shuler stated "...174,000 of the eligible residents
would move from private coverage to the government program if the state
expands Medicaid..."[591] For greed reasons, the lives of 200,000 or more
Louisiana Citizens have been casted down to the lowest rung of Dante's
inferno by Governor Bobby Jindal, the Louisiana Legislature, and the
Louisiana Ruling Class, which the former two work for, for a dollar bill.
Senate Bill 96 was thrown into Dante's Inferno by the Senate Health and
Welfare Committee's 6-2 vote in our demockerycracy. Imagine the number
of babies, when you pray tonight before going to bed, who will not be able
to see a doctor, or the number of elderly Louisiana Residents who won't,
who have worked all of their lives, and for doing so, they are rewarded with
a 6-2 vote. State Senator Fred Mills, who owns Farmers Merchant Bank in
Breaux Bridge, LA, was among the six individuals who rejected Medicaid
Expansion In Louisiana; we point out Senator Fred Mills because he owns
a pharmacy business in St. Martin Parish, and if Medicaid was expanded,
his business would stand to lose millions of dollars because Medicaid
Expansion would make acquiring prescription drugs much, much cheaper
than they cost in the so-called existing healthcare marketplace. People's
lives are nothing, and they are worth well less than a dollar in the Louisiana
Healthcare Marketplace.

Having taken a hands-off position on the environment, its health, and the
health of BP's Deepwater Horizon Oil Rig Disaster Cleanup Workers,'
Governor Bobby Jindal, in consistent fashion, is a staunch, and avid
opponent of a lawsuit filed against the Louisiana Oil and Gas Industry
by the New Orleans, LA East Levee Board, which claims the latter is
directly responsible for the on-going, massive Louisiana Coastal Erosion
and Wetlands Land Loss. We are not surprised by his opposition to the
mentioned lawsuit because it is in line with the Louisiana Ruling Class'
expectation of him when this class s/elected him Governor of Louisiana in
2007. Governor Bobby Jindal's opposition to the New Orleans East's Levee
Board's Lawsuit is a part of the implementation of the Louisiana Ruling
Class' neo-liberal economic policy.

---

[591] Ibid., p. 2.

One of Governor Bobby Jindal's Legislative Republican Allies, namely Senator Robert Adley, R-Benton, LA, put forward two bills for consideration during March 2014, which would give Governor Jindal total authority to prevent any legal action against the Louisiana Oil and Gas Industry related to Louisiana Coastal Erosion and Wetlands Land Loss. Jeff Adelson stated "Senate Bill 79, which in its current form would give the governor the ability to remove members of the Flood Protection Authority under certain circumstances, and Senate Bill 629, which would move the authority into the Governor's Office."[592] Before these two bills were put up for Legislative action, Governor Bobby Jindal had previously engaged in unethical conduct, by removing as many New Orleans, LA Levee Board Members, from their positions, who were proponents of the mentioned levee board's lawsuit. Specifically, Adelson stated "Jindal, a fierce opponent of the coastal-erosion lawsuit, has already replaced three of the nine members of the flood authority who voted to file the suit..."[593] This is how political corruption works: The Louisiana Ruling Class gave Mr. Bobby Jindal a majority of the $13 million he used to run for Governor in 2007; by March 2014, this money is paying off with great dividends because the Louisiana Oil and gas Industry, will not have to pay a single dime for the correction of the massive environmental destruction its oil and gas production has historically caused along the Louisiana Gulf Coast, and to its rapidly eroding Louisiana Wetlands. Moreover, once Senator Robert Adley's two bills are passed, any hopes oil workers previously had to gain compensation for their health problems will be dashed beneath the surface of t he Gulf of Mexico.

In addition, the passage of this proposed legislation will allow the Louisiana Oil and Gas Industry to police its own self. This is similar to a person who commits a homicide and is allowed by the criminal justice system to determine if he or she should serve any time for committing the mentioned crime. Millhollon stated "The governor said Adley's legislation will:

---

[592] Adelson, Jeff, 'Ladies in red' back in Capitol to fight for independent levee boards," The Advocate, April 26, 2014, p. 3.

[593] Ibid., p. 2.

- Encourage more operators to make admissions that will result in increased regulatory cleanups prior to lengthy and costly litigation.
- Clarify the types of damages that can be recovered and the standards for recovering those damages.
- Provide a common sense definition of contamination that makes it clear it must rise to an unsafe or unsuitable level before claims can be supported."[594]

C. The Coming Drowning Of New Orleans, LA And The Louisiana Gulf Coast

In short, the above simply means that the Louisiana Coast, and its Wetlands, will continue to erode, and in our lifetime, we will witness New Orleans, LA, and other low-lying cities along the coast, become submerged under Gulf of Mexico's water. Who cares about the life of people?; this is only about money, and the sinking of New Orleans, LA, and its people, are a reasonable tradeoff because nearly all of us *loves money more than we love our own children's lives, and we should not overlook the fact the Earth is an objective force. Neo-liberalism economic policy allows coastal erosion and wetlands land loss, then the Gulf of Mexico will, in unbiased and non-racial fashion, submerge cities and communities underwater.* By 2030, we will see this come to pass based on historical and modern day policies, which favor money over human and environmental life. While Governor Bobby Jindal is traveling all over America, Bob Marshall provides more information that shows Senator Robert Adley's two bills already mentioned will only hurry up the submergence of Southeast Louisiana, and New Orleans, LA in particular, underwater due to sea level rise. He wrote the following warning:

> "Stunning new data not yet publicly released shows Louisiana losing its battle with rising seas much more quickly than even the most pessimistic studies have predicted to date. While state officials continue to argue over restoration projects to save the state's sinking,

---

[594] Millhollon, Michelle, "jindal unveils legislation to solve oil and gas legacy lawsuits," The Advocate, March 27, 2014, p. 2.

crumbling coast, top researchers at the National Oceanic and Atmospheric Administration have concluded that Louisiana is in line for the highest rate of sea-level rise "on the planet." Indeed, the water is rising so fast that some coastal restoration projects could be obsolete before they are completed, the officials said. NOAA's Tim Osborne, an 18-year veteran of Louisiana coastal surveys, and Steve Gill, senior scientist at the agency's Center for Operational Oceanographic Products and Services, spelled out the grim reality. When new data on the rate of coastal subsidence is married with updated projections of sea-level rise, the southeast corner of Louisiana looks likely to be under at least 4.3 feet of Gulf water by the end of the century."[595]

No doubt, if the Louisiana people do not wake up soon, and make significant changes to the existing economic system, which is allowing greed to outweigh human reason and good practical, common sense, Southeast Louisiana, and other low-lying areas along the Louisiana Coast, will be under nearly 5.0 feet of Gulf of Mexico water well before the end of the Twenty-First Century-permanently. Marshall added "Southeast Louisiana — with an average elevation just 3 feet above sea level — has long been considered one of the landscapes most threatened by global warming. That's because the delta it's built on — starved of river sediment and sliced by canals — is sinking at the same time that oceans are rising. The combination of those two forces is called relative sea-level rise, and its impact can be dramatic."[596] Moreover, while Governor Bobby Jindal spends most of his time traveling out-of-state on personal business related to his own political ambitions, our entire Louisiana Gulf Coast is projected to go underwater within the next 30 years, and, little or nothing is being done now by our Road Scholar Governor to prevent the coming catastrophe. Jeff Adelson signaled the alarm of this pending disaster in his May 8, 2014 article in which he wrote the following:

---

[595] Marshall, Bob, "La. coast facing grim reality," The Advocate, February 21, 2014, p. 1.

[596] Ibid., p. 2.

"Grand Isle is sinking beneath the waves at a faster rate than any other area of the country and may be the most dramatic example of subsidence in the world, with estimates suggesting water levels there could rise between 4 feet and nearly 9 feet over the next century, according to data from the National Oceanic and Atmospheric Administration. The readings from the Grand Isle station, which are used to gauge relative sea-level rise for the entire area, could signal New Orleans and surrounding parishes are sinking even more rapidly into the Gulf of Mexico. Relative sea-level rise is calculated as a combination of rising water levels and sinking land. The newly posted water-level data, which look at five years, represent a confirmation of what many who have looked into the issue have feared for years: that the region is rapidly sinking, Southeast Louisiana Flood Protection Authority-East Commissioner Stephen Estopinal said... an engineer who has studied subsidence throughout his 40-year career. Between 2007 and 2011, the average sea level at a monitoring station at Grand Isle rose about 1.32 inches, according to NOAA's data. Extrapolated to today, that would mean the water now is about 2.1 inches higher than it was in 2007, according to the agency."[597]

Earlier, we pointed-out that the Louisiana Legislature is strongly considering passage of two pieces of legislation, which would destroy the power of the Southeast Louisiana Flood Protection Authority. Senate Bill 79, when passed during the March 2014 Legislative Session, would give Governor Bobby Jindal, and his predecessors, the power to remove members from the Southeast Louisiana Flood Protection Board, or any others, who make any attempt to hold the Louisiana Oil and Gas Industry accountable for creating the environmental conditions that are currently promoting inevitable flooding of the entire Louisiana Gulf Coast, including New Orleans, LA. The Louisiana Ruling Class, which is Governor Bobby

---

[597] Adelson, Jeff, "Water has risen 2 inches at Grand Isle since 2007, data show," *The Advocate*, may 8, 2014, p. 1.

Jindal's political sponsor, is leaving nothing to chance because another pending piece of legislation, namely, Senate Bill 629 moves the authority of flood protection in the Louisiana Governors Office. These bills are moving through house and senate committees without any resistance. In addition, another Senate Bill 469, is rapidly moving toward passage aimed at stopping a lawsuit brought by the Southeast Louisiana Flood Protection Authority, which seeks to make "...97 oil and gas companies...[take responsibility for] environmental damage to the marshes... A state Senate panel forwarded legislation Thursday that would kill a New Orleans-area levee board's lawsuit against the oil and gas industry... The lawsuits claim that energy companies dug about 10,000 miles of canals through the wetlands, which led to the erosion of the buffer that mitigated hurricane storm surges."[598] To show the unethical and corrupt character of this action, we already know that when Senate Bill 629 is passed, the power to monitor sea level rise will be placed in the Louisiana Governors Office. Thus, Mark Ballard added "SB469 would allow only government agencies with a Coastal Zone Management Plan to bring legal claims involving allegations in coastal areas."[599] When the Louisiana Governors Office takes over total authority for flood protection, all dissenting voices aimed at getting the Louisiana Oil and Gas Industry to stop destroying the Louisiana Gulf Coast any further, so sea level rise will be reduced to normal, will be silenced. This unethical activity is currently taking place in the highest committee rooms in Louisiana State Government, where plans are supposed to be made to save the Louisiana Gulf Coast and New Orleans, LA from catastrophic flooding. To the contrary, the political corruption we see taking place will only speed up the day when thousands of Louisiana Citizens will lose their lives, and billions of dollars of property will be permanently destroyed by floodwater.

As it is, we see even when so-called restoration projects are considered, in which billions of dollars are being sunk, the beneficial outcomes are small. Many such projects are obsolete before they are even completed because the neo-liberalism economic policy switch is still turned-on, and

---

[598] Ballard, Mark, "Oil lawsuit-killing bill advances," The Advocate, May 1. 2014, p. 1.
[599] Ibid., p. 1.

the same addiction to money and corruption trumps any positive changes that might help hold back sea rise. Marshall stated ""People are already questioning the wisdom of spending huge sums to protect Louisiana," he[Osborne] said. "The state needs to make sure they're proposing plans that will last more than a few decades, that they aren't asking for billions to build things that might be ineffective before they are even finished being built."[600] Actually, many such "golden calf coastal restoration projects" are not really meant to do anything that has a lasting impact; this money is mostly seen as a source of revenue for private business. This reminds us of cancer research donations; since our childhoods, cancer has been researched, and after 60 years, we are no closer to finding a solution than we were in 1950; yet, billions of dollars have been spent, with no overall conclusive results.

Of everything we have mentioned throughout this book, we hope that, by this time, the reader has arrived at a point of asking one simple question, namely, is this social, economic, environmental, and political destruction actually taking place in Louisiana,? Or, is this just a dream written for some Hollywood Science Fiction Movie? There are more than 500 references cited in this book, which provides more than sufficient information for anyone to conduct their own independent research in advance of political action. We are not talking about voting one politician out and another one in; we are talking about our *freedom, dignity, and integrity to live in a society free of all of this calculated conflict that is being promoted by greed, graft, corruption, and a total disregard for human life, regardless of age, race, color, or religion.* The murder of Michael Brown in Ferguson, MO is evidence of the change needed in Louisiana, and all over America today. No one is independent of life, or the rising Gulf of Mexico's waters. Just because you see someone's name, or picture on a poster board, this does not mean you know this person, or you know that person has your best interest at heart. We have to create a new society, one that is totally different from the one we now live in, or rather exist in, because most of us are just existing day-to-day, trying to get by any way that we can.

Lastly, this book is a micro-analysis of Louisiana Political Economy, and

---

[600] Ibid., p. 3.

it can be easily replicated by others in every state in America. There is one common denominator, namely neo-liberalism economic policy. In the numerator, is taxpayer dollars that are being siphoned out of social programs developed to help people all over America to live a decent, affordable life. Because of millions of dollars poured into political campaigns at all levels of government, there is no grassroots participation in the American Democracy, or more accurately, Demockerycracy. Louisiana Working Class people, and working class people all over America, do not have millions of dollars to give to a political candidate, who, once s/elected, will pass laws that safeguard human life, and insure that all working class people's basic needs are wholly met, regardless of race, color, or religion. Even President Barack Obama, and we know how you feel, that is, he is the first black person ever elected President of the United States; however, although this is partly true, the other half of the story is he was given roughly $750 million to run for President by the American Ruling Class, which includes both Republicans and Democrats. Louisiana Working Class people barely have enough money to pay their electric bills and car notes, let alone contribute $5 or $10 thousand dollars to some political candidate who is running for some office, which, underneath everything, an examination would reveal the political office is already bought by the "highest bidder."

Our survival, therefore, and in the end, depends on Louisiana Working Class people waking up from 400 years or more of Chattel Slavery and Modern Day Wage Slavery. During the American Slavery Institution, 100% of the African Slaves labor power was owned by the slaveowner. Today, we have a new variable called surplus value at work in the American workplace. Americans everywhere are hired as wage earners, which mean a large portion of every wage-worker's labor power is subtly taken by the private business owner because he or she bought John or Mary's labor power in the marketplace just like Mary and John buys a pair of shoes at the Mall. The owner of the shoe store set the cost of the shoe, and Mary and John pays the set price; the Chinese Wage Earner was paid $2.50 per hour to manufacture the shoe. But, at the Mall of Louisiana, and malls all over America, the same pair of shoes, for example, sale for $70; after the capitalist pays the Chinese Wage Worker $20 for his or her 8 hours of work, the storeowner pockets the surplus $50, minus overhead costs, simply because he owns the shoe store. The Chinese Wage Worker who made the shoes lost $50 of their labor power in the form of surplus value, which is exclusively owned by the capitalist. When this surplus value is multiplied by hundreds of Chinese Wage Workers over a specified period of time, the unpaid surplus value extracted from the former easily adds up to millions of dollars of profit every year.

Finally, we have much study, including political education, economic, social, environmental, and social, before us to do. Have you started the process of re-education, and the transformation of yourself into a critical thinker; as this life-supporting work is engaged, our consciousness changes; and as our consciousness changes, our understanding of self changes; and as our awareness of ourselves changes, we become more conscious of our human purpose, namely, to create a personal life, free of scarcity, fear, hunger, and, by working together for the social good of All working people, in an atmosphere of cooperation, we can collectively create a new economic system, in a new society totally free of exploitation and greed, which, to the contrary, is different from the society we currently live in that only serve the needs of the American Ruling Class. The new society, unlike the old one we live in now, that is driven by scarcity and private ownership, would be based on the simple premise that there is enough resources to satisfy the basic needs of everyone without any concern that one group or another's basic needs must go unmet in order to satisfy the basic needs of only one-half of one percent of the total American Population. As it is now, the Louisiana Working Class produce all use values with their labor power; we would merely use them productively to nourish the mind, body and spirit of every human being in the new society, from birth to death, regardless of the color of anyone's skin, eyes, or religion.

The main political hurdle we all must work together to remove, before we can begin the real work of building a new society, is bringing to an abrupt end the Louisiana Ruling Class' neo-liberalism economic policy, which, continues to act as a cancer on the Louisiana Department of Treasury's Budget, and its public sector in particular. Because of the privatization, tax breaks, and tax incentives mania sanctioned by Governor Bobby Jindal since 2008, the former has operated in the "red" since the latter became governor in 2007. Nothing has improved, and nearly everything has gotten awfully worse because private businesses are being allowed to bleed the state treasury dry. Millhollon wrote the following in support of this fact:

> "The Jindal administration asked State Treasurer John Kennedy for a $40 million funding seed this week to ensure higher education can pay its bills next month. There's just one problem: The state's general fund is running at a $172 million deficit, meaning Kennedy already is shuffling dollars to keep the state in the black...
> "The general fund is in cash flow deficit as of today and is currently having to inter-fund borrow to meet daily cash flow needs. So the fulfillment of any seed funding request at this point would require the Treasury to inter-fund borrow that much further in order to meet that new 'borrowing,' " Jason Redmond, deputy state treasurer, said Friday... Roughly $340 million, or 40 percent of the funds colleges and universities expect to get from the state, is so-called "one-time" money. The "one-time" money is supposed to materialize from property sales, legal settlements and back taxes the state expects to collect."[601]

Its the same old song: Budget shortfalls and deficits. The $172 million state general fund deficit is nothing more than the latest amount of Louisiana Taxpayer Dollars that Governor Bobby Jindal has allowed private businesses to steal from the Louisiana Department of Treasury. In an attempt to patch the deficit hole, Governor Bobby Jindal, road scholar, is seeking to put a band aid on the deficit with "one-time money that is suppose to materialize from property sales, legal settlements, and so forth. Any serious-minded business graduate student at Harvard, Yale, or Grambling State University, for example, would flunk out of graduate school, if they wrote a dissertation, claiming the way to operate state government is by using "one-time money to pay state government bills. This is ludicrous,

---

[601] Millhollon, Michelle, "State running low on money," The Advocate, April 25, 2014, pp. 1 and 2.

but because the vast majority of Louisiana Working Class people were still asleep by April 2014, the Jindal Administration is enabled, as a result, to give real money to private business, and in its place, use "Maybe Money" to support higher education, for example. Which Louisiana University will be forced to declare bankruptcy next? Millhollon and Addo sounded the following wake up call:

> "Legislators are especially concerned about a line in a report by the Legislative Fiscal Office. The office — staffed by financial experts — looked at the governor's budget and concluded that "$982.5 (million) may require another source of revenue in FY 16." In other words, nearly $1 billion in fiscal obligations could need a new funding source in a year's time."[602]

Therefore, by 2016, the last year of Governor Bobby Jindal's second term in the Governor's Office, the Louisiana State Budget will have a $1 billion deficit. This sum, more than likely, will mushroom higher because recently, the federal government's Center for Medicare and Medicaid Services (CMS) refused to approve Governor Bobby Jindal's privatization financing plan for the closed Louisiana Public Hospitals we discussed earlier. Marsha Shuler wrote the following:

> "The federal government Friday rejected the Jindal administration's financing plan for privatizing the administration of LSU hospitals. The U.S. Centers for Medicare and Medicaid Services questioned the administration's use of $260.8 million in advance lease payments to prop up the deals involving six public hospitals, including those in New Orleans, Lafayette and Houma. If the decision stands, the state would have to find another way to cover those payments... The private hospital companies leasing the state's charity hospitals agreed to pay up-front a larger proportion of their long-term leases,

---

[602] Millhollon, Michelle and Addo, Koran, "funding questions surround Jindal's budget," The Advocate, April 13, 2014, pp. 1 and 2.

which would result in paying lesser amounts toward the end of the contracts. But Tavenner[Administrator of the Centers for Medicare and Medicaid Services] wrote the arrangement amounted to Louisiana trying to get extra federal Medicaid dollars to repay private managers for those advanced lease payments... Tavenner wrote that constitutes a "hold harmless arrangement" that is not allowed under the federal rules."[603]

Mrs. Marilyn Tavenner caught Governor Bobby Jindal "red-handed," who, as we have already seen thus far, had set the greed table for the private businesses, which he allowed to privatize the Louisiana Public Hospitals. This robbery of the American Taxpayer was stopped just in time. The capitalists plan was rejected; however, to make it all look innocent and honest, the very first Louisiana Legislative Session conducted during Governor Bobby Jindal's first term in office, dealt primarily with ethics. This was done to create an atmosphere that Louisiana State Government was going to operate in an atmosphere of honesty and truth after not doing so for many, many years; yet, everything we have discussed throughout this book suggest a steady rising tide of corruption in Louisiana State Government now more so than ever. Before the federal government rejected the Jindal Financing Plan, the latter had already signed-off on contracts to give millions of dollars to private business, and the vast majority of the rest of us will be forced to pay the cost of it in the form of unemployment, layoffs, social program cuts, higher costs of all consumer goods, and because thousands do not have healthcare insurance, many thousands of children and adults, across the State of Louisiana, will pay for the deficit with their lives.

What is equally puzzling and contradictory is during Governor Bobby Jindal's fist and second term in office, higher education and K-12 Education in Louisiana both have taken one of the worst financial beatings imaginable. Louisiana's "Best and Brightest' Teachers, from kindergarten to the post-secondary level, have been laid-off, overworked, constantly threatened

---

[603] Shuler, Marsha, "federal government rejects Jindal hospital plans," The Advocate, May 3, 2014, p. 1.

their tenure and employment will be taken away from them, and, worse, teacher pay has been connected to student achievement in the classroom without any regard whatsoever for the social and economic conditions of the vast majority of Louisiana Households. The solution to all of the academic failures across the Louisiana Academic Landscape is, according to the Jindal Administration, threefold: (1) Institute something called "Common Core" in K-12 Public Education, and (2) Force colleges and universities to layoff tenured professors, and sharply reduce the number of academic program offerings at the university level, and (3) Set up Charter Schools for the primary purpose of funneling millions of dollars of Minimum Foundation Program Funds to private business. While all of this turmoil is bubbling in the ethics corruption crater like an exploding volcano, Louisiana's school age children currently lead the nation based on their diagnosis known as *attention deficit hyperactive disorder.* Kyle Peveto wrote the following about many Louisiana school age children, who must be sedated, or prescribed drugs, so they can sit in their classroom seats during the school day. He wrote,

"Childhood attention disorders have gone up dramatically nationwide in the past decade, but few states have seen their rates climb as high as Louisiana. Nearly 16 percent of Louisiana children have been diagnosed with attention deficit hyperactivity disorder, placing the state third behind Kentucky and Arkansas, according to the latest statistics from the federal Centers for Disease Control and Prevention, gleaned from a 2011 phone survey of parents. The national average is 11 percent, up from al-most 8 percent in 2003. However, when it comes to medication, Louisiana leads the nation, with 10 percent of the state's youngsters ages 4 to 17 on ADHD drugs. Dr. Steven Felix, a Baton Rouge developmental pediatrician, said children with ADHD can "have issues with school failure, low self-esteem, early drug use and higher rates of juvenile delinquency. So it is a major problem... Louisiana outpaces the nation in ADHD cases...Four of the top five states for ADHD diagnoses are also among the 10

most impoverished states. Louisiana ranks third in its
poverty rate, according to U.S. Census Bureau data. Yet
New Mexico, which ranks second in poverty, has a rate
of ADHD diagnosis only half as high as Louisiana...
Many children who show symptoms of the disorder must
deal with other issues. About 40 percent have learning
disabilities, he said, and many have high anxiety, sleep
disorders or oppositional defiant disorder, a condition that
includes a pattern of tantrums and arguing."[604]

Louisiana's ADHD problem speaks for itself. How can Charter Schools
reverse this deep-rooted social problem whose roots run very deep into the
massive poverty in which a vast majority of Louisiana Residents live today?
Through his use of social media and prepared statements released to the
public, Governor Bobby Jindal thinks otherwise. He thinks all it takes is
classify a public school as failing, and simply enroll the children with ADHD
in a Charter School, his or her academic performance will *miraculously
change from failing-"F-"to excelling at an "academic achievement-"A-" level.*
This is nothing but fantasy coated with false generosity in view of the
fact Louisiana leads the nation in ADHD cases, for school age children
between 4 and 17 years old. Although Louisiana is at the bottom of nearly
every national social index, this does not phase Governor Bobby Jindal
inasmuch as he, once again, regularly traveled out-of-state to campaign for
president. On May 10, 2014, Governor Bobby Jindal traveled to Virginia
Liberty University. According to Michelle Millhollon, "...the college has
become a part of the White House campaign trail. Mitt Romney spoke
there in 2012 as a Republican presidential candidate."[605] As the social and
economic climate for the vast majority of Louisiana Working Class people
continue to worsen, Governor Bobby Jindal is still being a road scholar,
and, in the process, he is intentionally sticking to his pre-programmed
game plan, which calls for the consistent ignoring of the human rights of
the Louisiana Working Class.

---

[604] Peveto, Kyle, "Louisiana ADHD increase among highest in nation," The
Advocate, May 11, 2014, pp. 1-3.
[605] Millhollon, Michelle, "Jindal to revisit religious freedom at Liberty University,"
The Advocate, May 9, 2014, p. 1.

On the other hand, Governor Bobby Jindal is proud of what he has done for the Louisiana Ruling Class, or the half-of-one percent of the Louisiana population. In the Epilogue that follows, we include information that sums up the overall purpose of the Louisiana Ruling Class' neo-liberalism economic policy, which, as we have already seen throughout this book, is the accumulation of capital by the mentioned class, and an increase in the income gap between the "Haves and the Have Nots."

EPILOGUE

NEO-LIBERALISM POLITICAL CAPTURE OF NATIONAL AND STATE GOVERNMENT, AND THE CREATION OF GROWING INCOME INEQUALITY IN LOUISIANA AND AMERICA

On May 4, 2014, Forbes published an article written by Governor Bobby Jindal titled "How We Achieved Louisiana's Economic Surge." In the latter, Governor Bobby Jindal, in his own words, outlined how the Louisiana Neo-Liberalism Economic Policy generated millions of dollars for the Louisiana Ruling Class, or the richest one percent of the population. Governor Bobby Jindal stated "the data speak for themselves...How have we done it?"[606] In this book, we included an extensive section that pertains to the private businesses that Governor Bobby Jindal gave tax breaks to lure them to Louisiana. Oftentimes, those private businesses were exempted from paying any taxes! Thus, the first thing Governor Bobby Jindal did to achieve his so-called economic surge was to eliminate taxes on private businesses. According to Governor Bobby Jindal,

> "First, we worked to create an environment where businesses can launch, relocate, grow, and thrive. We passed the largest income tax cut in Louisiana's history, and eliminated taxes that were hindering economic growth and discouraging business investment in our state."

Its easy to see how the largest income tax cut in Louisiana's history has fueled the unheard-of accumulation of capital, in the hands of one-percent

---

[606] Jindal, Bobby Gov., "How We Achieved Louisiana's Economic Surge," Forbes, http://www.forbes.com/sites/realspin/2014/05/04/how-we-ach, May 04, 2014.

or less of the Louisiana population, since Governor Bobby Jindal was s/ elected governor in 2007. We do not need to be a "rocket scientist" to connect the dots here. Such an unprecedented business tax cut, it follows revenue collection, by the Louisiana Department of the Treasury, was very low during Governor Bobby Jindal's first and second terms in office. And, as we have seen, during this same time, the Louisiana State Budget has been plagued with on-going "shortfalls and deficits." To patch up the holes in the budget, nearly all social programs in the Louisiana State Budget, which serves the basic needs of the Louisiana Working Class, from higher education, K-12 public education to the closure of every public hospital, have-All-been cut drastically, and thousands of Louisiana Working Class people have been laid-off. This financial carnage was planned and carried-out by the Jindal Administration, for one primary reason: With less people to serve, less money would be needed to serve them. In spite of all the social program cuts, the Louisiana State Budget, which by constitutional mandate, must be balanced by the start of each new fiscal year, and, as we have already seen, the Governor Bobby Jindal is using accounting "gimmicks," or one-time money from real estate sales and etc to create the illusion that the state budget submitted by him is balanced. How could it be balanced when such huge amounts of Louisiana Taxpayers' dollars have been given carte blanc to private business.

In his own words, Governor Bobby Jindal wrote another statement that verifies the extent to which he had to cut the Louisiana State Budget after giving private businesses one of the largest tax cuts in Louisiana's history. He wrote the following:

> "Second, we got our state's fiscal house in order. We cut the state budget by $9 billion or 26 percent, reducing the number of government jobs by over 28,000; we shifted from a government-run hospital system to a health system that embraces ingenuity and efficiency of experienced private partners... Per-capita income in our state is at its highest level ever."[607]

---

[607] Ibid.

Governor Bobby Jindal is right on the target when he stated per capita income in Louisiana is higher than its ever been since 2008. Earlier, we provided data that showed the number of newly minted millionaires in Louisiana rose sharply since Governor Bobby Jindal was s/elected governor in 2007. As a reminder, from 2012 to 2013, there was a 0.35 change in the percentage of Louisiana Households with investable assets of $1million. Before 2013, Louisiana ranked 41th in millionaire households. However, the corruption juggernaut unleashed by 2013 had the effect of causing Louisiana's rank to rise 10 spots nationally to number 32. The $9 billion budget cut, and everything we have discussed in this book thus far, worked together, in a calculated manner, to create a significant number of new millionaire households in Louisiana, which has benefited one percent or less of the total Louisiana population. It is necessary to add here that this great upsurge did not change the economic condition of the vast majority of Louisiana Working Class people. To the contrary, the average Louisiana Working Class person has less than $5,000 of investable assets.

Every since Governor Bobby Jindal began his tenure as governor in 2008, he has consistently said that the millions of dollars he gave away to private business, in the form of tax breaks, has created new, high paying jobs for Louisiana Working Class people. We have already seen how his tax breaks has increased the number of millionaires in Louisiana, and significantly changed the state's national rank regarding the number of millionaires. Unfortunately, we cannot say the same for the income of a majority of Louisiana Working Class people. In fact, contrary to Governor Bobby Jindal's emotional claims that his tax break program has been good for working people, an examination of the Louisiana unemployment rate, by parish, paints a vastly different and sorrowful picture. Table 1.21 below shows Governor Bobby Jindal's tax break Program has not had a positive impact on the unemployment rate across Louisiana by June 2014.

Table 1.21
Louisiana Unemployment and Obesity Rates, by the Third Year of the Second Term of the Jindal Adminstration, by Selected Parishes, June 26, 2014

PARISH	REGION	% UNEMPLOYMENT	% OBESITY
East Carroll	Northeast	15.7	53
West Carroll	Northeast	12.4	45
Morehouse	Northeast	11.6	46
Madison	Northeast	10.4	48
Richland	Northeast	8.7	47
Tensas	Northeast	10.2	47
Franklin	Northeast	9.9	45
Caldwell	Northeast	7.4	41
Catahoula	Northeast	8.5	45
Rapides	Central	6.3	41
Concordia	East Central	9.7	45
Grant	East Central	6.9	41
Winn	North Central	7.1	43
Jackson	North Central	7.3	41
Lincoln	North Central	8.0	40
Claiborne	Northwest	7.7	44
Caddo	Northwest	6.7	40
Webster	Northwest	7.2	43
Bienville	Northwest	7.4	44
De Soto	Northwest	8.3	45
St. Bernard	Southeast	7.1	39
Jefferson	Southeast	6.2	39
Orleans	Southeast	7.8	38
West Baton Rouge	Southeast	6.8	41
East Baton Rouge	Southeast	6.3	39
St. Mary	Southwest	7.5	45
St. Martin	Southwest	5.6	43
Calcasieu	Southwest	5.9	41
Cameron	Southwest	5.3	41
Evangeline	Southwest	7.2	41
Iberia	Southwest	5.7	41

Source: Flippen, Alan, "Where Are the Hardest Places to Live in the U.S.?, The Upshot, The New York Times, http://www.nytimes.com/2014/06/26/upshot/where-are-the-hardest,

June 26, 2014.

Moreover, for each of the selected Louisiana Parishes, we see the obesity rate consistently exceeds 40 percent except for St. Bernard, Jefferson, and Orleans. For East Carroll Parish, for example, 53 percent of the total population is obese! This would not be the case if the working people, who live in this parish and others, had a decent, well-paying job, which could afford them options to buy healthy foods to eat rather than fast foods and so forth. Louisiana has the worst obesity and diabetes problem in America! Kyle Peveto wrote the following about the obesity condition in Louisiana:

> "Diabetes is one of America's greatest public health battles. And Louisiana is on the front lines, with 49 of 64 parishes included in the "diabetes belt," a string of counties and parishes in the Southeast with high occurrences of the disease. The state ranks fourth in the nation in the rate of diabetes diagnoses, according to the U.S. Centers for Disease Control and Prevention, with 10 percent of adults living with the disease. The national average is 8 percent, a rate that has steadily climbed over the past 20 years. "It parallels the rise in obesity," said Dr. William Cefalu, executive director of the Pennington Biomedical Research Center. "It's a combination. We've become more sedentary, too." Diabetes sufferers have too much glucose, a form of sugar, in their blood. Too much of that sugar can cause irreparable harm, said Dr. Phillip Ehlers, a Livingston-based doctor. "It affects just about every part of the body," Ehlers told an audience at a Peoples Health forum. "You've got blood sugar floating around in your body, and blood has to go everywhere. It causes kidney disease, nerve damage."[608]

Strikingly, Louisiana leads the nation in the number of its citizens who are obese, and because so many of its citizens are grossly overweight, our state

---

[608] Peveto, Kyle, "High diagnosis rates on par with obesity in U.S., " The Advocate, July 13, 2014, p. 1.

is on the *diabetes front lines, where 49 of its 64 parishes are included in what Kyle Peveto calls the "diabetes belt."* Moreover, 77.0 percent of Louisiana Parishes are included in the diabetes belt. This means just about the entire state is being overrun by obesity and diabetes. The Centers for Disease Control reported 8 percent of the American people suffer with diabetes; in Louisiana, 10.0 percent of its people have been diagnosed with diabetes. All-in-all, a significant number of Louisiana Citizens are physically ill.

To determine the extent of "hunger" that exists in Louisiana and the nation, the August 2014 issue of the National Geographic magazine includes a special section on what it calls "Hunger In America." Tracie McMillan wrote the following in her article titled "The New Face of Hunger:"

> "More than 48 million Americans rely on what used to be called food stamps, now SNAP: the Supplemental Nutrition Assistance Program. In 2013 benefits totaled $75 billion, but payments to most households dropped; the average monthly benefit was $133.07 a person, less than $1.50 a meal. SNAP recipients typically run through their monthly allotments in three weeks...17. 6 million households in the U.S. don't have adequate resources to meet their basic food needs...72% of SNAP recipients are disabled adults, or the elderly"[609]

This is a humanitarian crisis of *epic proportion!* Yet, on August 7, 2014, President Barack Obama held a so-called Breaking News Conference, during which, he told the American People there is a humanitarian crisis in the northern mountains of Iraq, where some ethnic group faces starvation due to a revolutionary struggle going on in the area. We believe inhumanity against humanity, in any form, is absurd; however, given the deep-rooted hunger and starvation going on in America in 2014, it demands a *change by any means necessary.* Our American children and elderly, those individuals who are the future of America, and those who have toiled endlessly, to build America with their own labor power, should face, living, from day-today,

---

[609] McMillan, Tracie, "The New Face of Hunger," National Geographic, Vol. 226, No. 2, August 2014, p. 86.

with only minimal, if any, nutritious food to eat. Before President Barack Obama send food 10, 000 miles away to feed starving people in Iraq, he need to realize that there are American Working Class people living right there in Washington, D.C., only a few blocks from the White House, who go to bed hungry every night.

Take Louisiana for example. We have already seen 49 of 64 of its parishes have citizens living with diabetes in what has become known to scientists as the Diabetes Belt. There is a one-to-one correlation between the "Diabetes Belt," obesity, and Louisiana Working Class Citizens who receive SNAP assistance. According to Tracie McMillan's research, between 20 and 40 percent of Louisiana Residents received SNAP assistance in 2010.[610] The latter program does not mean a Louisiana Resident, who receives SNAP assistance, will consume a more nutritious diet. The data points to an opposite reality. For example, since 1995, the federal government spent $253.7 billion of taxpayers' money to support crop subsidies such as corn, cotton, wheat, soybeans, rice, and tobacco.[611] Tracie McMillan stated "today most subsidies go to a few staple crops, produced mainly by large agricultural companies and cooperatives."[612] While these *huge welfare subsidies directly benefit the American Ruling Class, and Louisiana's specifically, the subsidized crops mentioned do not lead to greater nutrition for the American Working Class, and Louisiana's in particular.* While the American Capitalists enjoy Subsidized Crop Welfare in the billions of dollars, Tracie McMillan added "Congressional cuts to SNAP last fall [2013] of five billion dollars pared…benefits from $205 to $172 a month."[613] The American, and Louisiana Working Class people, experienced a drastic drop in their SNAP benefits, while the American Capitalists' experienced an increase their Subsidized Crop Welfare Program. As we mentioned already, the subsidized crops are not used to produce whole foods that are life-supporting. To the contrary, most of them, such as "subsidized corn is used for biofuel, corn syrup, and mixed with soybeans, chicken feed. Subsidies reduce crop prices but also support the abundance of

---

[610] Ibid., pp. 86 and 87.
[611] Ibid., p. 86.
[612] Ibid., p. 86.
[613] Ibid., p. 72.

processed foods, which are more affordable but less nutritious. Across income brackets, processed foods make up a large part of the American diet." [614]

The typical dinner consumed by the average SNAP recipient in Louisiana, and those nationwide, consists of *fast food rather than a home-cooked meal, inclusive of whole food ingredients.* A common fast food meal consumed by SNAP recipients in Louisiana is as follows:

An expenditure of $10 usually is spent to purchase the **Typical McDonald Menu**, according to Tracie McMillan.

- Big Mac Sandwich.................................$3.99
- Large French Fries...............................2.40
- Fruit 'N Yogurt Parfait..........................1.00
- Three Cookies....................................1.00
- Large Soft Drink.................................1.49
- **Total..$9.88**

This diet is packed with refined, processed white sugar, sodium, saturated fats, and caffeine. Such a diet, among other fast foods consumed, has directly contributed to the development of a "Diabetes Belt" in Louisiana. This state also leads the nation in obesity as we have already discovered. Moreover, many of the Louisiana Cities in the identified parishes, which make-up the Diabetes Belt, consists of communities, villages, and so forth that are known as food deserts.

According to the Food Empowerment Project, "...a report prepared for Congress by the Economic Research Service of the US Department of Agriculture, about 2.3 million people (or 2.2 percent of all US households) live more than one mile away from a supermarket and do not own a car."[615] New Orleans, LA has one of the largest food deserts in the United States.

---

[614] Ibid., p. 87.
[615] _____Food Empowerment Project, "Food Deserts," www.food is power.org/food-deserts/

Hannah Duffany did a research study on the food desert in New Orleans, LA in 2013, and her findings confirmed this fact. She wrote the following:

"New Orleans is the largest metropolitan area in the state of Louisiana. It has a population of 360,740 people. Statistically, the city has proportionately higher levels of low income and minority citizens than the rest of Louisiana. The city has a relatively high minority rate of over 60%. Further, New Orleans suffers from an extremely high poverty rate of 25.7% (US CENSUS, 2010)...New Orleans, Louisiana is not a single food desert, rather, a compilation of various food desert neighborhoods or sections within the entire city...About one fifth of its citizens are food insecure (Feeding America, 2012), over a quarter live in poverty (US CENSUS, 2010) and many struggle to utilize the trifling number of full service grocers around the city. Although not true for all communities or individuals in New Orleans, food insecurity is a challenge for a number of neighborhoods within the city. With fewer than twenty full service grocery stores serving seventy-two distinct neighborhoods, equal access to healthy or fresh foods is severely compromised for those who have trouble reaching these stores. In neighborhoods that do not have ready physical access to grocery stores, residents must travel over a mile or more to access fresh fruits and vegetables on a consistent basis. The inconsistency and distance to full service retailer locations, along with poverty levels and individual transportation has been used as evidence to demonstrate that New Orleans has multiple food deserts (Ver Ploeg et al., 2009)."[616]

---

[616] Duffany, Hannah, Individual and Community Food Security in New Orleans: A Case Study on the Effects of Urban Agriculture in a Food Desert, Bennington College, Bennington, Vermont, webfac.bennington.edu/vinbruce/files/2012/01/Individual-and-community-food-security-in-New Orleans.pdf, June 1, 2013 pp. 28, 39, and 51.

Although hunger and malnutrition in Louisiana are widespread, Governor Bobby Jindal has found time to travel all over America making so-called plans to run for president in 2016. From the start of his first term as Louisiana Governor, Mr. Bobby Jindal has spent a significant amount of his time traveling outside of Louisiana. Elizabeth Crisp documented Governor Bobby Jindal's latest political campaign trip to Iowa on August 9, 2014. She stated "Gov. Bobby Jindal is in Iowa for several political events... Jindal... has been considered a potential contender for the GOP presidential nomination in 2016... The trip is Jindal's third to Iowa in a year. Next month, he's slated to travel to New Hampshire for several similar political events. Both Iowa and New Hampshire are major players in presidential primaries due to timing and media coverage."[617] Interestingly, Governor Bobby Jindal has done absolutely nothing for the Louisiana Working Class, yet, he is gallivanting all over America like he has figured out the solution to the Louisiana Diabetes Belt, or how to bring Louisiana's social index rank from nearly last in the nation to the "best" top five, regardless of the social index. But, there is goes down the Baton Rouge Airport Tarmac, professing to have an answer for the American Working Class, regarding how it can solve the social problems it faces. As the title of one of Billy Holliday's famous songs, this is certainly "Strange Fruit."

Moreover, what is his plan to solve this great obesity and diabetes problem in Louisiana is the question, among so many others, we have already raised? In addition to this very discouraging unemployment situation many Louisiana Working Class people currently face, thousands of us are at-risk for multiple catastrophic illnesses exacerbated by obesity. Diabetes is just the "tip of the iceberg." While this is the plight of too many Louisiana Working Class people, Governor Bobby Jindal has steadfastly refused to expand Medicaid in Louisiana, which would provided thousands of working class people an opportunity to receive some form of healthcare they so desperately need to address these and other health problems. Remember, we have already made the point before that health, which is a basic human rights need, has been turned into a commodity that is being bought and sold in the so-called *marketplace*. Anyone who cannot purchase healthcare, at a price determined by the capitalists, he or she is coldly left

---

[617] Crisp, Elizabeth, "Jindal politicking in Iowa," The Advocate, August 9, 2014, p. 1.

on the side of the road to suffer and eventually perish due to an untreated illness. Is this the 21th Century or the middle ages, better known as the "dark Ages?" Although we live physically in the 21th Century, human behavior, generally speaking, in the American Capitalist Society today, when human life is considered, has not progressed much since the Dark Ages several centuries ago. As the socio-economic, judicial, and political life, among a vast majority of Louisiana Working Class people, has steadily deteriorated since Governor Bobby Jindal was elected Louisiana Governor in 2008, he has, as we already know, spent more of his time traveling out-of-state campaigning for a 2016 run for President of the United States.

For instance, while Governor Bobby Jindal has refused to expand Medicaid in Louisiana, he simultaneously awarded the largest Medicaid Contract to a private business, which his Secretary of the Department of Health and Hospitals, Mr. Bruce Greenstein, formerly worked for before Governor Bobby Jindal appointed him to head this department during his first term in office. The Special Legislative Session called by Bobby Jindal, during his first months in office, to address *Corruption in Louisiana was nothing but a smoke and mirror tactic to cover up the corruption to come during his tenure as Louisiana Governor.* The largest contract awarded, by the Jindal Administration, to Client Network Services Inc., in the amount of $200 million, was a fraud for several reasons. Marsha Shuler wrote the following:

> "An anonymous whistleblower warned federal officials about problems "dangerously close" to fraud in connection with the state award of a lucrative, now-scrapped state Medicaid claims processing contract…[An] email shows that federal regulators had alerted state officials of the potential issues with the nearly $200 million contract prior to its award to a company that formerly employed the state's health agency chief. As secretary of the state Department of Health and Hospitals, Bruce Greenstein was in charge of the agency that oversaw the contract."[618]

---

[618] Shuler, Marsha, "Jindal warned about Medicaid contract," The Advocate, July 14, 2014, p.1.

Conflict of interest is written all over the approval of this contract by the Jindal Administration. Worse, the federal government informed Governor Bobby Jindal about the fraud involved, that is, Mr. Bruce Greenstein was in charge of the Department of Health and Hospitals, which oversaw the contract. This federal warning did not alter Governor Bobby Jindal by a hair; he proceeded with the award of the contract anyway! We already showed Louisiana Citizens arrested for possessing a small amount of marijuana were being sentenced to prison, for between 5 and 10 years or longer, at the same time Governor Bobby Jindal approved the $200 million contract. Shuler added "Greenstein repeatedly has said he was not involved in the decision to award the contract to his former employer, Client Network Services Inc., the Maryland-based technology firm known as CNSI. But phone records and other data included in the released documents show at least 2,882 contacts between Greenstein and CNSI executives and the company's lobbyist."[619] As we see, Mr. Greenstein coached CNSI how to bid on the $200 million contract based on the nearly 3,000 electronic telephone calls and texts exchanged between him and his former CNSI employer. Shuler confirmed this fraud when she wrote "The whistleblower claimed that CNSI's bid was too low and that the company could not meet a $6 million performance bond requirement. He said that speculation the firm got "preferential treatment" because of its relationship with Greenstein "unfortunately appears to be true."[620] Even though fraud is written all over the back channel way in which the $200 million contract was awarded to CSNI, Inc., no one, directly or indirectly involved, was arrested and sentenced to prison, although, as we have already mentioned, Louisiana Citizens, and African-American Working Class people in particular, are still being sentenced to prison daily. Anything goes, from hiding a commercial jetliner, or exploding one in mid air, when the accumulation of dollars is at stake. *Human life is rolled over under the heavy wheel of American Capitalism.*

Also included in Governor Bobby Jindal's article is a third factor, which has contributed substantially to the accumulation of capital by the Louisiana Ruling Class. Governor Bobby Jindal wrote the third factor as follows:

---

[619] Ibid., p. 1.
[620] Ibid., p. 1.

"Third, we worked to unleash the state's natural resources. We accelerated the elimination of the state sales tax on manufacturing machinery and equipment, and we eliminated the state sales tax on natural gas and business utilities."[621]

We intentionally placed these three factors in block quotation form so everyone can take a very close look at how Louisiana State Government, during the Jindal Administration in particular, has implemented the Louisiana Ruling Class' neo-liberalism economic policy, which, on one hand, created a surge in the number of Louisiana Millionaires, and on the other, simultaneously contributed to a widening of the income gap/inequality between the "Haves" and the "Have Nots." In order for the latter to take place, one primary pre-requisite *must be built as a foundation upon which the current income gap and income inequality can be built and enlarged steadily and continuously without any interruptions of any kind.* After doing some additional research, we discovered what the pre-requisite is in a recent OxFam Briefing Paper dated January 20, 2014.

According to this document, we discovered the following:

"... extreme economic inequality is worrying because of the pernicious impact that wealth concentrations can have on equal political representation. When wealth captures government policymaking, the rules bend to favor the rich, often to the detriment of everyone else. The consequences include the erosion of democratic governance, the pulling apart of social cohesion, and the vanishing of equal opportunities for all. Unless bold political solutions are instituted to curb the influence of wealth on politics, governments will work for the interests of the rich, while economic and political inequalities continue to rise."[622]

---

[621] Ibid.

[622] _____ WORKING FOR THE FEW: Political capture and economic inequality, 178 Oxfam Briefing Paper, www.oxfam.org., January 20, 2014, p. 2.

President Barak Obama received as much as $750 million, which he received from large special interests groups, to conduct his campaign for president in 2007. During the same time, Governor Bobby Jindal received approximately $13 million to run for the governor of Louisiana that year. In both cases, the income gap, or income inequality, has gotten much worse. Before President Obama was in office one month, he had already signed-off on an $850 billion bailout package needed in 2008 to keep Wall Street's capitalist system, characterized by unbridled speculation, greed, and human exploitation, from totally disintegrating. At the state level, Governor Bobby Jindal, as we mentioned earlier, cut $9 billion out of the Louisiana State Budget, which was money needed to take care of the basic needs of hard working, honest, Louisiana Working Class people. Instead of the $9 billion allowed to stay in the Louisiana State Budget, Governor Bobby Jindal gave it to private business in the forms of massive tax breaks and privatization of various government programs such as healthcare and prisons. *The only way this is made possible is the American Ruling Class, and Louisiana's in particular, is using its amassed wealth to capture government policymaking.* If any foreign government, or a so-called terrorist organization, had captured the Louisiana State Government policymaking apparatus, and, on top of doing this bend the rules to favor itself, we can be certain that this would be a direct cause and justification for war. Yet, as the income gap widens like the Grand Canyon in Arizona, the vast majority of Louisiana Working Class people are kept in a depression and stupor by the Louisiana Ruling Class. The latter instructs its privately owned social media, including all forms, to continuously fill up the former's minds with trivia, ranging from the Wheel of Fortune, soap operas, police blotters that are intentionally substituted for real news during the 5PM New Hour to various entertainment activities, including sporting events of all kinds, music awards shows, dancing with the stars, late night comedy talk shows, and hundreds of other ridiculous sit-coms. While in this mental state of depression and stupor, real-time actions taken by Governor Bobby Jindal for the purpose of further enriching the Louisiana Ruling Class, pass through the minds of Louisiana Working Class people totally unnoticed, or realized. For example, how many Louisiana Working Class people are aware that Governor Bobby Jindal gave a private consultant firm $5million to come up with ways to save state government money? How many of the former are aware that one of the ways Alvarez & Marsal recommended to the Jindal Administration to save money is the *closure of 18 Office of Motor Vehicles statewide?* Melinda Deslatte wrote this about the Louisiana State Government's Savings debacle:

> "The Jindal administration hired consulting firm Alvarez & Marsal under a $5 million contract to find ways to cut costs across state government through "efficiencies." Plans to close 18 Office of Motor Vehicles locations around Louisiana, limit ferry hours in Cameron Parish and consolidate transportation maintenance units were among the recommendations that hit resistance in the Senate Finance Committee...Generating the most criticism was a plan to save $2 million by closing 18 locations operated by the Office of Motor Vehicles, including in Oakdale, Donaldsonville, Bunkie, Kenner, Westwego, Mandeville, West Monroe, Sulphur, Golden Meadow and Eunice. The closures would come even as wait times at OMV locations have shot up to as much as an hour and half because of previous budget cuts."[623]

If this appears to be ridiculous, or outside of the bounds of common sense, then trust your own "gut" feelings. Remember, we mentioned earlier that there has been an unprecedented surge in the number of "newly minted millionaires" in Louisiana during Governor Bobby Jindal's first and second terms in office. This is how they are created at the Louisiana Taxpayers' expense. Where else can anyone get a consultant contract for $5Million, and then recommend something that makes no sense at all? Only here in Louisiana where ethics is highly cherished!!

Yet, as all of this greed unfolds every day, few, if any Louisiana Working Class people have an idea it is taking place. The best explanation for this mental disconnect between mind and actions was written by the Great Russian Writer-Leo Tolstoy. In his masterpiece titled *War And Peace*, which

---

[623] Deslatte, Melinda, "Senators pick through $74 M savings from consultant," The Advocate, May 16, 2014, p. 1.

was first written in 1869, and published in America in 1968, he wrote the following penetrating words that applied to the people of his day, and they still have the same fresh meaning in 2014 that they had 145 years ago:

> "Strange to say, all these measures, plans, and efforts, which were in no way inferior to others made in similar circumstances, had no effect upon the heart of the matter, but like the hands of a clock detached from the mechanism, revolved aimlessly and arbitrarily, without engaging the wheels."[624]

Today's-2014-political atmosphere in Louisiana, is characterized by a nearly complete indifference to the basic needs of the vast majority of the Louisiana Working Class people; and, the latter's indifference is manifested as being *satisfied with nothing*. From the perspective of the Louisiana Ruling Class, this indifference, on one hand, is designed to keep Governor Bobby Jindal out-of-state campaigning for president as much as possible, and on the other, it is designed to keep the Louisiana masses in a *constant state of struggle for survival*. In both cases, as Leo Tolstoy wrote more than a century ago, where the heart of the matter is concerned, the thoughts and feelings in the mind behave "...like the hands of a clock detached from the mechanism, revolved aimlessly and arbitrarily, without engaging the wheel." The mechanism is symbolic of the human brain; and the thoughts and feelings are symbolic of the hands of a clock, which revolves aimlessly and continuously without ever engaging the wheels of *critical thinking located inside the brain, including intellectual knowledge and spiritual intuition*. It is in this political atmosphere that Governor Bobby Jindal, and his Louisiana Legislative allies, were able to drastically widen the income gap between the Louisiana Ruling Class and the Louisiana Working Class. Governor Bobby Jindal believes, albeit naively, that the $9 billion budget cut is good for the Louisiana Working Class, and the latter believes one day it will *miraculously be the recipient of billions of dollars too*. Consistent with Dr. Martin Luther King's "I Have A Dream" Speech in 1963, we are, generally speaking, still dreaming all of these years later. However, for the one percent of the world population, and the one-percent

---

[624] Tolstoy, Leo, *War And Peace*, New American Library, New York, 1968, p. 1200.

of the American population in each state, the latter has seen their incomes and property ownership increase astronomically. Consider the following information.

A. Income Inequality Worldwide, 2014

Income inequality is not unique to Louisiana; it is a growing and dangerous problem, which affects the vast majority of the nearly 8 billion people who live on Earth today. One percent of the world population own half of the wealth while the other 99 percent share the other half, which, when spread among close to 8 billion people, this amounts to hardly anything. Oxfam described the worldwide income inequality as follows:

> "Economic inequality is rapidly increasing in the majority of countries. The wealth of the world is divided in two: almost half going to the richest one percent; the other half to the remaining 99 percent. The World Economic Forum has identified this as a major risk to human progress. Extreme economic inequality and political capture are too often interdependent. Left unchecked, political institutions become undermined and governments overwhelmingly serve the interests of economic elites to the detriment of ordinary people."[625]

Given the fact political campaigns, at all levels of government, require millions of dollars to operate, for a candidate seeking political office, to win an election, it follows the existing political systems serve the special interests of one percent of the world population, and, the interests of working class people are ignored. A $5 campaign contribution is not going to get anyone elected to office in the current capitalist environment we live in. Who can reasonably debate this is not true when the Oxfam Briefing Paper Number 178 states "the wealth of the one percent richest people in the world amounts to $110 trillion. That's 65 times the total wealth of the bottom half of the world's population. The bottom half

---

[625] Op. Cit., WORKING FOR THE FEW: Political capture and economic inequality, January 20, 2014, p. 1.

of the world's population owns the same as the richest 85 people in the world."[626] This may seem like the bottom half of the world population own millions of dollars per person, but once the several billion people's incomes are considered individually, we cannot find 85 working class people's income listed in the Forbes Magazine. Therefore, the bottom half of the world population's income does not come anywhere close to that of "the richest 85 people in the world." Isn't it hard to conceive that the one percent richest people in the world have an aggregate income that amounts to $110 trillion? This is not all. Oxfam Briefing Paper Number 178 added "It is likely that the full concentration of wealth is in fact even worse, as a significant amount of wealth among those at the top of the scale is hidden away in tax havens. It is estimated that $18.5 trillion is held unrecorded and offshore."[627] "By comparison, the GDP of the US, the richest country on earth, is 15.8 trillion."[628] The total amount of aggregate income owned by only one percent of the world population comes to roughly $128.5 trillion, and the actually amount may never be known. What we do know for certain is close to 8 billion people's individual incomes do not come close to the amount of income owned by only one percent of the world population, or the individual incomes of the richest 85 people in the world. The same trend hold true for the United States.

B. Income Inequality In The United States, 2014

The income inequality that the Jindal Administration orchestrated is consistent with the income inequality generalized trend, which exist in every one of the 50 states without exception. In order to widen the income gap between the American Ruling Class and the American Working Class, both of which make up the class structure of each one of the 50 states, it is a primary pre-requisite of the former that it must *first capture all of the political institutions of the individual government of every state, ultimately inclusive of the political capture of the federal government and the U.S. congress.* The American Ruling Class is defined by the Oxfam Briefing

---

[626] Ibid., p. 2.
[627] Ibid., p. 6.
[628] Ibid., p. 18.

Paper Number 178 as follows: "…400 of the richest Americans have more wealth than the 150 million citizens who comprise the poorest half of the population…"[629] This is not an accident, nor is it due to the laziness of American Working Class people. In order to make it appear that the great, growing chasm between the "Haves and the "Have Nots" is primarily due to some special connection the wealthy has with the *Divine*, the "Haves" use their great wealth strategically to support political candidates who will take actions that generate them increasingly higher profits. In short, the American Ruling Class uses its great wealth to capture the social, economic, judicial, and political systems. Policies are easily bent to favor the "Haves," and, once their thousands of dollars in campaign contributions are decisively used to s/elect favorable political candidates, most all legislation, especially those dealing with the potential to realize massive wealth, is passed that favor capital formations to the general exclusion of the American Working Class person. Oxfam stated "Concentration of wealth in the hands of the few leads to undue political influence, which ultimately robs citizens of natural resource revenues, produces unfair tax policies and encourages corrupt practices, and challenges the regulatory powers of governments."[630] With vast sums of concentrated wealth to use to s/elect their political candidates, regardless of whether the candidate is democrat or republican, the American Ruling Class' political candidates are placed, by the members of this class, in key elected government seats, ranging from President Barack Obama of the United States to the man or woman s/elected to serve on the police jury in some small village located in the Deep South. Recently, Senator Mary Landrieu was defeated by Dr. Butch Cassidy, who will replace her as a Louisiana Senator, beginning in January 2015. Interestingly, together, both candidates spent more than $26 million during the 2014 senatorial campaign, a sum that is more than had ever been spent on a senate campaign in Louisiana History.

According to Oxfam, the main goal of the American Ruling Class is to expand its stupendous ownership of wealth by capture of the government apparatus. Specifically, Oxfam stated "as we have seen, the influence of wealthy groups leads to imbalanced political rights and representation.

---

[629] Ibid., p. 22.
[630] Ibid., p. 11.

The outcomes include the capture of legislative and regulatory decision-making functions by those powerful groups."[631] As we mentioned earlier, "...the preferences of wealthy Americans are *overwhelmingly* represented in their government, compared with those of the middle classes. By contrast, the preferences of the poorest people demonstrate *no* statistical impact on the voting patterns of their elected officials."[632] Wealthy Americans, or one-percent of the total population in Louisiana, has already captured the Louisiana Legislature.

The most obvious way we know the Louisiana Ruling Class has already captured the Louisiana Legislature is simply based on the decisions it makes, and which class, or economic group, they favor a majority of the time. For example, during the current Louisiana Legislative Session, which began in March 2014, a number of bills being advanced especially support overwhelmingly the economic interest of the Louisiana Ruling Class. Specifically, Mark Ballard wrote the following:

> "A Louisiana House committee...voted [May 21, 2014] to specifically kill the lawsuit filed by a New Orleans-area levee board. The House Committee on Natural Resources amended Senate Bill 469 to say that the Louisiana Legislature wants this measure to apply retroactively, and that lawmakers oppose the lawsuits filed last year by Southeast Louisiana Flood Protection Authority-East against 97 oil and gas companies claiming environmental damage to the marshes. The panel then voted 13 to 6 to send the amended legislation to the full Louisiana House. "We want a statement by the Legislature saying this is retroactively applied," said Jimmy Faircloth, the Pineville lawyer who was the primary author of SB469 and represents large landowners. He is a former executive counsel for Gov. Bobby Jindal...The levee board lawsuits claim that energy companies over the years dug about 10,000 miles of canals through the wetlands, which led to

---

[631] Ibid., p. 11.
[632] Ibid., p. 11.

the erosion of the marsh buffer that mitigates the impact of hurricane storm surges on populated areas… Jindal and the oil and gas industry oppose the levee board lawsuits"[633]

Political capture of the Louisiana Legislature is clearly shown by Mark Ballard because Jimmy Faircloth, lawyer, "…was the primary author of SB469…"[634] and Mr. Jimmy Faircloth was employed by Governor Bobby Jindal as his executive counsel before the March 2014 Legislative Session. And, the members of the Louisiana House Committee, who voted in favor of killing the New Orleans-area levee board lawsuit, are equally indicative of the current political capture of the Louisiana Legislature. SB469 primarily favors the economic interest of the Louisiana Ruling Class, which owns the Louisiana Oil and gas Industry, either collectively or jointly, with other members of the ruling classes of other states. Moreover, less than a week later, Mark Ballard stated "the Louisiana House on Thursday rejected the lawsuit filed against 97 oil and gas companies by a New Orleans levee board by approving legislation that would retroactively kill the litigation, which claims the companies caused environmental damage to the state's wetlands. The voted 59 to 39 for Senate Bill 469…"[635] Ballard added "SB469 effectively immunizes the oil and gas industry from bearing any responsibility for the environmental damage caused over the decades, [Rep. John Bel] Edwards [D-Amite] said, asking his colleagues, "Who runs this place?"[636] With the oil and gas legislation-SB469-dead, a victim of the political capture of the Louisiana Legislature by the Louisiana Ruling Class, and by removing the latter from taking responsibility for, in many instances, irretrievably destroying the Louisiana Wetlands, this has made thousands of Louisiana Working Class people's homes and other properties vulnerable to flooding, and hurricane storm surge. According to The Advocate,

---

[633] Ballard, Mark, "La. House committee votes to kill levee board lawsuit," The Advocate, May 22, 2014, p.1.
[634] Ibid., p. 1.
[635] Ballard, Mark, "Louisiana House votes to kill levee board lawsuit," The Advocate, May 30, 2014, p. 1.
[636] Ibid., p. 2.

"Louisiana trails only Florida in the number of homes at risk for damage from hurricane-driven storm surge, according to CoreLogic, a global data analysis services firm. In Louisiana, 738,165 single-family homes valued at $161.1 billion are at risk for "storm-surge inundation." That's the third-highest amount of potential home damage. In Florida, 2.5 million homes valued at $490.4 billion are at risk. CoreLogic also ranked metro areas by storm-surge risk. New Orleans ranked No. 5 with 381,149 total properties valued at $85.7 billion. Lafayette was No. 14 with 106,166 properties valued at $21.3 billion."[637]

More than half a million Louisiana homes are placed at even greater risk of flooding due to the Louisiana Legislature's rejection of SB469. We wonder if anyone who voted to kill this lawsuit against the oil and gas industry live in homes that are consider at high risk for hurricane storm surge? The more troubling point here is $161 billion worth of properties are located in areas already devastated by the oil and gas industry, making them highly prone to flooding and economic loss. Who cares? Who even knows this is happening? Most of us spend so much of our time engaged in the superficial consumption aspects of life that during *political election times, we vote people into office paid for by the Louisiana Ruling Class, and they are the ones who voted to kill SB469, leaving a significant number of Louisiana Citizens' homes vulnerable to hurricane storm surge and general flooding from rainfall.* On top of this worrisome situation, Louisiana has found its way back at the top of another "Bad List," namely, delinquent debt. The Advocate Staff reported the following:

"Louisiana tops a bad list: a study of delinquent debt. The bad number is 8.7 — the percentage of Louisiana residents who are shown on credit reports as having past-due debt, according to the Urban Institute… Among the nation's 100 largest metropolitan areas, 8.6 percent of residents of the Baton Rouge and New Orleans regions

[637] _____ La. ranks 2nd for homes from hurricane storm surge, " The Advocate, July 10, 2014, p. 1.

had past-due debts... A higher portion of Louisiana's residents with credit files, 43.8 percent, had been reported for debt collection... the average amount they owed [was] — $4,194... In the Baton Rouge area, 43.7 percent of borrowers with credit files averaged $4,561 that was sought by debt-collection teams. The numbers for the New Orleans area were 41.5 percent and $4,251... Only about 20 percent of Americans with credit records have any debt at all."[638]

Only the Louisiana Ruling Class, for example, falls into the category of having "any debt at all." Everybody else, generally speaking, is saddled with mounting debt on their backs, ranging from hospital bills to home mortgages. Can we vote this problem away? The actions of the politicians voted into the Louisiana Legislature, by the Louisiana Working Class, provides an answer to this important question.

This brings one question to mind: Why do we need House of Representatives and Senators, given the fact most bills, similar to SB469, are written by other personnel and not by elected officials? In addition, democratic freedom and justice for the average Louisiana Citizen have been greatly reduced, or eliminated, because Mark Ballard stated "Louisiana legislators... have launched what has become the largest assault in 20 years on access to the civil court system for individual victims...Robert E. Kleinpeter, a Baton Rouge lawyer...[stated] Corporations are unrelenting on their attacks on the civil justice system. They don't want to be fair."[639] In short, corporations do not want any Louisiana Citizen to bring them to the civil court system, seeking any justice.

Another example of political capture of the Louisiana Legislature, by the Louisiana Ruling Class, is the Louisiana House of Representatives rejection of placing $38 million of advanced lease payments made, by several private

---

[638] Advocate Staff and Wire Report, "Louisiana tops nation on debt delinquency list," The Advocate, June 30, 2014, pp. 1 and 2.
[639] Ballard, Mark, "Legislature cracks down on lawsuits," The Advocate, May 25, 2014, p. 1.

businesses, which were allowed to takeover Louisiana Public Hospitals. Michelle Millhollon stated "The Louisiana House rejected an attempt Thursday to put $38 million in escrow until a resolution is reached on the Jindal administration's hospital financing plans. At issue is the federal government's rejection of the way Gov. Bobby Jindal structured the finances for private hospitals treating the poor on the state's behalf. Private hospitals now are taking care of patients once seen by LSU public hospitals."[640] This rejection means rather than Governor Bobby Jindal wait to see how the federal government plans to resolve a financial plan set in motion by him "...without waiting for federal approval. CMS had problems with the plan's use of more than $260 million in advance lease payments provided by two entities taking over operation of LSU hospitals in New Orleans and Lafayette."[641] If this money is placed in an escrow account, it would no longer be available for Governor Bobby Jindal to give to the Louisiana Ruling Class. Political capture of the state government organization, from top to bottom, is the reason the escrow account will not be set up. Moreover, if CMS does not allow Governor Bobby Jindal to stand, then the money, if placed in an escrow account, would be needed by the Jindal Administration to pay for the healthcare needs of the Louisiana Citizens. The health needs of thousands will continue to go unmet. Moreover, we discussed in this book a section that covers the Louisiana Criminal Justice Plantation System (Our added name). It was shown that Louisiana imprisons more of its citizens than any country in the world because the Prison Industry Complex is very lucrative. Thus, to keep Louisiana Prisons filled to capacity, the Louisiana Legislature must consider, and pass legislation that make it possible to generate increasing profit off of crime. Without the political capture of the Louisiana Legislature, this would not be possible. As it is, "the Louisiana Senate on Tuesday [May 27, 2014] advanced legislation that would create 14 new assistant district attorney positions across the state. The Senate voted 34-0 for the measure, which now heads to the House for debate."[642] In short, more assistant

---

[640] Millhollon, Michelle, "House says 'No' to putting millions of dollars in escrow," The Advocate, May 22, 2014, p. 1.

[641] Ibid., p. 1.

[642] _____ "Senate OKs more assistant prosecutors," Capitol News Bureau, May 27, 2014, p. 1.

prosecutors will mean more Louisiana Citizens can be rushed through the Louisiana Criminal Justice System; sentenced for a number of years; and thrown into a prison to serve time. Each day, the Jindal Administration pays local, sheriff operated and state-run prisons a daily fee to house old and new inmates, ranging from 1 year of incarceration to life. This is a multi-million dollar a year business!

Furthermore. Earlier, we mentioned that Louisiana State Law requires that Governor Bobby Jindal submit a balanced budget to the Louisiana Legislature for approval, for t he next fiscal year. In this case, the Louisiana Legislature approved Governor Bobby Jindal's state budget for the 2014-2015 Fiscal Year. Because of political capture of Louisiana State Government, by one-percent of its population, including the Louisiana Legislature, the mentioned state budget was approved, by the Louisiana Legislature, and, ethically speaking, it was approved by the latter, although it is not balanced as Louisiana State Law mandates. Michelle Millhollon wrote the following:

> "In a 75-22 vote, the House sent HB1 to the governor's desk... State Rep. John Bel Edwards, D-Amite, raised the only objections, complaining that HB1 sets up legislators to find nearly $1 billion in new revenue the following year. More than $900 million in recurring expenses will be paid with dollars likely to only materialize once."[643]

In short, Governor Bobby Jindal's 2014-2015 Fiscal Year State Budget has a $1 billion hole in it, and, this means it is not balanced because, by using "accounting gimmicks," it appears balanced, although $900 million "in recurring expenses will be paid with dollars likely to only materialize once." What happens after the bills are paid with dollars that do not ever materialize again? The Louisiana State Budget will have a $1 billion deficit or more once Governor Bobby Jindal's second term in office is over. As you may recall, the $1 billion deficit is the money Governor Bobby Jindal gave to private businesses, in the form of tax breaks and incentives, during

---

[643] Millhollon, Michelle, "house OKs budget with little discussion," The Advocate, May 30, 2014, p. 1.

his first term in office. Regarding ethics, when Governor Bobby Jindal signs his 2014-2015 Fiscal Year Budget, he will violate the Louisiana Constitution, which mandates that he sign a state budget that is balanced, and not dependent on "non-recurring money" to pay "recurring expenses."

The ultimate example of the political capture of the Louisiana Legislature, and state government in general, is Governor Bobby Jindal's absence and failure to participate in the Louisiana Legislative Session, which began in March 2014. Governor Bobby Jindal, as we already seen, is reduced to a Road Scholar, who is unable to exert any independent influence on any legislation that affects the daily lives of millions of Louisiana Citizens. According to the Capitol News Bureau and the Associated Press,

> "As the Senate Finance Committee listened to the public's concerns about the $25 billion state budget, Gov. Bobby Jindal settled into an airplane seat. Jindal flew to Denver, where he attended meetings for his national nonprofit organization, America Next, and spoke at a reception for the Alliance for Choice in Education. Jindal has visited more than a dozen states since January. He's been to California, Texas, Michigan, Minnesota, Illinois, Florida, New York, New Hampshire, North Carolina, Alabama, Georgia, Indiana and Tennessee. He's also visited Washington, D.C. America Next, the nonprofit that Jindal launched to find solutions for national problems, drives a lot of his traveling. He conducts what his press office simply calls "meetings" for America Next across the nation. The meetings are more likely fundraisers."[644]

How ironic and tragic, similar to a Greek Tragedy-Comedy Play. When the Senate Finance Committee took a discussion of public concerns related to Governor Bobby Jindal's $25 billion state budget, he was settled in his seat on an airplane headed to Denver, Colorado to participate in a fundraiser!! This is pure political capture of Louisiana State Government

---

[644] _____ "Governor deflects questions over travel," Capitol News Bureau and the Associated Press, May 25, 2014, p. 1.

by the Louisiana Ruling Class. Apparently, when the most important item on the March 2014 Legislative Agenda came up, Governor Bobby Jindal decided it was more important to fly to Denver, Colorado to participate in a fundraiser than be present in t he Louisiana Legislature working to help Louisiana Teachers, Louisiana Children, Louisiana Farmers, Louisiana Citizens, and many more. As clear as these facts are, it continues to evade the minds of just about everyone, regardless of education, occupation, or education and so forth. The voting conditioning runs deep in the minds of the average American Working Class individual. He or she, for the most part, still believe *if they go to the voting poll and vote for a political candidate, there is a chance he or she may win the election, and then, pass legislation or other that will improve their lives in some way or another.* For example, when Barack Obama was s/elected president of the United States in 2007, the vast majority of American Working Class people, especially the middle class, believe it was their votes that elected Barack Obama president of the United States, and not the *political capture of the legislature and general government regulatory and decision-making functions.* Thousands and thousands of American Working Class people traveled to Washington, DC in January 2008 to say later to someone that they participated in the Inaugural Celebration of the first elected Black President of the United States in American History. Very few, if any of these people knew, at the time, that Barack Obama was given $750 million in campaign contributions, most of which was donated by one percent of the American population. This may seem like a lot of money; however, it is a very small amount relative to the $850 billion Wall Street Bailout Package signed by President Obama in January 2008.

The 2008 massive bailout of Wall Street could not occur if beforehand, the political capture of the federal government, including its three branches- executive, legislative, and judicial-had not been achieved politically, by one- percent of the American population. The Oxfam Briefing Paper Number 178 verifies this fact. To set in motion the greatest concentration of wealth among the richest one-percent of the American population, and as we have previously discussed, Oxfam wrote,

"From the 1980s onwards, the financial and banking sectors pumped millions of dollars into undoing regulations put in place after the stock market crash and Great Depression of the 1930s. Deregulation has had two major ramifications: corporate executives associated with the banking and financial sectors have become exceptionally wealthy, and global markets have become much more risky, culminating in the global economic crisis that began in 2008."[645]

As we see, deregulation, or undoing government regulations since the Reagan Administration, was made possible by one percent of the American population spending millions of dollars of its wealth to politically capture the American Government. For example, as we already know, former President Bill Clinton was s/elected president of the United States to undo the Glass-Steagall Act, which became law after the 1929 Great Depression. Since the 1970s, not one word about this fact was taught to American Public Education Children in Civic or Free Enterprise Classes across America. And yet, it is this generation, and the unborn ones to come, that will be "Taxed" to pay for the growing multi-trillion deficit caused by deregulation. Politicians, from the federal to the local level of government, all, regardless of party affiliation, sing the song "No Tax Increase." However, *deregulation is a tax break for the one percent of the American population, and a tax increase for the other 99.0 percent, which consists mainly of the American Working Class.*

After the 2008 Great Depression, reform minded politicians went through an exercise to give the appearance that some concrete regulations would be put in place to prevent Wall Street Capitalists from making good on their promise to destroy their own American Capitalist System in the name of *greed.* For example, because the one percent of the American Population has already politically captured the American Government operations, the attempt to implement new regulations to prevent another 2008 Great from

---

[645] Op. Cit., Working for the Few: Political capture and economic inequality, January 20, 2014, pp. 11 and 12.

happening failed. Oxfam reported the death of the latest attempt by the Obama Administration to enact new reforms as follows:

> "In 2010, President Obama signed into law the Wall Street Reform and Consumer Protection Act (known as the Dodd-Frank Bill). The objective of this legislation is to regulate financial markets to protect the economy from a second major crash. However, the financial industry has spent more than $1bn on hundreds of lobbyists to weaken and delay the Act's full implementation. In fact, in 2012 the top five consumer protection groups sent 20 lobbyists to defend Dodd-Frank, while the top five finance industry groups sent 406 to defeat it. Even though Dodd-Frank was signed into law more than three years ago, only 148 of its 398 rules have been finalized, and the financial system remains just as vulnerable to crash as it was in 2008."[646]

As bad as the 2008 Great Depression was for the vast majority of American Working Class people, we see the same Wall Street Capitalists, who crashed their American Capitalist System in 2008, are the same ones who spent $1 billion to weaken and prevent the enforcement of any new regulations that would prevent them from crashing their American Capitalist System again. Nothing has changed, and the American Capitalist System is "… just as vulnerable to crash as it was in 2008.[647]

In sum, from the very beginning of this book, we have systematically outlined, in the clearest manner possible, how Neo-Liberal Privatization Economic Policy benefited the one percent of the Louisiana Population, and on a national scale, one percent of the American Population. Since Governor Bobby Jindal was s/elected governor in 2007, Louisiana's national rank, regarding the number of multi-millionaires, changed, from Number 32 to 12, during his first and second terms in office. To politically capture Louisiana State Government to make this economic outcome possible, one percent of the Louisiana Population contributed $13 million

---

[646] Ibid., p. 12.
[647] Ibid., p. 13.

or more to s/elect Mr. Bobby Jindal Governor in 2007. One percent of the American Population contributed $750 million to s/elect Mr. Barack Obama President in 2007. For the richest one percent of the American Population, in both Louisiana and the nation as a whole, this has meant a record increase in its income. Oxfam stated "In the US, the wealthiest one percent captured 95 percent of post-financial crisis growth between 2009 and 2012, while the bottom 90 percent became poorer."[648] Moreover, Oxfam gave a specific breakdown of the income distribution among the richest one percent of the American Population:

> "The United States is the country with the highest inequality level and poverty rate across the OECD, Mexico and Turkey excepted. Since 2000, income inequality has increased rapidly, continuing a long-term trend that goes back to the 1970s... Rich households in America have been leaving both middle and poorer income groups behind. This has happened in many countries, but nowhere has this trend been so stark as in the United States. The average income of the richest 10% is US$93,000 US$ in purchasing power parities, the highest level in the OECD. However, the poorest 10% of the US citizens have an income of US$5,800 US$ per year – about 20% *lower* than the average for OECD countries. The distribution of earnings widened by 20% since the mid-1980s... This is the main reason for widening inequality in America... Social mobility is lower in the United States than in other countries like Denmark, Sweden and Australia. Children of poor parents are less likely to become rich than children of rich parents."[649]

Every decision and action taken by the Obama Administration and the Jindal Administration, and state government administrations nationwide, regardless of party affiliation, collectively created the above income

---

[648] Ibid., p. 13.

[649] _____ COUNTRY NOTE: UNITED STATES, www.oecd.org/els/social/inequality, p. 1.

inequality in America through their implementation of the richest one percent of the American Population's Neo-Liberalism Economic policy.

For some people, this conclusion may still be difficult to believe or understand. The preponderance of the evidence presented, in this book thus far, is supported by a recent series of research articles published by The Advocate during November and December 2014. They shed more light on the Jindal Administration's massive Taxpayer Dollar "Giveaways" to private business, in the form of tax breaks, tax incentives, and privatization, during the former's first and second terms, from 2008 to 2014. We have included some of the information taken from The Advocate Review, and included it in the following section.

AFTERWORD

For the purpose of clarity, and ease of understanding of the gross amount of Louisiana Taxpayers' Dollars that have been "Given away" to private business since Governor Bobby was s/elected governor in 2007, it is best to open this analysis with an overview of the funds taken primarily from the public sector to *grow the Louisiana Economy.* According to Gordon Russell, "most of the lost revenue is contained in a relatively small number of the 462[tax] breaks on the books. In fact, just 12 of them account for roughly two-thirds of the $7.1 billion in revenue that the Department of Revenue estimates is lost to such giveaways each year."[650] Since 2008, Governor Bobby Jindal's implementation of neo-liberalism economic policy has added as much as $1 billion in Giveaways in the form of tax breaks, tax incentives, and privatization of social programs. All of the Giveaways have significantly impacted the public sector. What makes Governor Bobby Jindal's Giveaways different and dangerous is the vast majority of them go to private business, and not government agencies charged with caring for the basic needs of Louisiana Working Class people.

Gordon Russell's research shows just how wreck less the Jindal Administration's Giveaways is when he wrote the following:

> "Duck Dynasty" is the most popular show in the history of A&E. Wal-Mart is the world's largest retailer. Valero is America's biggest independent refiner, earning $6 billion

---

[650] Russell, Gordon, "Giving Away Louisiana: An Overview," The Advocate, file:///G:/ Giving%20Away%20Louisiana%20%20An%20overview%20%C2%AB%20 The%20Advocate%20Special%20Reports%20December%202%202014.html, December 2. 2014, p. 10.

in profits last year. But despite all that success, they're all receiving generous subsidies from the taxpayers of Louisiana, through programs that funnel more than a billion dollars every year to coveted industries."[651]

We have always been taught in school, regardless of the level, that owning one's own business is a good way to build our community. We were taught to save our money, then, take a risk by investing it in some venture, hoping that one day the business venture would prove successful. The danger we mentioned earlier is since Governor Bobby Jindal took office in 2008, he has allowed Louisiana Public Sector Funds to be given away to private business as investment capital, while the latter does not *take any upfront risks with their own money.* For example, Gordon Russell wrote,

> "Every time the Robertson clan films another episode of "Duck Dynasty," Louisiana is on the hook for nearly $330,000, at last count. During the past three years, state taxpayers agreed to fork over nearly $700,000 to Wal-Mart to build new stores in two affluent suburbs. And when Valero announced an expansion of its Norco operations, creating 43 new jobs, Louisiana promised to cover $10 million of the cost, or nearly a quarter of a million dollars per job."[652]

It should be recognized here that the above tax giveaways occurred after Governor Bobby Jindal's much publicized Special Legislative Session, during which Ethics Reform Laws were passed, which were suppose to prevent this type of corruption. Why do Louisiana Taxpayers, most of whom are working class people, have to pay Valero nearly $200,000 for each job it creates in the marketplace? It is also highly doubtful that any working class man or woman, who barely earns $30, 000 per year, agreed to giveaway $700,000 to Wal-Mart to build two new stores in two different affluent suburbs, a place where many of them cannot afford to live on the wages they are paid. Since Governor Bobby Jindal's Special Legislative

---

[651] Ibid., p. 1.

[652] Ibid., p. 1.

Session to address Ethics Reform, Gordon Russell stated "Louisiana's giveaways to businesses...have been growing at a much faster rate than the state's economy."[653] As we have already seen, its been a "Tax Giveaway Bonanza." Ironically, Governor Bobby Jindal has persistently held to his position of *no tax increases during his administration; yet, he has, and continues to giveaway more taxpayers' dollars, which exceeds the growth of the Louisiana Economy.*

According to Gordon Russell, "when Blanco took office, the state gave away a little over $200 million in taxpayer money...That number is now almost $1.1 billion annually, and it's been growing by an average of 17 percent a year..."[654] Next, we will take a brief look at the various industries that have been given the largest amounts of tax break giveaways and others, during the Jindal Administration's first and second terms in office. We begin with a consideration of the Film Industry Tax Incentives.

A. Film Industry Tax Incentives By December 2014

Says Gordon Russell, "Louisiana's film tax incentive program is one of the state's most popular and fastest-growing giveaways, and thanks to its industry-friendly provisions, the Pelican State has eclipsed Hollywood as the feature film production capital of the nation."[655] How could a good old, down home place like Louisiana become the feature film capital of America, if it were not for the Jindal Administrations massive Tax Giveaways to the Hollywood film making industry? Russell stated the great tax giveaway as follows:

> "Last year, 107 such projects qualified for help from Louisiana taxpayers, at an upfront cost to the state budget

---

[653] Ibid., p. 1.

[654] Ibid., p. 1.

[655] Russell, Gordon, "Giving Away Louisiana: Film tax incentives," <u>The Advocate</u>, file:///G:/Giving%20Away%20Louisiana%20%20Film%20tax%20incentives%20%C2%AB%20The%20Advocate%20Special%20Reports%20December%202%20 2014.html, December 2, 2014, p. 1.

of about $250 million. Stephen Moret, Jindal's secretary of Economic Development, says he thinks that figure could double within a few years. The program, the richest of its kind in the country, covers between 30 and 35 percent of in-state production costs, including eight-figure actor salaries, as long as a film's local costs top $300,000. The subsidy is so large that it completely changes the economics of filmmaking. And its size has probably contributed to the program's history of corruption as well, tempting some dishonest film producers into padding their expenses so they can recoup more money."[656]

This one industry was given $250 million since Governor Bobby Jindal has been in office, and this is more tax break money than all of the private businesses received during former Gov. Kathleen Blanco's one term in office. Russell added "Louisiana's film incentive program cost state taxpayers $251 million last year and returned less than 25 percent of that to state coffers in the form of taxes…It's no wonder: State taxpayers cover 30 percent of the cost of movies filmed here, including eight-figure star salaries such as the estimated $20 million paid to Tom Cruise for 2013's "Oblivion."[657] Can Louisiana's Public Sector afford to pay Tom Cruise $20 million to make the identified film? This payment is enough to operate the Southern University System for at least three years, yet, the latter was forced into bankruptcy in October 2011, two years before this outrageous sum of taxpayer dollars was given away to Tom Cruise, not counting the money given away to the other actors involved in making the film-Oblivion. The oil industry, especially those corporations involved in Fracking, have received a bonanza of Jindal Administration tax break giveaways.

B. Hydraulic Fracking Tax Incentives By December 2014

First, what is Hydraulic Fracking? Mark Ballard defined it as follows: "The

---

[656] Ibid., p. 1.
[657] Russell, Gordon, See Footnote 651, p. 3.

well bores two miles into the Earth's crust, and then runs horizontally for another mile. It cost about $15 million to drill... everything changed when energy companies in the last decade figured out how to combine horizontal drilling with hydraulic fracturing, or fracking, making gas and oil reserves locked in shale rock deposits accessible."[658] Having worked out the fracking technology, and instead of oil companies risking their own investment dollars to unlock the oil in the shale formations several miles beneath the Earth surface, the Jindal Administration graciously gave away millions of taxpayer dollars to oil companies engaged in fracking. Ballard stated the following:

> "...as the natural gas-rich Haynesville Shale in the northwest part of the state was tapped, an exemption that had cost Louisiana less than $1 million in lost taxes in 2008 had ballooned to $239 million two years later. Since then, the state has given back $1.2 billion in tax receipts due to the horizontal-drilling exemption. (The tax rebate applies to both oil and gas wells... The money lost to rebates could soon spike much higher: If the much larger Tuscaloosa Marine Shale, where the Blades well is located, lives up to geologists' expectations, Louisiana could soon be returning $1 billion or more in tax revenue to drillers every year."[659]

Since 2008, the first year of Governor Bobby Jindal's first term, the tax giveaway to oil companies engaged in oil fracking production increased 23,800 percent! Once again, tax giveaways by Louisiana State Government removes competition in the marketplace. If oil company (X) invests its own $15 million to drill a fracking oil well, and oil company (Y) receives state government tax giveaways to cover the same cost to drill its oil well, it is clear which oil company will succeed in the marketplace. Gordon Russell

[658] Ballard, Mark, "Giving Away Louisiana: Fracking tax incentives," The Advocate, file:///G:/Giving%20Away%20Louisiana%20%20Fracking%20tax%20incentives%20%C2%AB%20The%20Advocate%20Special%20Reports%20December%204%202014.html, December 4. 2014, p. 1.
[659] Ibid., p. 1.

stated "there's little evidence the tax break stimulates drilling."[660] The $240 million worth of tax break giveaways is not promoting competition but rather monopoly-capitalism. The next tax break giveaway that is draining the Louisiana State Budget, and the public sector in particular, is Enterprise Zone Incentives.

C. Enterprise Zone Tax Incentives By 2014

In theory, the above tax break giveaway was supposed to make it economically attractive for some private businesses to relocate to decaying areas of various cities statewide. Rebekah Allen described some of the communities in which enterprise tax incentives were given to help revitalize them. She wrote,

> "North Baton Rouge doesn't have high-end retail shopping centers or fancy restaurants. There are no movie theaters. The hospital has been shuttered. Instead of traditional grocers, there are convenience stores fueled by alcohol sales. Community leaders have dubbed it a "food desert" for its dearth of healthy food options, and elected officials have for years cried out for economic development measures that would stir job growth. The area, which includes neighborhoods like Scotlandville and Glen Oaks, has East Baton Rouge Parish's highest concentration of families below the poverty line and the lowest household incomes. It's among the poorest urban areas in the state. In short, it's precisely the kind of place that the state's Enterprise Zone program — which gives taxpayer money to businesses willing to relocate or expand in depressed areas — was designed to revive. But that's not what it's doing."[661]

---

[660] Russell, Gordon, See Footnote 651, p. 3.

[661] Allen, Rebekah, "Giving Away Louisiana: Enterprise Zone incentives," The Advocate, file:///G:/Giving%20Away%20Louisiana%20%20Enterprise%20 zone%20incentives%20%C2%AB%20The%20Advocate%20Special%20 Reports%20December%202%202014.html, December 2, 2014, p. 1.

To the contrary, Louisiana Taxpayers' Dollars are being used to assist some private businesses to locate in wealthy areas. Allen stated "the program, which has cost the state an average of $69 million a year for the past five years, more often than not pays businesses to set up shop in wealthy areas. It gives hundreds of thousands of dollars in tax credits, and sometimes millions, to some of the largest companies in the nation, among them Wal-Mart..."[662] We realize how redundant this may sound; however, Governor Bobby Jindal's Ethic Reform is nothing short of his attempt to make working class people feel *corruption ended when he became governor in 2008.* For example, Allen provided information that shows corruption is alive and well in Louisiana State Government. She wrote the following:

> "Since 2011, for instance, the state has approved nearly $700,000 in tax credits for Wal-Mart to build new stores in Covington and Mandeville, two of Louisiana's most affluent suburbs. In Baton Rouge's Perkins Rowe retail and residential district, where a one-bedroom apartment can rent for $1,500 a month, shops that got Enterprise Zone tax credits include Anthropologie, Fresh Market and Urban Outfitters. Critics — including some of the program's overseers — say the state is giving away tens of millions of dollars every year without doing much to stimulate investment in low-income areas, as the Enterprise Zone program originally was meant to do."[663]

What kind of economic system is this where Louisiana State Government, and the Jindal Administration in particular, is giving away public sector tax dollars to private businesses so they can build new buildings, stores, and so forth? Socialist countries have been criticized by almost everyone for engaging in so-called central planning, where the state allocates economic resources to business cooperatives to develop productive enterprises for the masses. What has aided private businesses to be exempt from having to set up their business operations in economically depressed areas, although

---

[662] Ibid., p. 1.
[663] Ibid., p. 1.

they are being given millions of dollars of public sector money? Rebekah Allen uncovered the corruption in her research; she summed it as follows:

"In large part, that's because the Legislature in 1999 got rid of the rule that businesses needed to actually invest in a designated Enterprise Zone to qualify for money from the program. Once that constraint was gone, the program attracted much broader interest — and, perhaps predictably, most of the projects that got Enterprise Zone money were outside the poor neighborhoods that were meant to benefit. Worse, much of the money has gone to subsidize retailers and restaurants, though economic development experts almost unanimously agree that it's foolish — and sometimes even harmful — to spend government money in those sectors."[664]

What is interesting here is when Governor Bobby Jindal called a Special Session of the Louisiana Legislature in 2008, did he know, at the time, that in 1999, the same law-making body abolished the law that required any private business that received an enterprise zone tax incentive to establish its business operation in an economically depressed community? Apparently, he did not know, and if someone told him about the change, he either simply ignored the matter, or realized he could not do one thing about it. Allen used East Baton Rouge Parish as an example of how public sector money has greatly benefited private business, and left thousands of its working class citizens behind in poverty. She wrote the following about this corruption:

"In East Baton Rouge Parish, 135 businesses received Enterprise Zone tax incentives between 2008 and 2013. But only 21 of them were located in North Baton Rouge, the poorest part of the parish. Excluding downtown, only 35 projects, or about one in four, were north of Florida Boulevard, typically seen as a dividing line separating rich and poor. The heaviest concentration of Enterprise

---

[664] Ibid., p. 1.

Zone awards were located in the southeastern part of the parish, where the highest-earning residents live, where the roads are already flush with business and where a move has been a foot to incorporate as a separate community with its own school district…Louisiana's poorest parishes — Madison, Tensas, East Carroll, St. Helena, Catahoula, Winn, Morehouse and Evangeline — had a total of 11 Enterprise Zone projects approved between 2008 and 2013. By comparison, there were 70 such projects approved in St. Tammany Parish, which is regularly ranked among the top three richest parishes in the state. Ascension and St. Charles, also among the five wealthiest parishes in the state, had 42 and 13 projects approved, respectively."[665]

We have often wondered what *is* the catalyst behind the so-called move to establish a "breakaway city," or new city within Baton Rouge, LA? St. Georges is the proposed name of this new city, and to date, at least 18,000 people have signed a petition in favor of establishing it as an independent municipality. This action is amazing! It is--because an entire new city is being established based on the use of enterprise zone incentives. In other words, the Louisiana Public Sector is funding the development of a new city of gold, and the communities in which private businesses were suppose to relocate their business operations continue to decay, and, worse of all, too many innocent working class people, who live in them, fall victims to violent crimes every day. Just watch your 6 PM news reports…Moreover, is the enterprise zone incentives paying for "White Flight?"

In sum, Gordon Russell stated "Louisiana's Enterprise Zone program has done little to spur investment and job creation in poor areas, its original intent. Instead, the bulk of the taxpayer money the program doles out — an average of about $70 million annually in recent years — has gone outside of the designated zones, much of it for dubious uses, such as to subsidize retailers offering low-paying jobs. And even though the state officials who oversee the program have long criticized it, reform has been

---

[665] Ibid., pp. 2and 3.

elusive."[666] If the above Louisiana State Government tax Giveaways raises the hair on your head, then consider those given to private businesses in the category called industrial tax incentives.

D. Industrial Tax Incentives by 2014

Since Governor Bobby Jindal was s/elected governor in 2008, he has presided over the giveaway of millions of dollars to attract industries to Louisiana, and much of the money used to do so came from the public sector. Richard Thompson stated "...Louisiana has handed out some of the biggest corporate giveaways seen anywhere in the country. Those gifts must be approved by the state Board of Commerce and Industry, which typically approves the breaks before it without discussion."[667] Between 2008 and 2013, "... the state's industrial property tax exemption dwarfs all the others; more than $8.5 billion in breaks were granted in the same six-year span...that program...does reduce how much is available to pay for public services in Louisiana — and local governments have no say in whether to grant the relief."[668] Governor Bobby Jindal says all of these industrial tax incentives will create new jobs for working class people. However, what he stopped far, far short of informing the Louisiana Public about is how much taxpayer dollars are paid to a private business to create a job. How does the Louisiana Economy benefit from attracting a new industry here if the Jindal Administration voluntarily pays millions of dollars for every new job it creates? Where are the logics in this equation? Take the Quality Jobs Program for example.

It is another conduit designed to pay millions of Louisiana Taxpayers' Dollars to private businesses to create jobs. Richard Thompson explained the tax giveaway as follows:

---

[666] Op. Cit., Russell, Gordon, See Footnote 651, p. 3.

[667] Thompson, Richard, "Giving Away Louisiana: Industrial tax incentives," The Advocate, file:///G:/Giving%20Away%20Louisiana%20%20Industrial%20tax%20incentives%20%C2%AB%20The%20Advocate%20Special%20Reports%20December%203%202014.html, December 2, 2014, p. 2.

[668] Ibid., p. 2.

"The Quality Jobs program, which targets new full-time jobs paying at least $14.50 an hour in a half-dozen growth industries, refunded about $100 million per year, on average, in payroll expenses and in sales and use taxes from 2008 to 2013...Among the 240 megadeals reviewed by Good Jobs First, the fifth-most expensive in the nation went to a major liquefied natural gas export facility that Cheniere Energy is building along the Sabine River in Cameron Parish...The state approved almost $1.6 billion in property tax relief for Cheniere, in addition to $117 million in workforce training costs and payroll rebates... The whole package works out to a cost to taxpayers of nearly $7.5 million per new or retained job, making it the most expensive mega-deal that Good Jobs First reviewed, on a per-job basis. And that was arguably generous, given that one-third of the 225 positions used to arrive at that number were existing positions that Cheniere simply pledged to "retain." Each new job cost nearly $11.4 million."[669]

What could possibly be the rationale, or benefit to the working class man or woman, for the Jindal Administration to pay Cheniere Energy $11.4 million to create a new job, or retain one it already has created? What kind of economic system is this? How can a Louisiana Schoolteacher encourage her students to get involved with *free enterprise, when, in the shadows, the businesses he or she might have to compete with, are being paid millions of dollars by the Jindal Administration to create new jobs?* Where is the so-called competition in this "Giving Away of Louisiana?" The playing field is far from being level; is there one at all is the question? Another aspect of the production process that the Louisiana Public Sector is subsidizing, in the form of taxpayer dollar "Giveaways," is called the Inventory Tax Refund.

E. Inventory Tax Refund By 2014

Gordon Russell stated this "fast-growing program is responsible for massive

---

[669] Ibid., pp. 2 and 3.

hole in state budget."[670] As you drive around in your local community, we are certain you have seen the large number of various commodities sitting on the lot of various private businesses. New and used cars are a highly visible example. Russell added the following:

> "While many, if not most, Louisianans probably have never heard of the business inventory tax, it's a big deal for…businesses…The tax also comes at a huge cost to the state, one that is growing rapidly. Louisiana's inventory tax refund program, approved by the Legislature in 1991, is responsible for a massive hole in the state's budget that totaled $427 million last year. And the number is growing rapidly: …the cost of the refunds has shot up by 120 percent over the last seven years, raising questions about whether the refund system is being gamed by businesses. The state does little to ensure that it's not. Robert Travis Scott, of the nonpartisan Public Affairs Research Council, which is studying the issue, expects the cost to the state to swell to $600 million in the next couple of years thanks to a slew of new industrial projects."[671]

Given Governor Bobby Jindal's interest in Ethics Reform, which was the first major topic on his Legislative Agenda, it is very ironic that Russell stated above that Louisiana State Government, during the Jindal Administration, has done nothing to stop the massive Inventory Tax incentives Giveaways to private business. If nothing is done immediately to end this giveaway, this tax break could increase by 40.5 percent over the next several years. Again, private business is not taking hardly any financial risks because, more and more of them can stockpile their inventories, and, those commodities that they do not sell, the Jindal Administration kindly send them a reimbursement check for the unsold inventory. The money

---

[670] Russell, Gordon, "Giving Away Louisiana: Inventory tax refund," The Advocate, file:///G:/Giving%20Away%20Louisiana%20%20Inventory%20tax%20refund%20 %C2%AB%20The%20Advocate%20Special%20Reports%20December%205%20 2014.html, December 5, 2014, p. 1.

[671] Ibid., p. 1.

used to cover the hole in the state budget usually comes from the Louisiana Public Sector. Later, we will provide some information that shows the Jindal Administration is already preparing to make more deep cuts public sector social programs, especially higher education.

F. Solar Energy Tax Credit By 2014

With the recent emphasis placed on green technology, Governor Bobby Jindal has given his approval of the Solar Energy Tax Credit. Jeff Adelson research shows this tax giveaway is also adding to the gaping hole in the Louisiana State Budget. He stated "the state alone has paid for half the upfront cost of the renewable energy systems since 2008 through a program that has cost Louisiana taxpayers $151 million. It is the most generous subsidy of its kind in America…it has grown exponentially, costing the state 122 times as much last year as the highest estimates bandied about when the measure was debated in 2007."[672] The cost of the Solar Tax Credit Giveaway rose every year since Governor Bobby Jindal been in office. As it was, Jeff Adelson wrote the following:

> "When it was first conceived in 2007, the solar program was expected to cost the state just $500,000 a year, enough to provide systems for 40 to 100 customers. As with many of the state's incentive programs, those estimates quickly proved far too low, with almost $1.5 million in credits being claimed in the first year by 259 residents. By the next year, the program's cost had soared to $8.3 million. By its third year, which started in 2010, more than $13 million in credits went to more than 750 residents and businesses. It would continue that explosive growth in each of the ensuing years, with about $61.1 million claimed for solar systems by 1,556 residents and businesses in the state's most recent fiscal year. The cost, and the fact that so much

---

[672] Adelson, Jeff, "Giving Away Louisiana: Solar energy tax credit," file:///G:/ Giving%20Away%20Louisiana%20%20Solar%20energy%20tax%20credit%20 %C2%AB%20The%20Advocate%20Special%20Reports%20December%206%20 2014.html, December 6, 2014, p. 1.

of it is borne by taxpayers, doesn't sit well even with some
who support renewable energy."[673]

The Louisiana State Budget, and its public sector, is similar to a shower head through which water continuously pours out as long as it is in use. Since Governor Bobby Jindal became governor, taxpayer giveaways have been pouring out of the public sector like the water coming through a shower head in use.

In view of these tax giveaways, and all of the ones that we have previously discussed in this book so far, together, they have created a massive hole in the Louisiana State Budget, and, by January 1, 2015, it is projected to be as large as $1.4 billion. Gordon Russell stated Louisiana is "... staring down a $1.4 billion budget shortfall..."[674] Melinda Deslatte stated "Gov. Bobby Jindal's administration has started sifting through agency budget proposals as it works on a plan to close next year's[2015] $1.4 billion shortfall...[Commissioner of Administration, Kristy Nichols said] cuts will have to be made."[675] One can be certain that the budget cutting trend will continue with more massive cuts made in the Louisiana Public Sector Program Budgets. More economic hardship, for working class people is, no doubt, on the way because the Jindal Administration, beginning January 1, 2015, maybe called "Lame-Duck." And, even if it were not called the latter, none of the tax giveaways will be terminated to prevent any more social program cuts. The Louisiana Public Sector is on the verge of total collapse. Mark Ballard added "...Nichols, Gov. Bobby Jindal's chief budget aide, said her staff are looking for ways to reduce the $1.4 billion hole in next fiscal year's revenues."[676]

---

[673] Ibid., p. 3.

[674] Russell, Gordon, "Giving Away Louisiana: 2015 governor's race," The Advocate, file:///G:/Giving%20Away%20Louisiana%20%202015%20governor%E2%80%99s%20race%20%C2%AB%20The%20Advocate%20Special%20Reports%20December%207%202014.html, December 7, 2014, p. 1.

[675] Deslatte, Melinda, "Jindal administration working to close budget gap," The Advocate, December 11, 2014, p. 1.

[676] Ballard, Mark, "Dropping oil prices continue to impact state budget," The Advocate, December 13, 2014, p. 2.

In sum, nothing else needs to be said about how Neo-liberalism Economic Policy has played a significant role, leading to the near collapse of the Louisiana Public Sector since Governor Bobby Jindal was s/elected governor in 2008. He was elected for this purpose inasmuch as the preponderance of the evidence points to this single conclusion. This statement is not made offhandedly, or without careful consideration. The research that went into this book is thorough in that many documents were researched to determine what is underlying the massive budget cuts that have become a hallmark of the Jindal Administration. In every instance, we found tax giveaways and privatization of social programs given to private business, and on the other, we consistently found information that led us, time and again, back to a long, growing trail of budget cuts in Louisiana Public Sector Programs, which were designed to help working class people meet the social and economic challenges they face in their lives every day. This trend shows no signs of slowing down inasmuch as the CBS News Network recently gave some coverage to the extreme "tax break giveaway corruption" taking place here in Louisiana. National attention was given to the Film Industry Tax Break Giveaways because the latter has changed the location where feature films are currently being produced. According to CBS News correspondent Anna Werner,

> "California isn't the epicenter of movie making anymore.
> The business has left the Gold Coast and gone south, to
> Louisiana. While Hollywood is traditionally thought of as
> the global film capital, there's one big reason most of the
> lights, cameras and action have moved thousands of miles
> away, reports CBS News correspondent Anna Werner.
> "Dallas Buyers Club, "12 Years a Slave," "The Curious
> Case of Benjamin Button" -- all of these award winning
> blockbusters were not filmed in California -- they were
> made in Louisiana..." It's very difficult to justify shooting
> in California when you have these type of incentives, "he
> said. Berger isn't talking about Louisiana's Cajun cuisine
> or lively nightlife -- he's talking about money. In 2002,
> Louisiana began offering a unique tax credit -- 30 percent

for productions shot in the state. Movie producers can get
even more money back by hiring local crews…"[677]

The "money," that is Louisiana Taxpayers' money, is bankrolling feature
film production at a rate that exceeds California and Canada. On December
27, 2014, an Advocate Staff Report included data that shows the extent
to which this film tax break giveaway corruption is eating a bigger hole in
the Louisiana State Budget, making more, and deeper budget cuts by the
Jindal Administration necessary. The following was reported:

> "Last year, 107 film and TV projects qualified for help
> from Louisiana taxpayers, at an upfront cost to the state
> budget of about $250 million. Stephen Moret, Louisiana
> Gov. Bobby Jindal's Secretary of Economic Development,
> says he thinks that figure could double within a few
> years…The program, the richest of its kind in the country,
> covers between 30 and 35 percent of in-state production
> costs, including eight-figure actor salaries, as long as a
> film's local costs top $300,000. The subsidy is so large that
> it completely changes the economics of filmmaking. And
> its size has probably contributed to the program's history
> of corruption…"[678]

This tax break giveaway corruption has not been slowed down by Governor
Bobby Jindal's so-called Ethics Reform Law passed at the beginning of his
first term in office. Unfortunately, Louisiana Working Class people are
continuously paying more of their hard earned income in taxes, and more
of it is being sunk into this type of massive corruption, including the others
we have already discussed. Poor, and impoverished families for example,
located in the poorest parishes in Northeast Louisiana, are paying the
eight-figure actor salaries while most earn minimum wage if they are lucky,

[677] Werner, Anna, "Louisiana: The new Hollywood," http://www.cbsnews.com/
news/louisiana-the-new-hollywood/, 2014, p. 1.
[678] Advocate Staff Report, "CBS News highlights Louisiana as 'the film production
capital of the world'", **http://theadvocate.com/news/11186618-123/cbs-news-
highlights-louisiana-as,** December 27, 2014, pp. 1 and 2.

and many others have no job at all. Did Mr. Bobby Jindal tell us that he was going to give our tax dollars away during his campaign for governor in 2007? And, if anyone can find a tape of a town hall meeting where he told us he was going to do this, then, we do not need to be upset or surprised by the giveaway of our tax dollars and the economic hardships we are now experiencing in our daily lives. Moreover, the industrial renaissance Governor Bobby Jindal proclaimed in taking place in Louisiana has had an influence on getting a growing number of Louisiana Working Class back to work. To the contrary, there was a noticeable increase in the number who filed unemployment claims by December 2014. According to The Associated Press, the Louisiana Department of Labor stated "...first-time claims for unemployment insurance in Louisiana for the week ending Dec. 20 [2014]increased to 2,531 from the previous week's total of 2,506... Continued unemployment claims for the week ending Dec. 20 increased to 20,837 compared to 20,322 the previous week. The four-week moving average for such claims increased to 20,327 from the previous week's average of 20,059."[679] As we see, more than 20,000 Louisiana Working Class people were continuously unemployed by the end of the second year of Governor Bobby Jindal's second term in office. These unemployment figures will likely continue to increase, although, as we have already seen, millions of dollars of Louisiana Taxpayers' Dollars have already been given away to various private businesses, in the form of tax breaks, to "grow the Louisiana Economy." Yet, unemployment has remained persistently high. No doubt, more Louisiana Working Class people will experience more financial strains during 2015.

With this dim prospect lurking on the horizon, and as early as March 2015, or shortly thereafter, we expect to hear about new social program cuts approved by Governor Bobby Jindal, in his desperate attempt to patch up the widening hole in the Louisiana State Budget. By the end of December 2014, the hole had grown to $1.4 billion, and this sum could rise higher in view of the fact *Louisiana has been given away in the form of lucrative tax breaks, tax incentives, and privatization of social programs.* Business layoffs will also add to the overall dismal plight of Louisiana Working

---

[679] THE ASSOCIATED PRESS, "Initial unemployment claims rise in Louisiana," The Advocate, December 29, 2014, p.1.

Class people. Moreover, we can also warn everyone that the austerity budget cutting will most likely continue to lead to more and more violent crimes in communities across Louisiana, including attacks against men, women, children, and the elderly. We can see the effects of these negative outcomes broadcasted on the 5PM daily newscasts, which are shown on local television in communities throughout Louisiana. The purpose of such broadcasts is *to confuse cause and effect, where the effect, crime for example, is presented as the cause of problems in a community, while the cause, namely Neo-liberalism Economic Policy, goes unpublicized, unaddressed, unanalyzed, unseen, undetected, and unnoticed by the vast majority of Louisiana Working Class people.*

BIBLIOGRAPHY

PREFACE

_____ "New rules on banks' risk in mortgage bonds eased," Associated Press, October 21, 2014, p. 1.

[2]McQueen, Michel, "House Panel Votes To Trim Medicare By $8.7 Billion," The Wall Street Journal, July 31, 1987, Section 2, p. 34.

[3] The Advocate Staff, "Sasol gives final approval to $8.1 billion Louisiana Project," The Advocate, October 28, 2014, p.1.

[4] _____ "Hercules Offshore to lay off 324 workers," The Advocate, November 5, 2014, p.1.

[5] _____ "Initial unemployment claims rise in Louisiana," The Advocate, November 8, 2014, p. 1.

[6] _____ The Council of Economic Advisers and the Department of Labor, Executive Office Of The President Of The United States, THE ECONOMIC BENEFITS OF EXTENDING UNEMPLOYMENT INSURANCE, http://www.whitehouse.gov/sites/default/files/docs/uireport-2013-12-4.pdf, December 2013, p. 1.

[7] Ibid., p. 11.

[8] Ballard, Marsha, "Bobby Jindal: Only office I'd seek is presidency," The Advocate, October 22, 2014, p. 1.

[9]Crisp, Elizabeth, "UNO Poll: Louisiana headed in 'wrong direction,'" The Advocate, October 30, 2014, p. 1.

CHAPTER I

[10] _____ Boundless Political Science, http://www.boundless.com/politicalscience/textbooks/boundless-political-science-textbooks/American-politics-1/

[11] _____Enlightenment, www.history.com/topics/enlightenment

[12] _____Boundless Political Science, Op. Cit.

[13] Wilson, Peter H., "The Causes of The Thirty Years War, 1618 -1648," English Historical Review, CXXlll (502): pp. 554-586. (Abstract)

[14] Stuart, Andrea, *Sugar In The Blood: A Family's Story Of Slavery And Empire*, Vintage Books, New York, 2012, p. 13.

[15] Ibid., p. 12.

[16] Ibid., p. 26.

[17] Boundless Political Science, Op. Cit.

[18] Goodman, John C., "What Is Classical Liberalism?," www.ncpa.org, Washington, D. C., 2010, p.1.

[19] Stuart, Andrea, Op. Cit., p. 10.

[20] Ayers, Edward L., Schulzinger, Robert D., et. al., American Anthem: Modern American History, Holt, Rinehart and Winston, 2007, p. 767.

[21] Stuart, Andrea, Op. Cit., p. 43.

[22] Ibid., p. 43.

[23] Ibid., p. 16.

[24] Ibid., p. 52.

[25] Prochaska, Frank, "The American Monarchy," HistoyToday, http://www.historytody.com/frank-prochaska/american-monarchy, Published in History Today (/taxonomy/term/43)Volume:57Issue:8 (/taxonomy/term/108) ,2007 (/taxonomy/term/14781), pp. 1, 2, and 3.

[26] Ibid., p. 3.

[27] Ibid., p. 4.

[28] Ibid., p. 4.

[29] Ibid., p. 5.

[30] Ibid., p. 7.

[31] Goodman, John C., "What Is Classical Liberalism?," www.ncpa.org, national Center for Policy Analysis, Washington, DC, 2010, p. 1.

[32] Ayers, Edward L. Schulzinger, Robert D., Teja, Jesus F. de la, White Gray, Deborah, and Sam Wineburg, *American Anthem: Modern American History*, Holt, Rinehart And Winston, New York, 2007, p. 38.

[33] Ibid., p. 38.

[34] Ibid., p. 38.

[35] Ibid., pp. 38, 39 ,and 40.

[36] Ibid., p. 41.

[37] _____ "Jefferson and Slavery," The Monticello Classroom, http://classroom.monticello.org/kids/resources/profile/263/Middle/Jefferson-and-Slavery/, 2007 Thomas Jefferson Foundation.

[38] Ibid.

[39] _____ "Slavery," George Washington's Mount Vernon, file:///G:/Founding%20Fathers-George%20Washington%20Slave%20Ownership.htm

[40] Gates, Henry Louis, Jr, George Washington's Runaway Slave, Harry, The Root, http://www.theroot.com/articles/history/2012/12/george_washington_slave_owner_and_the_people_he_owned.html

[41] Twohig, Dorothy, "That Species of Property": Washington's Role in the Controversy Over Slavery," http://gwpapers.virginia.edu/history/articles/species/#2

[42] Ayers, Edward L., et. al., Op. Cit., p. 46.

[43] Ibid., p. 49.

[44]Lopresti, Rob, which U.S. Presidents Owned Slaves?," file:///E:/ FoundingFathers%20U.S.%20Presidents%20Owned%20Slaves-George%20Washington%20to%20Ulysses%20GrantCivil%20War.htm, p. 1.

[45] _____ Justia U.S. Supreme Court, Plessey vs. Ferguson, 163 U.S. 537 (1896), U.S. Supreme Court Case, Plessey vs. Ferguson, No. 210, Argued April 18, 1896, May 18, 1896, https://supreme.justia.com/cases/federal/ us/163/537/case.html

[46] Lorenz, Charles, "If You're So Smart, Why Are You under Surveillance? Universities, neoliberalism, and New Public Management," Critical Inquiry, Volume 38, The University of Chicago, Spring 2012, p. 603.

[47] Ibid., p. 599.

[48] _____ "Ronald Reagan on Budget & Economy," On The Issues, http://www.ontheissues.org/Celeb/ Ronald_Reagan_Budget_+_Economy.htm

[49] Ibid.

[50] Lorenz, Op. Cit., p. 601.

[51] Thorsen, Dag Einar and Lie, Amund, What is Neoliberalism?, Department of Political Science, University of Oslo , http://folk.uio.no/ daget/neoliberalism.pdf, p. 2.

[52] Lorenz, Op. Cit., p. 602.

[53] Harvey, David, A Brief History Of NEOLIBERALISM, Oxford university Press, New York, 2005, p. 2.

[54] Lorenz, Op. Cit., p. 602.

[55] Ibid., p. 603.

[56] Ibid., p. 605.

[57] Boone, Timothy, "Rent stress felt most in rural areas of Louisiana," The Advocate, October 9, 2014, p. 1.

[58] Ibid., p. 1.

[59] Crisp, Elizabeth, "Southern board member calls for Mason's resignation," The Advocate, August 22, 2014, p.2.

[60] Crisp, Elizabeth, "Southern submits improvement plan," The Advocate, October 28, 2014, p. 1.

[61] Crisp, Elizabeth, "Grambling leader outlines plan to address deficit," The Advocate, October 31, 2014, p. 1.

[62] Crisp, Elizabeth, "Southern system president's term to end in 2015," The Advocate, August 24, 2014, p. 1.

[63] Lorenz, Op. Cit., pp. 605 and 606.

[64] Ibid., p. 606.

[65] Ibid., p. 606.

[66] Ibid., p. 608.

[67] Ibid., p. 608.

[68] Bagdikian, Ben H., *The Media Monopoly*, Beacon Press, Boston, 1983, pp. xv and xix.

[69] Ibid., p. xvi.

[70] Shenk, David, *DATA SMOG: Surviving the information glut*, HarperEdge, San Francisco, 1997, p. 30.

[71] _____ "Media Consumption to Average 15.5 hours a day by 2015," Science daily, University of California, Marshall School of Business, http://www.sciencedaily.com/releases/2013/10/131030111316.htm, October 30, 2013.

[72] Shenk, Op. Cit., p. 94.

[73] Ibid., p. 159.

[74] Ibid., pp. 124, 125, and 126.

[75] Ibid., p. 162.

[76] Jindal Bobby, Louisiana Gubernatorial Election Victory Speech, http://

www.americanrhetoric.com/speeches/bobbyjindallouisianagovvictory.htm. October 20, 2007, p. 2.

[77] Ibid., p. 3.

[78] Our Future: This is a phrase, similar to the often used one-American People-that, on an emotional level, would suggest that the opportunities and money to be derived, as a result of the implementation of neo-liberalism policies, will be shared equally by all Louisiana Residents, regardless of class, race, educational background, political affiliation, and religion among others not mentioned. The phrase our future is used to get the majority of Louisiana Working Class people, in a moment of emotional excitement, to believe that they will be included in the abundance, when in reality, the latter's taxpayer dollars will be used to pay for the Tax breaks and tax incentives and so on that were given to private businesses during the Jindal Administration's first term in office, from 2008 to 2012.

[79] Ibid., p. 4.

[80] Text of Gov. Bobby Jindal's inaugural speech, Associated Press, file:///G:/ JINDALADMINText%20of%20Gov.%20Bobby%20Jindal's%20 inaugural%20speech%20%20%20NOLA.com%20January%209%20 2012.htm, January 9, 2012, p. 3.

[81] Lorenz, OP. Cit., p. 601.

[82] Shuler, Marsha, Government workers down 30K over 6 years," The Advocate, October 13, 2014, pp. 1 and 2.

[83] Text of Governor Bobby Jindal Inaugural Speech 2012, Op. Cit., pp. 2 and 3.

[84] Ibid., p. 4.

[85] Sentell, Will, "Louisiana Supreme Court upholds state's teacher tenure law," The Advocate, October 16, 2014, pp. 1 and 2.

[86] Jindal, Bobby Governor, FULL TEXT: BOBBY JINDAL'S SPEECH TO THE RNC IN CHARLOTTE, http://illinoisreview.typepad.com/ illinoisreview/2013/01/full-text-bobby-jindals-speech-to-the-rnc-in-charlotte.html, FRIDAY, JANUARY 25, 2013, P. 1.

[87] Ibid., p. 2.

[88] Ibid., p. 3.

[89] Shuler, Marsha, "Federal questions on Medicaid funding worry Louisiana hospitals," The Advocate, October 19, 2014, pp. 1 and 2.

[90] Ibid., p. 5.

[91] Sentell, Will, "Officials: roads in 'deplorable state,' The Advocate, October 5, 2014, p. 1.

[92] Full Text of Governor Bobby Jindal Speech to the RNC, Op. Cit., p. 6.

[93] Ibid., p. 6.

[94] Thompson, Richard, "River corridor between N.O., BR is home for much of state's industrial boom," The Advocate, November 17, 2013, p. 1.

[95] Crisp, Elizabeth, "State face $1.2 billion budget shortfall," The Advocate, August 15, 2014, p. 1.

[96] Ibid., p. 1.

[97] Ibid., p. 1.

[98] Shuler, Marsha, "Budget panel defers action on surplus," The Advocate, October 17, 2014, p.1.

CHAPTER II

[99] Wolff, Richard, Democracy At Work: A Cure For Capitalism, Haymarket Books Chicago, Illinois, 2012, p. 24.

[100] Fram, Alan, "Background check bill faces likely Senate defeat," The Advocate, April 17, 2013, p. 1.

[101] Blum, Jordan, "Landrieu votes "yes" but gun control fails in U.S. Senate," The Advocate, April 18, 2013, p. 1.

[102] Joint Economic Committee Congress Of The United States, 94th Congress, 2nd Session, A Study: Estimating The social Costs Of National Economic Policy: Implications For Mental And Physical Health, And Criminal Aggression, October 26, 1976, Prepared For The Use Of The Joint Economic Committee Congress Of The United States, U.S. Government Printing Office, Washington: 1976.

[103] Ibid., p. III.

[104] Ibid., p. 2.

[105] Ibid., p. 4.

[106] Ibid., p. 7.

[107] Ibid., p. 22. The three sources of economic distress and stress are as follows: (1) Increased unemployment

[108] Ibid., p. 23.

[109] Ibid., p. vi.

[110] Ibid., p. 13.

[111] Ibid., p. iii.

CHAPTER III

[112] Page 936.

[113] *Hoskins, Richard Kelley, In The Beginning…:The story of the International Trade Cartel*, Virginia Publishing Company, 1995, p. 98.

[114] Ibid., p. 99.

[115] Ibid., p. 104.

[116] Griffin, G. Edward, *THE CREATURE FROM JEKYLL ISLAND: A Second Look at the Federal Reserve,* American Media, Fifth edition, 2010, pp. 219, 220, and 383.

[117] Schweizer, Peter, *THROW THEM ALL OUT*, Houghton Mifflin Harcourt, New York, 2011, pp. xxiii and xxiv.

[118] Anderson, Ed, "Jindal 'bats a thousand' at session," The Times-Picayune, http://blog.nola.com/news_impact/print.html?entry=/2008/03/jindal_bats_a_thousand_at_…, Published Friday, March 14, 2008, 10/22/2010, p. 1 of 3.

[119] Ibid., p. 1.

[120] Ibid., p. 1.

[121] Ibid., p. 2.

[122] Sentell, Will, "Schools chief to set rules for subsidies, " The Advocate, April 4, 2012, p. 1A.

[123] Millhollon, Michelle, " State budget $100 million in red in last fiscal year," The Advocate, October 6, 2010, p. 1A.

[124] Ibid., p. 1A.

[125] Ibid., p. 1A.

[126] Millhollon, Michelle, "Jindal aide to do DWIprogram," The Advocate, February 8, 2012, p. 1B.

[127] Millhollon, michelle, The Advocate, "Rainwater to do community service on DWI arrest," The Advocate, February 08, 2012.

[128] Millhollon, Michelle, "Report: Tax breaks benefits unclear," The Advocate, March 06, 2012, pp. 1 and 2.

[129] Monaghan, Steve, Your LFT Connection, September 2010.

[130] Ibid., p. 2.

[131] Ibid., p. 2.

[132] Ibid., p. 1.

[133] Ibid., p. 2.

[134] McCormick, Brett H., "Donaldsonville plant gets $2.1 billion expansion, " The Advocate, November 02, 2012, pp. 1 and 2.

[135] Boone, Timothy, "5 fertilizer plants planned in Pointe Coupee, The Advocate, February 28, 2013, p. 1.

[136] Allen, Rebekah, "EBR Metro Council approves incentives deal," The Advocate, May 08, 2013, pp. 1 and 2.

[137] Boone, Timothy, "IBM selects BR," The Advocate, March 27, 2013, pp. 1,2 and 3.

[138] Mitchell, David J., "BASF announces $42.6 million project, 22 jobs," The Advocate, September 12, 2013, p. 2.

[139] Thompson, Richard and Ballard, Mark, "Entergy to layoff 240 in La.," The Advocate, July 30, 2013, p. 1.

[140] Ballard, Mark, "Entergy seeks bill increase to pay for nuclear plant repairs," The Advocate, September 7, 2013, p. 1.

CHAPTER IV

[141] Williams, Bob, The Bob Williams Report, State Budget Update January 23, 2013, http://www.statebudgetsolutions.org/The_williams_report, 2013, p. 1.

[142] Oliff, Phil, Mai, Chris, and Palacios, Vincent, "States Continue to Feel Recession's Impact," Center on Budget and Policy Priorities, http://www.cbpp/cms/index=view&id=711, June 27, 2012, p. 5.

[143] _____NCSL FISCAL BRIEF: STATE BALANCED BUDGET PROVISIONS, National Conference of State Legislatures, http://ncsl.org/documents/fiscal/statebalancedbudget, October 2010, p. 2.

[144] Hall, Tom, "Louisiana governor plans cuts t oeducation, health care," http://wsws.org/en/articles/ 2011/03, March 3, 2011, p. 1.

[145] Shirley, Victoria, "Louisiana budget cuts: higher education on chopping block," http://www.knoe.com/story18441433/louisiana-budget, May 16, 2012, p.1.

[146] Gaharan, Alyson, "Midyear cuts were more modest than anticipated," The Daily Reveille, January 13, 2013, p. 1.

[147] Addo, Koran, "Board urged to stop education budget slashing," The Advocate, January 12, 2013, p. 1.

[148] Ibid., p. 1.

[149] Ibid., p. 1.

[150] Talley, Edie, "Jindal's latest higher ed proposal: More cuts, shaky money, higher tuition, Driftwood, http://driftwood.uno.edu/jindal's-lates-higher-ed-prop, March 17, 2013, p. 1.

[151] Addo, Koran, "College funding in question," The Advocate, March 18, 2013, p.1.

[152] Pope, John and Adelson, Jeff, " Regents claim Jindal proposing more cuts to higher education next year; greater reliance on one-time revenues, tuition," <u>Times-Picayune: Greater New Orleans</u>, March 21, 2013, pp. 1 and 2.

[153] Blum, Jordan, "SU Board OKs exigency," <u>The Advocate</u>, October 29, 2011, pp. 1and 2.

[154] Ibid., p. 3.

[155] Blum, Jordan, "AAUP censures Southern," <u>The Advocate</u>, June 15, 2013, p. 1.

[156] Ibid., pp. 1 and 2.

[157] Ibid., p. 2.

[158] Gyan, Joe, Jr. "Lawyers face off over Slaughter asset transfer," <u>The Advocate</u>, June 13, 2013, pp. 1 and 2.

[159] Gyan, Joe, "Judge: Assets transfer done to defraud SU Foundation," <u>The Advocate</u>, June 27, 2013, pp. 1 and 2.

[160] Ibid., p. 1.

[161] _____ Louisiana Household Income, Department of Numbers, http://deptofnumbers.com/income/louisiana/, 2011, p. 1.

[162] Ibid., p. 1.

[163] Addo, Koran, "Southern to welcome Brazilian students," <u>The Advocate</u>, July 03, 2013, p. 1.

[164] Ibid., p. 1.

[165] Oliff, Phil, Palacios, Vincent, Johnson, Ingrid, and Michael Leachman, "Recent Deep State Higher education Cuts May Harm Students and the Economy for years to Come," Center on Budget and Policy Priorities, March 19, 2013, P. 4.

[166] Blum, Jordan, "Higher ed leaders see funding method flaws," <u>The Advocate</u>, March 21, 2012, p. 1.

[167] Addo, Koran, "BACKLOG," <u>The Advocate</u>, May 19, 2013, p. 1.

[168] Ibid., p.2.

[169] Ibid., p. 5.

[170] Ibid., p. 9.

[171] Ibid., p. 10.

[172] Ibid., p. 15.

[173] Ibid., p. 15.

[174] Ibid., p. 15.

[175] _____Public School Funding in Louisiana, Minimum Foundation Program (MFP), Cowen institute For Public Education Initiatives, Tulane University, March 2010, p. 5.

[176] _____Department of EDUCATION, http://wwww.louisianabelieves.com/funding/revenue.

[177] Ibid.

[178] _____ *Webster's Ninth New Collegiate Dictionary,* A Merriam-Webster Inc., Publishers, Springfield, Mass., 1984, p. 1323.

[179] _____ Education Reporter, http://www.eagleforum.org/publications /educate/july1 , July 12, 2012.

[180] Ibid.

[181] Ibid.

[182] _____ PK-12 Public Education in Louisiana: 2011 Regular Session of the Louisiana Legislature, Cowen Institute Report, Tulane University, April 2011, p. 3.

[183] A public education student, who attends a so-called failing public school, usually has a low academic achievement history. The charter school is presented to him or her as a magical wand that can reverse his academic underachievement, and, in just a very short period, bring the affected students academic performance up to grade level and above. This sounds good to the affected students since their academic performance is at its lowest level, and any option that claims it can work an academic miracle

is grabbed for like a drowning man reaching for a rope as his last and only hope before drowning.

[184] Lussier, Charles, "State denies plan for two EBR schools to avoid takeover," The Advocate, July 12, 2013, pp. 1 and 2.

[185] Sentell, Will, "EBR charter schools win approval," The Advocate, August 14, 2013, pp. 1and 2.

[186] Lussier, Charles, "EBR School board to take up strategic plan, charter school request," The Advocate, August 15, 2013, P. 2.

[187] Sills, Marsha, "BESE approves charter schools in Lafayette," The Advocate, October 17, 2013, p. 1.

[188] Zeese, Kevin and Flowers, Margaret, "Obamacare: The Biggest Insurance Scam in History," Truthout, http://www.truth-out.org/opinion/item/19692-obamacare-

[189] Sauter, Michael B., Alexander, E. M., and Frohlich, Thomas c., "America's Richest (and Poorest) States," 24/7 Wall st., September 19, 2012.

[190] The term "poorest" must be placed in the proper context. Regarding the aggregate value of oil and natural gas for example, each year the oil and gas industry produce as much as $10 billion worth of oil revenues and an equal amount or more of natural gas annually via its onshore and offshore oil and natural gas drilling wells. The vast majority of this revenue does not go toward social program development for the Louisiana people. When other Louisiana industries are considered, the pattern continues to hold true. Thus, it is this reason that Louisiana is erroneously called a poor state by historians, sociologists, businesspeople, and politicians among many others in the social media.

[191] Sentell, Will, "Voucher payments under review," The Advocate, May 9, 2013, p. 1.

[192] Ibid., p. 1.

[193] Ibid., p. 1.

[194] Sentell, Will, "State's school voucher funding questioned," The Advocate, May 12, 2013, pp. 1 and 2.

[195] Sentell, Will, "Budget deal includes teacher pay raise, " The Advocate, June 06, 2013, p. 2.

[196] Ibid., p. 1.

[197] Ibid., p. 2.

[198] Vanacore, Andrew, "Legal challenge from Obama contends Louisiana vouchers collide with integration efforts, " The Advocate, August 28, 2013, p. 2.

[199] Millhollon, Michelle, "Jindal rebukes federal challenge of school voucher," The Advocate, August 25, 2013, p. 2.

[200] Vanacore, Op. Cit., pp. 1and 3.

[201] Millhollon, Michelle, "Jindal rebukes federal challenge of school vouchers," The Advocate, August 25, 2013, pp. 1 and 2.

[202] Blum, Jordan, "Jindal criticizes Justice Department letter on voucher lawsuits," The Advocate, September 26, 2013, p. 1.

[203] Ibid., pp. 1 and 2.

[204] Sentell, Will, "Vouchers aid desegregation," The Advocate, October 3, 2013, p. 1.

[205] Sentell, Will, "Jindal criticizes fed's new school voucher review plan," The Advocate, November 20, 2013, p. 1.

[206] Lussier, Charles, "Voucher participation on increase, but at a slower rate than expected," The Advocate, October 22, 2013, pp. 1 and 2.

[207] Ibid., p. 1.

[208] Sentell, Will, "Louisiana ranks low on nation's math, reading report card," The Advocate, November 7, 2013, pp. 1 and 2.

[209] Ibid., pp. 1 and 2.

[210] Sills, Marsha, "Lafayette schools budget talks to continue," The Advocate, May 15, 2013, p. 1.

[211] Dr. Pat Cooper's E-Mail to the Lafayette Parish School District Board Members and employed Lafayette Parish Schoolteachers, May 13, 2013.

[212] Bienvenu, Henri C., "Teacher positions at risk: school system facing $2.5 M budget shortfall," <u>Breaux Bridge Banner</u>, Vol. 27, No. 17, June 5, 2013, p. 1.

[213] In December 2010, the Board of Elementary and Secondary Education (BESE) set standards for schools to earn letter grades. BESE established its own Student Performance Scores (SPS). The new system's SPS Benchmarks are as follows: (1) Top-performing school must earn a 120 or above to receive a letter grade "A;" any school with a SPS of 65 or below will receive a letter grade "F." Based on this new BESE System, St. Martin Parish School District earned a District Performance Score (DPS) of 87.3 in 2010. Based on the BESE SPS System, St. Martin Parish School District's 87.3 DPS fell within the range 65.0-89.9, which means the latter's public schools across the school district cumulatively received a letter grade "D," or failing. In short, Dr. Lottie Beebe helped develop the BESE SPS System; the St. Martin Parish School District earned a "D" letter grade in 2010; and by June 2013, Dr. Beebe approved a budget reduction of $1.1 million to address a so-called budget shortfall caused by huge tax breaks given to private business by Governor Bobby Jindal. The game is on one hand, use the BESE SPS System to set up the Louisiana School Districts for failure, and on the other, politically get BESE to take MFP funds and place it in the General Fund line item in the Louisiana State Budget so it can be given to private business; the latter has set up numerous charter schools to receive MFP Funds that follow "academically –failing" children from "academically-failing" public schools to "flow-through" charter schools.

[214] Sentell, Will, "Panel sends public school funding bill back to BESE," <u>The Advocate</u>, May 16, 2013, pp. 1 and 2.

[215] Lussier,Charles, "DOE: 35 groups apply for charter schools, " <u>The Advocate</u>, May 17,2013, pp. 1 and 2.

[216] Sentell, Will, "La. students get aid to attend Arkansas schools," <u>The Advocate</u>, June 22, 2013, pp. 1 and 2.

[217]Sentell, Will, "Teach For America aid sparks heated arguments," <u>The Advocate</u>, June 27, 2013, pp. 1 and 2.

[218] Sentell, Will, "Education contracts spark questions," <u>The Advocate</u>, April 03, 2013, pp. 1 and 2.

[219] _____ "Louisiana House Approves Jindal's Reforms," Education News, http://www.educationnews.org/k-12schools/louisiana, April 10, 2012.

[220] Ibid., p. 2.

[221] Sentell, Will, La. schools get low marks," The Advocate, April 23, 2013, p. 1.

[222] Millhollon, Michelle, "Test results show some improvements," The Advocate, July 03, 2013, p. 2.

[223] Shuler, Marsha, "Teachers retiring in high numbers," The Advocate, July 10, 2013, pp. 1,2 and 3.

[224] Ibid., pp. 1 and 2.

[225] Ibid., p. 1.

[226] Ibid., p. 1.

[227] _____ "Schools Matter," http://www.schoolsmatter.info/2011/05/john-white-english-major-oligarchs-boy.html.

[228] _____ "Chiefs For Change," Biography, http://chiefsforchange.org/members/john-white/#sthash.TywairkO.dpuf

[229] _____ TeachForAmerica, http://www.teachforamerica.org/why-teach-for-america/

[230] Ibid.

[231] Ibid.

[232] Sentell, Will, "Tulane state leader of Teach For America ranks," The Advocate, September 7, 2013, p. 1.

[233] Ibid., p. 2.

[234] _____ "John White Appointed as New Louisiana Superintendent," Education News, http://www.educationnews.org/education-policy-and-politics/

[235] Ibid.

[236] Op. Cit., See Footnote Number 120.

[237] Sentell, Will, "La. superintendent reorganizes staff," The Advocate, October 12, 2012, p. 1.

[238] _____ Dave Lefty Lefkowitch, Zoominfo, http://www.zoominfo.com/p/David-Lefkowitch/1614/34. Mr. Lefkowitch received a BA degree from Yale University and a MBA degree from Stanford University both in the business field.

[239] _____ Hannah Dietsch, http://ZoomInfo.com/p/Hannah-Dietsch/1486655256.

[240] _____The Baltimore City teachers' Trust, Inc., http://www.bctt.org/aboutus.html.

[241] _____ "STATE SUPERINTENDENT ANNOUNCES TEAM OF DISTRICT SUPPORT LEADERS," http://www.louisianabelieves.com/newsroom/news-releases/2012.07/09/state-superintende...

[242] Ibid.

[243] Ibid.

[244] Op. Cit., http://www.louisianabelieves.com

[245] _____ "Louisiana Voucher Program Privatizes Education," Education Reporter, http://www.eagleforum.org/publications/educate/july12/1c, July 2012.

CHAPTER V

[246] Later, when we examine who pays the most taxes in Louisiana, we will, based on the tax and income data presented, define the Louisiana Ruling Class. It is common practice for the social media and politicians to talk about the middle class, but never do you hear any mention of the ruling class or working class. As far as the typical Louisiana resident is concerned, these classes do not exist; yet, they exist as surely as the oxygen we breathe on a moment-to-moment basis.

[247] Millhollon, Michelle, "Jindal cuts ribbon on medical education center," The Advocate, December 10, 2013, p. 1.

[248] Millhollon, Michelle, "Budgets for public hospitals depend on privatization agreements, " The Advocate, February 24, 2013, pp. 1 and 2.

[249] Ibid., pp. 2 and 3.

[250] Gregory, Don and Neustrom, Alison, Ph.D., A New Safety Net: The risk and reward of Louisiana's charity hospital privatizations, Publication 333, Public Affairs Research Council of Louisiana, December 2013, p. 8.

[251] Ibid., p. 8.

[252] Ibid., p. 4.

[253] Ibid., p. 9.

[254] Ibid., p. 9.

[255] Ibid., p. 9.

[256] Ibid., p. 10.

[257] Ibid. p. 10 and 11.

[258] Ibid., p. 11.

[259] Ibid., p. 13.

[260] Ibid., p. 15.

[261] Ibid., p. 15.

[262] Ibid., p. A1.

[263] Ibid., p. A2.

[264] Ibid., p. A2.

[265] Ibid., p. A2.

[266] Ibid., p. A2.

[267] Ibid., p. A3.

[268] Ibid., pp. A3 and A4.

[269] Ibid., p. A4.

[270] Ibid., p. A4.

[271] Ibid., p. A4.

[272] Ibid., p. A4.

[273] Ibid., p. A5.

[274] Ibid., p. A5.

[275] Ibid., p. A5.

[276] Ibid., p. A5.

[277] Ibid., p. A5.

[278] Ibid., p. A6.

[279] Ibid., p. A6.

[280] Ibid., p.A6.

[281] Ibid., p. A6.

[282] Ibid., p. A7.

[283] Ibid., p. A7.

[284] Ibid., p. A7.

[285] Ibid., p. A7.

[286] Ibid., p. A8.

[287] Ibid., p. A8.

[288] Ibid., p. A8.

[289] Ibid., p. A8.

[290] Ibid., p. A8.

[291] Ibid., p. A9.

[292] Ibid., p. A9.

[293] Ibid., p. A9.

[294] Ibid., p. A9.

[295] Ibid., p. A10.

[296] Ibid., p. A10.

[297] Ibid., p. A10.

[298] Ibid., p. A10.

[299] Ibid., p. A10.

[300] Ibid., p. A11.

[301] Ibid., p. A10.

[302] Ibid., p. 11.

[303] Shuler, Marsha, "Federal grand jury looks at Jindal administration contract," The Advocate, March 21, 2013, pp. 1 and 2.

[304] Deslatte, Melinda, "Greenstein resigns post, " The Advocate, March 29, 2013, pp. 1 and 2.

[305] _____ "Former DHH employee accused of swindling $1 M in Medicaid funds," The Advocate, June 04, 2013, p. 1.

[306] Shuler, Marsha, "CSNI files suit against state," The Advocate, may 7, 2013, p. 1.

[307] Millhollon, Michelle, "Jindal spending $4 million to find savings," The Advocate, January 3, 2014, P. 1.

[308] Shuler, Marsha, "Hospital privatization could impact thousands of state employees," The Advocate, march 11, 2013, p. 1.

[309] Shuler, Marsha ,"Loss of staff at EKL forces large reduction to activity," The Advocate, march 06, 2013, . 1.

[310] Ibid., pp. 1 and 2.

[311] Shuler, Marsha, "EKL layoffs of 700+ OK'd: Job losses effective April 15," The Advocate, April 02, 2013, p.1.

[312] Shuler, Marsha, "EKL closure will transfer prisoner care," The Advocate, April 13, 2013, p. 1.

[313] Ibid., p. 1.

[314] Ibid., p. 1.

[315] Ibid., p. 2.

[316] Ballard, Mark, "Legislator takes walk to illustrate bus problem," The Advocate, January 18, 2013, pp. 1 and 2.

[317] Addo, Koran, "State analyst defends Jindal policy," The Advocate, April 19, 2013, p. 1.

[318] Shuler, Marsha, "LSU board approves privatization for four more charity hospitals," The Advocate, May 28, 2013, pp. 1 and 2.

[319] Shuler, Marsha, "LSU approves blank contracts, " The Advocate. June 19, 2013, p. 1.

[320] Ibid., p. 1.

[321] Shuler, Marsha, "Panel approves hospital takeovers," The Advocate, June 10, 2013, pp. 1 and 2.

[322] Ibid., p. 1.

[323] Shuler, Marsha, "LSU Board votes t oclose charity hospital in Pineville," The Advocate, September 7, 2013, pp. 1 and 2.

[324] Zeese, Kevin and Flowers, Margaret, "Obamacare: the Biggest Insurance Scam in History," http://www.truth-out.org/opinion/item/1962-obamacare-the-biggest-insurance-scam-in-hi...

[325] _____Presidential Candidates: Selected Industry Totals, 2008 Cycle, http://www.opensecrets.org/pres08/select.php?pnd=H04.

[326] Op.Cit. See Footnote 172.

[327] Op. Cit.

[328] Op. Cit.

[329] Op. Cit.

330 Op. Cit.

331 Op. Cit.

332 Op. Cit.

333 Op. Cit.

334 Op. Cit.

335 Op. Cit.

336 Greenwald, Glenn, "The 'Public Option': Democrats' Scam Becomes More Transparent," http://www.commondreams.org/headline/2010/03/12-5, Tuesday, December 17, 2013.

337 Op. Cit., Zeese and Flowers.

338 Op. Cit.

339 OP. Cit.

340 Op. Cit.

341 Op. Cit.

342 Shuler, Marsha, "PAR seeks Jindal Medicaid explanation," The Advocate, march 12, 2013, p. 1.

343 Ibid., p. 1.

344 Shuler, Marsha, "house panel rejects Medicaid expansion, " The Advocate, April 24, 2013, p. 1.

345 Miller, Joel E., Dashed Hopes; Broken Promises; More Despair: How the Lack of State Participation in the Medicaid Expansion Will Punish Americans with Mental Illness Report, http://www.amhca.org/assets/contents/AMHCA_DashedHopes_Report_2_21_14_final.pdf, Alexandria, Virginia, February 2014, p. 1.

346 Ibid., p. 1.

347 Ibid., p. 1.

348 Ibid., p. 2.

349 Miller, Joel, PRESS RELEASE, American Mental Health Counselors Association, http://www.amhca.org/assets/contents/dashedhopesLouisiana, February 26, 2014.

350 Miller, Op. Cit., Dashed Hopes; Broken Promises; More Despair…, p. 25.

351 Ibid., p. 24.

352 Miller, Op. Cit., Dashed Hopes; Broken Promises; More Despair…, p. 7.

353 Ibid., p. 30.

354 Ibid., p. 27.

355 Ibid., p. 2.

356 Shuler, Marsha, "State scales back hospital request, " The Advocate, April 29, 2013, p. 1.

357 Lodge, Bill, "3 La doctors indicted after nationwide Medicare probe," The Advocate, may 15, 2013, p. 1.

358 _____ AMERICA'S HEALTH RANKINGS SENIOR REPORT: A CALL TO ACTION FOR INDIVIDUALS AND THEIR COMMUNITIES, United Health Foundation, 2013 Edition, p. 11.

359 Ibid., p. 11.

360 _____ America's Health Rankings, State Overview, 2013, www.americashealthrankings.org/seniors/2013.

361 Millhollon, Michelle, "Jindal cuts budget items," The Advocate, June 22, 2013, p. 1A.

362 Ibid., p. 1.

363 Millhollon, Michelle, "Gov. Jindal fires back on budget veto criticism, " The Advocate, June 25, 2013, pp. 1 and 2.

364 Ibid., p. 2.

365 Shuler, Marsha, "Changes to Medicaid expected, " The Advocate, July 01, 2013, p. 1.

366 Millhollon, Michelle, "La. Mental health program to cease," The Advocate, January 18, 2013, p. 1.

367 Ibid., p. 1.

368 Ibid., p. 2.

369 Jones, Terry L., "New Roads man accused of killing his grandmother," The Advocate, April 25, 2013, p. 1.

370 Millhollon, Michelle, "Legislative Audit questions lack of performance review of $363M contract," The Advocate, December 16, 2013, p. 1.

371 Ibid., p. 1.

372 Ibid., p. 1.

373 Advocate Staff Report, "La. improves one spot in health rankings to No. 48 out of 50," The Advocate, December 11, 2013, p. 1.

374 Addo, Koran, "Clinic opened to study childhood obesity," The Advocate, January 22, 2014, p. 1.

375 Advocate Staff Report, "report: Louisiana nursing homes second worst in U.S.," The Advocate, August 15, 2013, p. 1.

376 _____ Louisiana state budget (2008-2009), Sunshine Review, http://www.sunshinereview.org/index.php/Louisiana_sta, p. 1.

377 Ibid., p. 1.

378 Ibid., p. 1.

379 _____ Department of Environmental Quality, http://doa.louisiana.gov/OPB/FY13/SupportingDocum, p. ENVQ-14.

380 Ibid., p. ENVQ-15.

381 Ibid., p. ENVQ-18.

382 Harden, Kari Dequine, "Gulf health questions linger after oil leak," The Advocate, April 09, 2013, p. 1.

383 Wold, Amy, "3 years later, oil leaks effects still unfolding," The Advocate, April 03, 2013, pp. 1 and 2.

[384] _____ Restoring a Degraded Gulf of Mexico: Wildlife and Wetlands Three Years Into the Gulf Oil Disaster, The National Wildlife Federation, April 2013, p. 1.

[385] Ibid., p. 1.

[386] Wold, Amy, "Insects fall silent in oiled coastal marshes," The Advocate, April 23, 2012, pp. 1 and 3.

[387] Marshall, Bob, "La. Coast facing grim reality: Seas rising faster than predictions," The Advocate, February 27, 2013, p. 1.

[388] Handwerk, Brian, "New Orleans Sinking faster Than Thought, Satellites Find," National Geographic News, http://news.nationalgeographic.com/news/2006/0606(, October 28, 2010, p. 1.

[389] _____ "Vitter leads letter-writing campaign," The Advocate, April 23, 2013, p. 1.

CHAPTER VI

[390] Yen, Hope, "Poverty in U.S. increases: La. second in percentage of poor," The Advocate, September 14, 2011, p. 1A.

[391] Ibid., p. 1A.

[392] Bishaw, Alemayehu, Poverty: 2010 and 2011: American Community Survey Briefs, Issued September 2012, ACSBR/11-01, p. 3.

[393] Ward, Steven, "Study: Louisiana is saddest state in the U. S., The Advocate, February 20, 2013, pp. 1 and 2.

[394] Ward, Steven, "Poverty rises in Louisiana: Poor Louisianan ranks grew 75,000 between 2009 and 2010," The Advocate, September 25, 2011, p. 1.

[395] Ibid., p. 1.

[396] Ibid., p. 2.

[397] Kneebone, Elizabeth, nadeau, Carey, and Alan Berube, The Re-Emergence of Concentrated Poverty: Metropolitan Trends in the 200s Report, Metropolitan Policy Program at Brookings, Brookings Institutions, Washington, D.C., November 2011, p. 20.

[398] Ward, Steven, "Report: Poverty high in BR," The Advocate, November 3, 2011, p. 1.

[399] Ibid., p. 3. By January 2014, Louisiana ranked 50th in children living in poverty.

[400] Blum, Jordan, "Wealth gap hits black families in U.S., La," The Advocate, September 24, 2012, p. 1.

[401] Leonard, Barry (Editor), Estimating the Economic Effects of the Deepwater drilling Moratorium on the Gulf Coast Economy: Inter-Agency Economic Report, September 16, 2010, p. iii.

[402] Ibid., p. 7.

[403] Ibid. p. 3.

CHAPTER VII

[404] Rugaber, Christopher S., "Average U.S. household far from regaining its wealth," The Advocate, May 30, 2013, p. 1.

[405] Davis, Karl, Davis, Kelly, Gardner, Matthew, Heimovitz, Harley, Mcintyre, Robert S, Phillips, Richard, Sapozhnikova, Alla and Meg Wiehe, Who Pays?: A Distributional Analysis of the Tax Systems in All 50 States, 4th Edition, January 2013, p. 2. "This study was made possible by grants from the Annie E. Casey Foundation, the Ford Foundation, the Popplestone Foundation, the Stephen M. Silberstein Foundation, the Stoneman Family Foundation, and an extensive report-See Footnote 120-on which classes in Louisiana pay more and less taxes. The class with the greatest authority, power, and control of the state government apparatus *always pays less taxes, and the class with the least power and authority always pays the most.* The following tax data for Louisiana consistently supports this fact.

[406] Ibid., p. 62.

[407] Blum, Jordan, "La among lowest tax-burden states: But state has 'incredibly high' sales taxes that affect poor, working class," The Advocate,, October 24, 2012, p. 1.

[408] Ibid., p. 1.

[409] Ibid., p. 2.

410 The Institute on Taxation and Economic Policy, www.ITEPnet.org

411 _____ "Low-income taxpayers pay larger share in La.," <u>The Advocate</u>, January 31, 2013, pp. 1 and 2.

412 Davis, Davis, et. al., Op. Cit., p. 61.

413 _____ "Newly Minted Millionaires," <u>The Wall Street Journal</u>, Vol. CCLXIII, No. 14, January 17, 2014, p. A1.

414 Morath, Eric, "Where to Go If You Want To Marry a Millionaire," <u>The Wall Street Journal</u>, Vol. CCLXIII, No. 14, January 17, 2014, p. A2.

CHAPTER VIII

415 Wolff, Op. Cit., pp. 35 and 36.

416 Crawford, Corinne, "The Repeal Of The Glass-Steagall Act And The Current Financial Crisis, " <u>Journal of Business & Economic Research</u>, Volume 9, Number 1, January 2011, p. 127.

417 Wolff, Op.Cit., pp. 23 and 60.

418 Davidson, Paul, "BERNANKE DOWNPLAYS COST OF STIMULUS," <u>USA TODAY</u>, Section B, Money, January 17, 2014, p. 1B,

419 Fitzpatrick, Dan and Rapoport, Michael, "Profits show Biggest Banks Are Back From Brink," <u>The Wall Street Journal</u>, January 17-19, 2014, p. A1.

420 Ibid., p. A2.

421 Ibid., p. A2.

422 _____ "America's 25 Highest Paid CEOs", <u>Forbes</u>, http://www.forbes.com/pictures/mef45eghm/ and http://money.msn.com/investing/7-ceos-pulling-in-outsized

423 Foroohar, Rana, "The Myth Of Financial Reform," <u>Time</u>, Vol. 182, NO. 13, September 23, 2013, pp. 31 and 32.

424 Ibid., p. 32.

425 Calabresi, Massimo, "Oversight for Hire: The rise, and downsides, of

private bank examiners," <u>Time</u>, Vol. 182, No. 13, September 23, 2013, p. 36.

[426] Ibid., p. 36.

[427] Ibid., p. 36.

[428] Ibid., p. 38.

[429] Ibid., p. 38.

[430] Ibid., p. 38.

[431] Ibid., p. 36.

[432] Ibid., p. 38.

[433] Ibid., p. 38.

[434] Ibid., p. 38.

[435] Ibid., p. 38.

[436] Ibid., pp. 38 and 39.

[437] Fedoseyev, P. N., Bakh, Irene, et. al, *Karl Marx: A Biography*, Progress Publishers, Moscow, 1973, p. 383.

[438] Perkins, Tom, "Progressive Kristallnacht Coming?, http://www.wsj.com/news/articles

[439] Davis, Davis, et. al., Op. Cit., p. 1.

CHAPTER IX

[440] Sentell, Will, "Will Sentell stated Engineers say improvements needed, " <u>The Advocate</u>, january 19, 2012, p. 1.

[441] _____ High school diploma or higher, by percentage (most recent) by state, Statemaster, http://statemaster.com.

[442] _____ Revamp our workforce training programs, http://www.onthe issues.org/GovernorBobby_Jindal_jobs.

[443] _____ Databases, Tables & Calculators by Subject, Bureau Of

Labor Statistics, United States Department Of Labor, http://data.bls.gov/timeseries/?ASST220000003, 2003 to 2013.

[444] Ibid.

[445] Brenner, Harvey, Ph. D., Op. Cit., pp. Vi and Vii.

[446] Ibid., pp. 22 and 23.

[447] _____ Louisiana Per Capita Income Trends since 2005, Department Of Numbers, http://www.depofnumbers.com/income/louisiana/

[448] Brenner, Harvey, Dr., Op. Cit., p. 7.

[449] _____Recap Of suicides May 2002 through 2013, St Tammany Outreach for the Prevention of Suicide, http://www.stops-la.org/Stats.asp

[450] _____2013 Annual Report, AMERICA'S HEALTH RANKINGS, http://www.americashealthranking.org/LA/Suicide/2008-2008

[451] Chang, Cindy, "Louisiana is the world's prison capital," The Times-Picayune, http://www.nola.com/crime/index.ssf/2012/05/Louisiana_is_the, May 29, 2012.

[452] Ibid.

[453] Ibid.

[454] Ibid.

[455] _____ Statistical Briefing Book, Louisiana Department of Public Safety and Corrections: Corrections Services, http://www.doc.la.gov/pages/contact-us/headquarters/.

[456] Le Blanc, James M., Secretary, Demographic Profiles of the Adult Correctional Population: Fact Sheet, Louisiana Department of Public Safety and Corrections. http://www.doc.la.gov/wp-content/uploads/stats/2apdf, June 30, 2013, p. 31.

[457] Le Blanc, James M., Demographic Profiles of the Youthful Offender Population, Louisiana Department of Public Safety and Corrections: Fact Sheet, http://www.doc.la.gov/wp-content/uploads/stats/2g.pdf, June 30, 2013, p. 43.

[458] Ibid., p. 43.

[459] Forret, Jeff, "Before Angola: Enslaved Prisoners in the Louisiana State Penitentiary," <u>Louisiana History</u>, 54 (2013), p. 142.

[460] Blackmon, Douglas A., <u>Slavery By Another Name</u>, Doubleday, 2008, p. 53.

[461] Woll Peter and Binstock Robert H., *America's Political System*, Fourth Edition, Random House, New York, p. 569.

[462] Blackmon, Op. Cit., p. 6.

[463] Ibid., pp. 7 and 8.

[464] Pelaez, Vicky, "The Prison Industry in the United States: Big Business or a New Form of Slavery?" Global Research, http://www.globalresearch.ca/the -prison-industry-in-the-united.

[465] Blackmon, Op. Cit., pp. 4 and 47.

[466] Pelaez, Op. Cit.

[467] Weich, Ronald and Angulo Carlos, "Racial Disparities in the American Criminal Justice System," *Justice on Trial: Racial Disparities in the American Criminal Justice System* Report, 2000, pp. 185 and 186.

[468] Ibid., p. 187.

[469] Ibid., p. 196.

[470] Ibid., p. 199.

[471] Ibid., p. 199.

[472] Ibid., pp. 197 and 198.

[473] _____ Political Research Associates, DEFENDING JUSTICE: AN ACTIVIST RESOURCE KIT, Factsheet, <u>http://defendingjustice.org/factsheets</u>, p. 3.

[474] Leblanc, James M., Secretary, *Briefing Book: Louisiana Corrections*, July 2013 Update, p. 31.

[475] _____ State & County QuickFacts, United States Census, http:// quickfacts.census.gov/qfd/states/22000.html

[476] Leblanc, Op. Cit., p. 32.

[477] Weich and Angulo, Op. Cit., p. 205.

[478] Ibid., p. 205.

[479] Ibid., p. 204.

[480] Ibid., p. 197.

[481] _____Political Research Associates, Op. Cit.

[482] Pelaez, Vicky, "The Prison industry in the United States: Big Business or a New Form of Slavery?." http://www.globalresearch.ca/ the-prison-industry-in-the-united

[483] Davis, Angela, "Masked Racism: reflections on the Prison Industrial Complex," http://colorlines.com/archives/1998/09/ masked_racism_reflections, September 10, 1998.

[484] Ibid.

[485] Pelaez, Op. Cit.

[486] Ibid.

[487] Ibid.

[488] Ibid.

[489] Pelaez, Vicky, "The prison Industry in the United States: Big Business or a New Form of Slavery, " http://www.globalresearch.ca/the-prison-industry-in-the-united, March 2008.

[490] Ibid.

[491] Ibid.

[492] Chang, Cindy, "Louisiana is the world's prison capital," The times-Picayune, http://www.nola.com/crime/index.ssf/2012/05/ Louisiana_is_the_, May 29, 2012.

[493] Chang, Cindy, "North Louisiana family is a major force in the state's vast prison industry," http://www.nola.com/crime/index.ssf/2012/05/jonesboro_family, May 14, 2012.

[494] Ibid.

[495] Ibid.

[496] Ibid.

[497] Ibid.

[498] Ibid.

[499] Ibid.

[500] Ibid.

[501] Chang, Cindy, "Louisiana is the world's prison capital," http://www.nola.com/crime/indexssf/2012/05/Louisiana_is_the, may 29, 2012.

[502] Ibid.

[503] Ibid.

[504] Ibid.

[505] Chang, Cindy, "In world of prisons, some rural parishes' economies hinge on keeping their jails full," http://nola.com/crime/index.ssf/2012/05/in_world_of_prison, May 13, 2012.

[506] Ibid.

[507] Ibid.

[508] Ibid.

[509] Ibid.

[510] Chang, Cindy, "Louisiana is the world's prison capital," http://www.nola.com/crime/indexssf/2012/05/Louisiana_is_the, May 29, 2012.

[511] Chang, Cindy, "North Louisiana family is a major force in the state's vast prison industry," http://www.nola.com/crime/index.ssf/2012/05/jonesboro_family, May 14, 2012.

512 Chang, Cindy, Op. Cit., "Louisiana is the world's prison capital."

513 _____ DEATH PENALTY INFORMATION CENTER, http://www.deathpenaltyinfo.org/murder-rates-nationally-

514 Ibid.

515 Vetter, Kimberly, "High homicide rate plague Baton Rouge, The Advocate, February 26, 2012, pp. 1 and 2.

516 Ibid., p. 2.

517 Ibid., p. 3.

518 Gunn, Billy, "Homicides in Lafayette up, other crimes down," The Advocate, February 8, 2013, p. 1.

519 _____ Highest Murder rate US cities, http://shareranks.com/994,highest-Murder-Rate-US-Cities

520 Fuchs, Erin, "WHY LOUISIANA IS THE MURDER CAPITAL OF AMERICA," http://www.businessInsider.com/Why-is-the-murder-rate-high-

521 _____ Explore the Data: The State of Women in America, http://www.americanprogress.org/issues/women/news/2013/0

522 Blum, Jordan, "Wealth gap hits families in U.S., La.," The Advocate, September 24, 2012, p. 1.

523 _____ Explore the Data: The State of Women in America, http://www.Americanprogress.org/issues/women/news/2013/0

524 _____ When Men Murder Women: An Analysis of 2011 Homicide Data, Violence Policy Center, http://vpc.org/when-men-murder-women/, p. 1.

525 Stewart, Robert, "Study: Louisiana has highest rate of gun violence in U.S.," The Advocate, April 3, 2013, p. 1.

526 Ibid., p. 2.

527 _____ When Men Murder Women: An Analysis of 2011 Homicide Data, Violence Poli8cy Center, http://vpc/when-men-murder-women/, p. 5.

[528] Ibid., p. 23.

[529] _____ Explore the data: The State of Women in America, http://www. Americanprogress.org/issues/women/news/2013/0

[530] Castro, Martin, Thernstrom, Abigail, et. al., Sexual Assault In The Military, U.S. commission On Civil Rights, http://www.uscr.gov /pubs/09242013 Statutory Enforcement Report Sexual Assault in the Military, September 2013, pp. 3 and 4.

[531] _____ Service Women's Action Network: quick Facts, policy@ servicewomen.org, July 2012.

[532] Castro, Martin, Thernstrom, et. al., Op. Cit., p. 2.

[533] Ibid., pp. 5 and 6.

[534] _____ Service Women's Action Network: Quick Facts, policy @ servicewomen .org, July 2012.

[535] Hagel, Chuck, Department Of defense Annual Report on Sexual Assault in the Military, http://www.sapr.mil/, April 30, 2013, p. 28.

[536] Castro and Thernstrom, et. al., Op. Cit., p. 5.

[537] _____ "Army general avoids jail time, fined $20,000 in sexual assault case," New York Daily News.Com, March 20, 2014.

[538] Botelho, Greg and Baldacci, Marlena, "Brigadier general accused of sexual assault must pay over $20,000; no jail time," CNN Justice, http:// www.cnn.com/201403/20/justice/jeffrey-sinclair-court, March 20, 2014.

[539] Purpura, Paul, Louisiana national Guard's top enlisted adviser fired amid sexual harassment allegations," The Times-Picayune, NOLA.com, June 15, 2013.

[540] Hess, Alexander E.M., Sauter, Michael B., and Thomas C. Frohlich, "America's Least Healthy States: 24/7 Wall St.," http://huffingtonpost. com/2013/12/21/least-healthy-state, January 23, 2014.

[541] Ibid. http://24/7wallst.com/special-report/2013/12/17/america-most.

[542] _____America's Health Rankings: 2013 Annual Report, America'shealthranking.org/LA/cvdDeaths/2008

543 _____ Louisiana State fact Sheet, American Heart Association, http://www.heart.org/idc/groups/heart-public/@wcm/@adv/d, 2010.

544 Minino, Arialdi M., Murphy, Sherry L. B.S., Xu, Jiaquan M.D., and Kenneth D. Kochanek, M.A., National Vital Statistics Reports: Deaths: Final Data for 2008, Volume 59, Number 10, December 7, 2011, p. 94.

545 Kochanek, Kenneth D. M.A.,, Xu, Jiaquan,M.D., Murphy, Sherry L B.S.., Minino, Ariaaldi, M. M.P.H., and Hsiang-Ching Kung, Ph.D., National Vital Statistics Reports: Deaths: Final Data for 2009, Volume 60, Number 3, December 29, 2011, p. 84.

546 Murphy, Sherry L., B.S., Xu, Jiaquan, M.D., and Kochanek, Kenneth D., M.A., National Vital Statistics: Deaths: Final Data for 2010, Volume 61, Number 4, May 8, 2013, p. 86.

547 _____ Cardiovascular Deaths, AMERICA'S HEALTH RANKING, http://www.americashealthranking.org/LA/cvdDeaths/2008

548 _____ LouisianaLifeExpectancy: live longer live better, http://www.worldlifeexpectancy.com/USA/louisiana-heart-disease

549 Whiteaker, Chloe and Kuntz, Phil, Mapping America's Coronary Stent Hot Spots, Bloomberg View, http://go.bloomberg.com/multimedia/mapping-coronary-stent, September 26, 2013.

550 Waldman, Peter, Armstrong, Daniel, and Sydney P. Freedberg, "Deaths Linked to Cardiac Stents Rise as Overuse Seen," http://www.bloomberg.com/news/2013-09-26/deaths-linked-to, September 26, 2013.

551 Ibid.

552 Ibid.

CHAPTER X

553 Cruz, Gilbert, "Jindal Triumphant in Louisiana," Time, http://content.time.com/nation/article/0,8599,1674122,oc, October 21, 2007.

554 Ibid.

555 _____ "GOP Congressman Bobby Jindal Wins Louisiana Governor's

Race," Associated Press, http://www.foxnews.com/story/2007/10/21/gop-congressman, October 21, 2007.

556 _____Legislative Committee Analysis Tool (L-CAT), http://www. followthe money.org/press/ReportView.phtml?=42

557 _____ "How many registered voters in Louisiana,? Answers, http://wiki.answers.com/Q/How_many_registered_voters_in_Louisiana, 2007.

558_____2007 Gubernatorial general Election Results-Louisiana, http://useelectionatlas.org/RESULTS/state.php?fips=22&year=2

559 Hawkins, Dustin, "Profile of Louisiana Governor Bobby Jindal," About. com: US Conservative Politics, http://usconservatives.about.com/od/thinkersanddoers/p/profi

560 Ibid.

561 _____2011 Gubernatorial General Election Results, http://uselectionatlas.org/RESULTS/ state.php?year=2011&off

562 _____"Our Views: Mr. Jindal, road scholar," The Advocate, March 3, 2013.

563 Ibid.

564 Ibid.

565 Ibid.

566 Millhollon, Michelle, "Jindal on the road," The Advocate, April 10, 2013.

567 Ibid.

568 Ibid.

569 _____ "Gov. Bobby Jindal's out-of-state travel costs the state $175,000," The Associated Press, March 7, 2012.

570 Deslatte, Melinda, "Jindal out of state more than 2 months this year," The Advocate, November 11, 2013, p. 1.

571 Deslatte, Melinda, "Gov. Bobby Jindal's out-of –stsate travel costs the state $175,000," The Times-Picayune, http://www.nola.com/politics/index. ssf/2012/03/gov_bobby_jin, March 7, 2012.

[572] Melinda Deslatte, Jindal out of state morethan 2 months this year," The Advocate, November 11, 2013, p. 1.

CHAPTER XI

[573] Moller, Jan, "Louisiana has a budget surplus after all," The Times-Picayune, http://www.nola.com/politics,index.ssf/2009/10/louisiana_has_, October 17, 2009.

[574] Nossitier, Adam, "For Louisiana, Bons Temps Proved All Too Brief," The New York Times, http://www.nytimes.com/2008/12/19/us/19louisiana.html?_r=0, December 18, 2008.

[575] Alford, Jeremy, "Bobby Jindal's Bad Math: The republican wunderkind has failed Louisiana as a fiscal steward," gambit, http://www.bestofneworleans.com/gambit/bobby-jindal-bad

[576] Ibid.

[577] Millhollon, Michelle, "Critics say Jindal's budget strategies amount to 'accounting gimmicks,' The Advocate, march 1, 2014, p. 1.

[578] Ibid., pp. 1 and 4.

[579] Ibid., p. 5.

[580] Millhollon, Michelle and Addo, Koran, "Funding questions surround Jinal's budget," The Advocate, April 13, 2014, pp. 1 and 2.

[581] _____ "Jindal orders spending freeze to avoid shortfall," The Advocate, April 4, 2014, p. 1.

[582] Shuler, Marsha, "Treasurer John Kennedy: Louisiana in deficit spending; it's worse than past years," The Advocate, November 11, 2014, pp. 1 and 2.

[583] Wold, Amy, "Final stretch of Gulf coast removed from active cleanup status," The Advocate, April 15, 2014, pp.1 and 2.

[584] Ott, Riki, Sound Truth And Corporate Myths: The Laegacy of the Exxon Valdez Oil Spill, Dragonfly Sisters Press, Cordova, Alaska, 2005, pp. 393 and 395.

[585] _____ Report: Oil Is Not Gone; Impacts to Wildlife On-going,'

National Wildlife Federation, http://www.nwf.org/-/media/PDFs/water/2014/NWF_deepwater, 2014

[586] Ott, Op. Cit., pp. 29, 56, and 58.

[587] Marshall, Bob, "More massive tar mats from BP oil spill discovered on Louisiana braches," The lens: Focused On New Orleans And The Gulf Coast, http://the lensnola.org/2013/12/18/more-massiv-tar-mats-from, December 18, 2013.

[588] Thompson, Richard, "4 years after spill questions remain about health impacts," http://www.theneworleansadvocate.com/home/8950601-172/f, April 24, 2014.

[589] Ibid.

[590] Shuler, Marsha, "Medicaid expansion bill fails in Senate committee," The Advocate, April 23, 2014, p. 1.

[591] Ibid., p. 2.

[592] Adelson, Jeff, 'Ladies in red' back in Capitol to fight for independent levee boards," The Advocate, April 26, 2014, p. 3.

[593] Ibid., p. 2.

[594] Millhollon, Michelle, "jindal unveils legislation to solve oil and gas legacy lawsuits," The Advocate, March 27, 2014, p. 2.

[595] Marshall, Bob, "La. coast facing grim reality," The Advocate, February 21, 2014, p. 1.

[596] Ibid., p. 2.

[597] Adelson, Jeff, "Water has risen 2 inches at Grand Isle since 2007, data show," The Advocate, may 8, 2014, p. 1.

[598] Ballard, Mark, "Oil lawsuit-killing bill advances," The Advocate, May 1. 2014, p. 1.

[599] Ibid., p. 1.

[600] Ibid., p. 3.

[601] Millhollon, Michelle, "State running low on money," The Advocate, April 25, 2014, pp. 1 and 2.

[602] Millhollon, Michelle and Addo, Koran, "funding questions surround Jindal's budget," The Advocate, April 13, 2014, pp. 1 and 2.

[603] Shuler, Marsha, "federal government rejects Jindal hospital plans," The Advocate, May 3, 2014, p. 1.

[604] Peveto, Kyle, "Louisiana ADHD increase among highest in nation," The Advocate, May 11, 2014, pp. 1-3.

[605] Millhollon, Michelle, "Jindal to revisit religious freedom at Liberty University," The Advocate, May 9, 2014, p. 1.

CHAPTER XII

[606] Jindal, Bobby Gov., "How We Achieved Louisiana's Economic Surge," Forbes, http://www.forbes.com/sites/realspin/2014/05/04/how-we-ach, May 04, 2014.

[607] Ibid.

[608] Peveto, Kyle, "High diagnosis rates on par with obesity in U.S., " The Advocate, July 13, 2014, p. 1.

[609] McMillan, Tracie, "The New Face of Hunger," National Geographic, Vol. 226, No. 2, August 2014, p. 86.

[610] Ibid., pp. 86 and 87.

[611] Ibid., p. 86.

[612] Ibid., p. 86.

[613] Ibid., p. 72.

[614] Ibid., p. 87.

[615] _____Food Empowerment Project, "Food Deserts," www.food is power.org/food-deserts/

[616] Duffany, Hannah, Individual and Community Food Security in New Orleans: A Case Study on the Effects of Urban Agriculture in a Food

Desert, Bennington College, Bennington, Vermont, webfac.bennington. edu/vinbruce/files/2012/01/Individual-and-community-food-security-in-New Orleans.pdf, June 1, 2013 pp. 28, 39, and 51.

[617] Crisp, Elizabeth, "Jindal politicking in Iowa," The Advocate, August 9, 2014, p. 1.

[618] Shuler, Marsha, "Jindal warned about Medicaid contract," The Advocate, July 14, 2014, p.1.

[619] Ibid., p. 1.

[620] Ibid., p. 1.

[621] Ibid.

[622] _____ WORKING FOR THE FEW: Political capture and economic inequality, 178 Oxfam Briefing Paper, www.oxfam.org., January 20, 2014, p. 2.

[623] Deslatte, Melinda, "Senators pick through $74 M savings from consultant," The Advocate, May 16, 2014, p. 1.

[624] Tolstoy, Leo, *War And Peace*, New American Library, New York, 1968, p. 1200.

[625] Op. Cit., WORKING FOR THE FEW: Political capture and economic inequality, January 20, 2014, p. 1.

[626] Ibid., p. 2.

[627] Ibid., p. 6.

[628] Ibid., p. 18.

[629] Ibid., p. 22.

[630] Ibid., p. 11.

[631] Ibid., p. 11.

[632] Ibid., p. 11.

[633] Ballard, Mark, "La. House committee votes to kill levee board lawsuit," The Advocate, May 22, 2014, p.1.

[634] Ibid., p. 1.

[635] Ballard, Mark, "Louisiana House votes to kill levee board lawsuit," The Advocate, May 30, 2014, p. 1.

[636] Ibid., p. 2.

[637] _____ La. ranks 2nd for homes from hurricane storm surge, " The Advocate, July 10, 2014, p. 1.

[638] Advocate Staff and Wire Report, "Louisiana tops nation on debt delinquency list," The Advocate, June 30, 2014, pp. 1 and 2.

[639] Ballard, Mark, "Legislature cracks down on lawsuits," The Advocate, May 25, 2014, p. 1.

[640] Millhollon, Michelle, "House says 'No' to putting millions of dollars in escrow," The Advocate, May 22, 2014, p. 1.

[641] Ibid., p. 1.

[642] _____ "Senate OKs more assistant prosecutors," Capitol News Bureau, May 27, 2014, p. 1.

[643] Millhollon, Michelle, "house OKs budget with little discussion," The Advocate, May 30, 2014, p. 1.

[644] _____ "Governor deflects questions over travel," Capitol News Bureau and the Associated Press, May 25, 2014, p. 1.

[645] OP Cit., Working for the Few: Political capture and economic inequality, January 20, 2014, pp. 11 and 12.

[646] Ibid., p. 12.

[647] Ibid., p. 13.

[648] Ibid., p. 13.

[649] _____ COUNTRY NOTE: UNITED STATES, www.oecd.org/els/social/inequality, p. 1.

AFTERWORD

650 Russell, Gordon, "Giving Away Louisiana: An Overview," The Advocate, file:///G:/Giving%20Away%20Louisiana%20%20An%20 overview%20%C2%AB%20The%20Advocate%20Special%20 Reports%20December%202%202014.html, December 2. 2014, p. 10.

651 Ibid., p. 1.

652 Ibid., p. 1.

653 Ibid., p. 1.

654 Ibid., p. 1.

655 Russell, Gordon, "Giving Away Louisiana: Film tax incentives," The Advocate, file:///G:/Giving%20Away%20Louisiana%20%20Film%20 tax%20incentives%20%C2%AB%20The%20Advocate%20Special%20 Reports%20December%202%202014.html, December 2, 2014, p. 1.

656 Ibid., p. 1.

657 Russell, Gordon, See Footnote 651, p. 3.

658 Ballard, Mark, "Giving Away Louisiana: Fracking tax incentives," The Advocate, file:///G:/Giving%20Away%20Louisiana%20%20Fracking%20 tax%20incentives%20%C2%AB%20The%20Advocate%20Special%20 Reports%20December%204%202014.html, December 4. 2014, p. 1.

659 Ibid., p. 1.

660 Russell, Gordon, See Footnote 651, p. 3.

661 Allen, Rebekah, "Giving Away Louisiana: Enterprise Zone incentives," The Advocate, file:///G:/Giving%20Away%20Louisiana%20 %20Enterprise%20zone%20incentives%20%C2%AB%20The%20 Advocate%20Special%20Reports%20December%202%202014.html, December 2, 2014, p. 1.

662 Ibid., p. 1.

663 Ibid., p. 1.

664 Ibid., p. 1.

665 Ibid., pp. 2and 3.

666 Op. Cit., Russell, Gordon, See Footnote 651, p. 3.

667 Thompson, Richard, "Giving Away Louisiana: Industrial tax incentives," The Advocate, file:///G:/Giving%20Away%20Louisiana%20%20 Industrial%20tax%20incentives%20%C2%AB%20The%20Advocate%20 Special%20Reports%20December%203%202014.html, December 2, 2014, p. 2.

668 Ibid., p. 2.

669 Ibid., pp. 2 and 3.

670 Russell, Gordon, "Giving Away Louisiana: Inventory tax refund," The Advocate, file:///G:/Giving%20Away%20Louisiana%20%20Inventory%20 tax%20refund%20%C2%AB%20The%20Advocate%20Special%20 Reports%20December%205%202014.html, December 5, 2014, p. 1.

671 Ibid., p. 1.

672 Adelson, Jeff, "Giving Away Louisiana: Solar energy tax credit," file:///G:/ Giving%20Away%20Louisiana%20%20Solar%20energy%20tax%20 credit%20%C2%AB%20The%20Advocate%20Special%20Reports%20 December%206%202014.html, December 6, 2014, p. 1.

673 Ibid., p. 3.

674 Russell, Gordon, "Giving Away Louisiana: 2015 governor's race," The Advocate, file:///G:/Giving%20Away%20Louisiana%20%20 2015%20governor%E2%80%99s%20race%20%C2%AB%20The%20 Advocate%20Special%20Reports%20December%207%202014.html, December 7, 2014, p. 1.

675 Deslatte, Melinda, "Jindal administration working to close budget gap," The Advocate, December 11, 2014, p. 1.

676 Ballard, Mark, "Dropping oil prices continue to impact state budget," The Advocate, December 13, 2014, p. 2.

677 Werner, Anna, "Louisiana: The new Hollywood," http://www.cbsnews. com/news/louisiana-the-new-hollywood/, 2014, p. 1.

678 Advocate Staff Report, "CBS News highlights Louisiana as 'the

film production capital of the world'", **http://theadvocate.com/news/11186618-123/cbs-news-highlights-louisiana-as,** December 27, 2014, pp. 1 and 2.

[679] THE ASSOCIATED PRESS, "Initial unemployment claims rise in Louisiana," The Advocate, December 29, 2014, p.1.

Printed in the United States
By Bookmasters